THE  TIMES

GUIDE TO

THE SINGLE
EUROPEAN
MARKET

About the authors

Richard Owen was *The Times* Brussels Correspondent from 1985 to 1988, reporting extensively on EC affairs from around Europe. Educated at Nottingham University, Stanford University, California, and the London School of Economics, where he received a PhD in Government and Politics, Owen joined the BBC in 1973 and transferred to *The Times* as a leader writer in 1980. He was Moscow Correspondent of *The Times* from 1982 to 1985, and Jerusalem Correspondent from 1988 to 1991. His previous books are *Letters From Moscow* (1985) and *Crisis in the Kremlin: Soviet Succession and the Rise of Gorbachov* (1986), both published by Gollancz. Since April 1991 Richard Owen has been deputy Foreign Editor of *The Times*.

Michael Dynes joined *The Times* in 1986 as a reporter, and has written extensively about the internal market from both London and Brussels. He was educated at the University of Kent at Canterbury, the University of Indiana and Linacre College, Oxford, where he received an MPhil in International Relations. Before joining *The Times* he worked on the Middle and Far East desks at an Oxford-based commercial consultancy. He is currently *The Times* Transport Correspondent.

THE TIMES

GUIDE TO

THE SINGLE EUROPEAN MARKET

A Comprehensive Handbook
by RICHARD OWEN and MICHAEL DYNES

TIMES BOOKS
A division of HarperCollins*Publishers*

First published by Times Books
A division of HarperCollins*Publishers*
77–85 Fulham Palace Road
London w6 8jb

© Times Books, London 1992

British Library Cataloguing in Publication Data

Owen, Richard
　The Times guide to the single European market
　I. Title　　II. Dynes, Michael
　337.142

ISBN 0-7230-0470-6

Typeset by Rowland Phototypesetting Limited,
Bury St Edmunds, Suffolk

Printed in Great Britain by
Clays Limited, St Ives plc

CONTENTS

PREFACE

Since the first edition of *The Times Guide to 1992* was published in 1989 the world has changed out of all recognition—and with it the debate over the future of Europe. This *Guide to the Single European Market* builds on the earlier guide, which dealt with the formative stages of the 1992 programme for the internal market. The single market, which appeared relatively remote when conceived in 1985, is now upon us.

In keeping with the remarkable changes which have reshaped Europe, the new guide offers an updated account of the way business, finance, trade and politics will operate in the single market. It also discusses the impact on a frontier-free Europe of recent upheavals: the reunification of Germany, the democratization of Eastern Europe, the collapse of Communism in the Soviet Union after the failed coup of August 1991, the end of the Cold War and the creation of a European Economic Area through an EC–EFTA deal that gives EFTA nations (the European Free Trade Association) access to the single market (with soft EFTA loans and grants to the EC southern states), thereby creating a still wider European market of 380 million people. The entry of the pound into the European Monetary System's exchange rate mechanism and the departure of Mrs Thatcher—brought down, in no small measure, by the issue of Europe —to be succeeded as Prime Minister by John Major are also considered.

Nowhere has the debate about European unification been more fierce than in Britain. Some argue that the need to accommodate Eastern Europe is slowing down the pace of integration, making political and economic union—a federal Europe and a single currency—less desirable and less practicable. This, in effect, was the sub-text at the Maastricht summit of December 1991. If a Community of Twenty-four or Thirty rather than Twelve is no longer out of the question, the argument runs, then notions of a single currency, a European Bank (the 'Eurofed') and federal political institutions must be put on one side as impracticable. Instead of a united Europe centred around Brussels, there should be a broad free-trade area embracing both East and West Europe.

For others, by contrast, the opening up of Eastern Europe challenges the Twelve to proceed towards full integration at an even faster pace, so that the EC can consolidate political and monetary union while helping the East Europeans and, indeed, independent states formed from the former Soviet Union—including Russia—to develop democratic pluralism and free-market economies. Eventually, in this view, there will need to be new EC institutions, perhaps even a 'core' of EC nations organized along the lines of the United Nations Security Council, to govern a broader collection of states in a general pooling of sovereignty.

This debate has set 'wideners' against 'deepeners'. While it continues, the 1992 programme goes ahead, in an amended form—and it has fallen to Britain, after taking over the rotating EC presidency from Portugal in the second half of 1992, to preside over the final version of the single market.

The dilemmas posed by the challenge of responding to the new Eastern Europe and to EFTA arose just as the EC was dealing with the most difficult 1992 issues, such as car imports, border controls, the harmonization of company law and securities trading, and airline deregulation. The fact remains that scarcely a single area of political life is untouched by the European dimension, from taxation to defence, from transport to broadcasting. Similarly, almost every aspect of business and professional life will be affected by 1992, from accountancy to pharmaceuticals, from engineering to the law.

The Times can claim to have recognized earlier than most what the 1992 target date could mean for industry, commerce and finance, as well as for ordinary travellers and consumers, and ultimately for the UK's national sovereignty. This book draws on the work of *Times* home and foreign reporters on various aspects of 1992, as well as on our own experience and observation.

We owe thanks to Simon Jenkins, Editor of *The Times*, and Martin Ivens, the Foreign Editor. We have a debt, too, to Piers Akerman, former Deputy Foreign Editor, who as long ago as 1987 oversaw a week-long series on 1992 in *The Times* which provided the idea for the original *Times Guide to 1992*. As an Australian, and thus an 'outsider', he perceived perhaps better than many Europeans the significance of the integration process then taking shape.

Our thanks go, too, to Julia Owen for sustaining us since the beginning with encouragement and support.

Richard Owen and Michael Dynes
January 1992

INTRODUCTION

The single market arrives

In April 1990 the German economist Heiko Thieme ventured predictions for 1992 and beyond: Mrs Thatcher would not fight the next British election, but President Bush would be re-elected. Within five years Moscow would again have a stock exchange and a free economy. In Europe there would be full economic and monetary integration, with full political union by the end of the century. Six months later, at the extraordinary EC summit in October 1990 in Rome under the Italian Presidency, Mrs Thatcher lost patience with EC attempts to set a timetable for a European Bank and a single currency, accusing her fellow leaders of living in 'cloud-cuckoo land'. The following month, she stood down after failing to overcome a leadership challenge, and was replaced by John Major. 1990 also saw German unification achieved at a pace few had anticipated. The following year witnessed the end of Communism and the break-up of the Soviet Union following a bungled hardline coup against President Gorbachov in August, setting Russia on a path of reform and privatization. Will Herr Thieme's forecasts of EC monetary and political union be similarly fulfilled or have the upheavals of 1990–91 pushed 1992 off-course?

The Maastricht treaties of December 1991, formally signed by EC leaders in February 1992, kept the single market programme on target while at the same time pointing the way to a future Europe with common citizenship, common defence and common currency. The solutions to the differences between the Twelve, above all between Britain and its partners, were not especially elegant: as one official of the Dutch Presidency put it after the summit, Maastricht 'wins no beauty prizes for symmetry'. The arrangement whereby Britain reserves the right to opt in or out of a single currency in 1999 was ungainly, as was the compromise on the 'social dimension', under which the other eleven are to go ahead with common social provisions of their own. The eleven are to use the mechanisms of the EC to do so, thus excluding British ministers, who will 'opt-out' when social matters are debated in the Council, but not British MEPs at Strasbourg, who will vote on social laws with no application in the UK. Equally anomalous is the arrangement under which Britain will take part in the collective EC decision in 1996 on whether to proceed with a single currency while reserving the right not to trade the pound for the ECU.

Maastricht, in other words, papered over key points of difference between Britain and the rest over issues such as social policy, monetary union and defence. Behind these differences lies a broader, never-ending debate about how far European integration should go—whether the EC, in fact, is and should be much more than a free trade area. It also brought to the surface fears of German domination of the new Europe, fears reinforced by subsequent German behaviour over matters from Yugoslavia to interest rates.

Nonetheless, Maastricht was a milestone in EC history, a landmark event which agreed a single currency by 1999, with opt-out clauses for both Britain and Denmark; an eventual EC defence, with NATO preserved; common EC citizenship; common foreign policy, with implementation of agreed joint action by majority vote; greater powers for the European Parliament; and more funds for the poorer Southern countries, with the money paying for infrastructure projects and environmental legislation. All this is built on a programme which began as a plan for abolishing frontiers, and still has border-free trade at its heart. But there are still obstacles to such trade: in Germany, new environmentally friendly packaging laws were used to protect manufacturers against foreign products which do not conform to the 'Green' rules. Britain resisted the full abolition of frontier checks, claiming special status as an island, and came under pressure from Brussels to conform.

The plan for a Europe without frontiers had its origins in the Single European Act ratified in 1987. At its core lay a desire to bring down barriers to cross-border trade. But the act also swiftly acquired a political dimension, with federalist-minded idealists seeing in the single market the beginning of the United States of Europe. The plan grew as a result of a unique combination of circumstances: the determination of leading EC figures to fulfil the promise of the Treaty of Rome, the EC's founding document, by taking the EC further towards union; and the perception that only a pooling of resources could both match the economic strength of America and Japan on a global scale and guarantee growth and jobs within an expanded EC market. For some, the resulting vision was an exhilarating Euro-cause: for others, a disastrous slide towards the surrender of sovereignty.

Between the two extremes lies a third way, which seems likely to dominate the European debate after Maastricht: continuing integration and abolition of frontier barriers, tempered by a realistic attempt to cope with the obstacles which have arisen since 1987. The need to control the flow of illegal drugs was highlighted by a European Parliament report released just before the Maastricht summit at the end of 1991, which pointed to the rise of Turkish and Chinese gangs operating in Europe, some of them using Eastern Europe's new access to a united Germany. Attacks by IRA terrorists on British servicemen on the Continent also underline the problems of policing open frontiers. So, too, does the growing problem of immigration and asylum, with Britain concerned by the large numbers of refugees—economic and political—seeking asylum in the UK, and Germany and France alarmed by the social pressures and xenophobic violence resulting from the large numbers of immigrants in their countries.

Upheaval in Eastern Europe has complicated the picture, with the EC wanting to bring Poland, Hungary, Czechoslovakia and other nations into the democratic fold without abolishing the old East–West frontiers altogether (see Chapter 18). As *The Economist* noted in September 1991, there is a negative side to 'Euro-nationalism': the risk that the EC, as it abolishes internal controls, will try to 'keep out everything from American culture to Japanese computers, Ukrainian corn to Arab immigrants'. Nonetheless, eliminating internal barriers remains at the heart of 1992.

Abolishing frontier controls

In her controversial speech to the College of Europe in Bruges on 20 September 1988, Mrs Thatcher declared:

> Of course we must make it easier for goods to pass through frontiers. Of course we must make it easier for our people to travel throughout the Community. But it is a matter of plain common sense that we cannot totally abolish frontier controls if we are also to protect our citizens and stop the movement of drugs, of terrorists, of illegal immigrants.

The point was overshadowed by the furore over Mrs Thatcher's simultaneous tirade against the centralization of power in Brussels, the folly of trying to create 'an identikit European personality', and the vision of a 'European superstate'. But John Major, whose style on Europe is markedly different from that of Mrs Thatcher, refocused attention on the issue at the Luxembourg summit of June 1991, declaring: 'We must not be wide open to all comers just because Rome, Paris and London seem more attractive than Bombay or Algiers'. But this solution was not to hold up the abolition of frontier controls; rather, border relaxation inside the EC had to be accompanied by a 'tightening up of the perimeter fence' around the EC and better co-operation between EC police forces. Chancellor Kohl of Germany suggested an FBI-style European force in the run-up to Maastricht.

The heart of the internal market programme, in other words, remains the removal of physical, technical and fiscal barriers. In terms of everyday life and business it means that we—the 320 million citizens of the EC—should be able to move around Europe without hindrance in an integrated transport network based on free competition; to work in any of the Twelve member states on the basis of harmonized qualifications; to sell our goods in any other EC country as if it were our home market on the basis of harmonized standards; to deposit and borrow money anywhere in the EC, perhaps with a European Central Bank to control the money supply. In short, we must think, work and act as if Europe were one country.

The model for frontier abolition is the Schengen Agreement, signed in June 1990—symbolically, on a boat in the middle of the Moselle river —by France, Germany and the Benelux countries. The accord (named after the small town in Luxembourg, where it was first mooted) will remove all border controls between the five nations, harmonize visa requirements for third parties, and institute cross-border police procedures. These will include the exchange of information on 'criminals, undesirables and missing persons', common criteria for political asylum-seekers and the right of 'hot pursuit' on each other's territories. The Schengen Agreement cannot be applied without modification to other EC states. Italy, which wanted to join, was excluded because of its exceptionally long coastline, which makes control of illegal immigration more difficult; Denmark did not qualify because of its passport-free travel arrangements with other Nordic countries; and Britain has special status as an island.

Nonetheless, the abolition of frontiers remains the ideal, coupled with harmonization of standards and practices to ensure free cross-border competition. To reinforce protection against abuse, EC trade ministers agreed in September 1991 that there should be a single EC-wide computer information system linking customs, police and tax authorities—with built-in data protection for individuals. The impetus to overcome the obstacles to an internally coherent bloc thus remains strong. As Jacques Delors put it:

> Japan is spinning its spiders web over large areas of the Pacific;
> the US and Canada are closing together in a free-trade zone,
> doubtless with Mexico tomorrow—the world is beginning to build
> large regional assemblies. We have to move fast or Europe will
> become an archeological site where the Americans and Japanese
> come to dig over defunct ways of life.

The single market programme is, however, behind schedule. In its progress report on single market measures in June 1991 the European Commission reported that, of the 282 measures needed to create the internal market, only 193 had been adopted by all member states. Many barriers to the free movement of goods, services and people had been removed, but obstacles remained in vital areas such as investment, shipping and road haulage. Of the 89 measures still to be approved, 26 were in the internal market area, 28 in economic and financial affairs, 28 in agriculture, five in transport, one in the environment and one in social affairs (see Appendix 8).

As the 1992 ideal collides with reality, Martin Bangemann, the Internal Market Commissioner, has adopted the pragmatic approach which marked his time as German economics minister between 1984 and 1988. He dismisses the growing demand for protectionism from some industries such as cars and electronics, arguing that European companies should be more confident about free competition ('The Japanese cook with water like everybody else, fears of competing with them are ridiculous'). The Commission has drawn back from overregulation, with Bangemann refusing to intervene in a dispute between Britain and Germany over fireproof standards for mattresses, or to set EC standards for free-range chickens. 'How much range does a chicken need to be free'? he asked a farmers' delegation in Brussels, 'The Commission has no business trying to answer such questions.' The underlying principle here is 'subsidiarity', derived from a 1931 Papal encyclical: 'It is an injustice, a grave evil and disturbance of right order for a larger and higher association to arrogate to itself functions which can be performed efficiently by smaller and lower societies'.

Despite such reassurance, Euro-sceptics continue to fear that the 'federalists' will, in the end, impose not only a single European currency but also a European athletics team or a common European defence force. Under John Major, Britain continues to resist attempts to extend the abolition of physical and fiscal barriers to other areas such as the 'social dimension', with EC laws on minimum wages, part-time workers, conditions of work, or days off. Before Maastricht Douglas Hurd warned that such legislation would lead to a return to the 'bad old days' of 1960s strike-bound Britain—a stand described by Delors as reminiscent of Victorian arguments for child labour and other outdated practices.

Britain and EC integration

For Britain, the story of the Common Market began in earnest in 1973, with British accession. One of the dominant themes of British politics and history since then has been the nature of the relationship between Britain and the Continent. But the story of 1992 really began, not in 1973, but in 1957, with the signing of the Treaty of Rome. 'Europe will not be created at a stroke or according to a single plan. It will be built through concrete achievements,' observed Robert Schuman, one of the EC's founding fathers, and the man still revered in Brussels—together with Jean Monnet—as the originator of the post-war dream of a united Europe. If he has a modern successor, it is Jacques Delors, the former finance minister of France, whose second term as President of the European Commission ends in 1992. There is speculation that Delors may return to French politics: he continually refers to France as 'mon pays', has maintained his influence in Paris, and is thought to harbour prime ministerial or even presidential ambitions. Meanwhile, Delors' legacy as Commission President is the 1992 plan to realize the full Common Market envisaged by Schuman, Monnet and other pioneers in the 1950s.

In Britain, helped by the 1992 publicity campaign launched by the Department of Trade and Industry, national awareness of the implications has risen. As more and more single market measures are passed, thanks to majority voting in the EC Council of Ministers, much of 1992 is taking place of its own accord, with business activity refusing to wait for the official deadline. Occasional EC activities—the issuing of Euro-passports, the European Commission's monitoring of the Rover–British Aerospace deal, French takeovers of water companies or Hovis and HP Sauce—have alerted the UK public to the fact that an historic shift is taking place. It is a two-way process: while British property and construction firms are becoming more active on the Continent (especially as the Channel Tunnel nears completion), Dutch and other European property and financial institutions are already making inroads into the UK property market. In all areas of commerce, freer cross-border competition means that both Britain and its European partners and competitors in the EC will have to try harder—but the rewards will be much richer in a market of over 320 million people.

These changes in the professions, transport, tourism, banking, local government, takeovers and so on are taking place against a broader background of political and constitutional issues raised by 1992, such as the transfer of national sovereignty involved in the Single European Act. Behind the debate on Europe lies the still unsettled question of whether 1992 is a vehicle for free-market principles or a step on the road to a European national identity, an issue the fall of Mrs Thatcher brought into sharp relief but did not solve.

Thatcher to Major: a change of tone

The struggle in Britain between rival visions of European integration began with the arrival in Brussels of Lord Cockfield as the senior British Commissioner in 1985, his formulation of the single market programme and the signing of the Single European Act at the end of 1985 by all EC leaders, including Mrs Thatcher (see Chapter 3). But some apparently thought the programme could be confined to trade liberalization. EC energies were largely taken up with EC budget reform in 1986–87, but the Hannover summit of 1988 declared 1992 to be 'irreversible', and authorized Delors to proceed with a report on economic and monetary union.

After Hannover, Delors said monetary union was just one aspect of the rapidly developing programme for the abolition of barriers to trade and mobility in the EC by the end of 1992. There would have to be 'the embryo of a European Government in one form or another' by the mid-1990s. Chancellor Kohl agreed, saying that the European Parliament would, sooner or later, exercise powers 'not far below those enjoyed at present by national parliaments'. Delors went even further, observing that within ten years 80% of economic and social legislation would be passed at the European level.

At Madrid, the Delors report on the first phase of EMU was adopted (see Chapter 8). In November 1989, Delors proposed to MEPs a permanent European government or 'standing committee' of deputy prime ministers from the Twelve, with the Commission slimmed down to a leaner, more political body less involved in day-to-day management.

During the 1989 European election Edward Heath, the former Prime Minister, accused Mrs Thatcher of talking 'absolute rubbish' by expressing fears of a 'European superstate'. Michael Heseltine, also pro-European, attacked 'blind' and 'grudging' attitudes to Europe. Mrs Thatcher told the Commons she was a 'European idealist', but would not permit the single market either to take away from Parliament the power to run Britain's economy and taxation system or to introduce a 'detailed bureaucracy of standardization and harmonization'. She called for a 'Europe of enterprise' rather than a Europe of 'red tape and regulation, state intervention and control'.

For many, the charge of 'meddling' by Brussels struck a chord. But the government fared badly in the European vote, and opinion polls suggested Mrs Thatcher was out of tune with the public mood. Even the *Sunday Telegraph* called it a 'major blunder' to suppose that taking an anti-European stand won votes. John Major, briefly catapulted into the Foreign Office from his post as Chief Secretary to the Treasury in July 1989 in place of Sir Geoffrey Howe, sought to convince critics that the government was not 'lukewarm on Europe', telling the Economic Club in New York in September 1989 the suggestion was 'ludicrous'. 1992 opened up 'exciting prospects' for both Britain and Europe.

However, Europe remained a burning issue, and, in addition to Howe's removal from the Foreign Office, it hastened the departure of Nigel Lawson as Chancellor of the Exchequer in October 1989, following irreconcilable differences with Thatcher over her refusal to allow the pound to join the ERM. Major succeeded Lawson as Chancellor, with Douglas Hurd, long regarded as pro-European, becoming Foreign Secretary.

In June 1990 Major unveiled his plan for a 'hard ecu' as a parallel European currency to the pound, mark and franc rather than an alternative to them. In the run-up to the October 1990 Rome summit Major conceded that the 'hard ECU' could be the precursor to a single currency 'if that were the wish of governments and of people'—a position Thatcher herself adamantly opposed. Before Rome she condemned the single currency as a surrender of monetary and economic control to Brussels, and warned of German domination of the EC. At Rome—ostensibly called to discuss Soviet aid—she angrily accused the Italian presidency of incompetence for allowing the summit to agree a timetable for phases two and three of monetary union (see Chapters 8 and 9).

On 1 November Howe, who had remained Deputy Prime Minister, resigned, telling Thatcher her attitude on (EMU) had given him 'increasing grounds for concern . . . I am deeply anxious that the mood you have struck will make it more difficult for Britain to hold and retain a position of influence in this vital debate'. Two weeks later, Howe made a devastating attack on Thatcher in the Commons, saying her attitude to Europe was 'running increasingly serious risks for the future of our nation' and hinting that it was up to others to challenge her. Michael Heseltine duly did so. At the Paris Conference on Security and Co-operation in Europe (CSCE) in November Thatcher heard the news that she had failed—just —to win a majority in the leadership contest. 'I fight on . . . I fight to win', she declared. But on 22 November, after nearly 12 years in power, she resigned. Major, Hurd and Heseltine stood in the ensuing election, with Major emerging as the winner on 27 November.

As Prime Minister, Major has steered a careful middle way on Europe while making clear that he comes from a younger generation, more open to ideas of integration. In March 1991 he made a landmark foreign policy speech in Bonn, laying the ghost of the Bruges declaration. He urged harmony and consensus to achieve 'a safe and prosperous European home, with Britain at the very heart of Europe'. He added:

> Some people tend to see individualism and social responsibility as mutually exclusive. We make no such mistake . . . For many of my generation, Europe was a cause of political inspiration. We were barely adult when in 1963 Britain's Conservative government made the first application to join the Community.

The tone was very different. At Swansea in June 1991 Major declared:

> Europe is our continent, too. I do not intend to let Britain be sidelined in Europe. The potential damage to our trade, to the City of London and to our future prospects would be immense.

On the other hand, Thatcher retained the loyalty of many, and was given a rapturous reception at the Conservative Party conference at Blackpool in October 1991. She continued to speak out, warning against any commitment to federalism at Maastricht.

Objections to further integration

While the arguments over federalism continue (see Chapter 10 and the Conclusion), John Major has sought to maintain Mrs Thatcher's down-to-earth line but in a more pragmatic form. He, too, wants 1992 to mean that British firms will have as much chance of taking over Continental companies as European ones have of taking over British concerns, with covert barriers to British merger bids removed. What is unclear is that his view of those who see 1992 as a further stage on the road to the vision of the EC's founding fathers, who, when framing the Treaty of Rome in 1957, had more than a mere customs union in mind. The Six wished to lay the foundations of a united Europe which, through economic and political integration, would render unthinkable the kind of wars that had scarred and devastated Europe in the past.

In Britain, phrases or concepts with the prefix 'Euro' tend to arouse negative feelings, whatever personal or national regard we may have for the Dutch, Belgian, Italians or Danes. On the whole, this is due not so much to outright hostility to the EC as such (though this certainly exists) as to a feeling that EC membership has not brought the British people many tangible benefits since accession in 1973. There is an undertow of resentment at 'harmonization' measures, with earlier moves such as the decimalization of currency and metrification of measurements seen as part of a general process of 'Europeanization'. The new Euro-passport is accepted, but, rather like other new facets of modern British life such as the new-look telephone boxes, arouses few warm feelings and is disliked by many (some compare the Euro-passport's appearance, disparagingly, to that of a building society paying-in book).

The bloated Common Agricultural Policy (CAP), from which Britain benefits less than most other major EC states, has made the EC a laughing stock in British eyes. Even the British budget rebate—agreed after much painful negotiation in 1984—has not affected this perception of the EC as the home of butter mountains and wine lakes. Visitors have been known to arrive in Brussels looking for them (alas, EC surpluses are stored in the different Twelve countries). The image of 'fat cat' bureaucrats in Brussels has not helped, nor has the tendency of the UK's tabloid press to seize on lunatic fringe proposals and convey the impression that unhinged EC officials will not stop until they have harmonized everything, up to and including the rules of cricket. The European Commission often makes a useful 'whipping boy', and tends to be criticized even when what are really being attacked are decisions taken by the Council of Ministers, in which all Twelve nations are represented (see Chapter 2). To meet such criticisms—by no means confined to Britain—the Commission deliberately adopted a 'new approach' in 1985, continuing to press for harmonization where it believed it necessary but also relying on the mutual recognition of national standards (see Chapter 4).

To meet the well-founded British complaint that the CAP was an intolerable and inefficient policy, the Brussels summit of February 1988 passed—in modified form—the Delors package of financial reforms that included farm cutbacks and ceilings on farm spending. The CAP remains an albatross, however, and Ray MacSharry, the Commissioner for Agriculture, made a further attempt to reshape the CAP in July 1991, conscious that EC farm subsidies were holding up vital global trade negotiations in the Uruguay Round of GATT. As on previous occasions, MacSharry's attempts to cut the prices of milk, meat and cereals were blocked by farm ministers. Sceptics still claim that average British families spend an extra £10 a week on food because of the CAP system of guaranteed payments to farmers. One recent report—*Consumers and the Common Agricultural Policy*, from the National Consumer Council (NCC)—puts the figure as high as an extra £13.50 a week. Not surprisingly, the Commission rejects the NCC argument.

Single market hopes and fears

Attitudes in business and the professions vary, with some welcoming the opportunities of 1992, some fearing the risks, and others, even at this late stage, still largely puzzled by it. The enthusiasts include companies already prepared for business with the Continent; banks and insurance companies; firms which have European subsidiaries or have merged with European companies; haulage and smaller airline firms; and those in the computer and high-tech fields. One such is Roger Bellass, European Director for Customer Support at Tandem Computers. He argues that

> the computer industry is in a particularly good position to exploit the single market . . . After 1992 it will not be enough to pay lip service to customer service . . . customer expectations across Europe will rise to the highest common denominator. Just as the arrival of Japanese electronic goods in the West has given us higher expectations of what these goods should be like, and how reliable they should be, the advent of the single market will mean customers will expect the same standards from all companies as they get from the best ones, whatever country they are from.

1992, in other words, will benefit those who get customer service right.

Others believe that customer service will deteriorate. Michael Dobbs of Saatchi and Saatchi, the advertising agency, thinks 1992 has become 'too fashionable', a 'commercial virility symbol which is distracting and misleading trusting businessmen' who should be looking to markets elsewhere—for example, in the Far East. He points out that, with free cross-border competition, many companies will fail. The age of Europe Inc. and Euro-conglomerates leads to panic reactions, with 'partnerships sought in a hurry, often with confused motives and unsuitable partners'.

Others in the 'no' lobby include television authorities, who oppose the Commission's plans for Euro-regulation of television and satellite broadcasting (see Chapter 14). Britain's customs officers, who point out that over half of the illegal drugs which enter Britain do so from other EC countries, are increasingly aware of the implications of 1992, and initial hostility to the single market is giving way to acceptance of the need for cross-border co-operation. The European Police Union (EPU), which represents half a million police officers, is divided over the advisability of opening up frontiers. European police forces have already increased their co-operation through sophisticated computer methods. But, on balance, the EPU still fears that criminals of all kinds will find it easier to move around Europe after 1992 than the police seeking to catch them.

Somewhere between the optimists and the doubters are those business executives and professional people—probably the majority—who are not sure what 1992 will bring but are doing their best to prepare for it. In the legal profession the Law Society has set up a working party on 1992, on the assumption that the mutual recognition of legal qualifications (subject to 'top-up' tests in the country concerned) will mean changes in the structure of the legal profession within the UK. The distinction between barristers and solicitors could be eroded, for example, and restrictions in England and Wales against members of the Scottish Bar will look absurd in a frontier-free Europe. Meanwhile, lawyers in the UK could be in a good position to pick up Continental business, especially since a number of English law firms (mostly in the City) have already established major offices on the Continent: 17 have offices in Paris and eight have offices in Brussels. British construction firms and property companies have also begun to increase across the Channel. The European commercial property market is discussed annually at the MIPIM conference in Cannes.

Language and the single market

Behind these hopes and fears lurks the problem of language. English tends to be the language of international business, and is even used at EC summits (it is said that Helmut Schmidt of Germany and Giscard d'Estaing of France conversed in English in private when they were Chancellor and President). On the other hand, company and marketing executives will find after 1992 that it is a handicap not to be fairly conversant with at least one major European language, and preferably two or three. North Europeans—the Dutch, Germans, Danes—tend to speak good (if not impeccable) English as, increasingly, do those from southern Europe countries.

Some business executives think the dangers are exaggerated: Malcolm Miller, sales director of the mass-market computer company Amstrad, maintains that 'you can always make yourself understood, or find someone to translate'. Dr Michael Wintle, Director of the Centre for Modern Dutch Studies at Hull University, points out that British trade with the Netherlands has not been inhibited by the fact that few Britons speak Dutch. The two nations exchange 10% of each other's imports and exports, there are close links between the City and Amsterdam, and Unilever and Royal Dutch Shell are jointly owned. Therefore 'The implication that to do business with the Dutch you must speak their language is empirically a false one,' he said. A further test of the significance of language skills will be the performance of French companies in the unified market, since although the French expect others to learn their language they have traditionally been no more noted than the British for their mastery of other tongues—least of all, English, though it is a mark of the significance of English as the world's language of business that more and more French professionals now speak passable English.

Mastery of Continental languages will, nonetheless, be an important asset to both medium-sized businesses and the multinationals, and cassette tuition companies like Linguaphone, intensive language courses such as Berlitz, and residential 'immersion' language schools like the Business Language Consultancy in Devon expect an increase in interest. The government's contribution are new Language Export Centres, with London courses for business executives—some arranged at City offices —organized by the Polytechnic of Central London and financed by the government, industry and the language colleges themselves. Conversely, the City of London Polytechnic offers language courses for European business executives anxious to learn English.

Time, weights and measures and retailing

Other practicalities include the continuing lack of 'harmonization' between British Summer Time (or Greenwich Mean Time) and the setting of clocks on the Continent. At present, when British business executives telephone Amsterdam or Stuttgart just before lunchtime in London, or at the end of the afternoon, they are likely to find that their client, customer or supplier has already left the office. Conversely, when the Continental contact telephones London, Birmingham or Glasgow on arrival in the office the next day, the British business executive is still having breakfast at home or reading the paper on the train to work. In its report *Making the Most of Daylight Hours* the independent Policy Studies Institute argues that bringing British time into line with Europe would save energy, increase tourism and lead to fewer road accidents. But many— notably farmers, builders and Scots—object. A vote on time harmonization in the Commons in March 1990 was postponed because of Scottish opposition (it is significant that the Conservatives hold a mere handful of Scottish parliamentary seats; some claim that an important measure of business harmonization is being sacrificed for short-term electoral advantage).

Weights and measures are also due for harmonization following an EC draft directive on metrication, updating the 1979 directive—although the daily pint of milk appears safe. Imperial units such as gills, fluid ounces, inches and yards will go metric by 1994, although the therm and fathom will be retained until 1999. Britain wants permanent exemptions for the pint when used for milk and beer; for the troy ounce, used in bullion trading; and for the mile, which, however, is already giving way to the kilometre, just as pounds and ounces are being replaced in shops by kilos and grams.

This, in turn, is having an impact on retailing, as trans-frontier chain stores become more feasible. An 'International Council of Shopping Centres' has begun to meet annually in Nice. The Corporate Intelligence Group warns in its report *Retailing and 1992* that, although the UK retailing and distribution sector is one of the most efficient in Europe, it is tempting for Continental predators, since profit margins are high while legal restrictions on shops are less strict than on the Continent.

Another broad area related to European integration—though not yet covered by any 1992 directive—is health. Arrangements already exist between EC states to provide basic health care for each others' citizens on a reciprocal basis, but travellers are still advised to take out private insurance, and the prospect of a Europe-wide health service seems remote. According to the Office of Health Economics: 'The priority must be for cautious experiment'. The Commission has proposed an EC common-format health card containing a citizen's medical details (such as blood group) as a first step.

31 December 1992: no voice from the heavens

It is a mistake to suppose—in the words of one EC official—that 'neon lights will flash in the sky' at midnight on 31 December, 1992, and a voice from the heavens will proclaim an integrated Europe on 1 January 1993. In aspects of commerce and daily life from Vat to mergers or consumer safety, the programme will continue after 1992, and the European Court will have to deal with continuing disputes over 1992 directives. A further difficulty is that UK law is based on traditions which differ from that of the Continent, much of which derives from the Code Napoléon.

However, industry and the professions are preparing for a major change in the way we do business. The trade unions, too, are getting ready: after a record of hostility towards the EC, the TUC and its European equivalent, the ETUC (which represents 44 million workers), accept the 1992 programme, and want it to include the protection of employee rights. There may even be European unions to represent shopfloor workers in amalgamated European companies—a development which would have an impact on some of the TUC's more old-fashioned policies such as its opposition to single-union deals. Ford located a new electronics component factory in Cadiz in Spain in 1988, rather than in Dundee, and more recently moved the second stage of its programme for modernizing engine manufacture from Bridgend to Cologne.

Despite Delors' assurance that the Commission is 'not like Napoleon's Grand Army, it only intervenes when it must', many still suspect that 1992 is a vehicle for intervention by Brussels in daily life, from the environmental impact of motorways to pensions. But the single market presents both risks and opportunities for ordinary travellers and business executives. The growing number of executives who commute as naturally to Amsterdam or Paris as to Swindon or Liverpool are already involved in the realities of the new Europe, as are UK resort managers who have to abide by EC beach standards, or MOT garages which have to apply stricter standards for exhaust emissions. Whatever the wider arguments, the EC has already acquired a say in many areas once the preserve of national governments. As Lord Plumb, former President of the European Parliament, remarks: 'British firms should not assume that the old habit of doing things late and by halves will work this time . . . Continental companies are not going to wait until we are ready'.

1 THE IMPACT OF 1992

Twelve ways the single market is changing your life

The people of one English town—St Helens on Merseyside—are in no doubt about the impact of the single market on their lives. In October 1991 Pilkington, the world's largest glassmaker, announced that it was moving its headquarters to Brussels. Pilkington had been operating in St Helens for 165 years, but the management had decided that it could not afford to be 'on the periphery of the single market'. St Helens has been left with branch factories only, and the town has lost 750 jobs at a stroke, leaving the local community in a state of shock and a great deal wiser about the effects of 1992. For some companies and communities, on the other hand, a successful preparation for 1992 on their home ground will lead to job creation rather than job losses. Either way, life after 1992 will not be the same.

Imagine you are marketing manager for an office equipment company in Manchester. Shortly after the completion of the European single market on 31 December 1992 you put in a bid with the City Council for a contract to supply high-tech office equipment. But German, Italian and French firms are competing with you on an equal basis—and the German bid is accepted. On the other hand, you have just returned from Ghent, where, to the chagrin of the local Belgian firms, your bid for a major contract was successful. You also have high hopes of a supply contract at Lyons in France. You are learning to operate within a home market of twelve countries.

To relax from business pressures, you take your family for a break through France to Spain, using your new burgundy-coloured Euro-passports and putting your car—with EC-controlled exhaust emissions—on the new Channel Tunnel rail link with the Continent. While in Spain you interrupt your holiday at an EC-approved pollution-free beach to call on your brother, an accountant who works for a newly integrated Euro-telecommunications company near Madrid. On the way back to Calais you stop at a Barclays–Crédit Lyonnais Euro-bank and use your 'smart' electronic Euro-card to draw Danish kroner for your next trip to Copenhagen. How much easier it will be when the Ecu is finally introduced as a single currency, you think, controlled from the newly established European Bank based in London and Frankfurt.

Back home in the UK, you tune in to a variety of television satellite channels to watch the Euro-weather forecast and business news. Next morning, your managing director contacts you on your EC-compatible

car phone to warn you that you might have to go to Brussels to seek
permission for the proposed merger with your firm's Dutch subsidiary
—unless the Dutch take the firm over first. The prospect does not arouse
any particular anxiety, beyond the economic viability of the deal. You
think of yourself automatically as a Mancunian, an Englishman—and a
European.

Twelve benefits of the single market

This, or something like it, is what the world of post-1992 integrated
Europe is supposed to be like. The aim of 1992, as enshrined in the Single
European Act—a legally binding document amending the Treaty of Rome
—is to fulfil the original EC vision of a common market without obstacles
to the free movement of goods, services, capital and people. Not all the
Euro-developments projected above will come about, but 1992 will have
a major impact on the way we live and work in Europe. Among other
things it will mean:

- EASIER TRAVEL FOR PEOPLE. Frontier controls will be all but abolished at the EC's internal frontiers—though not at its external points
  of entry (if anything, external controls will be increased, to ensure
  that non-EC citizens do not find 'soft' entry points). Computer-read,
  single-format EC passports will cut down delays, and police and
  immigration forces will deal with crime more through discreet co-
  ordination than through frontier controls. Eventually, duty-free sales
  will disappear. This was originally scheduled to happen in January
  1993, but Britain has asked for a delay of between ten and 15 years
  because of the adverse impact on shops at ports and airports.

- EASIER TRAVEL FOR GOODS. Frontier delays for goods vehicles—
  many trucks and lorries wait at borders for eight hours or more—
  cost an estimated £17 billion, according to the European Parliament.
  Restrictions on tendering for public contracts cost a further £60 billion.
  The abscence of customs procedures should spare companies the
  need to fill in the 60 million forms at borders every year. It has been
  estimated that such border delays and bureaucratic red tape cost
  British and European consumers 80p for every £10 they spend.

- BUSINESS BOOM. 320 million customers await the efforts of EC business from Britain and Denmark to Greece and Portugal, with all firms
  competing on equal terms in a large open market. One of the key
  provisions obliges public authorities to give enterprises from any EC
  nation an equal opportunity to win high-value contracts.

- JOB RECOGNITION. A teacher from Glasgow will be able to teach
  in Lyons or Copenhagen, and an accountant from Brighton could

work in Naples or Frankfurt, all on the basis of mutually recognized qualifications and diplomas. Linguistic barriers will still cause problems—and will work against the British, since as a nation their grasp of Continental languages is still poor.

- FINANCIAL SERVICES. Restrictions on capital movements were lifted in 1990. EC citizens are now able to open bank accounts or take out mortgages anywhere in the Community, with some exceptions in southern Europe. Cross-border stockbroking is still being held up. But plans are well advanced for a European Bank, perhaps to be operational as soon as 1994, with a single currency shared by at least some EC members by 1997.

- CONSUMER PROTECTION. EC states are no longer able to block imports of foodstuffs or toys because they do not meet national labelling, health or safety standards. Broad criteria and common standards have been devised.

- FREE COMPETITION. Protectionist practices preventing free competition—including that in transport by road, sea and air—become illegal. The first stages of liberalization in aviation and road haulage are already in effect, preventing cartels and quotas and allowing smaller operators increased market access.

- VAT AND INDIRECT TAXES HARMONIZED. Britain successfully resisted plans for the abolition of Vat zero rating on basic goods such as food and childrens' clothes. But the basic principle of the 1992 programme is that, once border controls have gone, trade in the integrated market will be distorted if there are large differentials between Vat rates. A minimum floor of 15% has been agreed as the standard rate.

- TV AND BROADCASTING. Rules for satellite broadcasting across frontiers have been agreed. To prevent European TV being dominated by American or Australian soap operas, as much as 50% of programmes is to be of EC origin 'where possible'. The harmonization of technical standards for high-definition TV (HDTV) will mean improved picture quality and sound.

- THE TELECOMMUNICATIONS MARKET. This is being opened up following a decision to end the monopoly supply of customer terminal equipment and telecommunications services, including databases and electronic mailboxes. A similar move to break up the electricity and gas monopolies in the EC is under way. There is less hope, however, that electrical plugs and sockets will be standardized so that holidaymakers and business executives do not have to carry adaptors or change plugs. Similarly, there are still several incompatible types of cellular telephone systems throughout the EC, making it difficult to use mobile phones when crossing frontiers.

- QUALITY OF LIFE. As environmental protection increases, so quality of life should improve with it. Over 100 separate directives have been or will be implemented in the fields of energy efficiency, water purity and air pollution. This meets a growing demand for a change for the better in the environment.

- PENSIONS. The European Court of Justice has ruled that occupational pensions schemes must apply equal retirement benefits to men and women in cases of compulsory redundancy. Following a 1990 case brought by a male employee of Guardian Royal Exchange Assurance, the court ruled that a pension constituted 'pay' within the meaning of Article 119 of the Treaty of Rome, which prohibits discrimination between men and women.

Momentum of the single market

The momentum which produced this blueprint for change is partly political, partly economic. Much of the drive came from Lord Cockfield, for four years Britain's senior Commissioner in Brussels, with responsibility for the internal market. Formally speaking, the Single European Act and 1992 have their origins in a series of declarations by EC summits on the way forward, notably the Copenhagen summit of December 1982 ('We instruct the Council to decide . . . on priority measures to reinforce the internal market') and the Brussels summit of March 1985 ('We lay particular emphasis on . . . action to achieve a large single market by 1992, thereby creating a more favourable environment for stimulating enterprise, competition and trade'). The programme really began in 1985, with a European Commission White Paper, followed by the Single European Act agreed at Luxembourg in December the same year.

In 1985, 1992 seemed a pipedream to many, but in the seven years since then the single market legislation has been put in place piece by piece, to the point where it now increasingly governs our lives. As the programme's originator, Cockfield believed passionately in a Europe in which crossing from one country to another would entail no more formality for holidaymakers or lorry drivers than crossing from England to Scotland. The burgundy-coloured Euro-passports, now gradually replacing the blue, stiff-backed British ones of old, are part of this drive for a frontier-free Europe.

Lord Cockfield divided the internal market programme into over 300 specific proposals, or groups of proposals, which would then be presented to the Council of Ministers in a timetable geared to completion by

31 December 1992. The Commission has since reduced the number of measures to 282. It has been aided by a provision in the Single European Act which stipulates majority voting procedures in the Council of Ministers for internal market measures, thus effectively robbing individual nations of the power to veto proposals they found unpalatable. However, once passed by Council, the measures have to be incorporated into national law, and several countries (notably France, Greece, Portugal and Italy) have been slow in carrying this out. The Commission's sixth progress report on completion of the single market, issued in July 1991, criticized Italy in particular for adopting only just over half the agreed 1992 measures, and warned that it was turning its attention to rigorous enforcement of internal market legislation under powers given to it by the Treaty of Rome.

In the current Commission the Internal Market portfolio is held by Martin Bangemann of Germany, who, over the past four years, has pursued the 1992 programme with the same vigour as Lord Cockfield while observing the principle of 'subsidiarity': that the EC should only deal with matters best handled at European rather than national, regional or local levels.

Single market measures already in force

In the seven years since 1992 became more than a gleam in the eyes of Cockfield and Delors, the programme has continued steadily forward. Despite 'slippage', three-quarters of the 1992 measures have been passed into law—and EC law takes precedence over national law—with most of the remaining directives tabled and awaiting approval.

In other words, we are already being governed by 1992 directives in all four of the areas covered by the 1992 concept: people, goods, services and capital. Technical standards are being harmonized, with common standards for products from lawnmowers (and the noise levels they emit) to forklift trucks (including, for example, their forward and reverse gears). Some local authorities in the UK have begun to realize the implications. Bolton, in Lancashire, for example, has a 1992 action programme. Local surveys by the action group show a nearly 100% awareness of the single market—although 20% of local companies thought that it was irrelevant to them because they were 'not export orientated'. In fact, they and others like them could face competition on their home ground from elsewhere in the EC: the single market is a two-way process.

The idea of an integrated Europe may seem somewhat far-fetched if you are, say, an Englishman encountering obstacles when trying to buy a house in Italy, a Dutchman attempting in vain to settle a garage bill in France with a Eurocheque or a German infuriated at having to pay a motorway tax in Belgium. But under the 1992 process such irritations are beginning to be overcome. The process will be a long one, with many countries facing prosecution against outmoded protectionist practices in the European Court of Justice at Luxembourg. But the process *is* under way, for all that national governments often do their best to disguise it by presenting new EC laws as national legislation.

Take the problem of moving goods around the EC by road. In June 1988, after months of prevarication, EC transport ministers agreed to abolish all EC, bilateral and transit road haulage quotas by 1 January 1993. Ironically, this measure—a regulation, not a directive—was passed under German chairmanship, even though the Germans had been among the most vociferous opponents of free competition in road transport, fearing that their haulage companies would be at a disadvantage to more efficient Dutch or Belgian trucking ones—as indeed they may after 1992. To allay West German fears, the Commission, playing a role which is becoming increasingly common in controversial 1992 measures, agreed to undertake an informal review of lorry drivers' hours of work and rest, and to make tachograph inspections more strict. But the measure was passed, and is vital to the 1992 objective, given that over half of all internally traded EC goods are transported by road. Equally, 1992 involves the liberalization of air transport, inaugurating an era of greater competition and cheaper fares.

On the seas around Britain, British fishermen have found themselves obliged to compete with Spanish fishermen following a successful Spanish challenge to the 1988 Merchant Shipping Act which sought to stop Spanish-owned vessels taking up British EC fishing quotas by using 'brass plate' companies registered in the UK. To prevent this 'quota hopping', the Act had insisted that 75% of the ownership of such companies be vested in persons who were both UK nationals and resident in the UK. In July 1991 the European Court of Justice ruled that this was incompatible with EC law, which takes precedence over national law—the first time an Act of Parliament had been struck down by the EC. The government compromised by negotiating a deal with the Anglo–Spanish companies, under which they would have to land their catches in the UK and have properly registered UK agents. As *The Times* observed in an editorial, it seemed logical that 'those who flew the British flag should be the persons for whom the quotas were intended—the British'. On the other hand, the 1992 principle at stake was 'the right of any commercial company to set up in any EC member state'.

As another example, take the freedom of professional people to move around the EC as if it were one country. Shortly after the road haulage agreement by transport ministers, trade ministers met in Luxembourg to draw up common principles for the mutual recognition of diplomas by all twelve EC states. What this means is that after 1992, a surveyor from Birmingham will be able to practise in Barcelona without retaking surveyor examinations, and a lawyer from Leeds will be able to find employment in Frankfurt if he or she so wishes without resitting Bar Finals (although in some areas, such as the law and accounting, a local top-up test may be required to prove adequate knowledge of local law). The same, of course, applies in reverse—and Continental Europeans tend to speak far better English than British people speak European languages.

Another vital 1992 directive, on 'public procurement', obliges public authorities, including local government, to open up major public supply contracts to tender from any EC firm. If an Italian or Dutch company makes the best offer—as our imaginary office equipment supplier from Manchester found—it must be accepted, and the home-based British bidder will receive no sympathy. After 1992 there will also be intense competition between EC ports, especially once the Channel Tunnel is in place.

The challenge to Britain

In other words, much will depend on the confidence, energy and ability of British companies and professionals, and their willingness to meet the 1992 challenge both by facing competition from other EC nationals on their home ground and by trying to make inroads into domestic markets in the other eleven EC states. A CBI survey in 1988 showed that only 7% of companies had appointed an executive or team to prepare for 1992; the same percentage had introduced language training; 20% had carried out a 'strategy review'; 10% had done 1992 market research. Thirty-one per cent had done nothing at all. More recently a survey conducted by MORI in 1991 for the UK division of Epson showed that over half of the executives interviewed did not know who Jacques Delors was; under half knew what the letters CAP stood for, what the member states of the EC were, or in which city the European Commission headquarters was located. A remarkable 77% did not know what the letters ERM meant, and only one in three could say in German 'Good morning, my name is Mr Smith'. Fifty per cent still thought that 1992 would have little or no impact on their business.

Yet Britain stands to gain enormously from the single market, with the British economy perhaps best placed in the area of financial services. In July 1990 capital movements across EC borders were liberalized, despite earlier reservations on the part of the socialist government in France, which had argued that allowing EC citizens to move cash around the Community could only encourage tax evasion. In its now familiar role as honest broker, the Commission agreed to study ways of increasing tax inspection, thus overcoming French doubts and allowing the directive to go forward.

Coupled with a new 1992 banking directive allowing High Street banks to operate anywhere in the EC under a single licensing system, the capital movements directive means that EC citizens—including Britons—can deposit or borrow money anywhere in the Community, with exchange controls abolished (except, for a provisional period, in Greece, Spain, Portugal and Ireland). Whether National Westminster and

Barclays make more of an inroad into France than the Crédit Lyonnais or the Deutsche Bank in Britain will depend on the drive of the banks concerned. The same applies to insurance, where Britain also has a strong reputation.

There are, of course, drawbacks to these schemes. As Neil Hartley of National Westminster's 1992 policy unit points out, 1992 will mean job losses as well as job creation, through mergers and market penetration. Professor Peter Herriot of Birkbeck College, London, warns that Britain risks an exodus of skilled graduates to Europe ('designers to Dusseldorf, physicists to Freiburg, engineers to Essen'), a finding supported by the Institute of Manpower Studies at Sussex University in its report *The Graduate Labour Market in the 1990s*. Others caution that high salaries for, say, working in telecommunications in Frankfurt will be offset by high taxes and cultural dislocation. Headhunters Saxton Bampfylde, who recently surveyed managers responsible for 1992 in 130 large companies, say the successful Euro-executive will be the man or woman who knows the local culture well, rather than the 'Euro-yuppie' who stays in bland business hotels and is 'dressed out of the contents of a duty-free shop'.

The ripple effect of the single market

The single market stems from a complex of directives, regulations and other measures which together add up to a shift in the way the EC is organized—and in how we are governed. Whether we like it or not, 1992 is developing beyond the confines of the 1985 White Paper and taking on a life of its own. Almost any European-wide scheme, in fact, can now be related to the single market.

Broadcasting offers one example. Many governments and broadcasting authorities argue that harmonizing television standards and encouraging a 'European' culture in the media are not part of 1992. However, the White Paper refers to the need for 'a single Community-wide broadcasting area' on the grounds that the Treaty of Rome provides for 'a common market in services'. The Commission therefore drew up plans for common standards in advertising and the co-ordination of satellite technology and cable TV, arguing that television constitutes an economic service within the meaning of the Treaty, and that, because of the rapid development of satellite technology, there must be a framework to guide broadcasters and TV authorities in the integrated European market.

European policies directly affect products, from shoes (the British Footwear Manufacturers' Federation is appealing to the EC to act against a flood of foreign—i.e. non-EC—exports to the UK) to cigarettes. From 1 January 1993 cigarette packets must carry prominent, strongly worded health warnings. In 1991 the Commission debated proposals for banning tobacco advertising in newspapers and magazines and on hoardings, a measure which would mean revenue losses for the advertising industry amounting to £60 million a year, with similar losses for newspapers (especially colour supplements). Even horse racing and field sports are affected. Following a European Court case brought by Ladbrokes against Paris Mutuel, the French off-track betting organization, over its attempts to penetrate the UK betting market the Commission is considering EC-wide gambling legislation. If this is passed Britain might introduce a national lottery (it is the only EC state not to have one).

The air-liberalization package does not include the question of air-traffic control. Yet as Europe's skies become more congested, causing inconvenience and delays for air passengers (not least for those who have saved up for package tours), EC governments have begun to acknowledge that there should be a greater role for Eurocontrol, the under-used European air-traffic control centre at Maastricht in the Netherlands, even though Eurocontrol is not an EC body and has nothing to do with 1992.

Equally, there is no mention in the 1992 White Paper of defence. Yet it is increasingly assumed that, at some point, an integrated Europe will need some form of military integration—or at least military co-operation—to defend it. The Single European Act made provision for co-operation between EC states on 'the economic and political aspects of security'. It is a phrase that has given rise to varying interpretations, with the French and the Germans inclined to translate 'security' as 'defence' while the British prefer a far vaguer interpretation, implying only consultation on wider European security interests. But the Gulf War and the civil war in Yugoslavia provided further impetus towards a common defence policy, perhaps even the embryo of a European army following moves by France and Germany towards closer military co-operation.

There is growing recognition of the need to pool sovereignty in another area: environmental protection. Chlorofluorocarbons (CFCs), chemicals used in aerosols which harm the ozone layer, are to be phased out by the year 2000. Similarly, new standards have been set to cut noxious emissions from car exhausts (through catalytic converters) and power stations.

Education and the arts

No corner of life and commerce is likely to escape the long arm of Brussels. Even art dealers and auction houses, which might have thought themselves remote from arguments about harmonization and cross-border integration, face the prospect of a 1992 directive under which British dealers would have to impose Vat on works of art and antiques, thus risking (according to critics of the move) the loss of their current competitive edge and the transfer of international auction business to Geneva (Switzerland being outside the EC) and New York.

In education, traditionally regarded as a national prerogative, an International Baccalaureat (IB) could eventually challenge other certificates of higher education. The IB system, taught in 400 schools around the world, requires students to study three subjects in depth to the equivalent of A-level, but also to take three other subjects to a less exacting level, with a mix of science and humanities. Seventeen British schools and colleges teach the IB at present, with the examination board based at Bath University.

In higher education, the polytechnics have the edge in European business studies, with courses at Humberside College of Education, Kingston Polytechnic, Lancashire Polytechnic, Middlesex Polytechnic and Trent Polytechnic in Nottingham, which links up with the University of Paderborn in Germany and the Groupe Ecole Supérieure de Commerce in Toulouse. Such links are supported by the EC's Erasmus fund.

Dutch and French socialist MEPs have proposed a European history book in which national viewpoints on Waterloo, the Franco-Prussian war or the Second World War would be counterbalanced by other viewpoints and 'descriptions of events which occurred simultaneously in all member states, to stimulate an awareness of belonging to a single political entity'. Hugh McMahon, a former history teacher and Labour MEP for Strathclyde West, dismisses this as 'Euro-culture gone berserk': the EC cannot produce a 'sanitized version of the conflicts and wars which took place in Europe in previous centuries'.

There is, nonetheless, a detectable shift in arts syllabuses—and reading habits—towards European literature. Publishers at the Frankfurt Book Fair report a search for 'the big European novel rather than the big American novel'. One HarperCollins executive says that British publishers 'now spend more time at Frankfurt with the Europeans than with the Americans'. Publishers are buying European—rather than just UK—rights to American books to protect themselves against US editions being brought into the UK cheaply across unrestricted EC frontiers.

The advertising industry is also preparing for the single market, focusing on the concept of the 'European High Street'.

Eliminating the cost of twelve separate markets

The drive for integration, in other words, is as much political as economic. It stems not only from Euro-idealism (and not only from an impulse to complete the work of the EC's founders) but also from a fear that unless the EC works more closely together, not least in industry and technology, it will prove unable to compete effectively with other giant trading blocs, notably Japan/Asia and the United States.

The official Cecchini report on the benefits of the internal market —*The European Challenge 1992*—estimates that the integration of twelve national markets will save the EC £140 billion (about 5% of the Community's gross national product), will create millions of jobs and stimulate enough growth to 'put Europe on an upward trajectory of economic growth lasting into the next century'. This, the report declares, is 'a firm prospect, not a tantalizing chimera'.

The Cecchini report can be criticized for biasing the evidence in a way which suits EC officials who wish the single market plan to succeed. But even allowing for an element of Euro-wishful thinking on the part of the Commission, these are impressive claims. Cecchini could also have added that the countries which will benefit most from 1992 will be those which are best prepared for it. Unfortunately, despite the DTI campaign, awareness in Britain of how power in the EC works, and of the implications of the single market, is still at a low level compared to that of our Continental partners. In the following chapters we look at the decision-making structure of the EC, how the Single European Act which is changing our lives came about, and the significance of further revisions of the treaty of Rome to take the EC towards a single currency, a European Bank and closer political union.

2 DIRECTIVES AND DEMOCRACY

Who wields power in the European Community?

In framing the Treaty of Rome, which establishes the EC's institutions and defines their roles, the founders dealt with the most obvious political fact of life in the new European venture: that decisions taken in the name of the member governments (six in the beginning, and now twelve) would have to have the consent of all. Thus arose the Council of Ministers, which often puzzles outside observers since it does not exist in permanent session. It does, however, have a permanent secretariat and EC ambassadors in Brussels (known as Permanent Representatives), who take day-to-day decisions when the Council is not in session.

The Council, which has the last word in EC legislation, is simply made up of those ministers from the twelve governments with responsibility for the subject in question. Thus farm prices are settled (or not settled) by Agriculture Ministers, who then disperse back to their respective capitals and are replaced by their ministerial colleagues who deal with steel (Industry Ministers) or currencies (Finance Ministers) or pollution (Environment Ministers). The 1992 internal market directives are dealt with by Trade Ministers, unless they obviously fall within the purview of another set of ministers (financial services directives, for example, usually go to Finance Ministers).

One side-effect is that ministers from the twelve nations get to know each other intimately, and act almost as a European government. On the other hand, all ministers feel that they owe their first obligation to their national electorates. Once back home from a Brussels or Luxembourg meeting, they tend to disguise the extent to which they co-operate in the European cause and choose to emphasize instead the role they play (imagined or real) in defending national interests in an EC context.

The task of representing Europe as a whole, at least in the public eye, falls to the European Parliament in Strasbourg, with Euro MPs drawn from all twelve states, and to the European Commission, with its headquarters in Brussels. The European Parliament, however, was set up under the Treaty of Rome as a largely consultative body, initially called the European Assembly. It is only since direct elections in 1979 (and more recently since the advent of the Single European Act) that it has begun to acquire a more decisive role in EC affairs. Rightly or wrongly, therefore, the European Commission has come to appear in the public mind as the central EC institution, and the one that people regard as imposing its 'Brussels' will on EC citizens. The more the Commission tries to avoid this image, carefully pointing out that it is an executive body and that there is a constitutional balance to be observed between the Commission, the Council and the Parliament, the more power and influence seems to flow towards the Berlaymont, the Commission's star-shaped plate-glass headquarters in Brussels.

The European Commission

Despite its power and importance, the Commission is appointed, not elected. It is often described as the EC's executive branch or central bureaucracy. However, its function is more wide-ranging than this might suggest. It was established under Article 155 of the Treaty as the body which would originate draft legislation to put before the Council of Ministers and Assembly (Parliament), and which would then implement the resulting directives. However, Article 155 also gives the Commission the right to 'have its own power of decision and participate in the shaping of measures taken by the Council and the European Parliament'. The Commission can issue regulations of its own accord, without reference to the two legislative bodies—as it did, for example, after the Chernobyl nuclear accident, by imposing a *cordon sanitaire* around the EC against the importation of goods contaminated by radiation. However, the Commission also has the power 'to participate in the shaping of measures' which do pass through the Council and Parliament. It does this by sitting in on Council sessions, and by meeting at the Parliament building in Strasbourg once a month, when Euro MPs are in plenary session. Commissioners are therefore present—and active—at all three stages of the decision-making process: initiation of draft proposals, debate and implementation.

This is of particular importance where 1992 is concerned. Quite apart from powers given to it under the Single European Act, the Commission has been able to originate 1992 legislation; take part in, and even guide the modification process as 1992 directives pass through the Council and Parliament; and then implement the resulting laws. The key role in the first phase of the 1992 programme (1985–8) fell to Lord Cockfield, as Internal Market Commissioner: it now rests with Martin Bangemann of Germany, under the direction of President Delors. The Council and Parliament can overturn draft 1992 legislation if they are so minded, since they have the final say. However, in practice, the discussion of 1992 takes place within a framework defined by the Commission, and on the basis of proposals devised within the Berlaymont. This makes Delors and his 16 Commissioners potentially powerful figures. In the first Delors administration, for example, Peter Sutherland, the Irish Commissioner, matched Lord Cockfield's 1992 crusade with a forceful campaign of his own to exploit to the full the powers given to the Commission by the Treaty to intervene in mergers and takeovers if they distort competition.

The Commission is not, on the other hand, a 'foreign junta', as one peer memorably claimed in July 1988 during the debate in the House of Lords on the Rover–British Aerospace merger. Its national composition is carefully balanced, and Britain plays a full part in it—as in the Council of Ministers. In the present Community of Twelve there are 17 Commissioners—two each from Britain, France, Germany, Italy and Spain, and one each from Belgium, Denmark, Greece, Ireland, Luxembourg, the Netherlands and Portugal. The 17 Commission members are appointed by their national governments—in practice, their respective prime ministers, who discuss the appointments at the EC summit preceding the four-yearly change of staff at the Berlaymont. Heads of government naturally seek to appoint Commissioners who will represent the national interest. As a result of Maastricht, there are to be 12 Commissioners only.

By some unwritten law, however, Commissioners almost always 'go native'—the charge most often levelled at Lord Cockfield before his replacement by Leon Brittan—leading to perpetual tension between Brussels and the national capitals. The contradiction is built into the solemn oath Commissioners take on arriving in Brussels, which commits them 'to perform my duties in complete independence, in the general interest of the Communities'. Commissioners also vow 'in carrying out my duties neither to seek nor to take instructions from any Government or body'. The oath adds pointedly that all member states of the EC have undertaken to respect this principle and 'not to seek to influence Members of the Commission in the performance of their task'—a promise sometimes more honoured in the breach than the observance.

Each Commissioner is given one or more portfolios dealing with specific areas of policy (a list of the current Commission portfolios is given at the end of this book), with portfolios traditionally allotted by the Commission President over dinner at a chateau on the outskirts of Brussels, in a 'night of the long knives'. For Britain the most significant move in the Delors reshuffle of December 1988 was the allocation of the internal market portfolio, previously held by Lord Cockfield, to Martin Bangemann of Germany—albeit divested of responsibility for financial services and fiscal approximation. But the two British Commissioners were nevertheless given key portfolios. Leon Brittan took over from Peter Sutherland as Competition Commissioner, with responsibility for relations with the European Parliament and financial services, while Bruce Millan was put in charge of the Community's regional development funds. The controversial issue of fiscal approximation was given to the junior French Commissioner, Mme Christiane Scrivener, who is known to be sympathetic to the problems faced by Britain and Ireland over the proposed abolition of value added tax zero-rating. The powers of the European Commission President should not be exaggerated: he is not 'President of Europe', since power is shared with the other EC institutions, nor is he equivalent to a national prime minister, since Commission decisions are taken

Passage of Single Market Directives into EC Law

EUROPEAN COMMISSION
initiates legislation by
drafting directive.

COUNCIL OF MINISTERS
debates directive, either at
ministerial level or through
COREPER, the permanent
committee of ambassadors to
the EC.

EUROPEAN PARLIAMENT
amends directive. Single European Act gave MEPs limited power
of veto over 1992 legislation; Maastricht strengthened veto powers
in specified areas such as transport, the environment and
consumer protection.

**EUROPEAN
COMMISSION**
further modifies the directive
in the light of Council/
Parliament deliberations.

COUNCIL OF MINISTERS
votes on the directives, using
qualified majority system in
some cases and unanimity in
others. Directive becomes EC
law.

**EUROPEAN
COURT OF JUSTICE**
rules in cases where an EC
law is not observed by a
member state or causes
disputes between states and
the Commission.

**NATIONAL
GOVERNMENTS**
enact the new EC law by
putting it to vote in national
parliaments.

collectively, usually by majority vote. However, the President adopts an increasingly high profile, and attends Western economic summits alongside other Western leaders on behalf of the EC as a whole.

Each Commissioner has a staff or cabinet. The Commission bureaucracy is not as large as is sometimes imagined: including its 23 Directorates General, which report to Commissioners, it has about 15,000 staff (including interpreters and translators), less than the administration of Edinburgh —although the Eurocrats' high tax-free salaries and perks help to create the popular image of a bloated bureaucracy. It is also regarded as one of the most open bureaucracies in the world. The Council has a staff of 2000 and the European Parliament 3200.

The Commission meets on Wednesdays to review draft legislation, take legal action against recalcitrant states through the European Court of Justice, issue regulations and so on. A regulation differs from a directive in that it applies in detail to all member states. A directive, by contrast, lays down the aim and principle of a measure but leaves it up to national parliaments to put the new law into national form. In addition, the Commission administers EC funds, such as the regional fund or the farm support budget, and negotiates trade agreements on behalf of the EC.

The Luxembourg presidency draft on political union put forward in the first half of 1991, and used as the basis of the Maastricht summit at the end of 1991, offended Delors by proposing that the European Parliament should have co-decision powers with the Council of Ministers (see below), with the Commission still able to initiate legislation but less empowered to amend it. Delors described this as an inexplicable attempt to 'enfeeble' one of the institutions enshrined in the Treaty of Rome and a violation of the principles of the EC's founding fathers.

At the end of 1991 the Commission announced that it was abandoning the Berlaymont, which had become unsuitable and was, in any case, a health hazard because of the asbestos used in its construction. The Commission continues to be in dispute with Belgium, the host nation, over the siting and funding of a new headquarters.

The Council of Ministers

The Council represents the governments of the Twelve, and thus acts as a counterweight to the Commission, whose main focus is EC-wide rather than national. On the other hand, the Council also has to bear in mind the wider European interest. This is especially true of the twice-yearly EC summit, or European Council, which takes fundamental decisions about the Community's future direction.

As noted earlier, the Council does not meet continuously but is an *ad hoc* body made up of national ministers with responsibility for the policy area under discussion—Foreign Affairs, Agriculture, Transport, Industry and so on. The supreme body, therefore (the summit), is made up of prime ministers, or in one case (France) the president (hence the formal reference to 'the heads of state and government' at European Councils). Summits were not formally provided for in the Treaty of Rome, and only began in 1975. The institution of the twice-yearly (formerly thrice-yearly) European Council is now laid down in the Single European Act, and therefore in the Treaty. There is a growing tendency for the summit to deal with complex 1992 issues which in theory should have been sorted out at a lower level but which have proved intractable.

Unlike the Commission, which has a President appointed for two years (usually renewed, making a four-year term), the Council is chaired by each member state in turn for a period of six months. This rotating chairmanship is referred to—rather confusingly—as the presidency of the Council of Ministers, in addition to which the European Parliament has its own President (Lord Plumb). The three EC Presidents sometimes hold joint meetings (for example, to sort out a dispute over the budget).

The President of the Council is the prime minister of whichever country holds the six-month rotating presidency. In the first half of 1989 this was Felipe Gonzalez of Spain, in the second half of 1989 President Mitterrand of France (because France follows España in the alphabet of the country concerned). In 1990 the Council Presidents were the leaders of Ireland and Italy, followed by Luxembourg and the Netherlands in 1991, and in 1992 Portugal and Britain (United Kingdom). It will therefore fall to Britain to preside over the celebrations on 31 December 1992, handing on the presidencies of the single market to Denmark and Belgium in 1993. Since the foreign ministers meet regularly to deal with day-to-day Council business (when they become known as the General Affairs Council, rather than the Foreign Affairs Council), in practice the foreign minister of the Presidency nation is in the chair most often, and is therefore also referred to as President of the Council.

If the function of the Commission is to draw up draft legislation, including the draft EC budget, the task of the Council, in its various ministerial forms, is to examine the draft measures in conjunction with the European Parliament and in due course to amend, accept or reject them. Measures are usually examined first—and comprehensively—by EC ambassadors in Brussels, the Committee of Permanent Representatives, known collectively by the French acronym COREPER. When COREPER agrees unanimously on a measure (usually an uncontroversial one) it passes through the full ministerial Council on the nod, appearing on the agenda as what is called in the jargon an 'A Point'. Otherwise a directive can only become EC law when it has been passed by the ministers of the Twelve in the Council, sometimes by unanimity, sometimes by majority vote. The question of majority voting (strictly speaking, qualified majority voting, based on a complex mathematical formula) is crucial to the 1992 process, since under the Single European Act internal market measures can be passed by majority vote.

The system of rotating Council presidencies is also relevant to the 1992 programme, for the simple reason that each EC nation has different attitudes and priorities. Under the German presidency in the first half of 1988, for example, EC–Comecon *rapprochement* moved forward, and a large number of single-market measures were approved. Greece, which took over from Bonn for the second half of 1988, also pursued 1992 objectives, despite fears that the abolition of borders would expose the relatively weak Greek economy to cross-frontier competition. However, Council President Andreas Papandreou, the Greek prime minister, put the 1992 stress on social issues such as health and safety at work and (more controversially) worker participation in industry, a trend opposed by Mrs Thatcher, notably at the Rhodes EC summit (European Council) in December 1988, just before Greece handed over the presidency to Spain. Since Spain and France, which inherited the rotating presidency in the second half of 1989 (after the EC summit in Madrid on monetary union), broadly share the Greek outlook and also have left-wing administrations, social issues have come to the fore alongside 1992 economic and political ones.

Like Commission meetings, sessions of the Council are held behind closed doors, a practice which has increasingly led to the charge that EC decision making is unacceptably secretive. Ministers retort that—unlike Commissioners—they are elected in their home countries and are therefore accountable. Equally, there is a large Brussels press corps which is regularly briefed by national spokesmen, both during and between Council meetings, and which reports what goes on behind the scenes through contacts with officials. Nonetheless, concern is growing over what is known in EC jargon as the 'democratic deficit' or lack of democratic control over EC decision making, and there is pressure for the Council to open at least some of its proceedings to the public, with a press gallery at the Charlemagne building (the Council's headquarters, opposite the Berlaymont) on the lines of the press galleries at Westminster and other EC parliaments.

Ministers continue to argue that their deliberations are too sensitive to be exposed to the public gaze, partly because Council debates involve a great deal of bargaining between nations as ministers try to find a balance between national interests and the wider interests of the EC as a whole. Once back home, ministers sometimes find it convenient to blame an unpopular measure on 'Brussels'—but, in the last analysis, 'Brussels' means the Council, in which all twelve nations take an equal part.

For three months in the year (April, June and October) Council meetings are held not in Brussels but in Luxembourg. This practice is jealously guarded by the Luxembourgers, who have built a large European Conference Centre in the Grand Duchy, but it is a constant source of irritation to the large numbers of officials and journalists who have to make the 2½-hour journey to Luxembourg from Brussels. Moving documents and staff between the three EC centres (Brussels, Luxembourg and Strasbourg) is also estimated to cost the EC taxpayer up to £100 million a year. There is growing pressure to move the European Parliament from Strasbourg to Brussels as part of a campaign to centralize most EC functions, making Brussels the administrative and legislative centre for the single market and making good its claim to be 'the capital of Europe'.

Qualified majority voting

Since qualified majority voting in the Council is so central to 1992—and so strongly criticized by those who think that power is shifting to Brussels too far, too fast—it is perhaps worth looking at it in detail. Under the Single European Act, 1992 issues can be (and in practice are) decided by a system of voting under which each member state is given a number of votes more or less consonant with its size and importance in the EC. Thus Britain wields ten votes, together with Germany, France and Italy; Spain has eight; Belgium, Greece, Holland and Portugal have five each; both Denmark and Ireland have three; and tiny Luxembourg has only two. A qualified majority simply means 54 votes out of the total 76 from at least eight member states—meaning, in reality, that even two of the 'big boys' (for example, Britain and Germany) acting together cannot block a decision. It takes three of the larger countries (or two of them plus one or two smaller states) to muster enough votes to stop a 1992 decision going through. But qualified majority voting does not apply to fiscal issues, which remain subject to the national veto.

The question of majority voting is a sensitive one, since it strikes at the heart of the national veto—that is, the right of any member state to veto legislation it does not like. Originally, most EC laws had to be passed by unanimous vote, but in the 1960s pressure built up for a switch to majority voting. When this ran into difficulties (mainly because of French opposition) the Six (as they then were) agreed on an informal arrangement known as the Luxembourg Compromise. This said that majority voting would be gradually introduced, but that the right of national veto would be retained where 'very important interests of one or more partners are at stake'. In practice, this proved unworkable. The advent of qualified majority voting under the Single European Act seems to have ended the Luxembourg Compromise, at least for 1992 issues, although this will only really become clear in the course of time, as qualified majority voting is tested in practice (it is already being used increasingly). On non-1992 issues the right of veto is unaffected: on the other hand, the dividing line between 1992 issues and non-1992 issues is not always obvious. (For a discussion of whether the European Central Bank proposal can be vetoed, see Chapter 8.)

The Commission has come under fire for categorizing controversial proposals such as the European Company Statute as internal market legislation requiring only a majority vote. Similarly, the Commission has invoked Article 90 of the Treaty of Rome to bring in new directives liberalizing the telecommunications equipment market, a move contested by

France in the European Court of Justice. The Commission also drew criticism in 1989 for alleged corruption and excessive perks within its bureaucracy. Delors replied that such accusations amounted to a 'phoney war' to divert attention from key 1992 issues.

The European Parliament

It is sometimes supposed that Euro MPs are the decision makers in the EC, by analogy with Westminster. This is a misconception. The other widely held view of Euro MPs—that they enjoy a comfortable lifestyle with many perks—is less inaccurate, although MEPs can point to the arduous journeys they are obliged to make between their home constituencies and the Parliament's premises in Brussels and Strasbourg, or to conferences outside Europe (for example, for meetings with representatives of the ACP countries).

The Parliament has its origins in the European Assembly (initially the Assembly of the European Coal and Steel Community, before the EC proper was formed), to which national MPs were seconded. At first, the Assembly had 142 members; this was increased to 198 when Britain joined the EC in 1973 together with Denmark and Ireland, making an EC of Nine. However, the major change in the Parliament's fortunes came in 1979, when the first direct elections were held to a body of 410 seats, expanded to 434 seats for the next Euro elections in 1984, by which time Greece had joined the Community. The present Parliament has 518 seats, because of the entry of Spain and Portugal in 1986. After German reunification in October 1990 Bonn began to argue that Germany should have more than the 81 seats allotted to itself, the UK, France and Italy, but by the Maastricht summit this remained unresolved.

The last elections, in June 1989, saw victories for the Socialists and Greens and losses for the centre and right-wing parties which had dominated the previous Parliament. Voter turnout was 56% for the EC as a whole and 37% in the UK (higher than the 32% turnout of 1979 and 1984). The British Labour Party won 13 extra seats at the expense of the Conservatives, whose electoral campaign was described by Sir Leon Brittan as 'negative, damaging and confusing'. Even before the vote, the Spanish Partido Popular abandoned the Conservatives for the Christian Democrats.

The voting pattern throughout the EC was one of protest against ruling parties, with startling gains for the Greens in the UK and for the far right in France and Germany. However, because of the lack of a common electoral system, despite provision for one in the Treaty of Rome, the success of the Greens in the UK—with 2.3 million votes, or 15% of the vote, compared to the Conservatives' 34% and Labour's 40%—was not reflected in seats. Britain uses the first past the post system, whereas most other EC nations have some form of proportional representation (Ireland uses the single transferable vote). The Euro MPs, who sit in political groupings rather than national blocs, re-assembled in July 1989 with renewed confidence in their status as Europe's legislature. Lord Plumb (Conservative) was replaced as President by Enrique Barón Crespo, a Spanish Socialist, reflecting the new left-wing dominance of the chamber (260 seats, a narrow majority). On many 1992 issues, from the environment to workers' control, the Left and the Christian Democrats have informal understandings.

On the other hand, the Parliament did not become a true legislature even in 1979, and it took the Single European Act to give Euro MPs greater powers, especially with regard to 1992. Until this Act the Parliament was an almost exclusively advisory body in nearly all policy areas; Article 137 of the Treaty refers to its 'advisory and supervisory powers'. It offers 'opinions' which the Council can (and does) ignore, with one notable exception: the budget, where Euro MPs exercise joint control with the Council of Ministers in non-obligatory expenditure—that is, all spending except for farm support ('obligatory' in the sense that farm spending is a legal obligation laid down in the CAP).

Even here, however, the Parliament's powers are limited: farm spending, over which it has little or no control, still accounts for some two thirds of the budget, even after the Delors reforms, so that Euro MPs can only really influence one third of EC expenditure. They do so through a series of readings of the draft budget, which, after being drawn up by the Commission, goes back and forth between the Council and Parliament. However, the Parliament cannot increase expenditure beyond a 'maximum rate', which is set by the Council. This gives the Council the upper hand, and has in the past led to a wearisome annual tussle between the two institutions, often resulting in failure to adopt a budget at all and forcing the EC to resort to emergency monthly funding based on the previous year's budget (a system known as 'provisional twelfths') until a compromise is reached.

The Delors reforms, designed to prepare for 1992 by ridding the EC of budgetary wrangles, have greatly eased this problem, and annual budget crises no longer arise.

The Single European Act, moreover, gives the Parliament two further important roles in addition to its budgetary powers. Under the new 'co-operation' procedure (in effect, a second reading of 1992 legislation) the Council adopts a common position on a bill, taking into account the Parliament's opinion, and the Parliament then has three months to accept the proposal. If it does so, or takes no action, the proposal passes into law: but if MEPs propose amendments, or reject the bill, on its second reading by the Parliament, the Council can only pass its original version by unanimous vote. Otherwise it must accept Parliament's version, or drop the bill altogether. Second, a new 'assent' procedure gives the Parliament a final say in commercial agreements negotiated between EC and non-EC countries (and indeed in the admission of new member states to the Community).

In the European Parliament debates on the Single European Act after it was signed at the Luxembourg summit of December 1985 many Euro MPs argued vehemently that the Act should be rejected, on the grounds that the new powers it gave to Strasbourg were inadequate, even insulting. The majority view, however, was that the Act's powers could be used as a basis for Parliament's campaign to transform itself into a true EC legislature. Euro MPs have indeed made effective use of both the 1992 'second reading' and their power to accept or reject trade agreements (in the latter case, for example, by repeatedly holding up three trade protocols with Israel because of Israeli behaviour towards Palestinian Arabs). According to a study by James Elles, MEP, until the Single European Act the Commission took up wholly or in part about 85% of the Parliament's amendments to proposals—but the Council accepted far fewer.

Will the European Parliament ever become a true EC legislature? The weight of the EC's institutional structure, even as amended by the Single European Act, is probably against it. MEPs can put written questions to EC Commissioners and insist on a published answer (at an estimated administrative cost of £500–1000 per answer); ministers from the country which is in the EC chair must appear before Euro MPs to report on current EC issues and answer questions; and, in theory, Euro MPs can even dismiss the entire Commission—a power never so far used in practice. However, many Euro MPs themselves feel that the Parliament will not become the voice of the peoples of Europe until it has greater legislative powers and until its activities are centred in one place, preferably Brussels. At present, Euro MPs hold their plenary debates at their chamber in Strasbourg, in the Palace of Europe, and their committee and group meetings in Brussels, at the parliament building not far from the Commission and Council, while the Parliament's Secretariat is located in Luxembourg.

As part of the current rebuilding of the Brussels EC quarter to make a vast 'Euro City' for 1992 and after, a new debating chamber (described as a conference centre) is being built behind the Parliament's committee rooms. The Treaty of Rome, in fact, does not fix any seat for the Parliament, and in September 1988 the European Court overruled French objections to plans for holding plenary sessions in Brussels. A move by British MEPs in April 1990 to move the Parliament to Brussels was narrowly defeated.

In time, the pressures of the integrated market may force the Parliament to re-organize its work to resemble more closely that of a national parliament, with debates held continuously rather than for one week in four and increasing liaison between the European Parliament and national MPs. One estimate is that the Single European Act has increased the Parliament's workload by 30%. In Britain the House of Commons Select Committee on European Legislation sometimes scrutinizes EC laws only after they have been passed, because of the sheer volume. Options for increasing Westminster's scrutiny include a special question time on EC matters and allowing the Commons committee to see draft EC directives. (See also Chapter 10.)

In the summer of 1991 new arrangements were agreed between Strasbourg and Westminster, with British MPs allotted a special travel fund to enable them to visit EC institutions, and British Euro MPs given greater access to the Commons—reserved seats in the front two rows of the public gallery (MEPs previously had to queue with the public) and the right to reserve tables in Commons dining rooms (though for lunchtime only).

Strasbourg's powers were further tested in May 1990, when the European Court of Justice allowed the European Parliament to bring a law suit against the Council of Ministers for bypassing the Parliament when taking its decision to limit sales of food after the Chernobyl accident. The Court noted that the Council had used the Euratom Treaty as the basis for its action and not Article 100 of the Treaty of Rome, which would have required lengthy consultation with Strasbourg.

In July 1991, Euro MPs passed a resolution protesting that EC governments were still refusing to allow the Parliament to fill the 'democratic deficit'. In fact, of the 1,367 first reading amendments tabled by the Parliament from 1987 to 1990, 63% were accepted; and of the 357 amendments tabled on second readings, 55% were accepted. But the Parliament, in accordance with a recommendation by David Martin, MEP, wants the power to initiate legislation, coupled with 'co-decision taking' with the Council and Commission. Martin, the rapporteur on institutional reform, advocated a federal parliamentary republic of Europe, with the Council of Ministers as an upper Chamber (*European Union and the Democratic Deficit*, from the John Wheatley Centre). 'If the EC was a state and applied to join the Community it would be turned down on the grounds that it was not a democracy' he observed. Luxembourg, which held the EC presidency in the first half of 1991 and drew up the draft treaty revisions for Maastricht at the end of 1991, proposed co-decision making in specific areas: development aid, research, regional and social funds, and the environment.

In the event, Maastricht gave the Parliament powers amounting to co-decision making through a new 'negative assent procedure' laid down in article 189b of the political union treaty. Whereas Strasbourg had previously needed the backing of the Commission to get its amendments through the Council, it now has the right to negotiate directly with ministers on the changes it wants to see made, and to reject bills which fail to take account of those changes. The new powers cover laws on the single market, consumer protection, the free circulation of labour, the right of individuals and companies to establish themselves in any EC country, vocational training and health, as well as framework research and environment programmes. In addition, Maastricht required the assent of Strasbourg for structural funds, the rights of European citizenship and the harmonisation of electoral systems. The Commission and the Parliament are to run concurrently, and the Commission is reduced from 17 members to 12.

Maastricht did not, however, give Strasbourg a direct role in the new common foreign policy arrangements. Some MEPs welcomed the augmented powers: Enrique Baron Crespo, the outgoing President of the European Parliament, said Maastricht had at least acknowledged that the problem of the 'democratic deficit' was central to the EC and its future. But Egon Klepsch, his successor, said the Maastricht concessions were inadequate and 'Parliament must continue to fight for the extension of its rights'. Many MEPs deplored the decision to allow the UK to 'opt out' of common social policy, arguing that the move would create a 'two-speed Europe'.

The European Court of Justice

The 13 judges and six advocates-general of the European Court are nominated by member states and serve for a six-year term. They are required to be persons of the highest legal qualification 'whose independence is beyond doubt'. The Court, situated in Luxembourg, is the guardian of the Treaty and the EC's supreme legal body. It is not to be confused (but often is) with the European Court of Human Rights in Strasbourg, which is a Council of Europe body. (Still less is the European Court to be confused with the International Court of Justice in The Hague, as happened in one quality newspaper.)

EC law takes precedence over national law. Thus one function of the European Court is to give preliminary rulings on cases referred to it by national courts when a point of EC law is at issue. The national court then has to apply the ruling. However, cases can also be brought directly to the Court by individuals, companies or governments. In many cases it is the Commission which brings cases against both companies and member states for infringement of EC rules—including 1992 legislation. The first stage involves a written complaint and defence: there is then an oral hearing, in which both sides present their cases to the judges; in the third stage, the advocate-general gives an opinion; and finally, the judges deliver a verdict, arrived at by majority vote. The verdict usually (though not invariably) follows the advocate-general's opinion, as it did, for example, in rulings in 1988 against Britain over Vat exemptions.

The Court, like the Commission, is not an alien body but draws its members from all twelve states. Until recently, its President was a senior British judge. However, as 1992 approaches, its workload is becoming intolerable (it has only 500 employees), and in July 1988 the Council of Ministers agreed to the setting up of a lower-level EC Court of First Instance to sift cases before they reach the European Court proper. The new lower-level court should reduce the time taken to produce judgments in Luxembourg (currently anywhere between eighteen months and three years). However, there is no prospect of the Court's workload decreasing. On the contrary, as more and more 1992 directives are passed, an increasing number of test cases will be brought as the limits of single market legislation are probed—and as those who failed to stop 1992 laws passing through the Commission, Council and Parliament use the European Court as a last resort.

At the opening of the Court of First Instance in 1989, the presiding judge said that its workload highlighted the dual function of the ECJ. It has not only to decide matters of law but also to intervene in disputes over fact—customs classifications, agricultural regulations and the like. He also complained that the Court was overloaded with Commission cases brought under Article 169 against member states for their failure to implement EC directives. The UK has a good record in this regard; Italy and Greece are the worst offenders.

The Economic and Social Committee

This is an advisory body which brings together trades unionists, industrialists and other sectors of EC opinion to provide a sounding-board for ideas and to exchange news on current EC policies and proposals.

3 REVISING THE TREATY OF ROME

From the Single European Act to economic and political union

The Single European Act entered the world with a bang—literally. As European leaders gathered for the EC summit in Luxembourg in December 1985 a small bomb was thrown from a passing car onto the roadside near the Euro-Conference Centre on the Kirchberg. No motive was ever discovered: there had been a number of isolated, small-scale bombings in the Grand Duchy during the previous year, for no apparent reason, and this was assumed to be another such attack. Mrs Thatcher, who had survived the Grand Hotel bomb at Brighton the previous year, remarked calmly that bombs always caused anxiety but that the EC leaders had continued their deliberations unchecked.

Nonetheless the incident was perhaps symbolic, for the Single European Act, largely misunderstood or underestimated at the time, was itself a time-bomb. It was the culmination of 30 years of EC post-war history, and had given rise to a 'volcanic' display of opposition from Mrs Thatcher only six months before, at the Milan EC summit in June 1985, at the end of Italy's Presidency. The Act marked the first real attempt to bring the original Treaty of Rome up to date and shape the EC of the future. To understand its explosive content, it is necessary to go back to the Treaty of Rome itself and the beginnings of the Community.

The origins of European union

The idea of a European-wide system of government can be traced to medieval times, when the concept was one of a united Christendom. Scholars such as Aquinas or Erasmus thought of themselves as European, and moved freely from one university to another. In the seventeenth century William Penn, the Quaker, even proposed a European Parliament. In practice, however, European unification for the most part meant unification by force, through empires, from Charlemagne to Napoleon and Hitler. The rise of the nation-states in the eighteenth and nineteenth centuries, moreover, militated against the concept of unification, with notions of pan-European identity replaced by a balance of power between states, as at the Congress of Vienna in 1814–15. The First World War destroyed the old order but left Europe in a confused and disorganized state, prey to Fascist and Communist dictators.

It was the Second World War and its aftermath which produced a desire for union based on a determination to pool resources and make Europe into a peaceful force on the world stage. Hitler, it has been said, was the unwitting catalyst for democratic European unification. The apparently eternal problem posed by German power would be solved by bringing Germany (or at least West Germany) into a closely enmeshed, democratic Europe. The post-war enterprise had its roots in the 1948 Benelux Union between Belgium, the Netherlands and Luxembourg, and grew over a period of six years into the EC of Six, with Benelux joined by France, Italy and West Germany. This post-war process of integration was given added impetus by the two emerging superpowers—from the United States in the form of Marshall Aid and American support for European reconstruction and from the Soviet Union (less benevolently) in the form of an armed menace to Western Europe which had the effect of pushing the Europeans closer together for common protection. Britain, despite Churchill's rhetoric about the need for a United Europe, remained aloof.

In the early post-war years the impetus towards European union was simple and direct. As early as 1948 there was a defence dimension to the process in the form of the Treaty of Brussels establishing the Western European Union (WEU), which included Britain. In the 1950s the WEU became moribund, partly because of the formation of NATO, and attempts to form a European Defence Community (EDC) also foundered in 1954—because of a French veto. Instead, the emphasis was on economic union as a first step. However, it was always understood that the eventual aim was a union which had political and even defence implications as well as economic ones.

Monnet and the Franco-German axis

The main driving force came (as much of the 1992 impetus was later to come) from a Frenchman: Jean Monnet. Originally from a family cognac firm (and its pre-war salesman in Britain), Monnet helped to co-ordinate the economies of the Allies against Hitler, and became a passionate advocate of Anglo-French integration after the war. However, the fulcrum of European union was, in the end, Franco-German, with Britain still standing on one side. The French fear was that after two world wars, and centuries of Franco-German conflict before that, Germany would once again dominate Europe, through its possession of key coal and iron industries in the Saarland, a border region like Alsace, which had often caused bitter rivalry in the past. Together with Robert Schuman, the French Foreign Minister, who came from Alsace and who was also an ardent proponent of European integration, Monnet put forward a plan—which bore Schuman's name—for a European Coal and Steel Community (ECSC) to oversee the industries in a common supranational interest. This duly came about in August 1952, under Monnet's chairmanship, with the Benelux nations and Italy joining France and West Germany.

Three years later the same Six, under the influence of Monnet's Action Committee for a United States of Europe, began work on the Treaty of Rome, founding a European Economic Community with much wider powers than the ECSC. The 1955 meeting of the Foreign Ministers of the Six at Messina, in Italy, on the legal basis for a Common Market led two years later to the signing of the completed Treaty in Rome, on 25 March 1957. Euratom, the European Atomic Energy Community, was also established in Rome on the same day as the EEC. In 1967 the three 'Communities'—the ECSC, Euratom and the EEC itself—were merged. It is therefore technically correct to refer to the 'European Communities' —but in practice the EEC was the one that mattered. (The phrase 'European Economic Community' has since been almost universally shortened to 'European Community' as integration has proceeded and the Community's political character has developed.)

Largely due to continuing Franco-German *rapprochement*, helped by the personal relationship between de Gaulle and Adenauer, the EC made rapid progress towards its first goal: the removal of internal tariffs and quotas. As in the later case of 1992, the founding fathers laid down a target date for this customs union: 31 December 1969, 12 years after the signing of the Treaty. In the event, the removal of internal tariffs was completed over a year early, in July 1968, accompanied by the erection of a common external tariff to protect the new common market. The EC also fulfilled the Treaty's provision for a Common Agricultural Policy involving farm subsidies—a measure which was intended to support Europe's farmers and ensure food supplies but which was to consume a growing proportion of the EC's limited budget.

An ever-closer union

It swiftly became apparent, however, that the drive for integration went beyond a customs union and farm support. The subsequent history of the EC is a history of lurches towards the original goals of the Treaty preamble: 'To lay the foundations of an ever-closer union among the peoples of Europe . . . to ensure economic and social progress by common action to eliminate the barriers which divide Europe'. One early effort to fulfil this goal by creating a political as well as economic union was the Fouchet Plan (Marks I and II) of 1961, which proposed a joint foreign policy. However, this, like many other such plans, foundered on the objection—put forward most vehemently by de Gaulle—that foreign policy was a national prerogative not a supranational one. Similar objections ended the 1970 Werner Plan for Economic and Monetary Union by 1980; once again, governments declared that handing over control of monetary questions to the EC would be an unacceptable surrender of national sovereignty. The plan for European Union developed in 1976 by Leo Tindemans, then Belgian Prime Minister (and now Belgian Foreign Minister), also failed—not surprisingly, perhaps, since the Tindemans

Plan not only combined the two earlier failed Plans for a joint foreign policy and monetary union but added schemes for common regional and social policies, a common industrial policy and a programme for a Citizens' Europe.

Yet Euro-Plans have a way of lingering on EC shelves rather than disappearing. There is now a social and regional policy, co-ordination of foreign policy ('political co-operation') and a plan for a Citizens' Europe, while monetary union is obstinately back on the agenda. It became clear as early as 1959, when both Greece and Turkey applied for associate membership status, that the EC had a centripetal pull which would lead to its further expansion. The key development was Britain's decision—under Harold Macmillan's premiership—to apply for full membership, beginning in 1961 (barely a year, paradoxically, after Britain had been instrumental in setting up the rival EFTA, the European Free Trade Association). The British application was vetoed by de Gaulle—the first French 'non'—in 1963, on the grounds that Britain's ties were transatlantic rather than European. It was renewed by Harold Wilson in 1966, and again vetoed by de Gaulle. However, de Gaulle's nationalism and Gallic disdain were at odds with Community philosophy. He clashed frequently not only with Britain but also with leading statesmen such as Dr Walter Hallstein, the West German President of the European Commission, who favoured a switch to majority voting in the Council of Ministers.

Enlargement: Britain joins the Community

In 1969 de Gaulle resigned, and a year later he died. With Pompidou and Brandt leading France and West Germany, respectively, the British application was again renewed under the premiership of the pro-European Edward Heath, amid tough bargaining over the accession terms. Denmark, Ireland and Norway (which had submitted and withdrawn applications in accordance with Britain's applications and rejections) also applied. Britain, Denmark and Ireland finally became EC members in 1973, bringing the total from Six to Nine. All three ratified the decision in popular referendums—in the British case in 1975, after the new Wilson government had renegotiated entry terms to ensure a British budget rebate. A Norwegian referendum on EC membership in 1972, by contrast, produced a narrow majority against, with the result that Norway stayed out—although the 1992 process has brought renewed signs of interest in Oslo in full membership.

In 1975, the year of the British EC referendum, Greece put in its membership application, followed by Spain and Portugal two years later. Greece duly entered the Community in 1981, bringing the membership from Nine to Ten, and the entry of Spain and Portugal in 1986 completed the enlargement process for the foreseeable future, producing a Community of Twelve and providing further pressure for economic and institutional reforms as part of the 1992 process.

However, the development of the Community has been far from easy, and more a matter of 'two steps forward, one step back' than of smooth progress towards the dream of Monnet and Schuman. In the 1970s the CAP began to become unmanageable as the subsidies system for both production and storage gave rise to surpluses—the beginnings of the notorious food mountains. On the plus side, moves towards a common foreign policy took on new life, with the agreed Davignon Plan of 1970 on regular contact between EC foreign ministers in 'political co-operation', or POCO for short. Enlargement to Nine and then Ten failed to produce the expected economic benefits, partly because of the global oil crisis of 1973 and partly because of the lack of a coherent plan for EC growth. On the other hand, in 1974–5 the Regional Development Fund was set up to close the gap between prosperous and less-prosperous regions of the EC, and it was agreed that the European Parliament should be directly elected. In 1979, through the joint efforts of Helmut Schmidt, the West German Chancellor, Valéry Giscard d'Estaing, the French President, and Roy Jenkins, President of the European Commission, the European Monetary System (EMS) was founded, with an exchange rate mechanism designed to limit currency fluctuations by linking member currencies to a newly devised European Currency Unit—the ECU.

The 1980s thus found the EC advancing unevenly towards the vision of the founding fathers, facing institutional and budgetary problems inherited from the 1950s and 1960s, and suffering—after the de Gaulle–Adenauer and Giscard d'Estaing–Schmidt years—from lack of overall direction, guidance and leadership. Of the major EC statesmen, Mitterrand and Kohl lacked strong personal rapport and did not, on the whole, lend new dynamism to the Franco-German axis, the traditional motor of EC progress. Mrs Thatcher, continuing the British tradition of standing aloof (indeed, reinforcing it) did not appear to regard the European cause with any enthusiasm, to put it mildly. If anything, her instincts lay in another direction—the Anglo-American transatlantic relationship so feared in earlier times by de Gaulle. Mrs Thatcher's rapport was with President Reagan of the United States rather than with her Continental counterparts.

The early 1980s were dominated not by visions of the future but by Mrs Thatcher's determined—and justified—campaign to persuade Britain's EC partners that Britain's contribution to EC coffers was unacceptably high (Harold Wilson's renegotiated terms not having been fulfilled). With the help of President Mitterand, the campaign eventually led at the Fontainebleau summit of 1984 to a compromise involving a rebate to Britain of 66% of the difference between its Vat contributions to EC funds and its share of EC benefits—in other words, the difference between what Britain put into the EC and what it got out of it (less than France or West Germany, which gained more in farm support). The Fontainebleau settlement also involved an increase in the limit on overall

Vat contributions to the budget from 1% to 1.4%, with further rises to be discussed at a later stage.

All this had the merit of focusing attention on the chronic budgetary crisis and on the fact that the EC's 'own resources' were being outstripped by the cost of running a Community of Twelve. Reform was needed, but the shrill tone of Mrs Thatcher's campaign (and resulting anti-Common Market feeling in Britain) did not augur well for the reform effort. In the absence of convincing leadership from London, Paris or Bonn, much would depend on the new European Commission, led at the beginning of 1985 by a quiet, dapper Frenchman: Jacques Delors.

The Delors reform package

At the beginning of 1985 Delors made a tour of European capitals to introduce himself and to sound out opinion on four ways of moving the EC closer to the founders' goals:

1 Revival of the idea of a defence union;
2 Revival of the idea of monetary union;
3 Reform of the ECs institutional structure of Council, Commission and Parliament; or
4 Completion of the internal market through the complete dismantling of obstacles to trade (in other words, further development of the customs union).

In the end, the 1992 concept has come to embrace all four, either formally or informally, but in 1985 it was the proposal for completing the market which most appealed to EC leaders (Mrs Thatcher included), because it implied deregulation and freer competition. The difficulties began when Delors went on to argue that completing the internal market involved a mass of new legislation and that the Treaty of Rome would have to be amended—the birth of the Single European Act.

The practical basis of the Delors concept was simple: moves to harmonize EC standards and practices since the completion of the customs union in 1968 had come up against the obstacle of national protectionism. No state wanted to give up long-cherished practices in the wider interest. Therefore some supranational way would have to be found of persuading them to 'harmonize' or (as a first step, referred to as 'the new approach') mutually to recognize each other's standards. This became known in EC jargon as the 'Cassis de Dijon' ruling, after a celebrated case at the European Court of Justice in 1979. This arose when a West German firm found that it was prevented from importing Cassis de Dijon because it allegedly did not conform to exacting West German standards for liqueurs. The Court ruled that Bonn could only prevent the import of a French drink if it could prove that the liquid was harmful to health or contravened tax or consumer protection laws—which cassis (the basis of a popular aperitif called kir) did not.

In formulating their new plan for the internal market Delors and the Commission seized on the 'Cassis Principle' that, for goods to move around the integrated market unhindered, they need only conform to commonly agreed standards. Lord Cockfield, the Internal Market Commissioner, devised 300 measures to eliminate the technical, physical and fiscal barriers to intra-Community trade. In addition, the Commission took up earlier, unsuccessful ideas for institutional reform, monetary union and a common foreign policy. The last in this long line of failed visions was the Draft Treaty of European Union, devised by Altiero Spinelli, a veteran Italian Communist Euro MP, and adopted by the European Parliament.

The Milan summit: partial failure

The 1992 process which resulted is a diluted version of what union visionaries like Spinelli had wanted. On the other hand, the Single European Act goes further than sceptics had wished. When the EC Milan summit convened in June 1985 to take a first look at what was to become the Single European Act, Mrs Thatcher was highly suspicious of anything which went beyond the opening up of internal frontiers to facilitate movement and trade. Britain led the way in proposing a common foreign policy, going so far as to suggest a joint EC approach at the United Nations—which does not appear in the Single European Act as eventually agreed. However, Mrs Thatcher set her face firmly against changes to the Treaty of Rome, and—with the backing of Denmark—said that she saw no need for a special inter-governmental conference to agree such changes. Increased use of majority voting, the Prime Minister declared, could be covered by a 'gentleman's agreement' along the lines of the Luxembourg Compromise, with the national veto retained. Talk of European union was 'airy-fairy'.

The Milan summit was marked by bad feeling, caused by British anger over a Franco-German draft declaration on European Union which drew heavily on British proposals, and then went beyond them. However, at the end of the summit Mrs Thatcher was outvoted over the setting up of the Inter-Governmental Conference (IGC). President Mitterrand remarked tartly that the summit had sorted out 'those who favour a strong, united Europe from those who are hanging back'. The Milan summit communiqué (or rather, the Presidency's conclusions, since not all points were accepted unanimously) was the first mention of 1992 as a target date. It confirmed 'the need to improve the operation of the Community in order to give concrete form to the objectives it has set itself, in particular as regards the completion of the internal market by 1992 and measures to promote a technological Europe'. It also noted the need to improve decision-making procedures, partly by revising the powers of the Commission and the Parliament. The key section concluded:

> The summit discussed in detail the convening of a conference to work out the following with a view to achieving concrete progress on European Union: a treaty on a common foreign and security policy on the basis of Franco-German and United Kingdom drafts: and amendments to the Treaty of Rome . . . The required majority has been obtained for the convening of such a conference.

Amid the row over amending the Treaty it almost went unnoticed that the Milan summit had instructed the Council of Ministers 'to initiate a precise programme of action, based on the White Paper . . . with a view to achieving completely and effectively the conditions for a single market in the Community by 1992 at the latest, in accordance with stages fixed in relationship to previously determined priorities and a binding timetable'. The Milan meeting, in other words, was not as disastrous for EC unity as it appeared at the time. The only question was whether, when the EC leaders re-assembled in Luxembourg at the end of the six-month Luxembourg presidency, Mrs Thatcher would still be as adamantly opposed to Treaty changes.

The Luxembourg summit: Mrs Thatcher signs the Act

The Luxembourg summit began more auspiciously. The IGC Mrs Thatcher had so fiercely opposed at Milan took the modest form of a series of Foreign Ministers' meetings in autumn 1985. By the time the Luxembourg meeting convened, many of the basic issues had been agreed. The leaders were anxious to avoid a further display of disunity, and began by agreeing that Mrs Thatcher was right to put the 1992 emphasis on deregulation. Completion of the internal market would be designed to give a great impetus to the European economy, with special help for small and medium-sized enterprises. There was also initial agreement on giving the European Parliament a second reading of internal market legislation. However, France and Italy, with support from the Benelux nations, still wanted to turn the proposed Treaty amendments into an Act of European Union, creating a 'European space'—a phrase dismissed by the British as imprecise. They also wanted an expanded EC secretariat with power to co-ordinate EC foreign policy.

For Britain, again with support from Denmark, the priority was to make the existing EC institutions and mechanisms function more efficiently (for example, by revising the CAP) and to ensure that the move towards a frontier-free Europe did not imperil Britain's control as an island over drugs, immigration and plant and animal health. The summit eventually produced a compromise, but the tension between these two visions of 1992 has resurfaced in various guises ever since.

There was alarm on the second day of the summit when Denmark and Italy both threatened to walk out—the Danes because for them the draft agreement on 1992 went too far and the Italians because it did not go far enough. In a vivid if gory image, a distraught Delors protested that the changes insisted on by Britain amounted to a 'Texas chainsaw massacre'. However, in the end, late at night, the Single European Act was born, and the history of the EC had taken a major step. 'We decided to sit it out until we had a clear and decisive position,' a tired Mrs Thatcher told reporters after she had reversed her earlier opposition to Treaty changes—provided that they met British concerns. She still regarded amending the Treaty as unnecessary, 'but if they wanted it to be this way, so be it'.

Main points of the Single European Act

The Act laid down eight basic points:

1 1992. 'The Community shall adopt measures with the aim of progressively establishing the internal market over a period expiring on December 31 1992 . . . The internal market shall comprise an area without internal frontiers in which the free movement of goods, persons, services and capital is ensured in accordance with the provisions of this Treaty.' States could apply for exemptions, and the Act included a 'General Declaration' as follows: 'Nothing in these provisions shall affect the right of member states to take such measures as they consider necessary for the purpose of controlling immigration from Third World countries, and to combat terrorism, crime, the traffic in drugs and illicit trading in works of art and antiques'. On the other hand, the EC leaders agreed to avoid such continued national controls by introducing 'common measures' on police co-operation, visas, extradition and immigration. The Act also empowered states to take fellow states to the European Court if exemptions were 'improperly used' to restrict trade.

2 Practical steps to reduce the administrative and legal constraints on small and medium-sized businesses, with a Commission task force to oversee this deregulatory process.

3 In a concession by both Britain and West Germany, which had the strongest doubts about monetary union, the Act's preamble referred specifically to monetary union as an EC goal, to be 'progressively realized'. However, monetary union was not among the 1992 priorities laid down by the Act as legally binding, and Mrs Thatcher argued that the wording went no further than that of the Paris summit in 1972.

4 Disparities between richer and poorer regions of the EC were to be reduced (the policy known as 'cohesion') through the more efficient use of the structural funds or regional and social funds. To avoid a 'two-speed Europe', states would use their economic policies to promote 'harmonious development in the EC' and overcome 'the backwardness of the least favoured regions'. On Britain's insistence, this embraced 'declining industrial regions' in the north as well as rural areas in the south. The Act authorized the Commission to recommend 'amendments' to the structural funds —and at the Brussels summit of February 1988, the leaders agreed to Delors' proposals for the funds to be doubled by 1992.

5 The European Parliament was given a new 'co-operation' procedure, enabling it to amend legislation through a second reading and in some cases—notably commercial agreements—to have the final say. On most issues, if the Parliament rejected a bill on its second reading the Council could still have the last word by passing the measure unanimously.

6 Technological research to be encouraged within an agreed framework. Britain held up the resulting five-year (1987–91) research framework programme—eventually reduced to £4 billion (5.3 billion ECUs)—on the grounds that the technology projects involved had not been properly approved and there was too much research duplication among the EC nations. However, the programme—including information technology (ESPRIT), advanced telecommunications research (RACE) and industrial technology (BRITE)—eventually went ahead, albeit with a smaller budget than the 7.7 billion ECUs the Commission had wanted.

7 The environment. The EC was to take action to improve the environment, contribute towards the protection of human health and ensure 'a prudent and rational utilization of natural resources' on the principle 'that environmental damage should be rectified at source and that the polluter should pay'. Denmark's objections that its own standards were higher than those of the EC were met by a clause stating that the Act need not prevent member states taking 'more stringent measures' than the EC norm.

8 A separate Title provided for 'European co-operation in the sphere of foreign policy'—as distinct from external or trade policy, which is handled by the Commission, although it also impinges on foreign policy. The leaders undertook to formulate and implement a European foreign policy by consulting one another

'so as to ensure that their combined influence is exercised as effectively as possible through co-ordination, the convergence of their positions and the implementation of joint action', with Foreign Ministers meeting at least four times a year on political co-operation issues. Most controversial was paragraph 6a: 'The High contracting Parties consider that closer co-operation on questions of European security would contribute in an essential way to the development of a European identity . . . They are ready to co-ordinate their positions more closely on the political and economic aspects of security'. This should not conflict with the competence of either NATO or the WEU, the new Article said. A new foreign policy secretariat would be set up in Brussels (and duly was) but with purely administrative functions.

Ratification of the Act

The day after the Luxembourg summit, Delors declared that the EC could now undertake 'the adventure of progress towards union'. In fact, every EC summit since December 1985 had grappled in one form or another with the consequences of the Single European Act and of its inbuilt contradictions. Nonetheless, the Act is in force, and the arguments are about interpretation, not about repealing it—which is impossible. In the course of 1987 the Act was ratified by every national parliament, including Westminster, where the Lords almost staged a rebellion but in the end consented. Every ratification debate revolved around the degree to which the Single European Act involved a partial surrender of national sovereignty to the EC. In the case of two countries—Denmark and Ireland—it took popular referendums to resolve the question of the Act's constitutionality—in Denmark in March 1986 (56.2% in favour) and in Ireland in May 1987 (70.2% in favour).

The Act was passed, the Treaty was altered and with it the nature of the EC, even if some of the 1992 goals—such as monetary union—were put off to the distant future and others—such as foreign and defence policy co-ordination—were diluted or left ambiguous. The heart of the matter was the commitment to a single European market by 31 December 1992, and the agreement that the EC had the right to lay down policy throughout the Community in areas from taxation to tourism.

Further treaty revision: the Maastricht agenda

The Madrid summit of June 1989 gave Delors the go-ahead to develop a three-stage plan for economic and monetary union, with phase one beginning on 1 July 1990. But by the time of the Dublin summit a year later, at the end of the Irish presidency, pressure was building not only for economic and monetary union but for political union and institutional reform in the shape of further revisions to the Treaty of Rome. As with the Single European Act, preparatory moves took the form of an IGC—or, since two treaty revisions were proposed, two IGCs, one on monetary union and another on political union. The need for the latter was agreed in principle at the extra Dublin summit of April 1990, on a Franco-German initiative, to 'strengthen the democratic legitimacy of the union' and to ensure that the EC could 'respond efficiently and effectively to the demands of the new situation' created by events in East and Central Europe.

At Dublin in April and again in June Mrs Thatcher, perhaps surprisingly, raised no objections to the summoning of the IGCs, with their progress to be reviewed at the Rome summit in December 1990. In fact Mrs Thatcher praised the first report on political union, produced by EC foreign ministers for the June 1990 summit, on the grounds that it 'respected the separate identities of member states, reaffirmed that the Council of Ministers was the main decision-making body, and underlined the principle of subsidiarity'—meaning that EC institutions should only decide what could not be better handled at a lower level.

In October 1990, however, the Italian presidency, which had taken over from Ireland, called an extra EC summit, ostensibly to discuss aid to the Soviet Union, on the grounds that the December summit would be taken up with the IGCs. In fact, the October summit unexpectedly set the timetable for phase two of the Delors plan (the European Bank, beginning 1 January 1994) and phase three (the single currency, to start in 1997). Mrs Thatcher angrily denounced this outcome as 'putting the cart before the horse'. But the following month her role in shaping British policy came to an abrupt end when she was forced to resign as Prime Minister, with John Major succeeding her.

Luxembourg, which inherited the presidency in the first half of 1991, pressed ahead with draft treaties on monetary and political union to be adopted at the Maastricht summit at the end of the ensuing Dutch presidency in December 1991. In some respects the drafts were acceptable to the UK. On the social dimension, the Luxembourg summit of June 1991 agreed that social legislation had to be in accordance with national practices and traditions and would not affect national social security schemes, for example. Equally, Luxembourg defined the conditions for the introduction of a single currency. This would occur when EC economies had converged by achieving similar levels of inflation, interest rates and public spending. There would be co-ordination of police and immigration services; EC citizens would have the right to vote in any member state; and the Commission would be reduced from 17 members to 12 (one for each state).

However, Major made clear that the provisions in the Luxembourg draft for 'co-decision making' by the European Parliament (see Chapter 2) were unacceptable, as was majority voting on some foreign policy issues and above all the draft's reference to the EC's federal goal, or 'vocation'. 'Federalism' became an objectionable 'F word' in the British lexicon. 'We will insist on its removal before we sign any treaty at the end of December,' Major declared. The 'F word' was quietly dropped. In September Major disagreed with Mitterrand over the pace of integration, with Major insisting that the EC should be broadened to include the new democracies of Eastern Europe and Mitterand placing the stress on the integration of the existing Twelve.

The Dutch presidency, to the alarm and annoyance not only of Britain but also—in varying degrees—of France, Portugal, Ireland and Denmark, revised the Luxembourg text in an even more federalist direction. It firmly reinstated the word 'federal', made foreign policy and police and immigration affairs a matter of common policy agreed by majority vote, rather than co-operation between states, and increased the powers of the European Parliament further. After a stormy session of EC foreign ministers in the Netherlands at the end of September the Dutch text was withdrawn and the Luxembourg text reinstated as the basis for discussions at Maastricht. However, the impetus towards further treaty revision in the direction of a federal union remained strong.

The Maastricht summit

The outcome at Maastricht in December 1991 was seen as a disappointment by some arch-federalists, not least because Britain successfully manoeuvred to 'opt-out' of two key provisions: the introduction of a single European currency by 1999, and the application of Community legislation to social policies, on which the other eleven agreed to sign a separate protocol. On the other hand, the treaty on economic and monetary union provides for Britain to 'opt in' to the single currency, subject to Parliamentary approval, provided (as seems likely) Britain satisfies agreed criteria for economic convergence within the EC. Similarly, the overall thrust of Maastricht was toward closer union.

The Maastricht treaty on political union established a 'European Union'. In the final wording, the phrase 'ever closer union' (already in the Treaty of Rome) replaced the contentious draft phrase 'Union with a federal goal'. The aims of the Union were defined as the promotion of economic and social progress through the creation of an area without internal frontiers, and through economic and monetary union 'including, finally, a single currency'; the assertion of a European identity on the international scene through a common foreign and security policy, 'to include the eventual framing of a common defence policy'; the protection of citizens' rights through 'the introduction of a citizenship of the Union'; and close co-operation on home and judicial affairs, with co-operation across frontiers on asylum, immigration, drugs and terrorism, and a common visa policy to be agreed by unanimity in the Council until 1996, and by majority vote thereafter. Significantly, the Council has the power to introduce common visa requirements in the event of 'an emergency situation in a third country posing the threat of an inflow to the Community of nationals from that country'.

The Union is to have 'due regard to the national identity of its member states', however, and must also respect the European Convention on Human Rights, which results from 'the constitutional traditions common to the member states as general principles of Community law'. Article 3b enshrined subsidiarity in treaty form for the first time, declaring that the EC shall take action 'only if and insofar as the objectives of the proposed action cannot be sufficiently achieved by the member states and can therefore, by reason of scale or the effects of the proposed action, be better achieved by the Community . . . Any action by the Community shall not go beyond what is necessary to achieve the objectives of the Treaty'.

The political union treaty also re-defined the functions of the EC, adding the following to the wording of the Treaty of Rome and the Single European Act: measures concerning the entry and movement of persons in the internal market; economic and social cohesion; the environment; research and technological development; energy; consumer protection and tourism; the establishment and development of 'trans-European networks'; and for the first time the extension of EC competence into health ('the attainment of a high level of health protection') and education ('education and training of high quality and the flowering of the cultures of member states . . . as well as improvement in the knowledge and dissemination of the culture and history of the European peoples.'). The EC is to 'respect the responsibility of the member states for the content of teaching, the organization of education systems and their cultural and linguistic diversity' but will issue non-binding recommendations (adopted by the Council on a majority vote) to foster a 'European dimension in education' and encourage teacher and student exchanges. Health and education thus remain outside EC competence for the most part, but are brought into the EC orbit through co-ordination and co-operation.

The concept of European citizenship was also new ('every person holding the nationality of a member state shall be a citizen of the Union . . . every Union citizen shall have the right to move and reside freely within the territory of the member states'), with detailed arrangements to be worked out by the end of 1994 giving citizens 'resident in member states of which they are not nationals' the right to vote and stand as candidates in municipal and European elections.

On institutions, the Maastricht treaty gave the European Parliament extra powers of veto and amendment, and authorised it to scrutinise EC 'maladministration' and EC finances. The Commission was reduced from 17 to 12, with a term of office of five rather than four years as of 1 January 1995. The president of the Commission is to be appointed by EC leaders 'by common accord, after consulting the European parliament'. A new advisory body, the Committee of the Regions, was set up, with representatives from EC regions and local authorities appointed to it for a four-year term.

Finally, in a separate protocol, the eleven states other than Britain adopted common measures on social policy, with the treaty authorising them to 'have recourse to the institutions, procedures and mechanisms of the European Community' for this purpose. It remains to be seen what this means in practice. The protocol commits the eleven signatories to 'the promotion of employment, improved living and working conditions, proper social protection, dialogue between management and labour, and the development of human resources with a view to lasting high employment', with action to be taken by qualified majority voting. Unanimous voting is required for measures affecting social security, worker-management contractual negotiations, and conditions of work for third-country nationals living in the EC. John Major commented that all this represented unacceptable interference in national affairs, and would have 'handed over the government of this country to trades unions abroad' had he agreed to allow the social dimension to remain in the treaty proper. The Commission, however, has made clear that it still hopes to secure the agreement of all Twelve to a range of social policies by using existing powers to legislate on health and safety issues.

The Maastricht treaty is subject to review in 1996, when a further Inter-Governmental conference is to meet. The treaty states that 'any European State may apply to become a member of the Union', and it may well be that by 1996 the pressure for enlargement will have become so great that further treaty changes will be necessary to accommodate the needs of a wider EC.

4 STANDARDIZING INDUSTRY

Harmonization from pharmaceuticals to exhaust emissions

Imagine the frustration, delay, and unnecessary increase in costs faced by a British truck-manufacturing company trying to export its latest light-weight model to Italy, which has the vehicle's brakes dispatched to Turin to be inspected and approved by a recognized auto components inspector before receiving the licence needed to ship over the finished product for distribution and sale. There is no guarantee that the vehicle's brakes will be approved, even if they meet local technical standards, especially if the national government is determined to protect its domestic truck-manufacturing industry from external competition. Such obstacles have become all too familiar to EC manufacturers trying to export their products, whether cars, telephones or pharmaceuticals, to other EC member states, and have helped make a mockery of the European Commission's goal of creating a common market.

Conflicting product technical standards are by no means the only informal trade barrier likely to be encountered by companies seeking to develop markets in other EC countries. Because of the increased concern over industry's impact on the environment, some member states have been under great political pressure to introduce 'green' regulations on a wide range of industrial activities, processes and products, such as tighter controls on vehicle emissions. Although the political pressures that have given rise to such demands stem from a genuine concern over industry's impact on the environment, there are now widespread anxieties that a new hierarchy of 'green' standards could be used as a pretext for restricting the free circulation of goods around the EC. Consequently, the European Commission is engaged in drawing up new environmental standards for industry to provide increased protection for the environment without inhibiting trade.

However, the Commission's environmental initiatives go much further than simply ensuring that environmental concern is not distorted into creating new obstacles to commerce. Taken collectively, the proposed environmental protection package, which contains more proposals for legislation than any other aspect of the internal market programme, are aimed at nothing less than creating the conditions for a new 'ecological market economy'. Companies which have traditionally relied on 'end-of-pipe' solutions for the pollution created by their activi-

ties are now being asked to reassess completely their production processes, from the acquisition of raw materials to the delivery of the finished
product. In consequence, businesses, governments and consumers are
likely to face increases in costs expected to run into billions of pounds.

Proposals for a new energy tax alone, unveiled by Brussels in September 1991, are expected to raise £37 billion a year, as well as leading
to significant reductions in carbon dioxide emissions. Because of fears
that the so-called 'dark green' states—Germany, Denmark, and the
Netherlands—would take unilateral action and thereby create distortions
in the internal market, the Commission felt that it had no option but to
come up with a proposal of its own. Under the Commission's scheme, a
low-carbon tax would be introduced on coal, petrol and natural gas in
January 1993 and progressively increased until the year 2000. Most of the
tax would be likely to fall on the advanced economies in northern Europe,
leaving the poorer south able to pursue its development goals without
penalty.

Demolishing technical barriers

In June 1985 the European Commission published what has perhaps
become its most widely known White Paper, *Completing The Internal
Market*, which outlined an ambitious strategy and timetable for the task
of removing the Community's internal barriers to trade and merging
twelve disparate economies into one by 31 December 1992. It defined
three separate categories of internal barriers to the free movement of
capital, goods, labour and services. These were the fiscal, physical and
technical barriers to trade, whose existence had been identified by the
Delors Commission as being responsible for the 'economic balkanization'
of the Community.

The White Paper argued forcibly for the complete and effective
removal of all three categories of barrier. But it is the removal of the
technical barriers to trade, the plethora of different technical standards
for individual products drawn up by each member state (ostensibly for
health, safety and environmental reasons) which holds out the prospect
of creating a single industrial market of continental proportions, thereby
enabling Europe to compete more effectively with its competitors in Japan
and the United States.

Along with the creation of the Common Agricultural Policy, setting
up a Common Market, as specified under Article 100 of the Treaty of
Rome, was one of the fundamental objectives inspiring the foundation
of the EC. However, despite a promising start, the Community soon lost
its way. The first step towards the creation of the Common Market was
the establishment of a common customs tariff, completed well ahead of
schedule in 1968. It was followed ten years later by the adoption of the
Sixth Vat Directive, which formed the basis of the Community's indirect

taxation system and provided a common method for allocating revenues from national Vat receipts to the Community budget.

However, the impact of the two oil crises of the 1970s, and the unprecedented combination of inflation and recession that resulted, brought the promising progress of the Community's first 20 years to an abrupt halt. The impetus towards economic integration rapidly dissipated, and in many respects the Community began to move backwards. Member states, although required by the Treaty of Rome to dismantle all tariff barriers between them, showed a polite respect for the letter of the Treaty and systematically set about undermining its spirit by erecting a large network of non-tariff barriers, epitomized by divergent technical standards, in a forlorn endeavour to protect themselves from intra-EC competition.

The Community's preoccupation with the accession of new members during the 1970s and 1980s effectively ruled out any serious attempt to rectify this deteriorating situation. In this context, the Commission's efforts to harmonize every technical standard on a product-by-product basis were reminiscent of the labour of Sisyphus. In the mid-1980s the European Commission and the Council of Ministers launched a long-overdue resuscitation package for the ideals expressed by the founders of the EC.

A new approach to technical harmonization

Following recognition by the Council of Ministers that, in the field of technical standards and regulations, the goals of all national legislation were more or less identical, the European Commission was granted a licence to abandon its traditional one-dimensional approach to technical harmonization in favour of a new multi-dimensional strategy based on selective harmonization and mutual recognition.

The traditional approach, which required years of tortuous negotiations to arrive at a common position for a single product standard, was inherently bureaucratic, extremely unpopular and very time consuming. In many cases it had proved to be completely futile. By the time the new product standard had emerged from the bureaucrat's briefcase and onto the shopfloor it had often been made redundant by the rapid pace of technological development. The whole legislative process was rather like moving a mountain to bring forth a mouse, and it had brought into disrepute the Community's laudable efforts to create common industrial standards.

The most systematic expression of the new approach to the harmonization of technical standards was given by Lord Cockfield in the Internal Market White Paper. In this he called for a distinction in all internal market legislation to be made between 'what is essential to harmonize, and what may be left to mutual recognition of national standards'. In future, the traditional approach of legislative technical harmonization will be restricted to those areas where it is vital to create a uniform Continental market. Companies previously limited to national markets for products manufactured under national product standards will benefit from the economies of scale that the single internal market will create.

In 1985 the Commission acknowledged that exclusive reliance on Article 100 of the Treaty, which required a unanimous vote by the Council of Ministers to secure passage of all technical harmonization legislation, would be likely to present the same sort of difficulties experienced in the past. It therefore announced its intention to pursue legislative harmonization under Articles 30–36, which prohibited national governments from adopting policies which constituted an 'arbitrary discrimination or a disguised restriction on trade between member states'.

However, by the time the Single European Act had been ratified in 1987 the Commission's ability to secure legislative approval of technical harmonization measures by the Council of Ministers had been immeasurably strengthened. Article 100a of the amended Treaty introduced the principle of qualified majority voting for all measures 'which have as their object the establishment and functioning of the internal market'. The built-in institutional unanimity had been bypassed, allowing the Commission to press ahead with the task of laying the foundations of a single internal market. Henceforth, all legislative technical harmonization measures will be confined to establishing minimum health and safety requirements, conformity with which will guarantee manufacturers the right of access to the markets of other member states. In addition, legislative technical harmonization will be complemented by the systematic implementation of the principle of mutual recognition of non-essential national product standards. On the assumption that all such regulations are designed to lay down minimum health and safety standards, it follows that all governments have basically the same objectives in mind.

Following a series of seminal judgments by the European Court of Justice, notably the 1979 Cassis de Dijon ruling, which specified that Community law demands the mutual acceptance of goods from one member state by other member states, the Internal Market White Paper laid down that in future:

> The general principle should be approved that, if a product is lawfully manufactured and marketed in one member state, there is no reason why it should not move freely throughout the Community. The objectives of national legislation in this respect are essentially identical. Although they may take different forms, they amount to the same thing.

As a result, member states must now accept products from other member states which are manufactured to a different design but which nonetheless perform the same as those manufactured to national technical standards. This principle (which may in retrospect seem to be nothing more than common sense) is in fact little short of a revolution, given the historical context of Community attempts to harmonize technical standards. Moreover, working on the principle that it is better to privatize as much harmonization as possible, the task of establishing European-wide product standards has now been taken out of the hands of the bureaucrats and allocated to the new European standards institutes such as the European Committee for Standardization (CEN), the European Committee for Electrotechnical Standardization (CENELEC) and the European Telecommunications Standards Institute (ETSI). Most of the new European standards-setting procedure was completed in April 1990, with the creation of the European Organization of Testing and Certification (EOTC), a move widely acknowledged as a landmark on the long road towards the establishment of mutual recognition in testing and certification procedures throughout the Community.

Each organization, composed of industry experts and representatives of consumer bodies, has been authorized by the Commission to build on legislative technical harmonization by developing common industrial product standards applicable throughout the EC. Initially, Britain's participation in the new standard-setting organizations was extremely poor, and many of the key positions were allocated to Germany and France. At a meeting of 300 senior business executives in Glasgow in October 1988, Lynda Chalker, Minister of State at the Foreign Office, expressed the Government's concern that Britain was being overshadowed by its Continental rivals, and warned that: 'The common standards which get adopted in Europe are bound to bear the character of the countries which put the most effort into their creation'. Similarly, product testing and certification procedures, which are used by national regulatory authorities to ensure that imported goods actually comply with national technical standards and regulations before being granted authorization for sale in the national market, are now also subject to the principle of mutual recognition. However, with the appointment of Dr Ivan Dunstan, the director general of the British Standards Institute, as the president of CEN in 1990 and the appointment of Gordon Gaddes as head of CENELEC Britain had managed to make up some lost ground.

The old system of national product testing and certification procedures (which meant, for example, that before a British-made vehicle could be sold on the Italian market its brakes would have to be sent to Italian inspectors for testing before going back to Britain for installation and eventual shipment back to Italy) is finally on its way out. Member states who continue to protect their national markets from Community competition by taking refuge in Article 36 of the Treaty, granting them the right to restrict imports because they do not conform to their 'essential requirements', will no longer have grounds for doing so. If the new approach is successful, the different essential requirements of member states will be replaced by harmonized Community essential requirements.

In order that member states do not sabotage this strategy by continuing to lay down national product standards independent of the work of the new European standards institutes they are now obliged to notify the Commission in advance of their intention to introduce any new regulations and technical standards that could have an impact on other member states. Under a Directive on Mutual Information Procedures, which came into effect in January 1985, the Commission also has the power to prevent member states from implementing any new technical regulations until it has established whether they create any new barriers to intra-Community trade. To date, over 30 such technical standards have been blocked by Brussels.

According to Commission statistics, about 60% of the total number of complaints received from member states concerning other member states who fail to honour the provisions of the Treaty relate to the Common Market provisions of Articles 30–36. Because of its limited resources, the Commission has only been able to resolve less than half of these infractions, which has acted as a significant brake on progress towards the creation of a genuine internal market. However, under the new multidimensional strategy for harmonizing technical standards, Commission officials are confident that the combined impact of legislative technical harmonization, the principle of mutual recognition of non-essential national technical standards, the work of the new standardization organizations and the recently implemented mutual information procedures will produce a considerable improvement in the record of member states adhering to Community regulations. A new directive tightening up existing legislation on cross-frontier public procurement procedures (and another extending these procedures to the hitherto-excluded sectors of telecommunications, water, transport and energy) will give the Commission's strategy an additional impetus. Once adopted, these directives will require all public works and supply contracts to incorporate Community technical standards.

The new approach should also be strengthened as a result of the establishment in September 1988 of Eurocert, a Brussels-based organization, composed of national inspection and certification bodies from Britain, Belgium, France, Luxembourg, Portugal, Spain, Sweden and Switzerland, which is designed to ensure that product certificates issued by one member state will be recognized and accepted without difficulty by all other member states. The success of this initiative will depend on mutual confidence between the various national inspection and certification bodies, each of which will be required to have a stringent internal quality-assurance system, subject to regular audits by other members of Eurocert.

Yet for all its improvements over the traditional approach to technical harmonization, the new strategy is not without its problems. Where differing technical standards are not essential to cross-frontier trade, few difficulties should present themselves. However, in those cases where technical differences are essential (and they are many) the picture is considerably less optimistic. No amount of mutual recognition will, for example, enable a three-pin electrical plug to fit into a two-pin socket. Mutual recognition will not by itself establish the kind of European-wide industrial standards needed to create the economies of scale that would be offered by Community-wide industrial standards. It will be many years, perhaps decades, before the new technical standards authorities have completed the task of harmonizing essential technical standards.

In December 1990, after the European Commission had reviewed the progress made by the new standard-setting organizations, it was evident that their impact, although far from negligible, had been considerably more modest than anticipated. Admittedly, the number of European standards had grown from 56 in 1983 to 870 by 1990, including new standards for toys, pressure vessels, construction products, personal protective equipment, gas appliances and medical devices. But with the Commission calling for the introduction of more than 1,000 new standards by 1993, it was clear that the standard-setting process would have to be accelerated.

In its Green Paper on standardization the Commission recommended a further reorganization of the standardization machinery to create what it called a new European Standardization System (ESS), designed to give added impetus to the laborious task of standard setting. The Commission called for the new structure to be made up of a European Standards Council, composed of representatives from industry, consumers associations, trade unions, the presidents of CEN, CENELEC, ETSI, and Commission officials. The new body would be responsible for all aspects of policy making. In addition, a smaller European Standardization Board, made up of Technical officials, would be responsible for the management and co-ordination of the ESS. These bodies would oversee the standard-setting process, while at the same time bringing home to governments and industry the importance of creating European-wide technical and industrial standards at the rate needed to improve the Community's competitive position with America and Japan.

Furthermore, because European standards do not exist in their own right, the Green Paper called for the national standard-setting organizations to be made subordinate to the new Community organizations. The standards created by CEN, CENELEC and ETSI have no formal or legal status until they are transposed into the national standards arrangements of each of the Twelve. The Commission wants to see this replaced by the primacy of the European Standardization System. Finally, the Green Paper opposed the expansion of the technical bodies, such as CEN, CENELEC and ETSI, to allow technical officials from the new East European democracies access to the standardization process, although it did not object to granting them associate member status. The proposed reforms, however, could only come into being with the approval of the Council of Ministers, which has yet to respond to the Commission's initiative. Consequently, hopes for speeding up the standard-setting process are likely to remain in abeyance until well after 1993.

The cost of divergent technical standards

Less than a year after the Community's new harmonization procedures were fully in place the Commission published a report outlining its estimates of the total cost of all fiscal, physical and technical barriers to trade within the EC. The report, *The European Challenge 1992: The Benefits of a Single Market*, was the first to attempt to quantify how much European companies were losing as a result of border controls, protectionist public procurement policies and divergent national product standards.

The report was compiled under the chairmanship of Paolo Cecchini, a special adviser to the Commission, and was based on a survey of 11,000 business executives, conducted by 15 companies of consultants, academics, economists and Commission personnel. The central conclusion of this unprecedented two-year study was that effective implementation of the White Paper Internal Market programme would save European industry about £130 billion, the equivalent of some 5% of the Community's gross domestic product. The precision of the report's estimates has been the subject of a heated dispute, but few have denied that they are pointing in the right direction.

In addition to demonstrating the cost of maintaining twelve separate markets the report also highlighted the opportunities for economic growth, job creation, reduced costs, improved productivity, increased competition, greater professional and business mobility and enhanced consumer choice that were there for the taking. 'Now we have the hard evidence, the confirmation of what those who are engaged in the building of Europe have always known: that the failure to achieve a single market has been costing European industry millions in unnecessary costs and opportunities,' Lord Cockfield said in his foreword. However, even more revealing than the overall estimated costs of market fragmentation was the report's examination of the costs of market fragmentation in specific areas, such as border and administrative red tape, public procurement and divergent technical standards in particular.

According to the Cecchini survey, divergent national technical standards were the second most important obstacle to the creation of the internal market after administrative formalities and border controls. The operation of some 100,000 different technical specifications across European industry meant that European companies were compelled to operate in a technical Tower of Babel, which was losing them billions of pounds because of duplicated product development, lost economies of scale and an enforced competitive disadvantage in relation to their counterparts in Japan and the United States.

This situation was particularly acute in the high-technology sectors, where companies can no longer survive by selling solely in national markets. To have any prospect of competing with their Japanese and American rivals, European companies needed a domestic market of Continental proportions to achieve the volume of sales required to recoup the large expenditures entailed in research and development.

The automobile industry

Perhaps the most obvious beneficiary of the introduction of common technical standards across European industry is that of the automobile sector. In fact, the 1992 process should end the long-standing fragmentation of the European auto market and begin the age of the Euro-car. At present, the 12 million models sold annually in the European Community have to conform with a bewildering variety of national technical and safety standards, which deprive manufacturers of potentially substantial economies of scale.

Some countries (principally France and Italy) fear that the creation of a single market for the auto sector will enable external producers (such as Japan) to increase their penetration of the European market. However, the Commission appears set on introducing some 44 mandatory regulations—governing all aspects of auto production, from the depth of tyre tread and the brilliance of headlamps to the level of permissible toxic exhaust emissions—by the middle of 1992.

Anxieties over increased foreign competition may hold up the Commission's plans but they are unlikely to be prevented outright. Once installed, the new system will replace the existing patchwork of voluntary standards, enabling a vehicle made in one country to be sold freely in any other. Similar measures are also likely to follow for buses, trucks and motorcycles.

The telecommunications sector

In the telecommunications sector the costs of the divergent technical standards imposed on all three categories of telecommunications technology, customer premises equipment, such as telephones, facsimile and telex machines; transmission equipment, such as wire, cable and antennas; and the central office equipment needed to interface the growing variety of telecommunication services were estimated by the Cecchini report to be in excess of 25% of the £17.5 billion the European telecommunications market was worth in 1986. Moreover, these barriers were increasing at an alarming rate under the pressures of rapid technological innovation.

It is not necessary to look hard or far to locate the primary cause of this lamentable state of affairs. Hitherto, the various national telecommunications authorities, the government Post Telegraph and Telephone (PTT) organizations in Europe, such as the German Bundespost and the French Direction Générale des Télécommunications, as well as the privatized British Telecom in Britain, were responsible for establishing technical standards for the European telecommunications industry, through an organization known as the European Confederation of Postal and Telecommunications Administrations (CEPT).

Despite initially high aspirations, CEPT proved to be a failure. Production of telecommunications equipment continued to be carried out on a national basis, with the PTTs discriminating in favour of local manufacturers while relying on national technical standards to prevent European competition. Consequently, the harmonization of technical standards has been taken away from CEPT and allocated to the new Community standards organizations. Even more absurd has been the development of new telecommunications technologies on a national basis, notably packet-switching. This is a method of breaking down information into digital messages for transmission over telephone networks, used extensively by office workers in the form of electronic mail services and vital for office communications. However, because of the difficulties involved in tailoring each national system to another it is estimated that only three out of every four transmissions are successful.

However, the Internal Market White Paper, and the 1987 Green Paper on the liberalization of the telecommunications industry, is expected to bring about a considerable transformation in the Community's telecommunications sector. The deregulation programme called for the introduction of cross-frontier competition in the supply of terminal equipment by 1990, the end of national monopolies in the provision of value-added services such as electronic mail boxes, remote databases and voice messaging by the end of 1991 and some degree of price harmonization in an effort to bring tariffs into line across the Community by 1992.

Perhaps the most important single measure of all is the creation of ETSI, which is empowered to accelerate agreement on harmonizing European technical specifications and certification procedures. ETSI was established in Nice in March 1987, and had its inaugural meeting three months later under the directorship of Professor Diodato Gagliardi. Unlike CEPT, ETSI has its own building, a permanent director and a staff of twelve, with provisions for more staff once its workload begins to increase.

Most observers were very surprised by the speed at which the new organization was created, raising expectations that ETSI would register equally rapid progress in the field of establishing common technical standards for the high-growth digital mobile telephone sector. Keeping to time-honoured tradition, Europe had built its first generation of cellular telephone systems on the basis of incompatible technical standards. Any European business executive travelling by car from London to Paris and on to Rome, and who needed to keep in constant touch with head-quarters, would need three mobile telephones to do so.

During negotiations on technical standards for the second generation of mobile cellular telephones most European countries favoured the use of a narrow transmission band, while France and Germany proposed the adoption of the wide band. After months of difficult negotiations, France and Germany finally capitulated. The breakthrough was widely acknowl-edged to be unprecedented. However, the difficulty in arriving at common technical standards for the next generation of mobile cellular telephones showed the enormity of the task facing ETSI. Despite this success, even the most optimistic observers expect the standardization process to be slow and patchy, effectively ruling out the prospect of large-scale standardization in the telecommunications sector by 1992.

Technical standards as barriers to foreign trade

Shortly after the new technical standards organizations were in place, they were subject to many criticisms from abroad. American politicians in particular were concerned that one of the consequences of the new organizations would be European technical standards which would exclude US products from the European domestic market. Richard Mosbacker, President Bush's outspoken Commerce Secretary, accused the Commission of engaging in an ingenious form of protectionism through the standards-setting organizations. These fears were also expressed in a constant stream of US newspaper reports, which were given added credence by the House of Representatives Foreign Affairs Committee in its report on standards published in June 1988.

However, in a letter published in the *Financial Times* the same month, Roy MacDowell, the former President of the International Electrotech-nical Commission (IEC), a Geneva-based organization responsible for drawing up worldwide electrotechnical standards, challenged this 'pessi-mistic US view'. MacDowell pointed out that most electrotechnical stand-ards in Community countries were 'already based on standards written by the International Electrotechnical Commission'.

Furthermore, he pointed out that the IEC was a world organization whose standards are formulated by experts from all member countries—including the United States. America was therefore 'already in a position to participate directly in European harmonization through the inter-national forum provided by the IEC'. Moreover, the Commission has given an undertaking to the world trade body, the General Agreement on Tariffs and Trade, to adopt existing world standards as the new European ones.

MacDowell added that an agreement also exists between the IEC and its sister Community organization, CENELEC, 'under the terms of which information on European standardization and harmonization activities is transmitted to non-European countries via the IEC headquarters in

Geneva'. As a result, the 'principles of openness and transparency' demanded by Secretary Mosbacker were already in operation.

The pharmaceuticals sector

As in the telecommunications sector, the creation of a single market for the European pharmaceuticals industry, worth some £20 billion a year, faces complex problems. So far, the Commission's attempts to reconcile the need for strict control on the quality, safety and efficacy of new drugs with industry's desire for more efficient drug-registration and sales-authorization procedures have not convinced industry officials or national authorities that the objective of creating an internal market for the pharmaceuticals sector will be realized by 1992. Under the present system a pharmaceuticals company wishing to introduce a new product into a particular market must submit it to the appropriate national registration authority, which is responsible for establishing whether the drug is safe and actually does what the manufacturers claim of it. However, because each member state has its own registration procedure, acquiring twelve separate approvals to market a new pharmaceutical product (each of which can take in excess of two years), this is a laborious and expensive process which takes up the time allowed for drug patent protection.

Furthermore, the major purchasers of pharmaceuticals in the EC are the state-owned health authorities, which exercise considerable influence on the price at which drugs are sold. The great variation in national public health authority pricing policies (which invariably discriminate in favour of domestic drug manufacturers) also have a direct influence on company profits. Removal of such barriers would save the European pharmaceuticals sector an estimated 1% of the industry's annual costs. The pharmaceuticals companies maintain that, on average, it takes ten years to develop a new drug at a cost of £50 million, and unless the Community is able to introduce uniform registration, market-authorization and pricing procedures they are sceptical of their ability to compete effectively with their foreign rivals in the race to produce the next generation of high-technology drugs which require increasingly heavy investment in research and development—the return on which is never guaranteed. However, in the wake of the Thalidomide tragedy in the 1960s most European governments introduced complex and time-consuming drug-testing procedures (for example, Britain's 1968 Medicines Act) to reassure public opinion about the safety of the drugs they were consuming. Such anxieties have since been heightened by the appalling side-effects of the anti-arthritic drug, Opren.

As part of its attempts to facilitate the free circulation of medicines the Commission has proposed the creation of a Central European Medicines Agency (similar to the US Food and Drug Administration) to be responsible for testing all new biotechnology products. This would have the merit of streamlining national drug registration and authorization procedures, while permitting any new biotechnology-derived drugs to go on sale throughout the Community once they had been given the European seal of approval. Some industry officials have, however, already expressed fears that a European drug-licensing authority could become too bureaucratic. In addition, the Commission has also proposed that national testing agencies be retained for the licensing of the more traditional new products, supported by the principle of mutual recognition of member states' registration and marketing requirements where possible, and arbitration by the central agency in the event of unresolvable national disputes where necessary. But while this element of the proposal has been designed to avoid the dangers of excessive bureaucracy, it seems almost calculated to arouse national anxieties over whether other member states' testing procedures are as effective as their own.

As far as other aspects of the programme are concerned, the Commission has already produced a draft directive on price controls which would require the national public health authorities to make their pricing systems more open, thereby giving pharmaceuticals companies more certainty about the price at which their products will eventually be sold. A major breakthrough came in December 1986 with the adoption of directives setting out market-authorization procedures for high-technology medicines. This was followed in December 1991 by an agreement to extend drug patents by five years, thereby boosting pharmaceutical companies' profits and providing added incentives for new research. The Commission is still consulting the pharmaceuticals industry and the national regulatory bodies about their preference for a new EC drug regulatory system. The issue remains sensitive.

The construction sector

Contrary to popular perceptions, the European construction products industry is a major influence in cross-frontier trade. In 1985 the Community market for construction products was valued at around £70 billion, but the prospects for substantial future growth are tarnished by the enormous variations in customer specifications for building materials such as bricks, glass, plaster, concrete, aggregates, timber and steel. The cost of market fragmentation has been put at some £55 million a year, while their removal could generate £1 billion in extra business.

In Britain, the construction and construction products industry is already a highly competitive sector, where profit margins are tight. Consequently, British companies are more likely to find new business in Europe than Continental companies are likely to find in Britain. Leading British construction and construction product companies, notably Trafalgar House, Wimpey, Laing and Tarmac, have already established their presence in Continental Europe with a view to exploiting the potential offered by the creation of the internal market. Nonetheless, the British construction industry appears to be lagging behind some of its European rivals, particularly in France, where overall preparations for a European construction industry without frontiers appear to be considerably more advanced.

Unlike most industries, construction is both a service and a product. Prospective clients have an understandable preference for using construction companies with whom they are familiar and in whom they have confidence. This puts a high premium on having a physical presence in a given market and acquiring familiarity with the local environment. Such efforts would be to little avail if a construction company, having established itself in a particular market, was effectively prohibited from operating in it because the technical specifications of the construction products being used were unacceptable to the regulatory authority of the host country. However, the experience of one French company, which had to fight for five years to obtain the technical certification to sell its steel girders in Germany, demonstrated that such obstacles are all too frequent.

As in other major industrial sectors, technical specifications and product certification procedures are used to keep competition in the construction sector from other member states to an absolute minimum. The Cecchini report even claimed that the 'so called inherent divergencies in customer requirements may be largely a case of national tastes determined by national regulations'.

The Internal Market White Paper, in accordance with the harmonization and mutual recognition procedures outlined above, proposes a basic framework of European technical standards for construction products, in accordance with mutually accepted criteria of stability, safety and health. The standards organization (CEN) is currently drawing up a European code of technical standards for the construction industry, and although it is clear that the new standards will not be ready by 1992, the Commission has agreed to accept and enforce the mutual recognition of current national standards in the interim.

The foodstuffs sector

A similar approach has been used in the foodstuffs sector. Here the Commission's strategy involves the adoption of a series of general framework directives, governing the areas of additives, flavouring, labelling, packaging, public inspection and irradiation. These directives will establish the broad principles to which national food laws must adhere, leaving the details to be worked out largely by the Commission and the European Food Industry Association (CIAA) in a series of more specific foodstuffs directives.

The strategy is designed to capitalize on a succession of rulings by the European Court of Justice, notably the 1987 one against Greece and West Germany for prohibiting imports of beer that did not conform to national 'beer purity' laws and the 1988 ruling against Italy for prohibiting imports of pasta made from soft rather than hard wheat. The judgments have established that if a food product is legally manufactured and sold in one member state it can be manufactured and sold in all.

The new approach, as in so many other areas, represents a significant departure from the past. The old system of food standards harmonization focused on the specific composition of foodstuffs (known as recipe law) on a case-by-case basis. Attempts to lay down recipe law for particular foodstuffs gave rise to the popular misconception that Brussels' bureaucrats were trying to do away with the British sausage. Indeed, the BBC television series *Yes Minister* even had them trying to rename the British banger an 'emulsified high-fat offal tube'. The fact that British pork sausages can contain as little as 65% meat, defined as animal flesh, fat, skin, rind, gristle and sinew, while German sausages must contain 100% meat, defined as animal flesh only, seemed less important than the apparent assault on the traditional sausage as a symbol of Britain's national sovereignty. In any event, recipe law proved completely unworkable. In the field of additives alone there are an estimated 40,000 applications, making regulation of each a practical impossibility. On the principle that it is better to delegate as much harmonization to the private sector as possible, the CIAA, composed of the various trade bodies of the European foodstuffs industry, is now responsible for compiling compositional standards. As much research on foodstuff additives has already been carried out there is no need for the CIAA to start from the beginning, and the Commission has restricted its legislative activity to the protection of public health, consumer information, fair trading and public inspection. This change of direction represents a modest victory for Britain, which has persistently argued for the abolition of recipe law.

There is agreement on the immediate horizon on a host of quality and packaging regulations for the food and drink industry, including common procedures for verifying the quality of food imported from other member states (particularly important in the wake of growing public concern over salmonella and listeria poisoning), along with common rules on irradiated food and the labelling of health foods. The internal market for foodstuffs, excluding labelling, is therefore all but complete.

In March 1990 the Council of Ministers reached agreement on a new nutrition-labelling directive, which requires manufacturers and processors to specify the nutritional content of packaged foodstuffs where nutritional claims are being made for the product in question. The objective of the legislation is to provide consumers with an accurate picture of what is in a given foodstuff, and prevent manufacturers from providing only a partial account. As a result, manufacturers will no longer be able to say, for example, that crisps are high in fibre and ignore the fact that they are also high in fat and salt.

The implications of the successful creation of an internal market for the European foodstuffs industry (which now looks more optimistic than at any time since the White Paper was launched) are far-reaching. Small manufacturers, unless they are able to develop small national niche markets on a European scale, can expect much competition from their European counterparts. Many family food concerns, which owe their existence to the fragmentation of the European market and who are unable to form cross-border alliances, are likely to fail. Larger companies, who will benefit from the economies of scale that the abolition of trade barriers will produce, should find themselves facing the prospect of new markets emerging throughout the Community.

With a large European market now on the horizon it seems almost inevitable that foodstuffs manufacturers, processors and distributors will follow the trilingual labelling precedent set by the French manufacturer of Benedicta Mayonnaise, whose jars of salad dressing are already available in local supermarkets with a single French, British and Dutch label —assuming, of course, that the Commission keeps labelling requirements to a minimum. In the restructuring that is likely to follow the opening up of national markets some smaller companies may fall by the wayside, but consumers will benefit from lower prices brought about by increased competition and a significant expansion of the variety of food products available for consumption.

Concern remains, however, that the failure to specify what kind of products, and in what quantity, should go into particular foodstuffs, may force manufacturers to substitute cheaper ingredients in an effort to fend off competition from unscrupulous rivals. After all, how many consumers will have the time to read the various lists of ingredients used in competing products of, for example, apple pies, cream cheese or smoked ham? In an effort to prevent such substitution Commission officials have been under pressure to extend the Appellation d'Origine Controlée stamp used to prevent the fraudulent sale of wine to traditional and gourmet foodstuffs, although there appears little prospect of this happening at present.

Other sectors

The White Paper envisages applying the same strategy to every sector fragmented by divergent national technical standards, whether in the car, civil engineering or chemical industries. The same approach has also been applied to sectors outside manufacturing, including public procurement, air, sea and road transport, veterinary and plant controls, the free movement of workers and professionals, capital movements and financial services.

The White Paper singles out the liberalization of financial services, such as insurance policies, mortgages, consumer credit and unit trusts, as a potentially major source of economic growth and job creation. The Commission's proposals for deregulation are based on the co-ordination of national rules governing the authorization of companies wishing to operate in the financial services sector. The proposed Community regulatory system is to be based on the principle of 'home country control'. Supervisory responsibilities will lie with the appropriate authorities in the member state in which the company is based, regardless of which member state the company is operating in. Ironically, in most countries it is the governments of the member states who are pressing hard for deregulation, often in the face of bitter resistance from financial service institutions, such as those in Germany, who are very comfortable in their protected national markets and do not relish the prospect of competition from across the border.

Business and the environment

The environmental awareness that gathered pace during the 1980s assisted by a series of regional environmental disasters such as Bhopal, Chernobyl and the accidental dumping of 30 million tonnes of chemicals into the Rhine, the more global consequences of acid rain, the depletion of the ozone layer and the greenhouse effect have given environmental issues a political urgency that was unimaginable ten years earlier. After more than two centuries of unrestrained industrial activity, increased public anxiety about quality-of-life issues such as air purity and drinking water has forced politicians into counting the cost of the wholesale pollution of the land, sea and atmosphere. Although the new European environmental protection programme is in its formative stages, it is already clear that the clean-up effort will cost governments, businesses and consumers billions of pounds. The Clean Air Act, which was passed in 1990 by the US Congress, for example, is estimated to cost American industry $25 billion a year. The European Commission's new environmental protection programme is expected to dwarf that figure.

While environmental considerations were not seen to play a prominent role in the early stages of the internal market programme, they rapidly moved towards the centre of the political stage. Under Carlo Ripa di Meana, the Italian Environment Commissioner, there are now more proposals for legislation in the environmental arena than any other single sector of Community activity. An early indication of the newly found commitment to the environment came during the gathering of EC heads of state in their Dublin summit meeting in June 1990. Issuing a declaration on the environment, the Council said: 'The natural environment which forms the life support system for our planet is gravely at risk . . . the continuation of life could no longer be assured were recent trends to proceed unchallenged.' The declaration was widely seen as the first official attempt to reconcile the objective of increased economic growth contained in the internal market programme with the ostensibly antagonistic goal of sustainable economic development.

Prior to the Dublin declaration, the Community's commitment to protecting the environment, while far from negligible (witness the decision to reduce sulphur emissions from power stations by 60% from 1980 levels by the year 2003) fell far short of what many in the scientific community felt was required. The original Treaty of Rome makes no reference to the environment, and the Community's first environmental action programme did not begin until 1972. It was, however, the Single European Act which gave the Commission the legislative authority to take the initiative under Article 130, which stipulates that 'action by the Community . . . shall be based on the principles that preventive action should be taken, that environmental damage should as a priority be rectified at source, and that the polluter should pay'. Shortly after the Act was ratified, Jacques Delors, the President of the European Commission, remarked dryly: 'This victory went unnoticed in 1985–86.'

These three principles—preventive action, damage rectified at source, and the polluter pays—are in the process of transforming the face of European agriculture, industry and the consumption habits of tens of millions of its citizens. Between 1972 and 1991 some 100 separate pieces of environmental legislation were enacted, and the Commission is currently engaged in drawing up its fifth and most ambitious environmental action programme. This includes the unprecedented use of economic and fiscal instruments, such as taxes on carbon consumption, to lay the foundations of what is becoming known as the 'ecological market economy'. In short, the externalities of modern economic and industrial processes, such as the consumption of finite resources, waste, pollution and environmental destruction, will increasingly be factored into individual product costs.

British businesses received a taste of the new environmental regulatory regime following the introduction of the 1990 Environmental Protection Act. The legislation introduced two new pollution control systems, the first, enforced by HM Inspectorate of Pollution, imposing stringent controls on the land, sea and air emissions of some 5,000 industrial processes; and the second, enforced by local authorities, regulating the air emissions of some 27,000 less harmful industrial processes. Many British businesses are clearly struggling to cope with the new environmental regulations, which often involve large-scale structural change and substantial additional costs for large and small businesses alike. Unlike traditional end-of-pipe environmental remedies, the new regulations frequently entail a complete reassessment of production processes, from purchase of raw materials to the sale of finished products. Moreover, more exacting legislation is expected in the years ahead, and, as Michael Heseltine, the Environment Secretary, warned in May 1991, companies which fail to comply with the new environmental standards and take advantage of the opportunities presented by what he called the 'green renaissance' could face corporate catastrophe.

In one sense, because of the increase in popular support for environmental protection initiatives, the task of incorporating environmental considerations into all other sectors of Community activity is easier in the early 1990s than it was in the middle of the 1980s. Indeed, in a veiled comment on the former reluctance of some member states to support such initiatives, notably Britain and France, one recent Commission publication noted that: 'The last couple of years have been marked by a distinct jockeying for position on the diplomatic front with hitherto reluctant member states keen to be seen taking the lead on new initiatives'. That transformation is due, in large part, to the series of international conferences, such as the Vienna Convention on the Ozone Layer, the Montreal Protocol on Chlorofluorocarbons (CFCs) and the Basle Convention on the Movement of Hazardous Waste, which put environmental questions firmly on the international diplomatic agenda along with the great questions of war and peace. Now that national governments are eager to impress their domestic electorates with their commitment to environmental protection, the days when governments could deal with environmental issues under the heading 'globalony' have long since passed.

In another sense, however, it has become much more complex. One of the greatest problems faced by the Commission is preventing unilateral environmental protection initiatives by the 'dark green' countries such as Denmark and Germany from being opposed by 'light green' ones such as Spain and Portugal on the grounds that such measures constitute a new form of non-tariff barrier. New German laws, for example, will make it mandatory for the European packaging industry to collect and recycle virtually every box, can, bottle, tube and container sold in the Federal Republic. They have caused consternation among other member states. At the same time, the Commission is under constant pressure not to dilute its legislative programme to the lowest common denominator in an attempt to preserve some form of face saving by artificial green consensus.

Although the Commission's fifth environmental action programme is being finalized, the broad principles of the initiative, along with the principal areas of concern, are clear. In the five categories of concern—energy efficiency, waste management, air pollution, water purity and transport —almost 100 separate directives have been implemented or planned. In the energy conservation sector alone, some 14 legislative proposals are in the pipeline and designed to reduce energy consumption as the single most effective means of stabilizing carbon dioxide emissions—one of the principal causes of the greenhouse effect—at 1990 levels by the year 2000. The measures range from labelling the energy consumption of household appliances such as refrigerators, washing machines, tumble driers, ovens and lighting equipment (enabling consumers to make informed choices about the energy consumption of household implements) to the introduction of taxes on energy or carbon, known as a pollution added tax (PAT).

In the field of waste management, more than 20 directives have been implemented or are under consideration. Solving Europe's waste problem is one of the most formidable tasks facing the Community. According to Commission estimates, member states generate some two billion tonnes of waste a year, 150 million tonnes of which comes from industry and about 30 million tonnes of which is hazardous. Much of the remainder comes from household refuse and agriculture. With 60% of household waste dumped in landfill sites, 33% incinerated and 7% composted, there is already great pressure on existing disposal outlets. In many member states the infrastructure for disposing of and treating human waste is inadequate or even non-existent. In Italy, for example, 48% of the 1,580 sewage treatment plants no longer function, while in Spain, 80% of municipalities are without any treatment works. Moreover, contemporary intensive farming techniques have created a situation in some countries, such as the Netherlands, where the volume of animal slurry now far exceeds the soil's ability to absorb it.

Waste management directives have been drawn up to cover the entire spectrum of waste products, from the disposal of batteries to the removal and treatment of sewage, and the regulation of landfill sites to control of emissions from incinerators. The directives will introduce severe penalties for uncontrolled disposals, incentives for recycling and the use of cleaner technologies, and stringent regulations on the shipment of toxic and hazardous goods across frontiers. The Community's regional development funds will be used to help lay the sewers, build the waste-water treatment and incineration facilities needed to bring the poorer regions up to the same level of the more affluent regions, and help make the Community self-sufficient in the modern technologies of waste management.

No less than 24 directives have been adopted or are under discussion in the field of air pollution, including the total phasing out of ozone-depleting CFCs and halons by 1997, and a series of anti-pollution restrictions on emissions from cars, lorries and combustion plants. Few issues have, however, generated more column inches than the Commission's decision in 1989 to haul Britain in front of the European Court of Justice for its failure to comply with the directive on the purity of drinking water, one of the first pieces of legislation targeted against water pollution. The fact that France and Belgium were already before the court for similar offences, and that Germany and Luxembourg soon followed, failed to receive similar prominence in the British press. The drinking-water directive is one of 12 measures aimed at cleaning up Europe's rivers, lakes, beaches and seas. In an attempt to bring about a wholesale improvement in the aquatic environment, it would prohibit the discharge of untreated sewage and impose restrictions on agricultural production to prevent fertilizer nitrates seeping into the water table.

With traffic volumes forecast to increase considerably in the Community during the next decade, threatening to neutralize the reductions in carbon dioxide emissions obtained from imposing restrictions on other areas of economic activity, the transport policies of member states can be expected to come under increasing scrutiny from the Commission. Altogether, some 14 directives have been adopted or proposed. They are designed to encourage more environmentally benign forms of transport, particularly rail, and to reduce the consumption of oil and the production of carbon dioxide by harmonizing taxes on petrol, diesel and other fuels. In addition, initiatives such as the 1988 Environmental Impacts Assessment Directive, aimed at integrating ecological awareness into the planning stages of all agricultural, industrial, transport and regional development projects in the member states, could make it much harder for governments to destroy large tracts of countryside for new motorway and trunk road schemes. In October 1991, for example, Ripa di Meana, the Environment Commissioner, initiated legal proceedings against Britain for allegedly failing to comply with the directive on seven key construction projects, including the extension of the M3 through Twyford Down in Hampshire and the proposed East London River Crossing, which threatens the last ancient woodland in London.

However, while few could deny that Brussels has set about cultivating a new awareness of environmental issues, sceptics have been quick to point out the fundamental contradictions between the Commission's determination to accelerate economic growth and its environmental initiatives. Quite simply, the internal market will create more pollution —not less—and there is a widespread fear that, apart from a few nods in the right direction, little of substance will change. A report on 1992 and the environment compiled by Commission officials in 1991 noted that: 'Electricity generation and transport are major sources of air pollution, together accounting for around 60% of sulphur dioxide and 80% of nitrogen oxides.' It also pointed out that: 'Notwithstanding the favourable impacts which can be expected to result from the implementation of existing environmental policies, the growth impact of the Internal Market is likely to cause atmospheric emissions of sulphur dioxide and nitrogens of oxide to increase respectively by 8% to 9% and 12% to 14% by 2010'. The report proved so controversial that the Commission refused to endorse it.

Two recent developments, however, promise to strengthen the Commission's legislative programme for protecting the environment. The first involves a proposal to extend the qualified majority voting procedure to environmental initiatives. This received approval from the Council of Ministers and was incorporated into the treaty reforms agreed by EC heads of state at the summit meeting in Maastricht in December 1991. Unanimity will, however, be retained on all environmental issues dealing with taxation (such as the proposed carbon tax), town and country planning, land use, water and energy. The second involves the creation of a European Environmental Agency (EEA). There have been arguments over whether the EEA's role should be confined to the collection of scientific data or extended to embrace the enforcement and monitoring powers granted to atomic energy inspectors under the Euratom Treaty. The Commission is eager to follow the precedent set by Euratom, although the Council of Ministers remains adamantly opposed. The debate over inspection powers, however, is likely to remain somewhat academic until a location for the agency has been decided, and this is not expected to happen before the member states resolve their long-running dispute over the seat of other EC institutions. Unfortunately, the Maastricht summit highlighted yet again the Community's apparent inability to come to grips with this issue. Despite mounting pressure to agree on a location for the new agency, the French government insisted that Strasbourg must first be formally acknowledged as the home of the European Parliament.

Checklist of changes

- The traditional case-by-case approach to the harmonization of different product technical standards has been replaced by legislative harmonization where necessary and mutual recognition where possible.
- All essential technical harmonization measures will be brought into force by majority voting.
- These legislative measures will stipulate an obligatory minimum of health and safety standards, conformity with which will guarantee manufacturers the right of access to the markets of other member states.
- Legislative technical harmonization will be complemented by systematic implementation of the principle of mutual recognition for non-essential product standards, reinforced by the 1979 Cassis de Dijon ruling.
- The task of establishing European-wide technical standards has been allocated to the new European standards-setting organizations such as CEN, CENELEC and ETSI.
- The traditional system of national product testing and certification procedures will also be subject to mutual recognition.
- Under the directive governing mutual information procedures, the European Commission has the power to prevent member states from implementing any new technical standard likely to create additional barriers to trade.
- The White Paper programme calls for the introduction of cross-frontier competition in the supply of terminal equipment by 1990, the end of national monopolies in the provision of value-added services by the end of 1989 and some degree of tariff price harmonization by 1992.
- National drug registration and authorization procedures will be

streamlined with the introduction of either a central drug-licensing authority or mandatory Community-wide testing procedures, along with mutual recognition of member states' registration and marketing requirements.

- National public health authorities will be required to introduce more open drug pricing policies.
- Essential technical standards will be laid down for all other sectors, including the construction, car, civil engineering, and chemical industries. The same approach has also been adopted for sectors outside manufacturing, notably financial services and foodstuffs.
- Nearly 100 directives are expected, covering a wide range of environmental issues in the fields of energy conservation, waste management, air and water pollution, transport and the transport and treatment of toxic and hazardous substances.

5 TERRORISM, CRIME AND ILLEGAL IMMIGRATION

Internal frontiers and external borders

Complementing the European Community's attempt to demolish internal barriers to the free movement of goods, people, capital and labour is a parallel effort to strengthen its external frontier. Once internal restrictions are removed, many of the functions carried out by trade, security, customs and immigration officials will have to be transferred from individual internal frontiers to the Community's external border. The early years of the internal market programme were marked by a preoccupation with whether the new external barrier would result in greater protectionist pressures towards increased competition from non-Community countries. Attention has since shifted, however, to the more sensitive questions about whether the Community's defences against terrorism, crime and illegal immigration, are sufficiently effective or excessively stringent.

The IRA bomb which blew up the Visitors' Gallery at the London Stock Exchange in July 1990 and the car bomb which killed Ian Gow, the Conservative MP for Eastbourne, ten days later, were disturbing reminders of the apparent ability of terrorist gangs to operate throughout the Community with impunity. Record increases in the volume of drugs seized at Britain's ports and airports were seen as a testimony to the alarming growth of the international drug-trafficking trade. Finally, the increase in the number of residence applications from immigrants and refugees provoked bitter debates in many national parliaments over the effectiveness of existing immigration and asylum policies. Should the EC relax these policies or was Europe full up?

The promise of free movement

One of the main benefits of 1992 is the promise it holds out of free movement—the fulfilment of the dream expressed in 1951 by Ernest Bevin, Foreign Secretary in the Attlee government after the war, that one day he would be 'able to take a ticket at Victoria Station and go anywhere I damn well please'. Conversely, one of the main fears about 1992—expressed most forcefully in Britain but not only in Britain—is that it will create 'an internal market' for terrorism, crime and illegal immigration. In her forceful speech at the College of Europe in Bruges in September 1988 Mrs Thatcher supported 1992 in so far as it opened up markets, widened consumer choice and encouraged enterprise, but declared it to be a 'matter of plain common sense' that frontier controls could not be totally abolished if citizens were to be protected.

This demand for the retention of frontier controls contradicts the undertakings contained in Article 8a of the Single European Act, which defines the internal market specifically as an 'area without internal frontiers'. Andreas Papandreou, Greek Prime Minister and the then President of the Council of Ministers, accused Thatcher of 'putting in question, unilaterally, an Act which binds the Twelve by validated international treaty'. The Act does have a loophole, in the form of a General Declaration allowing states to 'take such steps as they consider necessary' to prevent drug smuggling, terrorism and illegal immigration. However, the Declaration is subordinate to the overall aim of abolition of frontiers, and EC leaders agreed to avoid national controls by laying down 'common measures' on visas, immigration and extradition while also intensifying police co-operation throughout the EC.

Under the 1992 process, in other words, as agreed in negotiations for the Single European Act, the apprehension of criminals and terrorists is provided for through the strengthening of external frontiers, European-wide police and intelligence co-operation, and common visa and immigration policies on the grounds that most arrests do not, in any case, take place at air- or seaports or border crossings. Where they do, the criminals have often in reality been tracked for miles through police co-operation (for example, from Spain or Italy to a Channel port) and the frontier is simply a convenient location for a police or customs operation.

As the impact of the Thatcher speech in Bruges demonstrated, the abolition of frontiers arouses fears of threats ranging from gunmen to rabies, and raises directly the issue of national sovereignty. It may be a mistake, however, to conclude that a majority of people therefore oppose the abolition of borders, provided that measures against crime are adequate. No aspect of the internal market programme has captured the imagination of European public opinion as much as the proposal to abolish the Community's internal frontiers and replace them with a single external one. In an age marked by ever-increasing amounts of intra-Community tourism and travel the prospect of being able to move from Britain to France, Germany, Greece or Spain without obligatory travel documents, inspection at internal frontiers and time-consuming delays is perhaps the single most tangible benefit of the Community's economic integration process. In a survey published in May 1991 by Euro-Barometer, the EC's public opinion research organization, most people in the Community believed that by the year 2000 they will be able to travel freely and work anywhere in an enlarged EC, be paid in a single currency and be defended by a common EC military force.

There can be little doubt that the Commission has been emboldened in its determination to press ahead with the abolition of internal frontiers by the decision of the so-called Schengen Group—the Benelux countries, Germany and France—to introduce their own border-free zone by 1990 —regardless of progress among the Twelve. The Schengen Agreement was finally signed in June 1990, although it will not go into effect until ratified by all five national parliaments, probably in the middle of 1992. The Commission clearly regards the Schengen initiative as the laboratory for its own proposals for a frontier-free Europe, and is confident that its anticipated success will help to force the more reluctant member states into following the Schengen example.

In February 1989, for example, Martin Bangemann, the Commissioner responsible for the internal market, announced the Commission's intention to press ahead with the introduction of common policies governing extradition, the right of asylum and the granting of visas. Bangemann's extraordinary claim that the entire edifice could be in place within six months seemed reckless in the extreme, but he also used the occasion to hint that the Commission might be prepared to accept the introduction of spot checks at frontier posts to replace systematic border controls, which observers in Brussels interpreted as an attempt to win Britain over to the controversial scheme.

Moving from one member state to another as one moves from Kent to Essex or Yorkshire to Lincolnshire is also a major attraction for European companies trading across national frontiers. Industry has been compelled to shoulder an immense burden as a consequence of the delays, red tape, form filling, and transport and handling charges associated with the maintenance of frontier formalities. The European Commission argues forcibly that the complete removal of these physical barriers to trade will not only reduce costs and stimulate competition but will also encourage many smaller firms (who have traditionally been inhibited from expanding beyond national borders because of the costs involved) to seek new markets throughout the Community.

The Commission's proposals have met much criticism. The fear that any attempt to abolish internal frontier controls to facilitate free movement for business executives, labour and tourists will have the potentially disastrous side-effect of laying the foundations of an internal market for terrorists, drug traffickers, criminals and dangerous diseases such as rabies has been most commonly expressed in Britain, Ireland, Denmark and Greece. Moreover, the difficulties posed by the pressures for increased immigration along the Community's external borders, particularly the anticipated rise in immigration from Eastern Europe following the collapse of the Communist dictatorships, will also have to be dealt with. Some observers fear that increased immigration from the East could lead to the displacement of existing migrant communities inside the Community, leading to a different kind of Fortress Europe, one in which European peoples are given preferential access to jobs and houses.

During a debate in the European Parliament in December 1985, shortly after publication of the Internal Market White Paper, the basic arguments of the anti- and pro-abolitionists were stated in terms that have been repeated in much the same form ever since.

Bob Cryer, the Labour MEP for Sheffield, challenged Lord Cockfield by saying: 'Would the Commissioner accept, with his well-known enthusiasm for the removal of all frontiers, that neither he nor anybody else has produced any solution to the question which keeps being raised . . . how one can control increased drug smuggling, how one can control rabies and how one can control the spread of plant diseases if customs supervision and frontiers are entirely removed as he wishes?' In his customary sardonic manner, Lord Cockfield replied: 'It was made clear in the White Paper that there were a number of problems, particularly in the field of terrorism and drug trafficking, which would require careful consideration before the full White Paper proposals are implemented.' The Commissioner then went on to give Cryer a lesson in how to work from first principles.

> If, for example, you were considering how to deal with the drug problem and assumed that you had no frontiers to start with, would you end up by saying that the right solution to the drug problem was the creation of national frontiers? I very much doubt whether you would. In fact most of the drug seizures are not made at national frontiers at all, nor are they made as a result of routine checks on every single person who goes from one country to another. I agree that these are very important problems, they need to be studied, and they need to be studied with an open mind.

The Commission's proposals, in fact, offer the basis for a fundamental transformation in the way the Community organizes its defences against terrorists, drug traffickers, criminals and plant and animal diseases. However, Britain is still looking for a 'balance of advantage' between free movement and control of crime.

The case for the abolition of internal frontier controls

Despite the abolition of customs duties and quantitative restrictions imposed on intra-Community trade by individual member states that followed the completion of the single external tariff in 1968, customs posts have remained a feature of national frontiers, even though they have been largely deprived of the function that gave them their name. Because there are no longer intra-Community customs duties on goods and services at internal frontiers, customs posts no longer really exist within the EC, even if the signs suggest otherwise. What are still often referred to as customs posts are in fact frontier control posts; they are only customs posts for goods entering member states from outside the

Community. Duty on alcohol and tobacco, for example, are excise, not custom duties.

The White Paper describes internal frontier controls as the most visible example of the continued division of the European Community into twelve national segments. Concomitantly, their removal would be the clearest sign of the integration of the member states into a genuine single market. The need to remove these internal frontier controls does not arise simply out of any idealistic or aesthetic sentiment. Rather, it stems from the practical necessity of stimulating economic growth by removing all physical barriers to trade as part of the Commission's overall strategy of making European industry more competitive in world markets.

According to Cecchini's report, the cost of these frontier controls is intolerably high, from both the perspective of the companies who have to go through them and the governments who have to administer them. The report estimates that some 25% of company profits are taken up by frontier control-related costs and delays, the equivalent of 2% of the value of each trans-frontier consignment of goods, which works out at roughly £6 billion every year. Frontier controls were identified by business executives as the single greatest obstacle to the expansion of intra-Community trade and a crippling burden on the smaller companies. Moreover, they cost Community governments an estimated £670 million a year in taxpayers' money to administer. The report also estimated that their removal could be worth around £10.5 billion in new trading opportunities, the equivalent of about 3% of the present value of intra-Community trade.

The Commission clearly shares the concerns of member states regarding the growth of terrorism, drug trafficking and major crime, and the role played by internal frontier controls in attempting to control these problems. However, the White Paper insists that:

> Frontier controls are by no means the only or most effective measures in this regard. If the objective of abolishing all internal frontier controls is to be met, alternative means of protection will need to be found or, where they exist, strengthened.

It accepts that many of the proposed changes will present difficulties for member states, and time will be needed for the necessary adjustments to be made. But it is quite adamant that such difficulties 'should not be allowed permanently to frustrate the achievement of the greater progress . . .'.

The White Paper then goes on to list all the internal areas in which common policies need to be developed, such as indirect taxation, plant and veterinary controls, the movement of individuals and the collection of trade statistics. Focusing on the movement of individuals, it points out that most of the Commission's initiatives (notably the introduction of the European passport) 'have been aimed at making checks at internal frontiers more flexible as they cannot be abolished altogether until, in line with the concerns expressed by the European Council, adequate safeguards are introduced against terrorism and drugs'. Meanwhile, the Commission envisages the gradual introduction of separate channels for Community citizens at sea- and airports, just as we already have for British nationals re-entering Britain at Gatwick or Heathrow, and the abolition of systematic controls over departures to other member states. Metal detectors at airports would remain in place, and member states would retain the right to re-introduce systematic frontier controls in the event of an emergency.

Crime and detection across frontiers

Turning to the external areas in which common policies need to be developed, the White Paper outlines a programme for the approximation of national legislation governing public security, illegal immigration, the possession of firearms, and visa and extradition policy, all of which will be enforced at the Community's external border. By 1992 the Commission hopes to arrive at the situation in which individuals can travel freely from one member state to another without having to undergo systematic checks on entry.

What lies behind the Commission's proposals, in addition to the attempt to reduce the costs borne by companies involved in intra-Community trade and the irritations endured by Community citizens travelling from one member state to another, is a recognition that terrorism, gun running, drug trafficking and major crime have long ceased to be national problems. As challenges to the fabric of both political and civil society everywhere in the Community, logic and reason would suggest that they are best dealt with on a Community-wide basis.

Furthermore, there is only a limited benefit to be obtained from effective frontier controls around Britain if British armed forces personnel on the Continent remain vulnerable to terrorist attacks. The continued fragmentation of member state policies in these areas works to the advantage of the terrorist, the drug trafficker and the major criminal. What the Community needs is a strict external frontier to act as the first line of defence against these organizations and individuals in the first place, backed up internally by increased co-operation between national law-enforcement and intelligence organizations. Such co-operation is already responsible for the great majority of terrorist apprehensions and confiscations of drug consignments, long before they get to internal frontier controls.

Addressing a London audience in November 1986, Lord Cockfield emphasized this point:

The way to deal with these problems is not simply to retreat behind national frontiers, to man the barricades against our fellow European citizens . . . There is no *a priori* reason to suppose that reinforcing the internal frontiers of the Community as we know them today is likely to prove the most effective way of dealing with these problems. And in so far as—inevitably—it obstructs the objective of creating a Europe without frontiers, it carries a heavy cost to trade, to industry, and ultimately to all our citizens . . . There are no customs officers on Hadrian's Wall, or immigration officials manning Offa's Dyke. That is what our ambition is to create.

Police and intelligence co-operation: the Trevi Group

The attempt to improve co-ordination between national police forces pre-dates the White Paper by a decade. Although the Treaty of Rome does not provide for measures designed to combat terrorism, drug trafficking and major crime, the Council of Ministers, meeting in Trevi, Italy, in December 1975, recognized the growing necessity of improving co-operation between the interior and justice departments of member states. Ministers agreed to set up three groups to deal with terrorism, drug trafficking and crime, which were supplemented with a fourth in October 1986 dealing with illegal immigration. Strictly speaking, the initiative, known as the Trevi Group or Trevi Process, exists quite independently of Community institutions, although for convenience it is often referred to as if it were a normal function of the Council of Ministers.

Despite a promising start, Interior and Justice Ministers did not meet again for almost ten years. However, as soon as Middle East conflicts began to spill over into the streets of European capitals the Community was forced to react. Since 1986, Interior and Justice Ministers, senior police and intelligence officers, and forensic scientists have been meeting in secret with increasing frequency to exchange information and ideas on how to stem the rising tide of international crime. These exchanges have been instrumental in breaking down traditional professional and national rivalries and laying the basis of trust and mutual respect, without which any attempt to increase cross-frontier co-operation would simply founder. At the same time, increasing concern is being expressed by civil liberties organizations about the activities of the Trevi Group, which are not subject to traditional parliamentary controls.

Following a series of bombing outrages in Paris in 1986 by the so-called Solidarity Committee for Arab Prisoners, who were attempting to intimi-date the French authorities into releasing three Arab terrorists, an emer-gency Trevi Group meeting was held in London at the request of Paris in September 1986, with Douglas Hurd, then Home Secretary, acting as President of the Council of Ministers. The meeting produced an agree-ment to improve the flow of intelligence and information, develop a co-ordinated response between member states, identify and close the loopholes through which terrorists gain entry into the Community and tackle the political problems which create terrorist violence in the first place.

At the end of the meeting Hurd described terrorists as being increasingly members of organizations which operate across national frontiers, who have access to substantial sums of money, arms, equipment, technical knowledge and training, which was forcing governments and their counter-terrorist agencies to organize themselves on a Community-wide basis. 'These new measures will help us to target terrorists' movements, supplies of money, arms and equipment, so that we can harry and disrupt them,' and would be followed up with further practical measures, the minister said.

In October 1986 Community Interior and Justice Ministers met to discuss the security implications of the Commission's proposals to abolish internal frontiers by 1992, in which the Commission was represented by Lord Cockfield. They agreed to launch a concerted assault against terrorists, drug traffickers, criminals and, for the first time, illegal immigrants, while simultaneously pledging themselves to the goal of free movement around the Community for all law-abiding citizens. The ministers agreed to consider the possibility of harmonizing member state visa and right of asylum policies, increase co-operation against the abuse of passports and exchange information gathered at spot checks on internal frontiers. Hurd publicly stated that the objectives of allowing free movement of Community nationals, while restricting criminals, were not irreconcilable. However, he then went on to insist that Britain would continue to conduct a full examination of every passport, reflecting Britain's actual but as yet unstated conviction that they were indeed irreconcilable.

Aspirations for closer and more effective action between member states appeared to receive a setback towards the end of the month, when Sir Geoffrey Howe, the then Foreign Secretary, demanded a united Community response against Syria, following evidence indicating Syrian complicity in the attempted bombing in April of an El Al airliner at Heathrow by Nezar Hindawi. The request was initially greeted with a mixture of caution, scepticism and outright hostility. After much agonizing, the Community, with the exception of Greece, agreed to a ban on all new arms sales and high-level visits to Syria, a review of Syrian embassy and consular staffs, and tighter security for the national carrier, Syrianair. Although Sir Geoffrey put a brave face on the agreement, he had clearly wanted much tougher action—much earlier.

The subject was also high on the agenda at the EC summit meeting in London that December. The meeting produced a communiqué committing member states to three principles: no concessions to terrorists or their sponsors, solidarity in preventing terrorism and bringing the perpetrators to justice and (in a veiled reference to the delay in reacting to the Hindawi affair) a concerted response to terrorist attacks. It was also revealed that the Trevi Group had produced a secret document listing those countries and organizations responsible for recent terrorist outrages and who continued to pose a serious threat to public security in the Community. Again, however, Greece refused to sign—a position that was modified substantially after the terrorist attack on the *City of Poros* cruiser in July 1988, which resulted in the death of 11 passengers.

Although the member states were moving in the direction of increased co-operation the increase in kidnappings in Beirut had placed an enormous strain on the Community's declared commitment to adopt a united front in the face of terrorist threats. During 1987, France and Germany, both of whom held known terrorists believed to be responsible for a variety of hijackings and assassinations, were under pressure to release them in exchange for their own nationals held hostage in Beirut. Throughout 1987–8 there were repeated reports that the United States, Germany and France had made significant diplomatic and financial concessions to secure the release of their hostages from Lebanon. Nonetheless, despite the temptation to waver from the principles outlined in the December communiqué it was becoming clearer that the only effective response to terrorism, whether internal or external, was a collective one.

At a meeting of Community Justice Ministers in Brussels in July 1987 member states took another step forward by agreeing to streamline extradition procedures, allowing nationals sentenced in one member state to opt to serve their sentence in their state of origin, and laying down that an individual could not be prosecuted more than once for the same offence anywhere in the Community. During the summit meeting between the leading industrialized countries in Venice in June 1987 an agreement to prohibit flights from any country failing to prosecute or extradite terrorists involved in offences involving aircraft was signed, adding considerably to the sanctions available against state-sponsored terrorism. During the EC summit meeting in Hannover in June 1988 Chancellor Helmut Kohl of Germany even went so far as to suggest the creation of a European police agency modelled on the American Federal Bureau of Investigation. The idea was not warmly received, but while it may still be premature to think along these lines it is likely to attract more serious consideration in the years ahead.

Indeed, at a meeting of EC justice and interior ministers in Dublin in June 1990 the Twelve agreed to set up a European Central Drugs Intelligence Unit (ECDIU), with the specific tasks of co-ordinating information and establishing a special training unit for drug-enforcement officers. If successful, the ECDIU could prove to be the model for further experiments in cross-border co-operation, which could conceivably develop into the European FBI or Europol suggested by Herr Kohl.

The next major breakthrough was made following a series of IRA attacks on British armed forces personnel in Germany and the Netherlands in 1988. Community Interior Ministers meeting in Munich in July 1988 agreed to further increases in exchanges of information and forensic evidence, a study on the security implications of 1992 and, perhaps most important of all, to launch an examination into possible Community-wide legislation to examine the bank accounts of terrorist organizations and seize their financial assets.

During its periodic review of the Prevention of Terrorism Act Britain had decided to introduce a new provision granting the government the power to inspect bank accounts (and confiscate their contents) where there was a suspicion that the money could be used to finance terrorist activities. However, Hurd was fully aware that there was little point in Britain acting in isolation. The legislation would be useless if terrorist organizations could move their accounts around Community banks. It was clearly apparent (although no government minister has yet conceded the point) that Britain could no longer take refuge in its island status from terrorists, drug traffickers or criminals.

However, the days when criminals can hide their ill-gotten gains in Continental retreats such as the Costa Brava may now be numbered. The success of the 1986 Drug Trafficking Offences Act, and the 1988 Criminal Justice Act (both of which gave British courts powers to confiscate the proceeds from drug trafficking and other forms of major crime), has encouraged the Home Office to try to persuade its Community partners to adopt similar laws.

Admittedly, France and Germany retain grave reservations over such a development, but progress has been particularly promising with Spain. Although still a long way off, the Home Office's ultimate objective is to facilitate the introduction of a fully harmonized system of judicial seizure for the proceeds of major crime—effectively preventing criminals from laundering money through Continental banks, and enabling the Community to establish a policy of 'no hiding place' for criminal fortunes. In December 1990, Leon Brittan, the Competition Commissioner, took the first step in this direction with the announcement that EC finance ministers had agreed to introduce a anti-laundering directive designed to reduce profits from drug trafficking and criminal activities. The measure, which came into effect in June 1991, will require anyone from January 1993 depositing more than £10,500 in a bank to identify themselves and the source of the money, thereby enabling the authorities to track the ebb and flow of proceeds from the international drugs trade.

In his recent book, *Terrorism, Drugs and Crime in Europe after 1992*, Richard Clutterbuck, a seasoned observer of European security issues, suggests that the dangers presented by the abolition of Europe's internal frontiers could be negated by using information technology to hamper the activities of terrorists, drug traffickers and major criminals. Such technologies, which include techniques to prevent impersonation by the digital recording of fingerprints, voice and vein patterns, linking Europe's national police computers and detecting explosives by vapour sniffing and neutron bombardment, are now all readily available. The difficulty facing Europe after 1992, he warns, will be how to protect lives and property, without unwarranted erosions of civil liberties.

The case against the abolition of frontiers

Nevertheless, the fact that terrorists such as Germany's Red Army Faction, or RAF (heirs to the notorious Baader–Meinhof Gang), the IRA and the Italian Red Brigades remain active gives cause for concern. The terrorists, too, are preparing for 1992, as was shown by the attempted murder in September 1988 of Hans Tietmeyer, a senior Bonn official, by the RAF with the active help of the Red Brigades, as part of a co-ordinated terrorist effort to disrupt an IMF ministerial meeting in Berlin. Similarly, the murder of Herr Alfred Herrhausen, the chief executive of Deutsche Bank, who was blown up in his bullet-proof Mercedes in November 1989, was yet another reminder that the RAF was still active. Partly because of such incidents, Britain's police forces, backed up by many of their Continental colleagues, have grave reservations about the proposed abolition of frontier controls.

During the annual meeting of the International Union of Police Federations (IUPF) in August 1988, which represents over 500,000 officers, a resolution was passed against abolishing frontier controls by a majority of one. However, most of Europe's police forces appeared to think that abolition was inevitable. But what irritated them more than anything was the failure of EC governments to consult them over the implications of abolition. This is a shortcoming which member states ought to rectify as soon as possible. Peter Tanner, the Secretary of the British Police Federation and President of the IUPF, also warned that if internal borders were to be abolished there would need to be rapid progress on establishing common procedures for extradition, criminal justice and the right of hot pursuit across borders, all of which the Commission hopes to have in place before the 1992 deadline expires.

The surprise announcement in November 1988 by the Belgian Cabinet to overturn the recommendation by the Belgian judiciary to extradite Patrick Ryan, the former Roman Catholic priest wanted by Scotland Yard in connection with four offences of conspiracy to commit murder and illegal possession of explosives, caused exasperation in Downing Street and overshadowed the forthcoming EC summit meeting in Rhodes. The rejection of the extradition request, originally made on 9 September, almost three months after Ryan had been detained by the Belgian authorities for entering the country with a false passport, was prompted by the Government's fear of possible IRA retaliation if Ryan, then on hunger strike in St Gilles prison in Brussels, died on Belgian soil. This was the first time that Belgium had denied an extradition request from a NATO partner for over 20 years, and it took the issue of increased co-operation against terrorism to the top of the Community's agenda.

During an otherwise low-key summit meeting at Rhodes in

December, Mrs Thatcher had some frank exchanges with her Belgian and Irish counterparts over the Ryan affair. However, the controversy at least resulted in a new initiative to tackle the problems of controlling terrorists, drug traffickers and criminals, in an internal market without frontiers. The twelve heads of government agreed to appoint a special official to take charge of intergovernmental negotiations on controlling terrorism, drug trafficking and illegal immigration, in advance of a Trevi Group meeting in December in Athens on the problems presented by international crime and the abolition of internal frontiers. Similarly, the decision by a Dutch court to acquit four suspected IRA terrorists of the murders of two Australian tourists in Roermond in 1990 provoked outrage from the Home Secretary, Kenneth Baker, who protested strongly about the decision during the Trevi Group meeting in the autumn of 1991.

Although the Commission is engaged in an attempt to wipe out a whole range of plant and animal diseases across Europe, British public opinion has tended to focus on the danger of rabies. These anxieties are not difficult to understand. *La rage* is a killer, and Britain has been free of the disease for over 60 years. However, there is much truth in the observation that Britain's island status, far from easing popular anxieties over the spread of rabies, has actually heightened them. In reality, the threat posed by rabies is marginal. In over 40 years of quarantine controls Britain has never found one animal with rabies. According to statistics collected by the International Organization of Epizootics, there were 19,000 cases of rabies recorded in the whole of continental Europe for 1985. Of this total, 14,000 were foxes, 3,000 were other wild animals and 200 were domestic animals. There was one recorded case of rabies among the human population—and that was in Finland.

Rabies is overwhelmingly confined to wild animals, most of which are foxes. Even so, the Commission is taking no chances. Officials have been monitoring closely a series of field tests with an oral vaccine for wild animals. If the tests prove successful the Commission is expected to launch a Community-wide rabies-eradication programme, which holds out the promise of eliminating the disease completely. Moreover, the Home Office has made it clear that Britain will retain its quarantine controls at sea- and airports. The Home Office has also been closely involved with the Eurotunnel contractors on devising ways to prevent animals from crawling along the floor of the tunnel. In short, Britain's defences against rabies will be as effective as ever. Equally as important, Europe's defences against rabies will be strengthened by the internal market programme.

Partly because there is still some time to elapse before the Community's external frontier is in place, Britain has shown a deep ambivalence towards the Commission's proposal to abolish all internal frontier controls by 1992, and is clearly leaning in the direction of keeping them intact. Reflecting on the Commission's proposals in October 1986, the Home Secretary said:

> A lot depends on the way we can strengthen our external frontiers. The more effective we are in keeping drugs, terrorists and major criminals out of the Community in the first place, the easier it will be to relax our internal controls.

Even so, the minister warned that 'it was not around the corner'.

Now 1992 is just around the corner, and the British position has hardened considerably. At the June 1988 meeting of the Trevi Group in Munich Hurd insisted that:

> Frontier controls do provide an effective means of dealing with these problems. They are not 100 per cent effective but they are more effective than internal arrangements.

Hurd seemed to be suggesting that Britain had its own ideas about European integration—a sort of internal market *avec frontières*. Addressing the annual conference of the Association of Chief Police Officers in Eastbourne a month before, the minister declared: 'We owe it to ourselves, and to our fellow citizens, to continue to do all we can to see that the terrorist, the drug trafficker or criminal, is not the unintended beneficiary of changes designed for the development of the Community, and the benefit of law-abiding Community citizens'. As a result of such anxieties, particularly after Britain's anger over the refusal of Belgium to extradite a suspected IRA terrorist, the Trevi Group, meeting in Athens in December 1988, agreed to examine the possibility of introducing a common extradition policy.

Controlling crime in the single market

These statements raise two fundamental questions about the proposed abolition of internal frontier controls. First, are these so-called internal arrangements—increased police co-operation, the creation of common policies on extradition, confiscation of terrorists' assets, immigration and the right of hot pursuit across national borders—more effective than internal frontier controls? British ministers think not, but at the same time acknowledge that without parallel legislation in other member states Britain's attempt to control terrorism and drug trafficking will be to little avail.

Moreover, while there are isolated examples of the efficacy of internal frontier controls, such as the chance apprehension of two IRA gunmen by a West German border guard in September 1988, the great majority of terrorists, drug traffickers and criminals are merely arrested at frontier control points, having been identified as a result of co-operation between

Community intelligence agencies long before. Furthermore, the most difficult internal frontier to monitor in the entire Community is the border between Ulster and the Irish Republic—which has no frontier controls.

Second, a major fear is that if Britain decides to keep its internal frontier controls there will be no changes benefiting law-abiding Community citizens. Movement in and out of Britain will remain more or less as time consuming and costly as it is at present. The Commission insists that one either has internal frontier controls or one does not—there is no half-way house—and it is disingenuous to suggest that we can have both.

At the kernel of the dispute over the abolition of frontier controls lies one of the many historic differences between Britain and its European neighbours. Continental Europeans have tended to rely more on individual identity cards than frontier controls for the apprehension of criminals—an idea which has never been particularly popular in Britain. However, at an address given at the Crime in Europe Conference in York in September·1988 David Faulkner, a deputy Under-Secretary of State at the Home Office, suggested that Britain might be forced to re-evaluate its traditional hostility to the introduction of a national identity card as a result of growing pressures for greater freedom of movement around the Community. At the Rhodes summit in December 1988 Mrs Thatcher raised the idea of EC identity cards without either endorsing or rejecting it.

This, coupled with intensive police and intelligence co-operation under Trevi arrangements and common EC policies on immigration and extradition, may point the way forward and allow the Single European Act's commitment to 'an area without internal frontiers' to be fulfilled. The alternative—the retention of national controls by Britain in isolation from the other Eleven—could lead to action against Britain in the European Court after 1992, which was not what the framers of the Act had in mind and is not what other members of the EC wish to see happen.

However, Britain is confident that the Single European Act does allow member states to retain internal frontiers. It has also challenged Lord Cockfield's claim that the great majority of drug seizures are made as a result of increased co-operation between national police forces.

A report released in Brussels in March 1989, based on statistics collected by the Home Office, showed that 36% of the volume of drugs seized in 1986 came from or via another EC country. That figure rose to 41% in 1987, and provisional data for 1988 shows an increase to 44%. While acknowledging that 'investigators depend on frontier staff to intercept intelligence targets', it nonetheless insisted that 'seizures made "cold" or according to "profiles" of likely smuggling types, depend on officers being at the frontier to observe, select, question and examine'.

Erecting the external frontier

EC interior ministers had begun work on erecting Europe's new external frontier long before September 1989, when the first images of thousands of Trabants spluttering from East to West Germany via Hungary and Austria flashed across television screens around the world. The exodus from the East did, however, have the effect of focusing the attention of governments on the urgency of tackling the problems presented by potentially large movements of people—the scale of which has not been seen since the nineteenth-century migrations from Europe to America—and efforts to complete the task before the 1992 deadline began in earnest. Simultaneously, human rights and refugee groups began to air misgivings about the new frontier controls, fearing that the Community was being panicked into taking excessively restrictive measures which would remove an essential avenue of escape for asylum seekers.

Under the 1951 refugee convention, a refugee is defined as someone who does not want to return to their country of origin because 'of a well-founded fear of being persecuted for reasons of race, religion, nationality, membership of a particular social group or political opinion'. The convention was drawn up at the height of the Cold War, when strict Communist border controls kept the flow of refugees from the Soviet Union and the East European satellites to a trickle, and when the lucky few who were able to cross the Iron Curtain were welcomed with open arms. Because these political refugees were so few in number, the Western tradition of granting asylum was never put under strain.

The migrations to Europe from Africa and Asia which occurred during the 1950s and 1960s were quite different. Although many of the new immigrants were fleeing political persecution, most came in search of a better life, often at the invitation of the host governments. But because of the large numbers of people involved, West European governments began to tighten their immigration controls during the mid-1970s, signalling the end of large-scale immigration to Western Europe. As the scope for immigration declined, the number of applications for asylum began to increase. By the mid-1980s, Community countries saw themselves confronted by the difficult and sensitive task of distinguishing between political refugees and economic migrants.

After years of simmering on the back burner, the issue was propelled to the top of the political agenda during the Luxembourg summit in June 1991, when John Major issued a call for urgent action to control what he described as the rising tide of economic migrants seeking a better life in the EC. 'We must not remain open to all comers, simply because Paris, Rome and London seem more attractive than Bombay and Algiers,' he said. Moreover, 'If we fail in our control efforts, we risk fuelling the far right, something we saw in the UK in the mid-1970s, and have since kept in check,' he added.

The Prime Minister's speech was not well received by Britain's immigrant community. In a front page article in the *Caribbean Times*, headlined 'Fortress Europe: Major Plans Iron Curtain II'', the Prime Minister was accused of making 'an extraordinary and highly offensive attack on the presence and contribution of visible minority people in Britain and throughout the European Community'. In fact, the attack was more imagined than real, but the incident served to highlight the difficulty the Community faces in erecting the external frontier without alienating existing immigrant communities.

As the negotiations on the external frontier went into a higher gear, a number of EC countries decided to embark on unilateral action. In July, after a series of suburban riots involving Arab minorities, Edith Cresson, the French Prime Minister, announced new controls on illegal immigration, and predicted that up to one million people could be deported. Following an increase in migrations from Yugoslavia, Romania, Turkey, Iran, Afghanistan, Poland and North Africa, Bonn also announced a tightening up of immigration laws. In addition, throughout the summer of 1991, television viewers witnessed the tragic spectacle of the thousands of destitute Albanian boat people arriving in Italian ports, most of whom were promptly sent back to their homeland.

With Britain receiving 1,000 applications for asylum each week, ten times more than in 1988, Kenneth Baker, the Home Secretary, announced a package of measures designed to reduce the number of people seeking asylum in the UK. The package included the withdrawal of legal aid for immigration and asylum cases, a doubling of the £1,000 fine imposed on airline and shipping companies under the Carriers Liability Act for allowing passengers to enter Britain without the proper documents, and the withdrawal of oral hearings in asylum and immigration cases the government regards as unfounded.

The announcement provoked an angry response from Britain's refugee and immigration organizations. The Asylum Rights Campaign, a steering group made up of a wide range of bodies, including Amnesty International, the Immigration Law Practitioners' Association, and the Refugee Council, denounced the measures for denying 'the victims of persecution and injustice the possibility of seeking and obtaining asylum'. On 3 July an editorial in *The Times* went further, insisting:

> Asylum is an honourable British tradition not to be abandoned even under the present pressure. Mr Baker should prefer the risk of admitting an 'economic refugee' by mistake to that of sending back to persecution, torture or death a single real refugee entitled to asylum.

In a letter to *The Times* in October, Louis Blom-Cooper, QC, the former chairman of the Press Council, described the Baker reforms as 'deeply worrying', and accused the government of 'not fully implementing the [1951] convention'. Responding to the allegation, Peter Lloyd, the immigration minister, insisted that: 'The threat to the institution of asylum does not come from the government but from the growing number of people who abuse it by making specious asylum applications in order to circumvent the normal immigration controls'.

Nonetheless, Baker's measures were seen by critics as a particularly blunt instrument for distinguishing between political refugees and economic migrants. The withdrawal of legal aid cut off access to Britain for the less affluent in both groups. In addition, the reliance on the Carriers Liability Act, which has resulted in fines exceeding £30 million since it came into effect in 1987, ignored the difficulties faced by genuine applicants attempting to obtain authentic travel documents from the very authorities responsible for persecuting them, and effectively made the airline and shipping companies the reluctant front-line arbiters of Britain's asylum and immigration law. Observers also predicted that the Community's new external frontier would incorporate many of the elements of the Baker package.

The need to erect an external frontier stems from the Internal Market White Paper's objective of abolishing internal frontiers. If Community citizens are to be able to travel freely within the EC, then member states' conflicting rules and regulations on the rights of asylum and entry have to be harmonized so that non-EC nationals are subject to the same set of checks. Hitherto, negotiations have focused on two new instruments, a convention on asylum and a convention on crossing external frontiers or a common visa policy. The convention on asylum, also known as the Dublin Convention, grants applicants the right to seek asylum in one member state only. In an effort to prevent what is known as 'refugees in orbit', rejection by one country means rejection by all. What remains to be agreed, however, are the common criteria by which applicants can be granted asylum status.

After assuming the Community presidency in July 1991 the Netherlands made the harmonization of asylum and visa regulations a priority. However, given the secret nature of these negotiations, few details about their content have been released. With predictions of a possible exodus from Eastern Europe of between two and four million migrants, combined with further large-scale migrations from Africa and Asia, refugee organizations fear that the Community is being stampeded into a panic reaction. Their greatest concern is that ministers will adopt policies similar to those in Britain. But predictions that EC governments will undermine the 1951 convention seem somewhat alarmist. Moreover, there are indications that the Commission is moving towards the recognition that the only effective way to restrain migratory pressures is to provide incentives for potential immigrants to remain in their country of origin by accepting more of their exports and providing increased Community aid and development funds.

In the run-up to the EC summit in Maastricht, Britain was in support of proposals to harmonize Community visa, asylum, and immigration procedures as part of the wider attempt to create the conditions that will allow free movement of people from 1993. But it remained adamant that the harmonization of conditions of entry should remain the responsibility of national governments working together through the Trevi Group of justice and interior ministers, rather than being transferred to Brussels. In the event, the Maastricht treaty acknowledged that immigration policy should remain the preserve of inter-governmental co-operation. The Commission was, however, given the power to define a common visa policy, which must be approved by Council on the basis of unanimity, unless faced by an emergency (such as a sudden influx from a particular country), in which case visa policy could be decided by majority voting. While the Maastricht compromise removed the delicate issue of immigration from the EC agenda, few observers expect it to remain that way for long. Elections in Austria, Switzerland, Belgium, France, Germany, and Italy have seen fresh gains for many of Europe's expanding right wing parties, much of which has been attributed to increased hostility towards immigrants, high unemployment, poor housing, and alienation from established political institutions. The Maastricht treaty could even exacerbate the difficulty by providing ammunition for right wing radicals to exploit growing fears about the effects of opening borders and pooling national sovereignty, particularly in France and Germany.

Checklist of changes

- The European Commission hopes to oversee the complete abolition of all internal frontier controls (the so-called physical barriers to trade) by the end of 1992.
- The abolition of internal frontiers will result in significant cost reductions for companies involved in cross-frontier trade, and will also make travel and tourism for the ordinary citizen considerably easier.
- The manpower and resources freed from internal frontier controls can then be redirected towards defending the Community from terrorists, drug traffickers and other criminals at the Community's external frontiers.
- The approximation of member states' fiscal taxation arrangements will eliminate the need to collect value added tax at internal frontiers.

- There will be increased co-operation between national police and intelligence forces in the fight against terrorists and criminals.
- Common Community initiatives on immigration, visa, extradition and right of asylum policies, the possession of firearms, confiscation of terrorists' and criminal assets, and the right of hot pursuit across national borders may also be introduced.
- Common programmes for the elimination of animal and plant diseases, possibly including rabies, will also be implemented.

6 PUBLIC WORKS AND PRIVATE TENDERS

Public purchasing across frontiers

As the barriers to free trade within the Community started to fall towards the end of the 1980s it became evident that many small, medium and even large businesses felt inundated by the directives designed to open up the European market for public contracts supplying equipment and services to local government, nationalized companies and other state organizations. Those companies that were quick to grasp the significance of the Commission's initiative rapidly assembled internal market management teams, fostered closer relations with Commission officials and started to test the uncharted waters of the new era of competition. Many more, however, appeared content to let things drift. In May 1991, Sir John Cuckney, the chairman of Investors in Industry, the venture capital group, warned that an alarming number of small and medium-sized British enterprises were in danger of losing out to their Continental rivals as the public procurement market started to open up. Observers attributed much of Britain's commercial complacency to a deep-rooted scepticism towards 'things Continental', and an equally embedded inertia towards change.

Although the principle of free trade is the cornerstone of the Treaty of Rome, the past 30 years have demonstrated that public procurement is the last area in which anyone would ever find it in operation. According to the provisions of Articles 30–36, member states are obliged to remove all quantitative restrictions (or any other measures having an equivalent effect) that obstruct the free movement of goods within the Community. Similarly, Articles 59–66 make it incumbent on member states to remove all obstacles in the way of the free flow of services across national frontiers. However, like so many other commitments entered into by national governments, these particular provisions were signed with the best intentions and promptly filed away.

The public purchasing programmes of central and local government (which includes their agencies and enterprises) have persistently reflected the defensive and parochial outlook displayed by the once-famous group of secretaries from Croydon who launched the 'I'm backing Britain' campaign in the 1960s. Both were motivated by the intensely patriotic (if somewhat economically misguided) conviction that buying national was the answer to Britain's economic difficulties.

During the past 30 years the growth of cross-border trade in goods and services in the private sector has been impressive. By comparison, the volume of such trade in the public sector has been comparatively static. There is a marked contrast between the demand by national governments for the private sector to adjust to the laws of supply and demand, on the one hand, and the way in which the public sector has been allowed to seek refuge behind national barriers, on the other. This raises charges of double standards.

The national bias of public purchasing bodies in favour of domestic manufacturers and suppliers covers three broad categories of goods and services:

1   All basic supply goods, ranging from office equipment to
   commercial vehicles and school and hospital supplies;
2   Public works such as roads, buildings, bridges and other civil
   engineering projects;
3   The so-called 'big-ticket items', which include sophisticated
   telecommunications and scientific facilities and
   power-generating and defence equipment.

The justifications used by member states to support biased national public procurement policies have depended on social considerations, economic necessity and outright national pride. At its most basic, governments have argued that domestic political exigencies have forced them to place public procurement contracts locally in order to reduce unemployment in declining industries or to support emerging industries in the early stages of development. More compelling, perhaps, has been the insistence that major industries such as telecommunications, aerospace and defence (which have massive research and development costs and where governments are frequently the only significant purchaser) would face collapse without government help. The implications of such a collapse, it is claimed, go far beyond considerations of social policy and regional development and into the realm of national security. All too often, however, economic necessity, social policy and strategic considerations have contained more than a hint of national pride. Governments have repeatedly asked themselves how an advanced industrialized country can be worthy of the name if it cannot support its own steel, car or defence industries.

However, it has become increasingly evident that the inescapable problem with a world view that stops at national boundaries will lead to long-term economic annihilation. Public procurement programmes that discriminate in favour of national champions reinforce the market fragmentation of the European economy, and cost the member states billions of pounds a year in unnecessary premiums to local firms. Market fragmentation denies companies the economies of scale they need to survive without government help, and leaves them vulnerable to competition from their larger external rivals. In the short term, discrimination in favour of local producers and suppliers may be a palliative for economically declining regions and companies unable or unwilling to survive without government assistance. However, in the long term it cannot generate the kind of competitive environment that companies need to survive in the increasingly competitive international economy.

The cost of national public procurement policies

According to the survey on the costs of European market fragmentation conducted on behalf of the European Commission by Cecchini in 1987, the value of all public purchasing contracts in 1986 was in excess of £355 billion, or £20 billion more than the value of all intra-Community trade during the same year. The sum of £355 billion is equivalent to 15% of the combined gross domestic product of all twelve member states, and therefore constitutes one of the most important single categories of European economic activity.

The Cecchini survey acknowledged that a sizeable portion of this sum was allocated to the purchase of goods and services that were inherently non-competitive, non-tradable or required in such small volumes that few manufacturers or suppliers outside the country in question would be prepared to compete against their domestic rivals. However, the survey insisted that, even making allowances for this factor, the estimated value of member states' annual public purchasing contracts were in the region of £230 billion. Of this total, less than 2% went to bidders outside national boundaries, which was costing the Community an estimated additional £14.5 billion a year. The assumptions and projections lying behind these figures have been the subject of a bitter dispute. The authors of the Cecchini study, in their enthusiasm to demonstrate the costs of discriminatory public purchasing policies, have been accused of considerably overstating their case.

It would be foolhardy, however, to accept the claim advanced by member states that the cost of national bias in public procurement programmes is negligible. No government likes to be accused, especially by bureaucrats in Brussels, of squandering public money. However, according to a report on the internal market published by Britain's independent Royal Institute of International Affairs in 1987, the costs of national discrimination in public purchasing was estimated at about £14 billion a year, thereby vindicating the Commission's estimates. It is therefore evident that national governments pay far more than they should for their purchases of works, goods and services, and in so doing finance inefficient and uncompetitive producers. An examination of some of the key sectors of the European economy would illustrate this point.

The European telecommunications market has become the classic example of the absurdity of protecting national markets from external competition by favouring national producers through biased public purchasing programmes. The Community market for telephone exchange systems is worth about £5 billion a year. However, the market is divided between eleven national producers, who are now installing no less than seven different exchange systems, five of which have been developed by European companies, most of whom are state owned.

If public procurement was opened to cross-border competition telephone exchange manufacturers would have a major incentive to link up, rationalize the number of exchange systems on offer and thereby reduce development costs, which would, in turn, be reflected in cheaper prices. In anticipation of 1992, a number of telecommunications companies have already begun to restructure their operations. The acquisition of AT&T's European interests by the French telecommunications company Alcatel, the purchase of the French company CGCT by the Swedish giant Ericsson and the link-up between the telecommunications divisions of GEC and Plessey represent the first wave of mergers in the European telecommunications industry.

Such distortions are also evident in other industrial sectors. The European locomotive industry, for example, is valued at about £70 million a year. There are no less than 16 locomotive manufacturers (compared to two in the United States) competing in an industry that has a 50% overcapacity and is characterized by little intra-EC trade. Boilermaking presents a similar picture. The market is worth an estimated £1.5 billion a year. There are 12 EC manufacturers (compared to six in the United States), and it is characterized by a phenomenal 80% overcapacity with negligible intra-EC trade. The same is true of turbine generator manufacturers. There are ten European manufacturers (compared to two in the United States) chasing orders in a European market that is valued at about £1.5 billion a year, and which has 40% overcapacity. Indeed, it would be difficult to identify a handful of industries that do not rely on the industrial equivalent of social security for their survival.

However, there is more to the cost of discriminatory public purchasing than simple market fragmentation. According to the European Commission, 'protectionist support, often portrayed as a shot in the arm for industry, is in fact a striking example of governments' shooting themselves, and their competitive ideals, in the foot'. Even more alarming is the report's prediction that 'unless restrictions on public purchasing are swept away, far from strategic industries being protected, whole areas of industry which have high multiplier effects on other sectors of manufacturing could cease to be viable'.

Opening up public procurement: round one

Because the member states had failed to honour the free-trade provisions of Articles 30–36 and 59–66 of the Treaty (and had shown no indications of ever doing so of their own volition) the need for additional legislation was abundantly evident. During the 1970s two directives were issued in an effort to remedy this situation, the 1971 Directive on Public Works and the 1977 Directive on Public Supplies.

The directives replaced divergent national procedures for issuing public procurement contracts with a Community-wide procedure governing all public works contracts over £670,000 and all public supply contracts over £134,000. Consequently, all public authorities responsible for awarding contracts falling above these thresholds were required to ensure that their invitations to tender were brought to the attention of companies and suppliers anywhere in the Community. This could be achieved comparatively easily by publication of tendering opportunities in the supplement to the *Official Journal of the European Communities*. The directives also made it illegal to split up tenders so that individually they fell beneath the two thresholds.

Under the new directives the contract-awarding bodies were explicitly prohibited from discriminating against non-national contractors or suppliers under the provisions of Articles 30–36. These articles prohibit all quotas on imports and exports between member states or any measure, whether by law, regulation or administrative practice, which has an equivalent effect. There are two exceptions to this requirement. First, member states are permitted to restrict trade on grounds of public morality, public policy, public health or public security. Second, they are permitted to restrict trade where the product in question fails to meet the member state's essential technical standards. However, any member state attempting to abuse these two let-out clauses could find itself before the European Court of Justice.

In an attempt to encourage public bodies to think in commercial rather than patriotic terms the two directives set out a series of objective criteria for evaluating competing tenders, and made it incumbent on the public bodies to award contracts to those companies who had submitted the lowest-priced or most economically advantageous offers. Where a contractor or supplier had evidence or suspected that it had been discriminated against by the awarding body it was empowered to register a complaint with the Director General for the Internal Market. The Commission could then conduct an investigation into the award procedure. If the investigation confirmed that discrimination had taken place, a formal letter could be sent to the member state asking it to answer the infringement allegation. If the member state failed to answer by the specified date, or if the answer was unsatisfactory, the case could be passed on to the European Court of Justice.

Although regarded as a major step forward in the cause of intra-Community free trade, the significance of the two new directives was soon demonstrated to be rather more apparent than real. In order to secure acceptance by the Council of Ministers the teeth of the original intention to open up public procurement to cross-border competition had been drawn out—one by one.

Under the terms of the two directives, a contract-awarding body had the choice of two basic types of tendering procedure which effectively enabled the authority to preserve its traditional national biases intact. The first is the open procedure, which requires offers to tender to be made available to all potential bidders. The second is the restricted procedure, in which only the contractor or supplier invited to tender may do so. Moreover, all construction and supply contracts awarded by the public authorities responsible for air, land and sea transport; the production and distribution of drinking water; the exploration, development and distribution of coal, oil, electricity and gas; and the development and maintenance of the telecommunications industry were excluded from the scope of the two directives. By the time they came into force, less than 20% of Community public procurement contracts were affected by them.

If this minimalist attempt to promote competition in public procurement became too onerous, the contract-awarding bodies were soon to demonstrate their ingenuity in finding new ways of evading the new works and supply directives in the limited areas in which they applied. Member states' failure to respect their commitments has varied from mild abuse of tendering procedures to outright violation and evasion. The two directives have still not been properly incorporated into national law in a number of member states, and failure to publish advance notification of contracts in the *Official Journal* has been widespread.

Most awarding authorities have insisted that contractors and suppliers adhere to national technical specifications, even in those areas where Community technical standards have been established. Tenders have been systematically divided up into separate contracts in order to fall below the thresholds at which publication in the *Official Journal* is mandatory. Use of the open tenders procedure has been kept to a minimum, while the conditions under which restricted procedures are permitted have been interpreted broadly. Some member states have not even bothered with such subtleties, preferring instead to ignore the conditions under which restricted procedures can be used while systematically eliminating tenders from other member states.

The Commission's powers of enforcement were no match for the ability of member states to ignore the two directives. It proved to be extremely difficult for construction or supply companies to produce evidence demonstrating that they had been discriminated against illegally. On the rare occasions such evidence was found, a company faced up to a two-year wait before the European Court of Justice could hear the case, by which time a construction project was invariably completed and a supply contract long consumed. There was, however, one lesson to come out of the public works and supply directives that was to prove invaluable in the future: how not to make the same mistake twice.

The White Paper and public procurement

Recognizing the political sensitivity surrounding the issue of national bias in public purchasing, the Internal Market White Paper announced the Commission's intention to establish the Advisory Committee on the Opening Up of Public Procurement. This was to be staffed by representatives from the Commission, the member states and the public bodies with responsibilities for awarding contracts. By examining the reasons why the public works and public supply directives had failed to prove effective, and by developing a closer understanding of the needs of the public purchasing bodies, the Advisory Committee set about drafting a strategy for the Commission's second assault on a practice it had denounced as 'economic incest'.

The White Paper gave an outline of the kinds of areas the Commission had identified as those in need of urgent attention. These included closing the loopholes in the existing public works and supply directives, tightening procedures for advance publication of tendering opportunities, providing construction and supply companies with effective means of redress where public purchasing procedures have been breached and, most sensitive of all, extending the contract-awarding procedures to the four excluded sectors.

In the eighteen months that followed the publication of the White Paper the atmosphere of foreboding concerning the prospects for opening up public procurement gradually gave way to cautious grounds for optimism. In three consecutive summit meetings (in The Hague in June 1986, London in December 1986 and Brussels in February 1987) an unprecedented consensus had emerged singling out progress on public procurement as one of the priority areas of the internal market programme.

Member states had finally taken the first tentative steps towards overcoming their traditional reluctance to submit their cherished public sectors to the laws of supply and demand. It was a long-overdue acknowledgement that, in the context of continued government retrenchment and persistent restraint on public spending, the contract-awarding bodies had to abandon their misguided patriotism and pay more attention to commercial considerations when awarding public purchasing contracts.

Opening up public procurement: round two

Reflecting the priorities laid out in the White Paper, and acting on the recommendations formulated by the Advisory Committee on Opening Up Public Procurement, the Commission first concentrated on the existing public works and supply directives. A new Public Supplies Directive was proposed in March 1988, amending the 1977 Public Supplies Directive, and became effective in January 1989.

The type of supply contracts covered by the new directive, ranging from office equipment to employees' clothing, was clearly defined, and the rules for calculating their value for the purposes of applying the £134,000 threshold at which it had to be published in the *Official Journal* (or *Tenders Electronic Daily*, the Community's online database) were made more explicit. The open tenders procedure was made the rule, and any attempt by a contract-awarding body to use the restricted tenders procedure had to be justified to the Commission. Procurement authorities are now also required to give advance notice of their annual purchasing requirements in an attempt to enable supply companies to prepare for potential contracts in advance. All public bodies, from the House of Lords down to the local High Street library, are now required to open all supply contracts over the designated threshold to cross-border competition.

A proposal to amend the 1971 Public Works Directive has proved somewhat more difficult to draft, but the broad outline of the Commission's intentions has already been made known. The existing £670,000 threshold at which all public works contracts have to be published in the *Official Journal* has been made obsolete by the rising costs of construction work over the past 15 years, and is to be replaced by a new £3.35 million threshold. Contracts for public works whose value exceeds the new higher ceiling will have to be advertised in the *Official Journal*. Both categories of contract will, however, remain subject to all other Community rules governing tendering procedures.

The Commission also intends to extend the scope of the existing directive on public works by introducing a wider definition of contract-awarding bodies subject to its provisions, including the non-governmental agencies financed from public funds. As in the case of public supply contracts, the availability of restricted procedures is to be sharply curtailed and the open procedure is to become the norm. In order to ensure that the contract-awarding bodies have adhered to the new tendering procedures they will be required to explain on request why they have decided to reject a particular bid and submit a report to the Commission on each award decision. In future, recognition of Community technical standards will be mandatory.

Following the emerging consensus on the need to ensure greater compliance with Community regulations governing public procurement, in July 1987 the Commission submitted to Council a draft directive on proposals to improve the means of redress available to companies who have been illegally discriminated against by public purchasing authorities. Because of the nature of public procurement (and the inordinate amount of time it takes the European Court of Justice to pass judgment on infractions of Community law) the Commission has focused its efforts on prevention rather than cure. Once a building has been completed it would be difficult, even for bureaucrats in Brussels, to demand that it be demolished because the awarding body had discriminated in favour of a national construction company.

The proposed prevention strategy contains three separate but interlocking elements. First, the Commission would be empowered to suspend for three months any contract award if the awarding authority failed to make adequate provision for cross-border competition. The awarding authority would then be required to make good its breach of Community tendering procedures by issuing a new call to tender complying with the provisions of the public purchasing directives. If an awarding body persisted in its error it would be incumbent on the government of the member states to compel the awarding body to respect Community law. Second, should this prove unsuccessful, the company would then be able to challenge national tendering procedures through the national courts without having to register a complaint with the Commission first. Violations of public purchasing directives are likely to be met with large fines. Finally, if all else fails, the Commission reserves the right to take the member state to the European Court of Justice under the provisions of Article 169 of the Treaty. The Commission has indicated that borderline cases will be overlooked, and that it will only act where there is evidence of a clear and blatant infringement of the rules. Council is expected to endorse the Commission's proposals for effective redress before the 1992 deadline is reached.

Acceptance of the proposed directive on compliance with Community tendering procedures has been described by the Commission as vital in order 'to increase the credibility of the Community's efforts to break down the psychological reluctance of traders, industrialists, and more particularly, small and medium-sized enterprises, to bid across frontiers for public works contracts'. In June 1988 the Commission unveiled its wide-ranging proposals to incorporate the four excluded sectors (telecommunications, energy, transport and water), which have so far remained immune from cross-border competition, into the Community's system for awarding construction and supply contracts, thereby fulfilling a priority commitment in its goal of completing the internal market by 1992.

Before making its proposals the Commission took into account the extensive analysis of the four excluded sectors conducted by the Advisory Committee on Opening Up Public Procurement. This examination demonstrated that biased patterns of public procurement could not simply be attributed to the public status of the organizations operating in the four sectors. Similar difficulties could be expected even if all four sectors were in private hands. Far more important was the actual structure of the sector itself, whether electricity, gas, coal or oil in the energy sector; the seaports, airports and rail networks and municipal mass transport systems in the transport sector; the purification and distribution functions of the water sector; and the development and supply of telecommunications equipment in the communications sector. The Advisory Committee found that all four sectors were inherently monopolistic, consequently insulated from competition and characterized by a highly developed propensity to 'buy national'.

The main reason for the excluded sectors being left out of the scope of the 1970s directives on public purchasing was that the pattern of ownership throughout the Community varied considerably from private to public or a mixture of the two, and the Commission faced great difficulty in trying to find some regulatory formula that adequately catered for the different forms of ownership. The new directive ignores this question, and focuses instead on the more important area of state influence. Any organization in the four excluded sectors (whether publicly or privately owned) that is subject to official or unofficial pressures to place public procurement contracts with local firms will be subject to the new directive. The intention is not to force these organizations to buy foreign, but to ensure that they are free to exercise their commercial judgement, independently of nationalistic public purchasing pressures.

Because the organizations operating in the excluded sectors are more sensitive to industrial and commercial considerations than the public and administrative bodies covered by the existing directives on public purchasing, the new directive provides a considerably more flexible tendering procedure. The organizations can choose between requesting tenders on a contract-by-contract basis or periodically calling for expressions of interest from would-be contractors or suppliers. They can also avail themselves of the option to maintain a pool of contractors and suppliers, on condition that the terms of entrance to the pool are made public and that foreign companies have the same rights of access as national companies. A new system (known as a negotiated procedure) has been introduced in which an awarding body can enter into talks with prospective contractors or suppliers, but only where the response from open or restricted procedures has been unsatisfactory, or where issues of national security or defence are at stake. As with previous directives, Community technical standards must be used wherever possible. The telecommunications sector was the subject of a separate directive in 1989, and electricity in 1990.

The excluded sectors directive will cover all supply contracts valued at £134,000 and above, which the Commission estimates is enough to buy 4.5 miles of fibre-optic cable, two buses or a small crane, and all works contracts valued at £3.3 million and above, enough to pay for 6.5 miles of standard or 1.5 miles of high-speed railway line or the dredging of a major port. Access to the Community's public purchasing market by organizations from outside the EC can be excluded where more than 50% of the value of the contract is provided by companies outside the twelve member states.

The directive opening up procurement in the excluded sectors to cross-border competition was finally agreed by Community industry ministers in February 1990. Although welcomed as a milestone in the creation of the single market, in so far as it discriminated in favour of Community suppliers the breakthrough was also denounced by foreign critics as protectionist. But the so-called 'Buy-Europe' clause in the directive, enabling purchasers to ignore non-Community bids up to 3% cheaper than Community tenders, was defended by trade officials on the grounds that it was temporary and would be removed if the GATT talks succeeded in abolishing such restrictions worldwide.

Completing the Commission's internal market programme in the field of public purchasing is a new directive covering the flourishing market for telecommunications, known as Open Network Provision. In December 1988, the Commission announced its intention to launch an ambitious and highly controversial plan to compel member states to open up their national telecommunications services industries to free competition throughout the Community by 1991.

The plan, which was implemented under the competition provisions of Article 90 of the Treaty of Rome, makes it incumbent on member states to relinquish their monopoly rights over the burgeoning telecommunications services sector. Only voice telephony and telex services will remain outside the scope of the directive. In a separate but related move, the Commission also submitted to the Council of Ministers a draft directive calling for the introduction of harmonized technical standards, in an effort to open up the telecommunications networks to all equipment manufacturers, and thus bring an end to the arbitrary power of the private and state-owned phone companies to decide who has access to the network.

But the telecommunications services plan, which would open up the vast majority of the Community's £44 billion telecommunications services industry to free competition, was confronted with bitter opposition from a variety of member states, principally Germany, France and Italy, all of whom continue to exercise a virtually exclusive monopoly over their telecommunications services sector. The plan also faced opposition from Britain, on procedural grounds (despite the UK government's commitment to the objectives of the proposal), because it was convinced that the Commission was overstepping the limit of its powers by refusing to adhere to the normal procedure of drawing up a draft directive for approval by the Council of Ministers.

The plan was originally scheduled for finalization in March 1989, and would have eliminated all telecommunications services monopolies by January 1991. However, it proved so controversial that the Commission was forced to consider a one-year extension of the liberalization timetable in order to defuse some of the angry reactions its ambitious proposals had generated.

The Commission was taken to the European Court of Justice by France, following its decision in June 1991 to issue its own directive forcing member states to open up the Community's terminal equipment market to cross-border competition. But the Commission, backed by the powerful commercial telecommunications companies, expressed confidence that the Court of Justice would uphold its authority to liberalize the telecommunications sector under the powers granted to it by the EC's founding treaty—as it already had done in the field of competition policy and the liberalization of the air transport industry.

The Commission also remained confident that it would emerge victorious in the battle over the proposed liberalization of telecommunications services. As one official said: 'Eventually, the member states will have to reconcile themselves to the fact that they are signatories to the Treaty of Rome'. Yet there is no disguising the growing anxiety among the governments of member states over the Commission's determination to ride roughshod over national sensibilities—using every power at its disposal, and forcing them to adhere to the Community's timetable for the completion of the internal market by 1992. The Commission hopes to implement a new directive by 1992 covering the liberalization of telecommunications services, which will include everything from electronic mail to data processing and teleshopping.

Reviewing the progress in opening up the Community's public purchasing markets in the sixth annual report on the internal market, published in July 1991, the Commission noted that 'work is proceeding satisfactorily'. The directive enlarging public procurement in transport, telecommunications, water and energy services has been adopted, while the Public Works and Public Supplies Directives came into force in January 1989 and July 1990, respectively. In order to ensure that the directives were being transposed into national law correctly, new monitoring procedures were also put in motion. Checks are now made on all contracts awarded in connection with programmes supported by the Community's structural funds, and infringements can be met with the freezing of structural fund payments. The report noted, however, that: 'Most difficulties are caused by ignorance of the directives.' Consequently, 'information campaigns are being conducted, and training courses organized for administrators at national and regional levels'.

Checklist of changes

- The loopholes in the 1971 directive on public works and the 1977 directive on public supplies will be closed and procedures for advance publication of tendering opportunities will be tightened up.
- Public bodies will be required to open all supply contracts worth more than £134,000 and all public works contracts worth more than £3.3 million to cross-border competition.
- In order to make sure that the contract-awarding bodies adhere to the new procedures they will be required to explain why they have rejected particular bids.
- There will be a wider definition of contract-awarding bodies, recognition of Community technical standards will become

mandatory, and all works contracts above £3.3 million will have to be advertised in the *Official Journal*.

- The means of redress for companies who have been illegally discriminated against by the public purchasing authorities will also be improved, and substantial fines are likely to be imposed on anyone violating the Community's public purchasing directives.
- The four excluded sectors (telecommunications, energy, transport and water) will also be incorporated into the Community's systems of awarding construction and supply contracts.

7 PROFESSIONAL MOBILITY

Living and working in the new Europe

As a result of legislation governing professional and worker mobility, EC nationals are entitled to take up employment or set up a business anywhere in the Community. Much of the impenetrable bureaucracy that used to confront people attempting to work abroad has been dismantled, thereby giving professionals, workers and even the unemployed unprecedented opportunities to pursue employment prospects outside their country of origin. Although Community nationals are still required to obtain residence permits, the need to obtain work permits has been abolished. Nevertheless, much work remains before the Commission's goal of creating a genuinely free market for labour is complete. Even before the advent of 1992, some member states (notably France) have been erecting new barriers to labour mobility in an effort to protect their own domestic labour markets.

The attempt to create a single European market would be fatally flawed without a single market for labour. Along with capital, goods and services, the free movement of labour, whether unskilled, skilled or professional, is one of the vital factors of production necessary for the efficient functioning of the Community's economy. Indeed, in many respects the internal market programme would simply not work without the abolition of national labour markets and the freedom for labour to move around the Community in search of more attractive conditions of employment and new opportunities to exploit.

The need to eliminate the barriers preventing the free movement of labour is particularly acute in the case of the service sector, which has recorded impressive rates of growth in recent years and will continue to do so only in an atmosphere of free competition. However, the benefits to be obtained from increased competition between goods, capital and services apply with equal force to every aspect of the labour market. The free movement of labour also constitutes one of the central elements of the European Commission's determination to create a 'Citizens' Europe', in which such freedoms are enshrined in Community law.

The Treaty of Rome already provides the legal basis for Community citizens to establish themselves in any member state and to be treated equally with the citizens of the host state. Article 52 lays down that 'restrictions on the freedom of establishment of nationals of a member state in the territory of another member state shall be abolished by progressive stages . . . such progressive abolition shall also apply to restrictions on the setting up of agencies, branches or subsidiaries by nationals of any member state established in the territory of any member state'. It also specifies that 'freedom of establishment shall include the right to take up and pursue activities as self-employed persons, and to set up and manage undertakings', while Article 57, as amended by the Single European Act, made it incumbent on the Council of Ministers to issue directives facilitating the mutual recognition of 'diplomas, certificates and other evidence of formal qualifications', enabling individuals who qualify in one member state to practise without hindrance in any other.

In an effort to allay the anxieties of member states about the employment of other Community nationals in certain sensitive sectors, principally those of national defence and security, the objective of creating the conditions for the free movement of labour cannot be allowed to prejudice the right of member states to regulate those sectors vital to 'public policy, public security and public health'. However, member states are explicitly prohibited under Article 53 from introducing any new restrictions on the right of Community nationals to establish themselves and take up their professions in any member state of their choosing.

As a result of two landmark rulings by the European Court of Justice in 1974, the right of Community citizens to work in any member state, without discrimination, was further reinforced. However, despite the theoretical right of establishment, a complex web of national regulations governing skills and professions in most member states has proved to be virtually impenetrable for non-nationals, unless they have been prepared to take their professional or vocational examinations all over again. Free movement has effectively been circumscribed by the various national regulations governing access to everything, from plumbing and carpentry to medicine and corporate law. Having qualified in a given field in one member state, the ability to work or practise elsewhere in the Community was frequently barred because of national differences in training periods and qualifications, or because member states simply refused to recognize equivalent qualifications obtained in other member states in order to protect their professional and labour markets from intra-Community competition.

Previous attempts to create a free market for labour

Because most of the barriers to the free circulation of labour arise out of different national educational traditions, reinforced by the fact that professions and skills are essentially nationally based, the European Commission had previously tried to eliminate the differences in member states' level and length of training requirements on a case-by-case basis. The negotiations co-ordinating professional qualifications were both difficult and protracted, but, by 1985, significant progress had been made. Some eight directives had been issued by the Council of Ministers, harmonizing national requirements to take up and practise a variety of professions in any member state. These included directives for doctors (1975), nurses (1977), dentists (1978), veterinary surgeons (1978), midwives (1980), architects (1985), pharmacists (1985) and general practitioners (1986), which was to become the last of the sectoral directives designed to facilitate increased professional mobility.

At the time, the directive governing training for GPs was seen as the dawning of the age of the Euro-doctor. The measure was basically a consolidation and updating of the 1975 directive on essential medical qualifications for GPs, based largely on the British model. British GPs are already required to undergo six years' basic training, followed by three years' practical experience in the National Health Service before becoming fully qualified. By 1990, all other member states also required two years' practical experience in addition to the basic training requirements. Yet while the measure established uniform Community training requirements for GPs, very few have so far availed themselves of their freedom to work in any member state. According to Commission estimates, there are some 600,000 doctors practising in the Community, only 2,000 of whom work in member states other than the one in which they qualified. Language, as in so many other areas, remains the single greatest obstacle to professional mobility in the internal market.

Although the negotiations which led to the implementation of the eight professional mobility directives have helped to build links between related professions in the twelve member states, they were nonetheless a laborious and time-consuming process. The negotiations for the directive governing architects took 17 years to complete, thus acquiring the dubious distinction of becoming one of the longest discussions over a single piece of legislation in the Community's history. Nor was this an isolated phenomenon. The negotiations for the directive for pharmacists came a close second, having taken 16 years to complete, while the proposal for the free movement of lawyers has been on the negotiating table for over a decade with no sign of a breakthrough. With some 80 or so professions still to go, the Commission will be fortunate to have completed the task of creating an internal market for professionals this side of 2092.

Along with many other of the Commission's 1992 initiatives in the internal market programme, the prospects for rapid progress were enhanced immeasurably by abandoning the traditional approach of case-by-case harmonization in favour of a mutual recognition. During the EC summit meeting at Fontainebleau in June 1984 member states gave their approval to a scheme designed to build on the existing legal foundations for the freedom of establishment by introducing the principle of a general system of mutual recognition for all higher education qualifications. With its mandate in hand, the Commission promptly set about drawing up radical new proposals for creation of an internal market for labour and the professions.

The Internal Market White Paper made a sweeping assault on the remaining barriers to the free movement of labour. It declared that:

> The Commission considers it crucial that the obstacles which still exist within the Community to free movement for the self-employed and employees be removed by 1992. It considers that Community citizens should be free to engage in their professions throughout the Community, if they so wish, without the obligation to adhere to formalities which, in the final analysis, could serve to discourage such movement.

It also pointed out that, as far as employees were concerned, free movement was now virtually complete, and a succession of rulings by the European Court of Justice had already severely curtailed the right of the public authorities in the various member states to reserve positions for their own nationals. However, certain problems still remained to be solved—for example, obstacles preventing the free movement and residence of Community migrant workers, particularly those living on the frontier of one member state and employed in another. Proposals to remove both the cumbersome administrative procedures governing the acquisition of residence permits in different member states and the taxation of frontier-migrant workers were put forward as potential solutions, and are still awaiting approval by the Council of Ministers.

In addition, the White Paper announced a two-stage programme designed to bring about the essential comparability of different member state vocational training qualifications. The first part of the programme called for the prompt approximation of vocational proficiency certificates among member states, while the second stage involved the introduction of a European vocational training card by 1990, serving as proof in all member states that the holder has been awarded with a universally recognized vocational training qualification.

In May 1987, and after much acrimonious debate between the Twelve, the Council of Ministers endorsed a multimillion pound Commission proposal to increase student exchanges between Community universities. Known as Erasmus, the programme (originally budgeted at £125 million and subsequently trimmed to £60 million) enables an estimated 5% of students in higher education to spend part of their courses in another Community country. Britain receives about £12 million, much of which is spent in the form of a travel allowance of about £1,500 for some 25,000 British students. The programme is to run for three years.

The Commission also declared its intention to propose legislation facilitating the mutual recognition of apprenticeship courses, as well as measures to ensure that freedom of movement is not restricted to only those gainfully employed. One of the most important initiatives in this respect is the 1987 programme to increase co-operation between further educational establishments, designed to promote increased mobility of students around the Community and act as an encouragement for the acquisition of language skills. However, while much of this work remains to be completed, member states have been able to agree on a general system for the mutual recognition of higher education degrees, which has been described as the single most important step towards the creation of a free market for people and services.

Mutual recognition of professional diplomas

In July 1985 the Commission put forward its proposal to create the basic conditions for the free movement of citizens who wish to take up a profession subject to regulation in another member state, and in which access is conditional on holding a specific degree of higher education. It was the first example of the Commission's attempts to create a 'Citizens' Europe', and is based on the principle that what was good for one member state was also good for all others. The proposal does not cover those professions already subject to sectoral directives, such as doctors, dentists and architects, but applies to everyone else, including surveyors, accountants, lawyers, physiotherapists, opticians and psychologists.

Initially, the Commission's proposals were greeted with some reservation by member states, notably Britain and France. Commission officials argued that the general recognition directive would only work on the basis of mutual trust and co-operation between member states. However, it was one thing to say that professionals from one member state would practise according to the requirements of other member states, and quite another to suggest that differences between member states in training and professional practice could be easily overcome on the basis of mutual trust and co-operation, combined with a probationary period of practical experience.

The legal profession, as represented by the Consultative Committee of European Bars, insisted that some mechanism (for example, an aptitude test to determine whether a lawyer from one member state was competent to practise in another) had to be incorporated into the proposal. The Commission objected to such modifications on the grounds that the professions were merely trying to preserve their closed-shop privileges, and that if it granted special concessions for lawyers, every other profession would soon be seeking preferential treatment, thereby undermining the whole purpose of the directive. Besides, one Commission official said indignantly: 'When it comes to the point, is a German lawyer really likely to seek to defend a client in a British court without knowing British law and being able to speak the language?'

At a meeting of the Council of Ministers in Luxembourg in June 1988 ministers agreed a compromise, allowing member states the freedom to decide whether to require non-national professionals to undergo a period of probation or sit an aptitude test before practising in their respective territories. Much to the irritation of the Commission, particularly Lord Cockfield, the compromise also made aptitude tests obligatory for all professions involved in legal work, provided that they were not another examination of 'the entire corpus of knowledge'. After a reading by the European Parliament, the directive was formally approved by the Council of Ministers at the end of 1988 and came into force in 1990.

The directive is predicated on four guiding principles. First, it is general in character, and will be applied to all regulated professions for which a three-year university degree is required. Second, mutual recognition is based on confidence and trust between member states, thereby avoiding the need to harmonize the different education and training schemes for the different professions among all member states. Third, the directive states that recognition is given to the 'finished product', defined as a fully qualified professional who has completed any training required in addition to obtaining a university degree. Foreign nationals can also use the same professional titles as domestic nationals. Finally, where important differences exist between the same profession among different member states, national authorities have the right to examine the competence of individual professionals by means of an aptitude test or a period of probation at their discretion.

The directive also makes special provision for the chartered bodies of Great Britain and the Republic of Ireland. These bodies, which regulate professional standards, are unique to Britain and Ireland. However, while membership of a chartered body is not based on the same level of higher education required in other EC member states in order to practise a particular profession, for the purposes of the directive there is no difference between them. Members of chartered bodies now have access to their sister professions in the Community, and, by the same token, their sister professions also have access to membership of the chartered bodies.

The agreement was described by Francis Maude, the junior trade minister, as 'an essential element in a genuine single market, leading to lower prices for services, and increased opportunities abroad'. It also gives European professionals greater freedom to move around the Community's internal market than is enjoyed by their American counterparts in their domestic market. However, proposals to extend similar rights of mobility to students, pensioners and the unemployed found considerably less sympathy from Britain, supported by Denmark, and remain effectively deadlocked. The Commission has, however, made clear its determination to prevent the new mobility freedoms from being restricted only to those gainfully employed, and will no doubt try again later.

In theory, the agreement on a 'general system for the recognition of higher education diplomas awarded on completion of professional education and training of at least three years' duration' provides an estimated 10 million Community professionals with the freedom to live and work in any member state of their choosing. As an instrument for the promotion of professional mobility, the initiative has been described by the Commission as being 'better than a passport'. However, the Commission is clearly unhappy about the incorporation of aptitude tests into the directive, and has declared its determination to monitor the situation closely in order to prevent the professions from erecting new barriers.

Any attempt by member states to preserve their national markets for professional services against foreign competition could provoke intervention from Brussels. One case of particular interest is the plan by the French legal profession to prohibit second-country lawyers from practising law in France from January 1992 unless they first join the French legal profession. Although the new law does not apply to non-French law firms already practising in France, there are fears that the measure could be used to exclude new entrants from gaining access to the profession. If such fears are borne out, the Commission will be forced to take action.

Proposals for a supplementary directive, known as the 'second general system for the recognition of professional education and training', have been under discussion since October 1988. The measures are designed to ensure mutual recognition for secondary levels of education and training, such as the ordinary national diploma, although they are still awaiting approval by the Council of Ministers. However, the proposed European Community Certificate of Experience, enabling, for example, hairdressers, retailers and hotel and catering staff to rely on the experience obtained in their country of origin when they apply for vacancies in other member states, has been endorsed by Council.

UK professions affected by the Mutual Recognition Directive

1 Institute of Chartered Accountants in England and Wales
2 Institute of Chartered Accountants of Scotland
3 Institute of Chartered Accountants in Ireland
4 Chartered Association of Certified Accountants
5 Chartered Institute of Loss Adjusters
6 Chartered Institute of Management Accountants
7 Institute of Chartered Secretaries and Administrators
8 Chartered Insurance Institute
9 Institute of Actuaries
10 Faculty of Actuaries
11 Chartered Institute of Bankers
12 Institute of Bankers in Scotland
13 Royal Institution of Chartered Surveyors
14 Royal Town Planning Institute
15 Chartered Society of Physiotherapists
16 Royal Society of Chemistry
17 British Psychological Society
18 Library Association
19 Institute of Chartered Foresters
20 Chartered Institute of Building

21 Engineering Council
22 Institute of Energy
23 Institution of Structural Engineers
24 Institution of Civil Engineers
25 Institution of Mining Engineers
26 Institution of Mining and Metallurgy
27 Institution of Electrical Engineers
28 Institution of Gas Engineers
29 Institution of Mechanical Engineers
30 Institution of Chemical Engineers
31 Institution of Production Engineers
32 Institution of Marine Engineers
33 Royal Institution of Naval Architects
34 Royal Aeronautical Society
35 Institute of Metals
36 Chartered Institution of Building Services Engineers
37 Institute of Measurement and Control
38 British Computer Society

The language barrier

Although welcoming the internal market programme as a much-needed stimulus for European industry, many critics have argued that, no matter how many technical, physical and fiscal barriers to trade are dismantled between now and 1992, the linguistic one will remain intact, effectively condemning the Community to permanent fragmentation. Even if all the directives are implemented by the deadline, language will remain the greatest single barrier preventing the creation of a genuine internal market. Linguistic differences are an unfortunate but brutal fact of life, and they will always be with us. They may be of minimal significance where member states have a long tradition of close economic ties, such as the historic relationship between Britain and Holland, but where no such relationship exists, any attempt to break new ground will be difficult —if not impossible—without the requisite linguistic skills.

At the institutional level the Community functions effectively only because it spends large sums of money on interpreters and translators, who account for about one in three of all Community employees. There are nine official languages in the Community: English, French, German, Italian, Spanish, Greek, Danish, Dutch and Portuguese, with Irish as an unofficial working language. Without the services of legions of interpreters and translators, the Community's modest bureaucratic machine, under strain at the best of times, would come to a precipitate halt. Few companies can afford to spend similar sums on interpreters and translators, so what hope is there for the internal market—especially for countries like Britain and France, which have a poor reputation for acquiring foreign-language skills?

According to a survey of 1,500 British companies conducted by Newcastle-upon-Tyne Polytechnic in 1988, the language barrier is far more significant than most British companies appreciate. This showed that a severe shortage of staff speaking European languages was costing British industry millions of pounds every year in lost contracts. Moreover, it found that while English has become the leading language in diplomacy, science and technology, it has been steadily losing ground to European languages in the fields of commerce and industry.

Perhaps even more alarming was the fact that this trend had been observed since Britain joined the Community in 1973, but a disturbing proportion of British companies had failed to take appropriate action, preferring instead to 'muddle through' by inundating foreign consulates with untranslated and (for the most part) 'unintelligible' trade literature. The survey discovered a direct correlation between export performance and linguistic competence, and found that Britain's trade deficit in manufactured goods, particularly in the car, textile, iron, steel, resins and plastics sectors, could be reversed if a more balanced trade relationship could be established with just three countries, Germany, Italy and Japan. Emphasizing the importance of language skills, the report noted that: 'It is not fortuitous that West Germany, Italy and Japan came respectively second, fourth and sixth in the rank order of foreign languages most lacking in British companies.'

Warning British firms that there was little doubt that the survival of manufacturing industry in Britain will come to depend on exports to non-English speaking countries, the authors stressed that: 'The key European languages—German, French, Spanish and Italian—are likely to play an increasingly important role in UK–EC trade if Britain is not only to maintain its market share, but also to increase it'. However, the omens are not favourable. In the decade between 1973 and 1983 the volume of manufactured goods imported into Britain from the Community rose by 300%, while Britain could manage only a modest 66% in the other direction. 'Other countries,' the report said, 'have mastered our language and market, but we have not reciprocated to the same extent. This deficiency, moreover, seems to apply to firms all over Britain'.

The survey also found that, in spite of a marginal increase in company awareness of the importance of language competence since the 1980s, there remained a marked reluctance for companies to employ individuals as much for their linguistic as for their technical skills. Many companies had been deterred from recruiting linguists because of the poor cost-effectiveness of employing a specialist if the frequency of foreign-language use was low. However, the consequences of underestimating the utility of linguists were inescapable. 'British companies are losing valuable trading opportunities for the lack of the right skills in the right languages, and many without realizing it,' the report concluded.

It is clear that it will be the linguists who will manage European industry and commerce in the 1990s. There is already a considerable premium in Europe for people with linguistic skills, and as the competition between European companies (as well as US and Japanese ones located inside the Community) intensifies, they are likely to become a scarce and extremely valuable resource—commanding ever-increasing financial rewards.

However, British students appear to be on course for allowing their Continental counterparts to take the largest share of the anticipated growth in the language market. David Smith, chairman of the 1988 Headmasters' Conference, a forum representing Britain's leading independent schools, warned his colleagues that many of Britain's schools and colleges were simply not prepared to cope with the challenge presented by 1992—particularly as far as foreign languages were concerned. Such predictions appear to be borne out by the statistical evidence. Despite the growing involvement of Japanese companies throughout the European (and especially the British) economy, British universities produce barely 50 Japanese-language graduates a year, while the number of university applications to study other foreign languages is declining steadily.

Although there is good cause to be concerned about the number of linguists produced by the education system, the problem is by no means confined to Britain. However, an attempt by the Commission to promote language teaching through the Lingua programme rapidly turned into an example of how Brussels, in its enthusiasm to promote the European ideal, has a marked tendency to overreach itself. The programme was an attempt to enforce the teaching of two languages at schools throughout Europe, as well as establish a new pupil exchange scheme.

In May 1989, Britain bitterly opposed the project, primarily on the grounds that the Commission had no powers under the Treaty of Rome to legislate in the field of secondary education. Downing Street also felt that the £160 million programme was 'poor value for money'. Domestic commentators felt that to have allowed the plan to be implemented, even for such laudable reasons, would have been to set a precedent that could have had serious repercussions for secondary education in the future.

Eventually, a compromise was reached in which the revised £130 million Lingua programme excluded all reference to secondary schools, and concentrated instead on promoting language teaching in post-secondary fields such as teacher exchanges, vocational training and language instruction for trainees in management, tourism and business studies.

Improving linguistic skills throughout the Community will not by itself be sufficient to encourage widespread mobility of labour and reduce existing disparities in the supply and demand for labour and skills. According to one survey produced by the City University Business School in 1990, demographic changes, combined with a demand for new skills, are likely to produce acute labour shortages in a wide range of sectors towards the end of the decade. Because of declining birth rates, the Community's labour force will begin contracting by 250,000 people a year from 1995 and by one million a year from the turn of the century.

With a decline in the number of young people entering the labour force, employers will find it difficult to make up numbers. Two obvious sources of supply—workers in the over-40 age group and women returning to work after having families—have frequently left school early, suffered protracted periods of unemployment and have had little or no retraining since they originally entered the labour market. Consequently, without the appropriate retraining programmes needed to equip workers with the skills required to fill the new jobs created by industrial change, employers could find themselves in the difficult position of being unable to recruit from surplus pockets of labour because of the lack of industrial and linguistic skills. Moreover, few governments have begun to tackle this issue on the scale many predict will be necessary if a crisis in the labour market is to be avoided by the end of the 1990s.

Checklist of changes

- Introduction of the general system of mutual recognition for all higher education qualifications will enable professionals to practise anywhere in the Community.
- Member states will be entitled to require an aptitude test or a period of probation for all professionals involved in legal work before allowing professionals from other Community countries to practise on their own territory.
- The eight sectoral directives governing professional mobility, passed prior to the White Paper programme, are not affected by the general directive on the mutual recognition of professional qualifications.
- The European Commission intends to introduce a two-stage programme designed to make member states' vocational training qualifications comparable, along with a European vocational training card serving as proof that the holder has been awarded a universally recognizable vocational training qualification.
- Student exchanges between Community universities and higher education colleges will be increased.
- Proposals for a directive governing the mutual recognition of apprenticeships will also be implemented.
- Legislation designed to remove the cumbersome administrative procedures governing the acquisition of residence permits in different member states and the taxation of frontier migrant workers will also be forthcoming.

8 ECONOMIC AND MONETARY UNION: 1

Cross-frontier banking and financial services

Plans for a single currency and a European Bank are part of a broad drive for economic and monetary union, which includes the liberalization of financial services across frontiers. Britain has, by and large, approved of the second but not of the first.

The desire for economic and monetary union derives ultimately from the Treaty of Rome. More recently, additional impetus has also come from the Treaty revisions debated between the Rome summit of December 1990 and the Maastricht summit of December 1991 (see Chapter 9). These, in turn, stem from the report on monetary union ordered by the EC summit at Hannover in 1988 and drawn up by a committee of experts headed by Delors. Key elements in the overall scheme for monetary union include:

1 A directive permitting banking across frontiers on the basis of a single licence, with associated directives on securities trading and other fiscal services;
2 The agreement fully to liberalize capital movements throughout the EC, which came into effect on 1 July 1990;
3 Britain's decision to commit the pound sterling to the Exchange Rate Mechanism (ERM) of the European Monetary System (EMS) in October 1990;
4 Economic convergence, with the Twelve reaching similar targets on inflation rates, interest rates, currency stability and budget deficits;
5 The Delors plan, which envisages a three-phase programme for economic and monetary union culminating in the creation of a European Bank ('Eurofed') to control the money supply in a united EC.

Much of the argument before and since Maastricht has been about the timing of the Delors programme—for example, whether the introduction of a single currency should precede or follow the setting up of a European Bank. But there are also fundamental points of principle at stake. Britain in particular has been reluctant to concede that a single currency is inevitable. Indeed, John Major repeatedly vowed in the run-up to the Maastricht summit that it would never be 'imposed' on the UK, though not least given his need to appease the pro-European faction of the Conservative party, he also made clear that it would be equally wrong to reject the possibility out of hand. Like all EC economic blueprints, the single-currency plan has powerful political overtones, with obvious implications for national sovereignty. Germany, too, has doubts about the pace of economic and monetary union following German re-unification. As the costs of German monetary union have risen, the guardians of the deutschmark at the Bundesbank have become less enthusiastic to agree a rigid timetable for EC currencies to unite. Equally, Germany saw concessions at Maastricht on political union as part of its price for allowing monetary union to proceed.

The Delors three-stage plan

The Delors Committee report, to which the heads of central banks and other financial experts contributed, was published in April 1989. At the Madrid summit in June 1989, EC leaders agreed that the first phase of the plan would amount to 'increased economic and monetary co-ordination' among the Twelve, beginning at the same time as capital movement liberalization in mid-1990. More controversially, and in the face of opposition from Mrs Thatcher, they also agreed to prepare 'completely and adequately' an IGC on stages two and three—understood by France, Germany and other countries to include the evolution of a federal banking structure, as recommended by the Delors report, and possibly a single currency. The Strasbourg summit of December 1989 acknowledged that this would require treaty revision; the Rome summit of October 1990 mapped out a timetable for monetary union and the Rome summit of December 1990 agreed that draft treaty amendments on economic and monetary union would be discussed at the Maastricht summit of December 1991.

Part of the debate at Madrid in 1989 revolved around the question of whether acceptance of phase one of the Delors plan necessarily entailed acceptance in principle of phases two and three. Britain, for example, has never accepted that this is the case. Nonetheless paragraph 39 of the Delors report stated: 'A decision to enter upon the first stage should be a decision to embark on the entire process'. The *Financial Times* commented that if Mrs Thatcher believed Britain could go along with phase one in the hope that the rest of the scheme would never come to fruition, she was mistaken: 'It should be burnt into the consciousness of the British Prime Minister that she may slow down an evolution on which all other members of the EC are resolved; she may influence its form; but she will not stop it'. John Major and his Chancellor of the Exchequer, Norman Lamont, take a subtly different line from Mrs Thatcher; they accept that the rest of the EC may proceed with a European Bank and a single currency, but argue that Britain retains the option to join in or not, as it deems fit.

The three proposed stages of the Delors plan were:

1 Greater economic convergence from 1 July 1990, with all currencies inside the EMS; central bank governors able to make proposals to the Council of Ministers; creation of a European Reserve Fund;
2 More collective decision making, though with national governments retaining ultimate control of fiscal and monetary policy; non-binding rules for national budget deficits; fewer exchange rate realignments; and the establishment of a federal European banking system through a European System of Central Banks (ESCB);
3 Fixed exchange rates; binding deficit constraints; ESCB (the Eurofed) to acquire far-reaching powers over national reserves and fiscal policy; finally, the replacement of national currencies by a single European currency.

Phase one—the least controversial—has been largely achieved. The Spanish peseta joined the EMS on 19 June 1989. At Madrid Mrs Thatcher, who had always insisted that the pound would only join the EMS fully 'when the time is ripe' (a phrase taken by many to mean 'never'), agreed to a list of specific conditions: the pound would join when UK inflation was down to the EC average; when France and Italy had emulated Britain in getting rid of exchange controls; when the internal market had been completed; when a free market in financial services had been achieved; and when competition policy had been strengthened.

Sceptics saw this as a delaying tactic: that is, Mrs Thatcher had joined the bandwagon with the aim of slowing it down. The then Chancellor of the Exchequer, Nigel Lawson, on the other hand, had long pressed for ERM entry, as had Sir Geoffrey Howe. Tensions came to a head within the Cabinet shortly after Madrid, with Sir Geoffrey Howe replaced (briefly) as Foreign Secretary by John Major. Then in October Lawson resigned over the issue, the immediate cause of his departure being Mrs Thatcher's refusal to sack her economic adviser, Sir Alan Walters, a noted opponent of British entry to the ERM. Major became Chancellor in place of Lawson, with Douglas Hurd moving to the Foreign Office from the Home Office.

However, the European monetary question remained an explosive one. In a bid to resolve the single-currency problem Major proposed a 'hard ECU', or parallel currency, as a halfway measure, and in October 1990 finally persuaded Mrs Thatcher that the time was 'ripe' at last for the pound to enter the ERM (see Chapter 9). The introduction of a more pro-European British 'style' since Major took over from Thatcher in November 1990 has helped to reduce tensions within the EC over monetary policy. As the run-up to Maastricht showed, key differences remain between Britain and the other eleven. But away from the public rows over the ECU and the Eurofed, quiet progress has been made in harmonizing other financial services, with Britain and the City of London playing a leading role.

Freedom of capital movements

The official EC Cecchini report on the anticipated benefits of 1992 suggests that deregulation and the absence of artificial barriers will have a major impact on financial services—banks, insurance and securities. To reverse the formula, freedom in financial services could provide the impetus for much of the 1992 programme as capital moves about the integrated market and banks compete across borders to offer services. EC officials estimate the 1992 saving to the financial services sector as between £14 and £15 billion. The four areas targeted for immediate 1992 integration are capital movements, insurance, banking and securities.

All 25 financial service proposals in the 1985 White Paper have been tabled. A number of directives have been in force for some time, such as the 1985 law liberalizing the marketing of mutual funds and unit trusts. However, British unit trust companies complain that they are still excluded from mutual trust markets in Europe, where distribution networks have been largely built up by banks and advertising is restricted. Other areas are even more complex, from motor insurance to 'own initiative' life insurance and group pension schemes. However, the governing principle of 'home country control' is firmly established, meaning that 'the home country supervising financial institutions should be responsible for the authorization of financial operators and the application of key prudential rules to those operators throughout the Community' (Geoffrey Fitchew, Director General of DG XV).

The liberalization of capital movements is already bringing closer an unrestricted market in financial services. The basis for this lies in Article 67 of the Treaty of Rome, which provides for member states to 'abolish all restrictions on the movement of capital belonging to persons resident in the Community'. Some loosening up of capital flows did take place after EC directives were passed in the 1960s, but it took the 1992 impetus to provide the final push. Britain, with its traditional strengths in the field, is likely to benefit more than most other EC countries from free capital flows, a prospect welcomed in the City and Whitehall. Britain abolished exchange controls as early as 1979, though this was more a consequence of the new Thatcher government's political philosophy than the result of developments within the EC.

The Cecchini report anticipates 'substantial economic gains' from the integration of financial markets, because of the pivotal role such services play in acting as the catalyst for European economies in general. The report calculates that the integration in 1992 of banking and credit insurance, brokerage and securities will save the Community 'in the order of 22 billion ECU'—about £15 billion. In the eight countries where financial integration is to take place—Britain, France, Germany, the Benelux nations, Denmark and Italy (Spain, Ireland, Greece and Portugal are excluded until after 1992, the latter two until 1995), the report found 'notably wide margins' in prices charged at present for mortgages, motor insurance and consumer credit. The 'competitive pressures of integration' will level these differentials out, to the benefit of the consumer, Cecchini suggests.

The first part of the Commission's two-stage plan for free capital flows across frontiers began in February 1987, with the liberalization of cross-border transactions in unit trusts, unlisted securities and long-term trade credits. The second phase, agreed in June 1988, completed the process by providing for full liberalization beginning in July 1990. There were some worries about the possible impact on the EMS, but in fact currencies have remained stable since July 1990. Though some countries maintained higher interest rates to restrain domestic demand, there was no excessive flow of funds from weaker economies, such as Italy's to stronger ones, such as Germany's, partly because domestic borrowers still find it troublesome to borrow abroad.

In banking, there is already a degree of free competition. In practice, however, as Cecchini noted: 'It appears difficult for many banks to compete successfully in other Community countries because new establishment involves considerable costs not borne by existing domestic banking networks'. The Second Banking Directive, tabled in January 1988 and adopted by the Council on 19 June 1989, deals with these hidden barriers —including restrictions on foreign involvement in local banks, prevalent in southern Europe—and lays the basis for a single licensing system, while seeking to allay US fears and to tighten up on possible abuses (see below).

Insurance in the single market

Similar restrictions are to be swept away in insurance and securities trading. There has been widespread irritation over barriers put up by insurance firms in Germany, where non-German insurance companies must have a permanent local establishment, pay penalizing tax rates which the Commission regards as discriminatory. The principle was tested in the European Court in 1986, when German insurers complained that they had been fined for obtaining for clients low-cost industrial and marine insurance in Britain. Due to these test cases, and qualified majority voting, a directive on cross-border competition in non-life insurance for commercial customers is already on the statute books.

In their study on Europe's domestic market, Jacques Pelkmans and Alan Winters write that 'insurance probably offers more scope for British gains from the European Domestic Market than does banking'. The 1986 ruling by the European Court freed co-insurance from restrictions, and set out once and for all the right of establishment for insurance companies in other EC states. As in other areas, barriers to cross-border trade in insurance were supposed to disappear in accordance with earlier directives, notably the 1978 directive on co-insurance. In practice it has taken the 1992 process to crack—or start to crack—a particularly tough nut.

The non-life directive, passed in June 1988, came into force in July 1990. It permits cross-frontier trade by larger companies, defined as those with a minimum turnover of 24 million ECUs (£16 million) or over 500 employees. It covers transport risks—marine and aviation, general liability, property and fire. Because national governments derive substantial income from life insurance tax, and because tax on insurance still differs from country to country, the directive concedes that tax can still be collected by the state within which the risk is insured. Sir Leon Brittan, the Commissioner for Competition Policy, observed that the existence of twelve separate markets for non-life insurance had 'cramped competition, pushed up prices and reduced consumer choice'.

Agreement on common insurance policies throughout Europe is still a long way off, but there are likely to be a growing number of cross-border mergers in insurance, as the recent acquisition of Equity and Life by the French Compagnie du Midi illustrates. Eagle Star has complained that French insurance companies, many of which are state-subsidized, are underpricing to win UK business. The business could just as well flow the other way: British companies such as Royal Insurance are actively expanding their Continental operations.

However, life insurance remains problematical. The Commission tabled its third directive on life assurance in draft form in February 1991. To meet objections from the insurance brokers, the draft proposes that customers would still be protected under the laws of their country of residence or nationality, regardless of where they bought the policy. Policy holders, moreover, would have a 30-day period during which to reconsider. John Redwood, the Trade Minister, said in June 1991 that Britain would use its EC presidency in the second half of 1992 to speed up adoption of the Commission draft directive. UK companies stand to do well, because they offer greater returns than their Continental counterparts. There are fewer restrictions on UK investment portfolios. A survey by Bacon and Woodrow, Actuaries, on behalf of the Association of British Insurers, shows that rates of return from 'with profits' insurance over 15 years averaged 8.2% in the UK compared to 6% in Germany and even less in other EC countries. This makes UK endowment policies attractive to other Europeans, whereas British buyers are unlikely to rush to take out European insurance (except for British citizens securing mortgages to buy property elsewhere in the EC and wishing to hold an accompanying endowment policy in the same local currency).

The main problem remains the German government's reluctance to allow foreign insurance companies into its protected market. Even in commercial insurance, which Germany has (in theory) agreed to open up to competition, rigid German regulations on premiums amount to a form of protectionism. There is, in addition, a German government monopoly on fire and property insurance, and special rules for health insurance. On the other hand, such restrictions may be undermined by cross-frontier banking, which is well advanced, as banks are permitted to offer a range of services across frontiers (insurance included).

Securities and stockbroking

The same applies to restrictions on stockbroking. The Commission's directives on cross-border dealings in securities and equities have been repeatedly held up. In the UK, the Securities and Investments Board and the Securities Association have lobbied hard in Brussels against directives which, they believe, will place tightly regulated British firms at a disadvantage to less-regulated Continental competitors. They also dislike the idea of an EC trading mentality, under which non-EC firms will be excluded where possible. The Commission issued proposals in this field at the end of 1988. The hope in Brussels is that by 1993 (if not 1992) the differing EC country regulations governing securities trading will be brought into line (see also the section on the Second Banking Directive, page 138). A harmonization directive on brokerage and investment houses is also under consideration in Brussels on the assumption that cross-border speculation will increase. A new draft 'recognition of particulars' directive would require any stock exchange in any EC country to accept a company for trading if its listing particulars had already been accepted by a stock exchange in another EC state. Under the directive, companies would have to have three years' trading experience to be listed. This presents few problems for countries like France, where similar regulations already apply, but creates difficulties for the London Stock Exchange, where the unlisted securities market requires a three-year track record but listed companies must have at least five years' trading experience.

However, resistance to cross-border securities trading comes mainly from the southern EC states—the so-called 'Club Med' of Spain, Italy and France—who want to protect their stock exchanges from competition for as long as possible. Given modern electronic technology traders could go ahead and deal across borders—directive or no directive—but protectionist-minded governments would almost certainly retaliate by requiring foreign investors to incorporate locally or set up local subsidiaries.

In May 1991 Andrew Hugh Smith, chairman of the International Stock Exchange in London, deplored the lack of progress on a single-licence trading system for securities. John Redwood, the Trade Minister, warned that if the directive was not passed the likely beneficiaries would be 'offshore centres' outside the EC such as Zurich. 'There is no economic law which states that the EC will always maintain a major financial services industry,' he said. 'Modern technology allows people to shift business around the world rapidly.'

Mortgages across frontiers

In theory, banks and finance houses across the EC will compete with each other after 1992 in offering home loans. The extent to which this happens will depend on how far home loan practices are harmonized. At present, they differ widely, as does home ownership, which is high in Britain and Spain (64% owner occupation) and in Ireland (74%) but low in Germany (37%) and the Netherlands (44%), where rented accommodation is the norm. The Commission has therefore not sought to table a mortgage finance directive, but instead is incorporating the mutual recognition of home loan standards into the Second Banking Directive.

French, Danish and Dutch finance houses have already set up subsidiaries in the UK to offer mortgages to home buyers. However, this is not seen as a real threat by any of the major building societies. They, in turn, are making modest forays into the Continental housing market: Abbey National has a Spanish subsidiary, Abbeycorp (with Swiss involvement) and the Midland Bank's French subsidiary is making inroads into the French mortgage business. Building society managers expect to see more cross-border activity of this kind in 1992. However, an EC-wide regulated home loan market is some way off, especially since countries like Germany operate strict rules for home loans through tightly regulated finance institutions, with home buyers obliged to prove that they have saved a high proportion of the value of the house. Some UK finance houses already offer ECU mortgages, based on the ECU basket of European currencies.

Export Credit Guarantees

Another intriguing question is whether the practice of using state agencies such as the Export Credits Guarantee Department (ECGD) to support trading ventures will continue to make sense either for intra-European trade or for EC-based trade with the rest of the world. It is possible that, as the financial barriers come down, credit insurance will increasingly pass to private rather than government institutions, or a combination of the two, along the lines of existing German private insurance companies, which reinsure with the government.

Export finance not only underwrites the export risk, it also insures the exporter against bankruptcy by foreign customers. However, in theory, a Dutch or French insurer could undercut the ECGD by offering British exporters the same service for exports to Holland or France, on the same terms as the ECGD but with the advantage of local knowledge. Moreover, the concept of 'national exports' will become increasingly outdated in the single market, and the concept of 'European' exports to non-EC countries will come to the fore.

This could lead in the long run to the development of a pan-European export credit agency. A step in this direction was taken in July 1991, when the Dutch group Nederlandsche Credietverzekering Maatschappij NV was given ECGD short-term business in the face of competition from other EC insurance groups, notably Assicurazioni Generali of Italy. There was disquiet in the House of Commons over the fact that the winning bid was not British. But the government replied that the Dutch company chosen had offered cash to help revitalize the ECGD, with the aim of helping British exporters by offering insurance against unusual risks such as buyer insolvency or even political upheaval.

Capital transfers and insider trading

The June 1988 directive on completing capital movements liberalization by July 1990 is a textbook example of the passage of a 1992 directive from draft proposal to law in the face of twelve differing national standpoints. Britain's initial objection was that the free flow of capital across frontiers should not be regarded as a step towards the harmonization of indirect taxes, over which the UK retains its veto. But others also had reservations.

France in particular, under the socialist government of Michel Rocard, expressed strong doubts, arguing that if EC citizens were able to move capital around the Community freely this could only encourage fraud and tax evasion. This objection was met by an undertaking from the Commission that it would report on ways of strengthening cross-border tax inspection to prevent abuses. France, unlike Britain, has no pay-as-you-earn (PAYE) tax system, and French tax officials rely on their right to obtain information from banks—a further reason for French objections to the directive. The City of London is bound to benefit from liberalization as EC capital flows to a proven financial centre, with market capitalization totalling $500 billion. Only Germany comes close, with $160 billion, while financial markets in France and Italy have $100 billion each. However, anxieties about fraud persist in London as well as in Paris. A further misgiving in London is that EC investors may regard the City as over-regulated under the 1986 Financial Services Act—drawn up by the government without thought of the implications of 1992.

Fears that the removal of restrictions on bank account movements within the EC could benefit tax dodgers and other villains rather than *bona fide* business executives and bank customers have been partly met by the new directive on insider dealing agreed by finance ministers in Luxembourg in June 1989 at the same time as the Second Banking Directive. The Commission's original proposals were adapted to meet the demands of the British Bankers Association and City institutions, to the point where they closely resemble UK legislation by laying down a narrow definition of insider trading, embracing both 'primary' and 'secondary' insiders who misuse information about a company they work for or are 'closely associated with', while allowing normal stock market activities to go ahead unhindered. The directive requires EC countries to co-operate across frontiers in tracking down illegal stock exchange activity. All states are obliged to bring their national laws into line with the directive by 1 June 1992, causing problems for Belgium, Italy, Ireland and Germany, which have little or no insider trading legislation.

Another proposal—for taxing bank interest and investment income at source—has had a less favourable reception. Such a withholding tax, proposed variously at 10% or 15%, would apply to National Savings and building society accounts, and would help—for example—to allay French fears of a diversion of savings to tax-free Luxembourg. However, when in July 1989 Pierre Beregevoy, the French Finance Minister, chaired a discussion on reducing tax evasion in an era of free capital flows, Mme Christiane Scrivener, the Commissioner for Fiscal Affairs, stressed co-operation against fraud rather than a withholding tax, a clear admission that the tax was unpopular. Britain described it as 'misguided', since it would add to business costs and raise interest rates. Germany announced in July 1989 it was abolishing its own unpopular 10% withholding tax and said it would seek 'a more viable tax on investment earnings' with its EC partners.

The Second Banking Directive: solvency ratios and reciprocity

The Second Banking Directive, adopted in June 1989, is a powerful force propelling the European banking world towards a financial revolution. Under the directive, due to come into force on 1 January 1993, any High Street bank in an EC member country will be able to operate throughout the Community on the basis of a single licence issued in its country of origin—not in the 'host' country. In other words, the directive accepts the principle that it is enough for banks to be properly authorized and supervised in their home country for them to be able to deal in deposits and loans of both cash and securities in any of the other states. The directive alters a situation in which banks can only open subsidiaries in another country, and then subject to local controls. Host countries retain the right to control bank liquidity for reasons of monetary policy.

Under the directive, Lloyds or National Westminster, for example, will be able to operate on the Continent without local authorization—and equally, Crédit Lyonnais or the Dresdner Bank can operate in Britain, competing with British banks in offering a range of services. British banks claim to be ready for the fray: Barclays, for example, says it has 3,200 offices 'from Munich to Murcia, Paris to Piraeus' with Barclays de Zoete Wedd particularly strong in France, Spain and the Netherlands (*1992: What Does the Future Hold for Your Business?*, Barclays Corporate Marketing Department). The Bank of England suggested in a survey in June 1989 (*The Single European Market: Survey of the UK Financial Services Industry*) that France, Italy and Spain offer the best markets for UK bank expansion.

Only post-1992 practice will show how far this can develop: for example, national home loan regulations will still differ widely. German home buyers have to prove they have saved one-third of the proposed mortgage. Banks licensed to operate throughout the EC must have a minimum working capital of £3.5 million and provide Brussels with information on their larger shareholders. Solvency ratios have proved a sticking point: under the Basle agreement of July 1988, reflected in an EC draft directive, the Group of Ten agreed that a bank's funds must constitute at least 8% of its risk-weighted assets. Both Germany and Denmark object that mortgage lending, which plays a large role in their banking objectives, is given too high a risk weighting both in the Basle agreement on solvency ratios and in the subsequent EC directive. (UK discount houses are exempted because of their 'special nature'.)

Ordinary bank customers will be more concerned with the standardization of cashpoint bank cards, beginning in Belgium, Germany, Denmark and—surprisingly—Portugal and Spain, with banks in those countries negotiating joint agreements on customer access to computerized networks. Such Euro-networks or even bank mergers will become a common feature. In the wake of the BCCI collapse in July 1991, the Commission proposed making countries in which banks are registered responsible for compensating depositors in other countries if one of their banks fails —a scheme designed to avoid 'brass plate' banks which avoid proper supervision.

Non-EC banks will have access to the EC, but the EC will retaliate by withholding approval for non-EC banking operations if EC banks are not given comparable treatment in third countries. This softens earlier proposals under which automatic penalties would have been imposed on non-EC banks from countries which created difficulties for European banks. According to Willy de Clercq, the then External Affairs Commissioner, speaking in Austria in August 1988:

> Our view is that Community credit institutions should have equal access to the financial markets of non-European countries. The Commission will check on a case-by-case basis whether similar institutions from all member states are given the same treatment in the non-Community country concerned.

However, in September 1988, Lord Young, the then Trade and Industry Secretary, told a meeting of the Italian Chamber of Commerce in London that the reciprocity proposal would erect a wall of protectionism round Europe and threaten London's position as a key financial centre open to all comers. His view is supported by the Bank of England, which opposed interference by Brussels which might, for example, prevent a US bank from opening in London because an undercapitalized Portuguese bank had been barred from the United States.

This had given rise to anxiety in the United States, where the federal banking authorities maintain that reciprocity would require radical changes in US interstate banking law. To meet this, the directive was reformulated to provide for 'case-by-case' negotiations with countries where commercial and investment banking are legally separate. It remains unclear, however, just how the EC's 1992 banking plans will overlap with the international supervisory regulations being drafted by the Bank for International Settlements (BIS) in Basle, although the BIS is involved in EC deliberations.

Remaining details to be cleared up involve how national laws requiring banks to disclose information for tax purposes will be retained. Governments retain their powers to control national instruments of fiscal policy such as interest rates—though this may also be eroded if the co-ordination of interest rates becomes a consequence of economic integration and EMS management in 1992 conditions. For Britain, a further problem arises in the field of securities, listed by the directive as one of the 'core activities' of banking, along with deposits, loans, credit, portfolio management and leasing.

The City is in a strong position, however, with a daily foreign exchange turnover of $90 billion, compared to $50 billion in New York and Tokyo. It attracts business because of its skills and its liberal regulatory system, both assets for 1992. This could put British banks in a strong position as cross-border banking strategies emerge: the cross-shareholding link-up between the Royal Bank of Scotland and Banco Santander of Spain—plus its German and Belgian subsidiaries—announced in October 1988 is just one example, though the first to involve a UK bank. The RBS and Santander are negotiating with a third partner, Crédit Commercial de France (CCF). Other link-ups include a deal between Amro Bank in the Netherlands and the Société Générale of Belgium; the purchase by the Deutsche Bank of Banca d'America e d'Italia; a joint venture between Belgium's Générale de Banque and the Amsterdam–Rotterdam Bank; and the acquisition by Crédit Lyonnais of a controlling interest in Credito Bergamasco of Italy. In July 1989 Hypotheken und Wechsel Bank of Bavaria took a 50% stake in Foreign and Colonial Management, the British fund management group, which said it was 'positioning itself firmly on the 1992 express'. In November 1989 Morgan Grenfell announced it had agreed to a $1.5 billion takeover bid by Deutsche Bank, a move said by the German bank to reflect 'the pre-eminence of London in Europe in corporate finance and asset management'. In 1991 the Dresdner Bank and the Banque Nationale de Paris exchanged 10% shares with a view to collaborating in international markets.

The attraction of such deals lies in increased capital assets and market access, but they also usually involve the harmonization of computerized cash-card services and point-of-sale systems, the most obvious benefit to customers. Consumer credit is a likely growth area, with further expansion by systems such as Eurocard and Visa. The European Council for Payment Systems, which groups 40 banks, is working on compatibility for all electronic card systems. In April 1990 larger banks and credit card companies issued a voluntary code of practice to forestall a Commission regulation on the subject. But the Commission believes that the code puts too much onus on the cardholder, who is obliged to 'take the necessary measures immediately to become aware of the circumstances of the theft or loss, and demonstrate that he took such measures'.

Checklist of changes

- All restrictions on movement of capital belonging to EC residents have been abolished
- Cross border competition in non life insurance for commercial clients is in effect.
- Cross border competition in life insurance should eventually be allowed.
- Restrictions preventing other EC nationals from trading in securities or acting as brokers are to be lifted.
- Any High Street bank will be able to operate throughout the Community on the basis of a single licence under the Second Banking Directive.
- A single licencing system for securities is proposed.
- Compatible credit/cash card technology to be more widespread.

9 ECONOMIC AND MONETARY UNION: 2
The European Bank and a single currency

Whatever the arguments over national sovereignty, many traders, customers and business executives support closer monetary integration on the grounds that changing money around the EC means sizeable financial losses, while transferring money from bank to bank within the Community is a haphazard and costly business. The European Consumers Bureau (BEUC) has concluded that, at the moment, banks do not listen to clients' instructions when making money transfers: fail to make clear the cost of a transaction in advance: and charge both sender and payee even where the remitter has agreed to bear the costs. As for *bureaux de change*, BEUC concluded that travellers making a round-trip of EC capitals would lose almost half their spending money just by paying handling charges—and by losing on official exchange rates. In 1990 Sir Leon Brittan, the Commissioner for Competition Policy, tabled proposals to eliminate currency handling charges, arguing—in the face of fierce opposition from High Street banks and agencies such as Thomas Cook—that in the run-up to a single currency, exchanging pounds for francs or marks need not be any different from exchanging English pounds for Scottish pounds—a cost-free transaction.

In Britain, however, the question of whether pounds, marks and francs should be replaced by the ECU, with money supply controlled by a European Bank, is seen not only as an issue of fiscal harmony but also as a matter of national sovereignty, with the pound sterling as a symbol of independence and national monetary control. Similar tensions lay behind much of the debate in 1989–90 over whether the pound should join the EMS, as provided for in phase one of the Delors plan.

Pressure for Britain to join the EMS became powerful after the 1989 Madrid summit, with Pierre Beregevoy, the French Finance Minister, observing that 'a common monetary policy cannot work effectively as long as Great Britain remains outside the EMS exchange mechanism'. Both Nigel Lawson and Sir Geoffrey Howe agreed, and Howe predicted that the pound would be inside the ERM by the time of the next UK election, in 1992. He was right—although the intense manoeuvring over whether and when the pound should join was part of the bruising Cabinet debate over Europe which led to his resignation, that of Lawson and, ultimately, Mrs Thatcher's too.

Opposition to ERM entry stemmed partly from the belief, expressed among others by Tim Congdon, economic adviser to Gerrard and National, that between 1987 and 1988, when sterling was informally pegged to the German mark, the effect on credit growth and inflationary pressures had been 'disastrous'. The EC nations, Congdon wrote in *The Times* on the eve of the Madrid summit, suffered from 'deep-seated financial incompatibility'. This was a view shared by Sir Alan Walters, Mrs Thatcher's economic adviser, who famously called the EMS 'half-baked'. Opponents of ERM entry argued that the merits of the EMS in keeping down inflation had been exaggerated; that sterling had a global as well as European role; and that once inside the EMS, sterling would be dominated by the mark, the most powerful European currency.

EMS: arguments for and against

The EMS dates from 1979, and was designed as a way of stabilizing currency fluctuations after the collapse of the post-war Bretton Woods fixed exchange-rate system, and the partial failure of the European 'Snake', which allowed fluctuations within agreed limits. Unlike the Snake, the EMS is a system for full currency management, under which currencies participating in the ERM have fixed rates against the European Currency Unit (ECU). The ECU in turn is based on the 'basket' of currencies participating in the EMS. Until October 1990 sterling was part of the ECU 'basket', but not of the ERM itself. When it joined it did so—like the Italian lira and the Spanish peseta—within the 'broad band' of 6%, that is, it could fluctuate in value up to 6% above or below its value at entry, giving a total potential fluctuation of 12%. (The 'narrower' band permits maximum variations of no more than 3% either way.)

The ERM currencies have their ECU rate realigned at sessions of EC finance ministers called for the purpose. Between realignment meetings the central banks intervene in foreign-exchange markets to support a member currency when it reaches its 'floor', drawing on a reserve called the European Monetary Co-operation Fund, based on members' gold and currency reserves. As the British debate continued, supporters of the EMS pointed to its stability since 1979 and to the steady reduction in inflation differentials. Many British executives argued that planning would be much simpler if the pound were part of a stable currency system. Delors marked the tenth anniversary of the EMS in March 1989 by saying it had 'given the rest of the world a concrete example of the Community's capacity to act together and create an island of stability in an ocean of monetary turbulence'.

Sceptics pointed out that France and Germany were—and are—often in conflict over monetary policy, despite their membership of the EMS and the existence of a Franco–German Finance Council, set up in March 1988. French officials express open anger when the Bundesbank raises its interest rates and sets off a European chain reaction without consulting its French counterpart. Indeed, French enthusiasm for a common currency and European Bank stems in part from the French desire to curb the dominant German currency and economy.

However, bankers and businessmen continued to urge ERM entry for the pound, and a Commons select committee report entitled *Financial Services and the Single European Market* said Britain should join the EMS 'as soon as possible' to enable the City to be 'the financial gateway to Europe' in 1992.

On 8 October 1990 John Major, who succeeded Lawson as Chancellor, announced full UK membership of the ERM, together with a 1% cut in bank base rates. The pound entered the ERM at a rate of 2.95 DM. Major said entry would reinforce firm monetary policy and help bring down inflation. Mrs Thatcher, a less convincing convert, declared that the conditions she had outlined at Madrid (see Chapter 8) had been met: 'The real thing that made this decision possible was the uncontestable signs that the economy is working in the way we intended it to in reducing inflationary pressures'. Lawson, not to be outdone, said in the Commons that the 'real tragedy' was that the pound had not joined the EMS five years earlier.

The move produced a euphoric surge in sterling on foreign exchange markets, and Beregevoy called it 'good news for Europe'. A year later, on the anniversary of the move, *The Economist* reported that it had been 'a great success', and ran a photograph of Lawson captioned 'Proved right', with another of Sir Alan Walters captioned 'Proved wrong'. Interest rates had fallen from 15% on the eve of entry to 10%, and inflation had fallen from nearly 11% to 4%—although a price had been paid in high unemployment. Analysts agreed that the timing of entry had not been particularly propitious, with German unification pushing German interest rates higher, a recession looming and UK wage inflation ahead of its EC partners—but any moment chosen would have had its drawbacks.

The ECU: a future single currency?

When sterling joined the ERM Major was careful to stress that this did not mean that Britain also agreed in principle to a single European currency. Indeed during his term as Chancellor, Major pioneered the concept of a 'hard ECU' in a bid to head off the single-currency idea. Delors was sceptical about sterling's entry into the ERM, telling EC foreign ministers in Venice that 'only the future will tell us whether this was a pretext for slowing down the process of integration'.

The 'hard ECU', as outlined by Major in June 1990, was intended as a 'parallel currency' alongside national currencies. Under the scheme, which received backing from Carlos Solchaga, the Spanish Finance Minister, a European Monetary Fund would be established (replacing the plan for a more ambitious European Bank), with powers to issue 'hard ECUS' and set ECU interest rates. Sir Leon Brittan took up the idea as an interim measure, observing that since British shoppers would be disconcerted to find their familiar pounds and pence replaced, 'our notes and coins could have a sterling value on one side and the ECU equivalent on the other'. Major, using language very different from that of Mrs Thatcher, conceded that the hard ECU could develop into a single currency if that was what peoples and governments wanted.

However, at the Rome summit of December 1990, which set out the timetable for proposed treaty revisions to be discussed at Maastricht a year later, Delors denounced the Major plan as a device for avoiding the single currency itself. As late as May 1991, on the other hand, Norman Lamont, Major's successor as Chancellor, was insisting that because a single currency was 'a long way down the road' and 'a leap in the dark with high risks', the hard ECU or parallel currency was still a valid initiative. *The Times* agreed, noting in an editorial that the hard ECU was no longer an 'unappealingly premature baby' and had some support from Spain, France and Italy as an evolutionary concept.

So far, the ECU remains largely a notional currency, used as a unit of account for EMS realignments and EC internal calculations. But it is increasingly also used as a unit of payment and reserve currency, and both travellers cheques and Eurobonds can be ECU-dominated. One EC country—Belgium—has even issued ECU coins bearing a portrait of the sixteenth-century Emperor Charles V. The coins—5 and 50 ECU pieces, minted in silver and gold, respectively—are intended primarily as collectors' items. In theory they are legal tender, but no restaurant or shop will take them, as we discovered when trying to pay with ECUs. Nonetheless, the issue is intended by Belgium as a gesture in the direction of a future common currency.

A clearing house for ECU transactions was set up in October 1986 by a consortium of seven European banks, including Lloyds and the Crédit Lyonnais. One Luxembourg bank has even issued Visa credit cards in ECUs. At present, less than 1% of business transactions in the EC are invoiced in ECUs, though this would change if it became a parallel currency. The European Parliament's Economic and Monetary Affairs Committee has urged use of the ECU for paying workers in EC border areas —for example, a Dutchman working in Germany might hold a bank account in ECUs and convert them to marks or guilders as required. One British firm, APV Baker, reported in 1991 being paid 71 million ECUs by the Soviet Union for food-processing equipment—but converted the ECUs into sterling. As the firm's finance manager observed, 'If you could feel a 50 ECU note, some of the resistance to using it [the ECU] might disappear'.

The ECU, meanwhile, remains little known in Britain, except to the money markets. When we offered Belgian-issued ECUs to London shopkeepers and bus drivers as an experiment while preparing *The Times Guide to 1992*, comments varied from 'What bright spark thought that one up?' (a bus driver) and 'We'd have to change all the tills and retrain the staff—try Harrods, they might take them' (a DIY store supervisor) to 'It might be useful if you did a lot of travelling, but people are already getting angry about Brussels having a say in what goes on over here' (a policeman in Trafalgar Square). 'I'm very British—it just wouldn't seem like England if we had a European currency. Why can't they all change over to our money?' was a typical reaction (in this case, a newspaper seller outside a London Underground station). There was no greater familiarity with the ECU when we tried again in 1991. Some object on the grounds that the ECU also happens to be the name of a medieval French coin.

In August 1988 the Treasury took the unusual step of issuing bills denominated in ECUs—the first such bills to be internationally tradeable. The aim was to diversify Britain's reserves while, at the same time, encouraging the development of an ECU market in London. Commission officials were quick to warn, however, that the issuing of ECU-denominated bills could not be a substitute for other moves towards monetary union—a warning they repeated over Major's 'hard ECU' plan.

The EC summit in Rome in October 1990 laid down a timetable for EMU, with phase two—the European Bank—set for 1994, and phase three—the single currency—set for 1997 (see Introduction). In May 1991 Delors announced a compromise formula under which the UK could sign a treaty at Maastricht allowing for a single currency, with the proviso that the UK Parliament could decide whether or not to join at a later date —an 'opt-out' clause. Before the EC summit in Luxembourg in June 1991, Major and Chancellor Kohl of Germany agreed that the summit would not rush into plans for a single currency and a European Bank, but would 'take stock'. Because of the cost of German monetary union following unification, Kohl's enthusiasm for a single currency has dimmed. 'No-one is ready to give up the stable deutschmark for an unstable currency— that is just stating the obvious' he remarked. Hans Tietmeyer, vice-president of the Bundesbank, said in Frankfurt in June 1991 that Germany needed a strong independent mark 'for several years ahead' because of the 'difficult situation' created by German unity.

However, in September 1991, when EC finance ministers met at Apel-doorn in the Netherlands under the Dutch EC presidency, Wim Kok, the Dutch Finance Minister, sought to force the pace by presenting a draft agreement under which any six EC members who met agreed economic criteria could go it alone on a single currency, leaving the others to join later. Lamont accepted this 'inner core' concept, noting that Britain would almost certainly qualify for the inner group if it chose—but emphasized that Britain might well choose to stay out. The Dutch came under fire for proposing, in effect, a 'two-speed EMU', but replied that what was proposed was a 'one-speed EMU' with countries like Britain or some of the southern EC nations granted 'temporary exemptions' if they so wished. This still implied, however—to Lamont's dissatisfaction—that countries which opted not to use the single currency would inevitably 'opt in' at some future date.

Theo Waigel, the German Finance Minister, said that Germany could accept the Dutch conditions for economic convergence before introduction of a single currency, with EC states having to converge on inflation, interest rates and currency stability, but argued that the 'core group' which met these conditions should consist of seven or eight countries rather than six. EC finance ministers could decide which countries qualified for a single currency, and EC leaders would confirm this at a summit. Under the Apeldoorn plan, however, plans for a European Bank would be delayed: instead of the Bank being established in 1994, with a single currency introduced later, a European Monetary Institute (suggested by Major as part of his 'hard ECU' scheme) would co-ordinate monetary policies throughout the Twelve, reporting by 1996 on whether convergence was sufficient to allow for a single currency, and transforming itself into the European Bank once this had been achieved.

In October 1991 EC finance ministers meeting in Luxembourg discussed a Dutch proposal that 'clear, strict and comparable' yardsticks for measuring budgetary convergence should be written into the Treaty of Rome amendments, including the power to fine an EC government which overspent. Germany backed a Dutch suggestion that an EC economy would be judged to have entered the 'danger zone' if it had a ratio of national debt to GDP of over 60%, and if its annual budget deficit amounted to more than 3% of GDP and/or exceeded capital investment. Greece and Italy opposed such rigid formulas, while Britain argued that economic performance should be measured over a period of years, not annually.

In the run-up to the Maastricht summit Major and Lamont vowed that they would never allow the EC to 'impose' a single currency on the UK. At the Conservative Party conference in October 1991 Lamont declared, to loud applause, that although Britain's future lay in Europe:

I will not allow a single currency to be imposed on this country.
Unlike the Labour Party, we do not want laws to be made and taxes to be raised in Brussels for which the British people have not voted.

Frankfurt versus London: the European Central Bank

The communiqué issued at the Hannover summit of 1988 which commissioned the Delors report did not include the words 'European Central Bank'. This was at Mrs Thatcher's insistence. She said she did not expect to see a European Central Bank in her lifetime and added flatly: 'I do not share the vision of a United States of Europe and a single currency'. On the eve of the summit Mrs Thatcher had remarked that a European Bank could only come about when Parliament was abolished and there was a European government instead.

However, a number of leaders had made it clear at Hannover that they regarded a European Bank or 'Eurofed' as an integral part of monetary union. The communiqué at Hannover recalled the objective of the 'progressive realization of economic and monetary union' affirmed in the Single European Act. The Delors committee set up by Hannover contained eleven EC central bank governors, including Robin Leigh-Pemberton (Governor of the Bank of England). The committee also drew on experts such as Alexandre Lamfalussy (general manager of the Bank for International Settlements), Niels Thygesen (a Danish economics professor), Miguel Boyer (a former Spanish finance minister) and Frans Andriessen (former Dutch Finance Minister and EC Agriculture Commissioner in the first Delors Commission, now External Relations Commissioner).

'We have a structure and a date' President Mitterrand of France declared after Hannover. 'If there is to be monetary union there must be a central body to manage it. What remains to be settled is its relationship to the existing central banks.' The options considered by Delors included:

1 The replacement of national central banks by a Bank of Europe;
2 Less radically, a European Bank, or federal reserve, controlled by the existing central banks;
3 Least radical of all, increased co-ordination among central banks.

Any of these options could be accompanied by the issuing of ECU's as a European currency to be used in parallel with national currencies—for example, for commercial transactions to pay travel bills. Under the Luxembourg and Dutch EC presidencies in 1991, however, a debate arose over whether the European Bank should take the form in the first instance of a 'European Monetary Institute', whose function would be to manage economic convergence—including co-ordination of the member states' medium-term economic strategies—and to preside over the gradual introduction of the ECU as a parallel currency before transforming itself into a fully fledged 'Eurofed'.

The Delors concept of an ESCB (European System of Central Banks) resembles option 2. However, even a central bank 'system' would entail new central banking institutions. There are fears in the City that, whatever form it takes, a future Euro Bank will be located in Frankfurt—unless Britain takes steps to ensure that, like the new European Bank for Reconstruction and Development (EBRD) to aid Eastern Europe, it comes to London or is shared with Frankfurt. British banking officials argue that a European federal reserve bank in Frankfurt would become the operational centre of official foreign exchange and money market intervention in the Community, thus threatening London's pre-eminence as a financial centre.

A further difficulty arises over the question of who would control the 'Eurofed'—the bankers themselves, on the model of the powerful and independent Bundesbank, or governments, through EC finance ministers? In November 1990, EC central bank governors drew up draft statutes for a future European Bank. These required central bank governors under the new system to be independent not only in relation to the Bank but also within their own national systems. Leigh-Pemberton placed a UK 'reserve' on these terms, arguing that Bundesbank-style independence would require changes not only in Britain (where the Bank of England is under Treasury control and directly linked to government instruments of monetary control) but also in France, where a similar system obtains.

The Rome summit of October 1990 envisaged January 1994 as the starting date for the European Bank, but with a three-year 'transitional period' to 1997 before it assumed full monetary responsibilities. The objective of the Euro Bank, under the draft statutes, would be to maintain price stability—a narrower remit than that of the Bundesbank, which is required, in addition, to promote employment and achieve balanced growth. In November 1990 Norman Lamont, in one of his first statements as Chancellor under the new Prime Minister, John Major, declared the Delors plan 'unworkable', noting that economic convergence was a long way off when inflation in the EC ranged between 2.5% and 22%, interest rates from 8.5% to 19% and budget balances from a 1% surplus to a 17% deficit.

In April 1991 the central bank governors, meeting at Basle for a session of the Bank for International Settlements, considered how profits from the European Bank or a European federal reserve might be distributed among the EC central banks, settling on GDP and population as the main criteria. But no decision was taken on whether the central bankers themselves or EC finance ministers should control Euro Bank interventions in foreign exchange markets. In the same month, London and Frankfurt both put in formal bids to house any future European Bank, as did Paris, Luxembourg and Amsterdam.

Single currency: the opt-out clause

In October 1991 the Dutch Presidency released the draft version of its proposed treaty on economic and monetary union, giving the UK parliament and indeed all other parliaments in the EC the right to say yes or no to a single currency by opting out within six months of a decision by other EC states to go ahead. Any country whose parliament 'does not feel able to approve of the irrevocable fixing of its currency' would be granted exemption from full EMU. In addition the Dutch proposed a non-binding declaration of intent on a single currency, alongside the treaty, in which states would declare it was their 'strongest intention to participate in EMU without exemptions'.

However Norman Tebbit, speaking for many anti-federalist Conservative backbenchers, warned that even a treaty which left options open still amounted to a long-term commitment to abolish the pound. As such, it should be rejected. Douglas Hurd agreed, saying: 'We are not going to commit Britain to joining a system called stage three, with a single bank and single currency. We are not going to make that commitment'. He added: 'We will not reach agreement at Maastricht on the final shape of Europe. That will probably be for our children. What we will have to try to decide is whether there is enough common ground for a further worthwhile step forward. I think there is'. Another EC summit on the issue after Maastricht was possible but not desirable, because 'it would be much better to deal with this in an orderly way during the Dutch Presidency and get on with the next stages in the Community,' such as enlargement and farm reform.

However, Wim Kok, the Dutch finance minister, said that any country which opted out of stage three would have little or no say in such matters as the make up and powers of the European Central Bank. Delors and the Commission expressed concern about the opt-out clause, pointing out that if Germany as well as the UK took advantage of it, economic and monetary union would be postponed indefinitely.

At the end of October, Downing Street dismissed the concept of a non-binding declaration as 'irrelevant', but left open the question of whether Major would sign the formal Dutch draft treaty, including the opt-out clause. Major told the Commons that Britain belonged 'in the mainstream of Europe . . . We cannot dictate what our children will make of the Community, but we must leave them in a position where they can effectively influence the shape of Europe'. He added that on EMU,

> it would be irresponsible for any government to ask the people to decide now that we should adopt at a future date a single European currency which will have far-reaching implications for the conduct of monetary and economic policy. A move to a single currency which was not backed up by convergence between the economies of the member states of the Community would be a recipe for economic disaster . . . I am not prepared to commit our country now to a single currency. We must be able to judge nearer the time— Parliament must judge nearer the time—whether a single currency is in the interests of Britain.

The Maastricht summit

At Maastricht Major stuck to the 'opt-out' clause, observing that the conditions laid down for economic convergence were in any case such that it was 'highly uncertain' when a single currency would be introduced. The final wording of the EMU treaty, however, defined the 'irrevocable fixing of exchange rates leading to the introduction of a single currency, the ECU' as an EC goal, and the German press was quick to record—with pangs of regret and doubt—the 'end of the Deutschmark'. The second stage of EMU—economic and monetary convergence—was set for 1 January 1994, and stage three—the European Central Bank—for 1997. The general impression left was that a single currency was all but inevitable, and Britain had not so much 'opted out' as reserved the right to 'opt in' at a future date.

The Maastricht treaty called for a single monetary policy to maintain price stability, sound public finances and 'a sustainable balance of payments', all in accordance with the open market and free competition. To co-ordinate national economic policies, the Council of Ministers is required—by majority vote—to adopt 'broad guidelines' for economic co-ordination. The summit agreed a vague formula for bringing recalcitrant EC members into line: if any country's national economic policies prove inconsistent with the guidelines, thus jeopardizing EMU, the council will make the 'necessary recommendations' for action against the EC state concerned.

To govern monetary policy the treaty duly established a European System of Central Banks (ESCB) made up of a European Central Bank (ECB) and the central banks of the member states. The tasks of the ESCB are given as the implementation of EC monetary policy; the conduct of foreign exchange operations; and the management of member states' foreign reserves. The European Bank President and other senior officials are to be appointed by EC leaders for a limited term of eight years and will run the Bank, together with the governors of national central banks, in a Governing Council. The bank is defined as independent—on the model of the Bundesbank—and is expressly forbidden to take instructions either from EC institutions or from member state governments.

The treaty prohibits 'excessive budget deficits', and obliges EC states to report their 'planned and actual deficits' regularly to the European Commission, which in turn is to monitor compliance with budgetary discipline. Maastricht gave the Council of Ministers teeth with which to enforce compliance through a graded scale of measures including fines 'of an appropriate size' and a requirement that the offending state shall make a suitable deposit with the EC 'until the excessive deficit has been corrected'.

The second stage of EMU is defined as beginning in January 1994, by which date all member states will have abolished restrictions on the movement of capital not only between states (as in stage one) but between member states and third countries. Similarly, by the same date they will have adopted—'if necessary'—multi-annual programmes to ensure 'lasting economic convergence' and have begun the process of central bank independence. At the same time, excessive budget deficits must also be avoided. 1994 also sees the setting up of a European Monetary Institute (EMI) to strengthen central bank co-operation, help co-ordinate monetary policies and oversee the development of the ECU. Above all, the EMI will prepare the way for stage three and the European Central Bank, setting up the 'regulatory, organisational and logistical framework' for the ESCB by 31 December 1996 'at the latest'.

The third and final stage of EMU, including the introduction of a single currency, should be fixed during 1997. But if no date has been fixed by the end of 1997, 'the third stage will start on 1 January 1999'. Thereafter the value of the ECU will be 'irrevocably fixed', and the ECU will become 'a currency in its own right'. By 1 July 1998, six months before the single currency comes into effect, the Council is to agree by majority vote, not unanimity, which member states qualify, according to agreed criteria: a rate of inflation close (within 1.5%) to that of the three best performing member states in terms of price stability; a consistent avoidance of excessive budget deficits, the guidelines being budget deficits of less than 3% of GDP and government debt below 60% of GDP; satisfactory performance within the EMS over a two-year period, with no devaluation against any other member state currency; and satisfactory long-term interest rates, that is, no more than 2% above the average in the three EC states with the lowest interest rates.

The opt-out clause, or protocol, for the UK reads: 'the UK shall not be obliged or committed to move to the third stage of economic and monetary union without a separate decision to do so by its government and Parliament . . . Unless the UK notifies the Council that it intends to move to the third stage, it shall be under no obligation to do so.' A Danish opt-out clause similarly allows an 'exemption' for Denmark should a Danish referendum on the single currency result in a no vote.

On the other hand, another protocol notes that all twelve states have confirmed 'the irreversible character' of the move toward a third stage simply by signing the EMU treaty: 'Therefore all member states shall, whether they fulfil the necessary conditions for the adoption of a single currency or not, respect the will of the Community to enter swiftly into the third stage of EMU, and therefore no member state shall prevent the third stage'. It seems likely that Britain will qualify for stage three, and so will be in a position to opt for the single currency if it wants to. John Banham, director general of the CBI, commented that Major had achieved what British business wanted: 'Agreement on economic and monetary union which leaves the way open for UK participation in a single European currency, with steps to secure the more even enforcement of Community legislation, but without an extension of Community powers that could threaten international competitiveness'.

Checklist of changes

- A Second stage of EMU to begin 1 January 1994, involving economic convergence, avoidance of budget deficits, and the establishment of a European Monetary Institute to strengthen central bank co-ordination.
- Third stage of EMU (introduction of single currency and European bank) to be fixed by 1997, and to start no later than 1999. ECU to be the common currency: countries eligible to join must meet agreed criteria involving rates of inflation, interest rates, budget deficits and performance within the ERM.
- UK 'not obliged' to join in single currency without a decision to this effect by UK government and parliament.

10 MERGERS AND ACQUISITIONS

European competition and industrial policy

In its annual report on competition policy in June 1991, the European Commission warned that the abolition of internal barriers to trade would fail to improve the competitivness of European industry unless companies, particularly those hiding behind walls of government protection, were forced to go out and compete with their rivals across the Community. Signalling his determination to extend the Commission's newly won powers of enforcement to every corner of commercial activity, Sir Leon Brittan, the Competition Commissioner, reminded governments and the captains of industry that: 'National champions in the Middle Ages generally fell off their horses under the weight of their own armour'. The illustration was designed to highlight the Commission's determination to eliminate unauthorized government subsidies to industry and to clamp down on illegal restrictive and monopolistic practices, rather than wait for protected and inefficient industries to fail in the face of foreign competition.

From the outset of the internal market programme, the European Commission's overriding objective has been to break down the fragmentation of the European economy into twelve separate and often conflicting components and create a single, unified market of 320 million producers and consumers. In essence, it is a strategy designed to benefit European business. The Commission believes that companies traditionally boxed into their national markets should be free to break out of their national confinement and link up with other European firms, whether through mergers, joint ventures or acquisitions.

Paradoxically, the Commission has two ostensibly irreconcilable goals:

1 To promote the restructuring of the European economy by allowing the various industrial sectors to consolidate their operations across national frontiers, shut down excess productive capacity, enhance economies of scale and reduce costs, thereby acquiring the kind of industrial strength needed to compete with American and Japanese companies on a more equal footing;
2 To prevent these newly restructured industries from engaging in the kind of practices that have earned big business a bad name the world over, such as illegal market-sharing arrangements, the abuse of dominant market positions to extract monopoly profits and

attempts to prevent new competitors entering given markets.

The internal market programme would be an exercise in futility if, at the very moment national barriers to trade were levelled, European companies immediately set about raising them by introducing a new set of commercial barriers to trade and engaging in ingenious forms of anti-competitive behaviour. The Commission was fully aware that there is a contradiction between allowing companies to co-operate with each other across national borders when the temptation to abuse such freedom is likely to prove irresistible. However, it proposed to reconcile the irreconcilable by introducing a comprehensive competition policy, granting it the power to appraise all large-scale mergers which have a Community dimension and decide whether the proposed merger should be allowed to go ahead, whether the terms of the merger should be altered in the interests of free competition or whether it should be prohibited outright.

Under the provisions of the Treaty of Rome, the European Commission already possesses considerable powers to monitor certain categories of business activity. Article 85 prohibits as incompatible with the common market 'all agreements between undertakings, decisions by associations of undertakings and concerted practices which may affect trade between member states which have as their objective or effect the prevention or distortion of competition within the common market'. In short, any agreement or conspiracy by companies, individually or collectively, to fix prices, limit production or divide up the market is illegal, and it can be broken up before or after the event has taken place, and the offending companies subject to heavy fines. However, the Commission also has the power to give its approval to any restrictive practice where such an agreement 'contributes to improving the production or distribution of goods or to promoting technical or economic progress', an increasingly controversial area known as industrial policy.

Similarly, Article 86 states that 'Any abuse by one or more undertakings of a dominant position within the common market or in a substantial part of it shall be prohibited as incompatible with the common market in so far as it may affect trade between member states'. Consequently, any business abusing its dominant position can find itself the subject of a Commission investigation, and, if found guilty, be compelled to stop and made to pay a substantial fine. Article 86 also applies to mergers that would create a dominant position likely to be abused, but here the Commission can only act after the event has taken place, a limitation regarded by successive Competition Commissioners as the Achilles' heel of the Community's competition policy.

In the separate but related field of government subsidies to industry, known as state aids, Article 92 grants the Commission the power to make a prior decision whether (and at what level) aid can be given. It can also compel companies who have received state aid without the Commission's approval to pay it back. The Commission can, however, give approval to government subsidies where they are designed to promote economic development in areas of economic decline, but only the Commission is empowered to decide what government subsidies fall within this criterion.

Collectively, the ability to police restrictive market agreements, dominant market positions, mergers that are likely to lead to dominant market positions and state aids is an impressive range of powers at the disposal of the Commission to regulate competition within the Community. However, the Commission felt that its inability to scrutinize mergers before they have taken place is an obvious deficiency in its powers of competition enforcement. The deficiency had become extremely acute as companies, in anticipation of the creation of the single internal market in 1992, have developed an appetite for US-style merger mania which has already led to a large increase in cross-frontier mergers and takeovers in an effort to strengthen their competitive positions. The Commission has been engaged since 1973 in a frequently acrimonious struggle with the Council of Ministers to fill this gap.

A comprehensive merger control policy

Few would dispute that until Peter Sutherland, the former Irish Commissioner for Competition Policy, joined the Commission in 1984 the attempt to obtain approval from the Council of Ministers for a directive on merger control had been given a low priority. No-one knew how the 38-year-old softly spoken Irishman would shape up to his new job. But for anyone prepared to look into his background, there was more than enough to indicate that here was a man who was going to upset the system.

Born the son of an insurance broker, he was educated at University College, Dublin, and the National University of Ireland, before becoming a barrister at the Irish, English and New York Bars. As the youngest-ever Attorney General in the government of Garret FitzGerald, he is credited with almost single-handedly persuading the Irish courts that IRA terrorists should no longer be able to evade extradition on the specious grounds that their actions were political and not criminal. Mr Sutherland was Ireland's fourth Commissioner since it joined the Community in 1973, and was to become universally acknowledged as one of the most rigorous Competition Commissioners Europe has ever had.

His success could be said to stem from a lifelong predilection for a good fight. During his university days he had a passion for rugby, and it is said that he fractured his nose no less than nine times, but refused to stop playing the game. He was to carry this enthusiasm for the scrum into adult life, and, in the course of his four-year term as Commissioner, forced many powerful corporate leaders and national politicians to leave the industrial playing field nursing their own bloody noses.

Presenting the Commission's sixteenth annual report on competition policy in July 1987, Sutherland gave notice to member states that he was determined to revive the stalled 1973 draft directive on mergers and takeovers. If they could not agree by the end of the year, at least in principle, to the necessity of augmenting the Commission's powers, he would use the full force of Articles 85 and 86 to try to fill the gap. Sutherland insisted that the new powers were needed to protect consumer interests, prevent mergers which distorted competition and provide companies with a predictable and effective Community-wide legal framework within which mergers and takeovers could be conducted.

Only Britain and France expressed reservations about the Commissioner's aspirations for new powers, and were confident that his threat to exploit existing legislation was little more than bluff. Then in November a decision by the European Court of Justice added considerable weight to Sutherland's warning. The Court approved an earlier decision by the Commission to allow the US company Philip Morris to take over a large minority stake in the UK-based company, Rothmans International, in the face of a legal challenge by British American Tobacco and R. J. Reynolds, on the grounds that the deal was against the interests of free competition.

However, in granting its seal of approval for the deal the Court also said that the Commission had a legal obligation to investigate any merger or acquisition that could lead to the creation or consolidation of a market dominance, and thereby violate the Community's competition code. It was a watershed decision. Hitherto, the Commission was under the impression that its powers under Article 85 were limited to investigations of price-fixing or market-sharing arrangements. However, the Court said that Article 85 could also be applied to mergers and acquisitions which might restrict competition (before the merger or acquisition went ahead), a decision which partially made up for the limitations of Article 86 governing mergers, which specifies that the Commission can act only after the deal has gone through. Now the Commission had the power to approve all mergers or acquisitions, except those between companies who do not have a dominant market position and whose combination would not lead to the creation of a dominant market position.

At an Internal Market Council the following month all member states except Britain and France (both of whom already have highly sophisticated merger control arrangements) granted their approval in principle to a comprehensive Community merger control policy. The Commission was then instructed to explore ways of overcoming the reservations expressed by London and Paris. A new, revised draft directive on mergers and acquisitions was tabled in March 1988, proposing that the Commission should have the power to regulate all mergers where the combined turnover of the companies involved exceeded £690 million, except where the company being taken over had an annual turnover of less than £33 million, or where 75% or more of the merged companies were in a single member state.

The proposal also called for a system of prior notification, powers to make dawn raids on company premises in search of incriminating evidence, fines of up to 10% of the combined company profits if the directive was violated and a commitment to speed up the bureaucratic process so that companies would be given a decision on whether the merger or acquisition could go ahead within a six-month period. 'Is it really acceptable,' asked Sutherland at a conference on 1992 in Paris the same month,

> that the same mergers between different companies in different member states should be subject to differing national laws, with the distinct possibility that conflicting decisions will be reached resulting from the fact that member states could apply different criteria? At least for important concentrations, which can have an impact on the internal market, the Community should be allowed to intervene.

Sutherland went on to warn that:

> Without a Community system of merger control, the door will remain open to the possibility that economic concentrations will be created in Europe which escape the existing rules. Clearly, such an outcome would contradict the very objectives that underpin the single market strategy—namely the creation of an environment for maximizing economic efficiency, competitiveness and technological progress.

Replying to Sutherland at the annual dinner of the Confederation of British Industry in May, Lord Young, the then Secretary of State for Trade and Industry, insisted that '1992 will not call for a sea change in mergers policy—just a further evolution of the approach we have taken for many years', effectively ruling out any British concessions on the Commission's demand for a comprehensive merger control policy. In Luxembourg the next month France decided to join its European neighbours and accept, in principle, the need for such a policy, leaving Britain the only member state to refuse to do so.

The junior trade minister, Francis Maude, denied that Britain was isolated on the issue of merger control. Did this mean that the rest of the Community was isolated from Britain? The minister could not be drawn into a reply, and took refuge in the statement: 'We are not prepared to say yes to the principle before we know the final form of the proposal'. In all fairness to the embattled minister, Britain may have been isolated on the question of the principle, but a number of member states had previously expressed grave reservations about the details. France had indicated that the £690 million threshold was too low, and Britain was not alone in its anxiety that the six-month period for decisions could jeopardize prospective mergers, even if the Commission could adhere to it.

However, no-one was prepared for the bombshell dropped by John Banham, the Director General of the Confederation of British Industry (CBI). In a June statement that brought him into direct conflict with government policy, Banham warned that:

> If counter-productive xenophobic arguments about hostile takeovers are to be avoided, it is essential that clear ground rules are set out and observed. The only pan-European agency able to ensure fair play in a free market is the European Commission.

Not content with pre-empting Lord Young, Banham went on to claim that one of the major reasons that British companies had not been able to link up sufficiently in preparation for 1992 was a fear of violating Britain's highly discretionary merger laws. According to Banham, not only were new EC controls necessary but the government's failure to accept the principle and get down to negotiating over the details was crippling the Department of Trade and Industry's campaign to prepare British business executives for the arrival of the internal market. Europe may have been open for business, Banham suggested, but Britain was not open for Europe.

Sutherland failed to get a merger control directive passed during his term of office, but he had managed to push the issue to the top of the European agenda. Moreover, he had won over eleven of the twelve member states to his point of view, leaving the British government isolated in Europe and cut off from its own business community. Despite this failure, he was nonetheless extremely effective in deploying the full weight of the Treaty of Rome against both companies and governments seeking an unfair competitive advantage over their rivals in the Community. It was left to Sir Leon Brittan, Sutherland's successor, to complete the negotiations on the new merger control regulation—which would probably have been impossible had it not been for the groundwork prepared by the softly spoken Irishman.

Sir Leon takes the helm

Sir Leon Brittan arrived in Brussels under the cloud of the Westland helicopter affair of 1986, which brought his meteoric political career to an abrupt halt and cast him into the domestic political wilderness. Born the youngest son of a Lithuanian doctor who had emigrated to London in 1927, he was educated at Haberdashers' Aske's School, before going up to Trinity College, Cambridge, to read English and Law, where he obtained a double first. After becoming a highly successful barrister specializing in libel actions, Sir Leon was elected to Parliament in 1974, and rose to Cabinet rank within seven years. During that time he had moved from the 'wet' wing of the Conservative Party, where he had been chairman of the left-of-centre Bow Group, to become one of Mrs Thatcher's right-hand men. From the outset of his political career, however, he had been an ardent and vocal supporter of Britain's membership of the European Community.

Prior to Westland, Sir Leon's political career had not been without incident. After being appointed minister of state at the Home Office in 1979, he became associated with the now-notorious government pamphlet, *Protect and Survive*, which urged householders to whitewash their windows for protection in the event of a nuclear war. Two years later, without any formal training in economics, he was appointed Chief Secretary to the Treasury, and was exposed to the accusation of being under the influence of his elder brother, Samuel Brittan, the noted economist for the *Financial Times*. Similarly, Sir Leon's elevation to the position of Home Secretary in 1983 coincided with Mrs Thatcher's 'short sharp shock' initiative, winning him the dubious accolade as the minister for 'Laura Norder'.

However, it was Sir Leon's conflict with the then Defence Secretary, Michael Heseltine, over whether the ailing Westland helicopter company should be bought out by American or European interests, and the revelations of dirty dealing in high places that followed, that led to his resignation as Trade and Industry Secretary in January 1986. His supporters insisted that he had been the scapegoat needed to assure Mrs Thatcher's political survival. But despite his loyalty, the promised recall to the front benches from the Prime Minister never materialized. In 1988 Mrs Thatcher offered him the position of successor to Lord Cockfield as Britain's senior Commissioner. After some hesitation, he accepted, becoming the Commissioner for Competition Policy in 1989.

Although some expected Sir Leon to become 'Mrs Thatcher's Commission poodle', the British members of the Brussels' press corps lost no time in placing wagers on how long it would take Sir Leon to 'go native', as his predecessor was widely reputed to have done. From the perspective of Mrs Thatcher, that transition must have occurred with uncomfortable speed. Although consistently opposing radical proposals for a federal Europe, Sir Leon rapidly set about extending competition policy into the energy sector. In addition, he frequently issued calls for Britain's full membership of the ERM, urged the government to participate fully in the negotiations on economic and political union, and never flinched from criticizing Mrs Thatcher's abrasive attacks on Community 'personalities and institutions'.

The enforcement of Articles 85 and 86

One of the most effective powers available to the Commission (powers denied to the Office of Fair Trading under British competition law) is the ability to make dawn raids on companies suspected of abusing a dominant position or engaging in a conspiracy to restrict free trade. In December 1985 the European Court of Justice found that Akzo, the Dutch chemicals multinational, had been abusing its dominant position by undercutting its prices in an attempt to force Engineering and Chemical Supplies Ltd, a small Gloucestershire-based firm, to withdraw from the organic peroxides market. The managing director of the company could obtain little protection under British law from the predatory pricing activities of a foreign rival. However, after receiving a complaint from the ESC, the Commission made a dawn raid on the Dutch company's premises and obtained all the incriminating evidence needed to secure a conviction. Akzo was fined £6.4 million, the ESC was still in business and the whole episode demonstrated how the Commission was able to come to the rescue of a small British firm (or indeed a small company anywhere in the Community) in the name of free competition.

In April 1986 15 international chemical companies (including the British firms ICI and Shell) were fined £38.75 million between them for engaging in an illegal price-fixing and market-sharing arrangement in polypropylene between 1977 and 1983, in violation of Article 85 governing conspiracies. However, in August the following year the Commission gave its approval for ICI and the Italian company Enichem to form the European Vinyls Corporation, a joint venture that planned to shut down 300,000 tonnes of excess capacity. Together, the two cases highlighted the Commission's dual approach towards business combinations. Agreements designed simply to fix prices will not be tolerated by Brussels, but agreements seeking to promote industrial restructuring are likely to get the Commission's blessing.

Although in December 1987 the Commission had given provisional approval of the conditions laid down by the Monopolies and Mergers Commission for British Airways' £250 million takeover of British Caledonian, it still had an obligation to make sure that the merger did not restrict the access of other carriers to routes shared by the two merged airlines as soon as the deal had gone ahead, under the authority granted it by Article 86. Once the Airlines of Britain Group (made up of British Midland Airways, Manx Airlines, Loganair and Eurocity Express) complained that the merger would lead to a restriction of trade the Commission launched its official investigation. The Community's powers to regulate the air transport industry had been severely circumscribed until the approval of a package of measures the same month, granting the Commission tough powers to monitor competition between the European airlines. The BA–BCal merger thus became a test case of the Commission's new authority to regulate the air transport industry.

By March 1988, when the Commission had announced its conditions on which the takeover would be authorized, it was abundantly clear that Sutherland was determined to carry out his threat to use the Treaty's competition powers to the full. British Airways was forced to surrender most of British Caledonian's European network to its smaller competitors, accept limitations on its use of landing and take-off slots at Gatwick Airport and comply with restrictions on extending its monopoly at Heathrow. Although these conditions were to remain in force for only four years, they were significantly more stringent than those demanded by the Monopolies and Mergers Commission. The deal was a major concession by Lord King, the company chairman, and another success for Commissioner Sutherland.

However, the significance of the affair went beyond the problems for the personalities involved. It emphasized the shortcomings of national merger regulation and highlighted yet again the case for impartial and effective merger control arrangements at Community level.

The attempt in 1988 by Nestlé, the Swiss foods group, to take over Rowntree, the British confectionery manufacturer, produced a nationalistic reaction almost identical to that which followed the attempt by the Italian entrepreneur, Carlo de Benedetti, to take over the Belgian conglomerate, Société Générale de Belgique. Both sides were motivated by the 'buy now or get bought later' ethic that has dominated Europe in the past few years. According to Gary Hamel of the London Business School, the large increase in cross-border mergers and acquisitions was the result of a realization by European companies that 'By 1992, all the good-looking girls on the dance floor will have partners'.

At the same time, the two bids were a reminder that—at least psychologically—many businesses (and most member states) had yet to understand the implications of the European single market. Both bids were characterized as an assault on the very fabric of the nation by some outside predator intent on stealing a national asset. In an article in *The Times* in May 1988 Kenneth Dixon, the chairman of Rowntree, portrayed Kit Kat, Polo, Smarties and After Eight as an integral part of Britain's heritage, similar in stature only to the Crown Jewels, the Union Jack and the Houses of Parliament. The distinction between the company's interest and the national interest was lost completely, and the two concepts were projected as being identical and inseparable. By arguing (mistakenly, as it transpired) that the bid should be stopped because Swiss law prevented Swiss companies from being taken over by foreign companies, Dixon had inadvertently implied that if British companies enjoyed the same rights in Switzerland that Swiss companies enjoyed in Britain, he would have no ground to stand on. Likewise, de Benedetti (known in the Italian press as 'Carlo-Grab-It-All') was presented in Belgium as a swashbuckling marauder in search of foreign plunder. Observers felt that unless Société Générale was able to fend off the attack, Belgium would find itself under Italian domination.

In both cases the acquiring companies were not as predatory as the victims made out. Nestlé had been in Britain for 120 years, and as the manufacturer of Branston Pickle, Findus Frozen Foods and Nescafé coffee, was as much a part of the English cultural heritage as any box of Quality Street. Furthermore, it is simply not true that Swiss law prohibits foreign firms from taking over domestic ones. As Helmut Maucher, Nestlé's managing director, pointed out in his reply to Dixon's article in *The Times* the following week, Swiss companies can provide in their articles of association a provision granting them the right to refuse to register a shareholder, thereby making it extremely difficult for them to be taken over. However, companies who do this pay a heavy price, as unregistered shares trade at a much lower price than freely transferable ones. Besides, similar mechanisms are available to British companies seeking to protect themselves from unwelcome takeover bids.

Despite the rather colourful language of the Italian press, neither could de Benedetti be described as an avaricious raider. His companies, which include a variety of computer, publishing, car component, food and financial service concerns, employ over 100,000 people in Europe. Like Nestlé, his bid for a foreign company was motivated by a determination to be prepared for 1992. In the end, de Benedetti lost, and Nestlé was cleared by the Monopolies and Mergers Commission to go ahead with its bid for Rowntree. The experience of the two besieged companies was a salutary lesson for every other sleepy European firm that thought 1992 would not affect them. Sutherland could not intervene in either case, as there was no prima facie evidence for an investigation under the conspiracy or market dominance provisions of the Treaty. However, the bids demonstrated beyond doubt that, despite the promise of a European single market by 1992, economic nationalism remains a powerful force to be reckoned with by any company seeking to acquire firms in other member states.

While the Commission was unable to act in the Nestlé or de Benedetti bids, a bizarre combination of circumstances enabled it to intervene in the attempt by GC&C Brands to take over the Irish Distillers Group (IDG) with a £169 million bid before the deal went ahead—an event unprecedented in the history of Community competition policy. GC&C Brands, the consortium created in May 1988 by Grand Metropolitan, Allied Lyons and Guinness for the specific purpose of acquiring and then dismembering IDG, could barely disguise its surprise when it learnt on 29 July that the Commission was investigating it for conspiracy under Article 85. IDG, the makers of Jameson, Powers, Paddy and Bushmills whiskies, had complained to the Commission that GC&C was attempting to deprive its shareholders of the possibility of more competitive individual bids by creating the consortium.

In these circumstances the Commission's ability to approve mergers was not restricted to Article 86. Article 85 also applied, reinforced by the decision of the European Court of Justice over the Philip Morris case in November 1987. Commission officials could not recall another example of a joint venture takeover, but were delighted at the opportunity to show their strength in a takeover bid before it took place. The Commission's performance was widely seen as a test case, demonstrating how quickly and effectively it would be able to deal with mergers should the proposed directive on merger control ever get approval by the Council of Ministers.

The Commission issued its decision on 17 August—a record 20 days after the complaint was made—forcing the break-up of the consortium but allowing its individual members to go ahead with new individual bids. To emphasize the point, Sutherland issued a statement saying that: 'The Commission's intervention in the IDG case shows that it can and will act quickly and effectively to ensure that collusive practices restricting competition do not take place'.

Anyone who expected Sutherland's successor to relax his tough line against violations of Community competition policy was in for a rude awakening. In December 1990, ICI of Britain and Solvay of Belgium were fined a staggering £36 million—one of the largest penalties ever imposed by Brussels—for operating a cartel in soda ash, a raw material used in glass making.

The enforcement of Article 92

The Internal Market White Paper provides member states with a reminder of the Commission's declared intention to restrict illegal state aids with a rigorous application of Article 92. 'As the Commission moves to complete the internal market it will be necessary to ensure that anti-competitive practices do not engender new forms of local protectionism which would only lead to a re-partitioning of the market.' It goes on to point out that there is a tendency among some member states

> to spend large amounts of public funds on state aids to uncompetitive industries and enterprises. Often, they not only distort competition but also in the long run undermine efforts to increase European competitiveness.

Any government thinking that they were somehow exceptional was soon to receive a rude awakening. Initially, Delors had wanted Sutherland to adopt a soft line on government subsidies, but the Competition Commissioner insisted on a strict interpretation of the Treaty, and eventually got his way.

The Commission had already cut back large amounts of state assistance from the Community's ailing steel and ship building sectors before it turned its attention to the car industry. In March 1986 Sutherland launched an inquiry into plans by the German motor group, Daimler-Benz, to build a £577 million car plant in Baden Württemberg. The local authorities had offered to pay for the preparation of the greenfield site and connect the plant to essential services. The Commission insisted that the offer constituted an illegal subsidy, and the offer was eventually withdrawn.

In December 1987 the British government was forced to trim £70 million from its £750 million aid package for the Rover Group as a condition of the sale of Leyland Trucks to DAF of the Netherlands. Three months later it was the turn of the French government to come under the Commission's scrutiny. It was given permission to give the state-owned company, Renault, a £1.9 billion subsidy, somewhat smaller than the government had initially sought, but only on the condition that its status was changed from a public to a private company subject to commercial law. It was also made clear that failure to carry out this commitment would be met by a demand that the subsidy be repaid. When Roger Fauroux, the French Industry Minister, announced in September 1988 that he had decided to keep Renault's public status intact, Sutherland made it abundantly clear that such action would give the Commission no option but to withdraw its consent for the proposed debt write-off. If France decided to go ahead with this write-off it would be summoned to the European Court of Justice.

The Commission is also currently investigating a £9.7 million subsidy from the Italian government to Alfa Romeo in 1985 and the sale of Alfa Romeo to Fiat in 1986. It considers that the price paid by Fiat was much lower than the value of Alfa Romeo, and thus involved an undisclosed illegal subsidy. Despite the evident reluctance of the Italian government to have its state aids subject to external scrutiny, the Commission has refused to back down.

By the time the British government had completed its plans for the privatization and sale of the Rover Group to British Aerospace in March 1988 for £150 million there should have been no doubt in anyone's mind that the deal could only go ahead after receiving the seal of approval from Brussels under Article 92—but there was. Professor Roland Smith, the former chairman of British Aerospace, told MPs in parliament that if the Commission stepped in and demanded changes in Rover's proposed £800 million debt write-off he would pull out. Such talk may have been designed to intimidate the Commission, but it was to little avail. When the deal finally went through in July, Smith was forced to accept a £253 million reduction in the government's proposed cash injection into Rover.

The Commission had saved the British taxpayer millions of pounds in excess subsidy, and, as far as it was aware, had fulfilled its obligations to make sure that the disposal of a major public company did not confer an unfair advantage on the new owner in relation to other European enterprises operating in the same sector. The National Audit Office, however, subsequently accused the government of under-valuing Rover's assets, prompting the Commission to demand an explanation. A formal investigation was launched, and evidence of illegal actions by government ministers was disclosed.

Under the provisions of Article 92, Sir Leon had no option but to demand in June 1990 that the British government recover £44.4 million of illegal state subsidies or 'sweeteners' paid to British Aerospace when it acquired Rover in 1988. But, like the report by the House of Commons Trade and Industry Committee (which was also to investigate the sordid affair), Sir Leon was unable to find any evidence to justify Opposition allegations that Rover's assets were considerably undervalued. The case did, however, highlight the difficulty of deciding what is a fair price for an industry, especially if, as was the case with Rover, the government had ruled out competitive bidding. The government accepted the Commission's decision, although British Aerospace announced its intention to challenge the Commission's verdict in the European Court of Justice. When the case came before the Court in October 1991, Commission lawyers accused Lord Young of trying to hide millions of pounds in illegal government aid to British Aerospace. The court was told that Lord Young advised the chairman of BAE in writing to 'keep things quiet' or risk alerting the European Commission. Contrary to popular perceptions, the Commission's action was motivated by a desire to ensure that the competition rules were enforced equitably, not to make life difficult for Britain.

In July 1989, for example, the Commission approved a £731 million aid package for Short Brothers, the ailing Ulster-based aerospace company. The greater part of the package was for writing off accumulated debts and anticipated future losses, in an effort to make the company more attractive for sale to a foreign buyer—a practice traditionally disapproved by Brussels. However, because of the vital role the company plays in the economy of Northern Ireland, accounting for 10% of manufacturing employment in the region, the Commission was moved to make an exception to the rules against subsidies. Justifying its action, the Commission insisted that 'the social and economic consequences of a closure would be far reaching, and would inevitably result in a loss of confidence amongst potential outside investors who are crucial to Northern Ireland's economic development'. A year later, however, the Commission announced that it was launching a formal investigation into allegations that the £700-million plant being built in Derbyshire by the Japanese car manufacturer, Toyota, had received a hidden subsidy in the form of undervalued land for the new plant.

In addition to following the precedent of fighting illegal state aids and restrictive practices set by his predecessor, such as the new investigation launched against the European steel industry in April 1991, Sir Leon also began to apply the Community's competition regulations to areas hitherto untouched by Community Competition law, notably the energy sector. Aware that only 5% of Community electricity was traded across borders, the Council of Ministers approved a Commission proposal for a new electricity and gas transit directive in 1990, thus enabling power utilities in one member state to be able to buy and sell electricity and gas in another.

The 1990 power transit directive was limited to cross-border trade. Sir Leon's aims, however, are far more ambitious. They amount to little more than the total restructuring of the European electricity and gas industries. The Commission's objective is to enable large industrial consumers to shop around the Community for the cheapest source of supply; to oblige national electricity grids and pipeline networks to act as carriers between producers and consumers; and to increase competition by allowing new producers to enter the market. In March 1991 Sir Leon fired his opening shot. Letters were sent to the national electricity utilities in ten member states, requesting information on their compliance with the Community's competition laws. Following the privatization of Britain's electricity industry, only France, Ireland, Portugal, Italy and Greece have publicly owned electricity industries. Nonetheless, it is clear that the Commission is convinced that most are engaged in some form of monopolistic trade.

The initiative provoked a bitter debate throughout the Community over the liberalization of EC energy markets, especially after the European Court of Justice aproved the Commission's use of Article 90 to open protected markets with or without the approval of the Council of Ministers. Defending his action, Sir Leon said that 'such monopolistic companies have to justify their existence if they want to remain in business'. Competition, he added, 'and the freedom to export and import are essential components of the policies needed to create an internal energy market'. The move against the electricity sector was widely seen as a rehearsal for the more formidable task of opening up the Community's gas market. Here, however, the Commission will have to act with greater caution if liberalization is to avoid creating conditions of uncertainty, thereby threatening investment in new infrastructure, as happened in the United States.

Comprehensive merger control endorsed

Capitalizing on the groundwork laid by his predecessor, Sir Leon Brittan began to break new ground in the quest for a comprehensive merger control regulation. In January 1989, Lord Young, the then Trade and Industry Secretary, indicated that for the first time Britain was prepared to endorse new Community powers to approve all large-scale mergers. After his meeting with the 17-member Commission, Lord Young said that while Britain retained reservations about the proposed merger control regulation, it nonetheless accepted the necessity of avoiding the problem of 'double jeopardy', where mergers had to be approved by both national and Community authorities. He suggested that it might be possible to reach an agreement whereby large mergers were approved by the Commission while smaller ones would be left to national bodies such as the Monopolies and Mergers Commission. Although he gave no indication of the turnover threshold that might initiate a Commission investigation, it was clear that the end of the Commission's 16-year campaign for new powers to regulate mergers was in sight.

In April Sir Leon unveiled a new proposal which would grant the Commission powers to approve in advance all mergers where the combined turnover of the merged companies exceeded 5 billion ECUs (£3.5 billion). The revised turnover threshold was transitional, effective until 1992, when it would fall to 2 billion ECUs (£1.4 billion). After further talks in Brussels in October, Britain, France and Germany agreed on the 5-billion ECU turnover threshold tabled earlier by Sir Leon. Agreement on the compromise proved elusive, however, because of the determination of Italy and a number of smaller member states to hold out for a 1-billion ECU threshold, largely because they had little or no effective merger control apparatus of their own, rendering them reliant on Brussels for the enforcement of competition policy.

The Council of Ministers finally accepted the Commission's case for comprehensive merger control in December 1989, and the Commission's new powers came into effect in September 1990. Under the new regulation, the Commission has the authority to monitor all mergers where combined global turnover exceeds 5 billion ECUs, although mergers between companies with more than two-thirds of Community turnover in one member state are exempt. Companies are required to provide the Commission with prior notification of an intention to merge, along with copious amounts of business information. Firms failing to meet these requirements face fines of up to £50,000. The Commission then has one month to decide if the proposed merger is subject to the regulation, and four months to reach a decision on whether to 'bless or block' the combination.

The Commission monitored its first business merger under the new regulation in November 1990, when it gave approval for the link-up between Renault and Volvo, as part of the wider effort to restructure the European car industry. The procedure was completed without incident or delay. By September 1991, when the new merger control regulation had reached its first anniversary, 53 mergers had been approved. But it was the decision to block the proposed Franco-Italian takeover of de Havilland, the ailing Canadian aircraft manufacturer, which marked the first real test of the Commission's new powers. The Franco-Italian bid, the first to be blocked under the new regulation, was disallowed on the grounds that it would have created a 'powerful and unassailable dominant position in the world market for turboprop aircraft'. Sir Leon insisted that the acquisition would have simply increased the market share of the bidders without bringing improvements in competitiveness. But the decision caused bitterness in Paris and Rome, provoking demands for a revision of the merger control regulation.

Early indications suggest that most companies have adjusted to the Commission's new powers, and approve of the clear demarcation between national and Community merger control law. Nevertheless, much disquiet exists over other aspects of Commission competition policy. Apprehension over the proposed 13th directive on company law announced in January 1991 on the regulation takeovers is acute in Britain. Following the exposure of the international fraud carried out by senior executives of BCCI in the summer of 1991, Sir Leon announced that the Commission was to consider prohibiting certain kinds of corporate structure in an effort to prevent financial institutions from abusing the new commercial freedoms created by the internal market. BCCI had been able to sidestep direct regulation because it was not classified as a bank under Community law. But any attempt to tighten up the banking laws could provoke protests from the Community's powerful financial institutions. Finally, the Commission's determination to extend its control on illegal state aids, highlighted in July 1991 by the demand that governments provide financial information about national enterprises, can be expected to meet fierce resistance from countries like France and Italy, which continue to have large public-sector manufacturing and industrial interests.

The European Company Statute

Since June 1988, when Jacques Delors announced his intention to revive a long-standing Commission proposal to table plans for a European Company Statute as part of his personal commitment to add a 'social dimension' to the internal market programme, EC governments, companies and trades unions have been preparing for what promises to be a major showdown over the controversial issue of workers' rights.

In essence, the proposed European Company Statute would act as an alternative for companies currently required to register their existence and activities under national law. By incorporating under the European Company Statute, companies involved in cross-frontier mergers would be freed of the present requirement to adopt the company law of either member state. In addition to simplifying the legal situation, the Commission declared that the European Company Statute will also allow companies with operating losses in one member state to offset them against profits in another.

However, the proposal has a sting in its tail. In exchange for the benefits offered by the European Company Statute, companies would be required to accept certain minimum standards of worker participation in the running of the industries in which they are employed. Incorporation under the proposed legislation would be optional, not mandatory. The proposal has already received much criticism from Britain, which regards it as 'irrelevant', bitter opposition from UNICE, the European Employers' Federation, which fears it could become a millstone around the neck of European companies, and considerable scepticism from the European Trade Union Confederation, which insists that the proposals do not go far enough.

The idea of a European Company Statute is by no means new. The original proposal was made in 1970, following an initiative by France, but it proved so controversial that it was eventually shelved in 1982—a fate which befell all other attempts to revive the idea thereafter. It has, however, been brought back to life by Delors, in the conviction that the internal market programme could be placed in jeopardy unless the Community's workers believe that there is something in it for them too.

In a consultative document on the company statute circulated in the summer of 1988 the Commission outlined three models for worker involvement in company decision-making structures, each with varying degrees of worker participation. Officials have insisted that the proposal represents 'a modern approach for employer–worker relations through-out the EC', and that if consultations between governments, industry and trades unions showed enough support for the move, the Commission will go ahead and draft the legislation.

During preliminary discussions in Luxembourg in October 1988 the Commission expressed fears that, once the internal barriers to trade had been demolished, companies located in the more affluent Northern regions of the Community might be tempted to move some of their operations South, to avail themselves of cheaper labour costs and less stringent worker-protection legislation.

However, the Commission's argument received a hostile reception from member states anxious about the consequences of imposing new burdens on recently deregulated business, and from those who feared that the European Company Statute could provide a loophole enabling companies to bypass their own more restrictive worker-protection legislation. Francis Maude, the junior trade minister, told his European colleagues that the government had already consulted British companies about the proposal, and most saw little or no need for company law to be harmonized throughout the EC.

In her forthright speech in Bruges the previous month, Mrs Thatcher warned that the Community 'certainly does not need new regulations which raise the cost of employment, and make Europe's labour market less flexible and less competitive with overseas supplies'. The Prime Minister went on to state that if Europe was to have a company statute it must contain the least possible regulation, and warned that Britain would fight any attempt to introduce 'collectivism and corporatism' at the European level.

The European social dimension

Alongside the Commission's attempt to secure approval for the Company Statute lies a related but separate effort to give the 1992 impluse a human face in the form of what has become known as the 'social dimension.' In essence, this is an attempt to ease the social consequences of market deregulation with improved protection for workers. After his speech to the TUC in Bournemouth in September 1988, Jacques Delors won over the anti-EC tendencies in the British trade union movement, thereby helping to create a clear division on social policy between Labour and the Conservatives. But the conversion of the British trade union movement to what the Conservatives dismissed as 'continental type socialism' led to even more bitter exchanges between the two parties. In the run-up to the Madrid summit in June 1989, Mrs Thatcher increased her assault on the social dimension by declaring: 'From the accounts that I have received about the social charter it's more like a socialist charter.' As a result when in 1989 the other eleven member states decided to implement the Social Charter, Britain decided to exclude itself.

Mrs Thatcher's departure from the European stage in November 1990 and replacement by John Major was accompanied by expectations in Brussels of a more measured approach by Britain towards Community social legislation. Initially, the omens appeared favourable. In January 1991, after accusing Britain of jeopardizing the internal market because of its opposition to the social charter, Vasso Papandreou, the Employment Commissioner, noticed what she called 'a change of style' following talks with Michael Howard, the Employment Secretary. During the talks, Howard had agreed to the social charter 'in so far as it generates employment', but he reiterated the British government's view that some of the proposals would 'add to business costs'.

In April the Commission recommended the creation of a formal employee consultation machinery for companies with workforces in more than one member state. The recommendation was a greatly watered-down version of the proposed Vredeling directive of 1980. It was, nonetheless, rejected, and was met by a counter-proposal from Howard for consultation procedures based on a voluntary approach. Howard's proposal was then dismissed by Norman Willis, the TUC General Secretary, as a 'smokescreen'. By now, many commentators felt that Britain and the Commission had become locked in a sterile debate on industrial relations more appropriate to the 1970s than the 1990s. An article in the *Financial Times* the same month, while sympathetic to the goal of improved worker–management relations, doubted that legislation was the correct way to bring it about, especially as Japanese management techniques, involving employees directly in working arrangements, were in the process of transforming British industry.

However, while Howard's opposition to worker-participation schemes appeared to generate little interest in Britain, his opposition to other elements of the social dimension proved more controversial. Opposition to Commission proposals in June to grant working women 14 weeks' paid maternity leave and impose a 48-hour ceiling on the working week provoked an outcry. The media were quick to point out that Britain has one of the poorest records for maternity provision in the Community, second only to Greece's. Howard insisted, however, that the Commission's proposals would cost employers millions of pounds a year in additional costs, while at the same time impairing the employment prospects of large numbers of people.

Although Britain's negotiating style had become more conciliatory since the fall of Mrs Thatcher, it was clear by the autumn of 1991 that the Conservative government could not reconcile itself to the Commission's vision of a new social dimension or social charter for Europe. Ministers no longer fought over every aspect of social policy, but they continued to object strongly to a dozen or so of the charter's 50-odd legislative proposals. By and large, proposals in the field of improved health and safety caused little difficulty. But where those proposals extended to social policy or industrial relations, Britain remained hostile. During the Maastricht summit in December, the impasse forced Britain's European partners to opt for an inter-governmental accord embracing the aspirations set out in the social charter, thereby avoiding a political showdown.

Checklist of changes

- Proposals to grant the European Commission new powers to monitor all large-scale cross-frontier mergers with a combined turnover of £3.5 billion have now been approved.
- The Commission will continue to exercise all its powers to appraise state aids to companies in both the private and public sectors in order to prevent governments engaging in anti-competitive practices.
- An optional European company statute, enabling companies involved in cross-frontier mergers to incorporate under European rather than national law, will also be introduced, along with measures designed to facilitate some degree of worker participation in company decision making.
- New health and safety standards governing working practices will be introduced. Measures to increase worker rights will also be implemented, but they will not apply to Britain.
- A series of measures aimed at providing European companies with a common framework for conducting their operations will be implemented, including a Community trade mark, a European patent law and legislation harmonizing variations in national audit and fiscal procedures.

11 OBJECTIONS TO THE SINGLE MARKET

Arguments against 1992 from Right and Left

The programme for the completion of the single market by 1992 is designed to benefit businesses, consumers and travellers, but it does not arouse universal enthusiasm. There are fears that free movement will help criminals and terrorists in Europe and (mostly on the centre and right of the political spectrum) that 1992 will entail a serious loss of national sovereignty and enmesh Britain in European-style socialism. John Major's new style on Europe has, to some extent, calmed Euro-fears on the Right. But many still believe that, as Mrs Thatcher put it at Bruges:

> It is ironic that just when those countries such as the Soviet Union which have tried to run everything from the centre are learning that success depends on dispersing power and decisions away from the centre, some in the Community seem to want to move in the opposite direction. We have not successfully rolled back the frontiers of the state in Britain only to see them re-imposed at a European level.

The Left, while on the whole approving of 1992 after initial hostility, fears that cross-border activity by multinationals will benefit big business rather than ordinary employees, and lead to the erosion of workers' rights and health and safety standards—the 'social dimension'. Many business executives, for their part, fear that their companies will suffer commercial losses, or even fail.

Most of the critics of 1992 accept that, in Mrs Thatcher's words, 'by getting rid of barriers, by making it possible for companies to operate on a Europe-wide scale, we can best compete with the United States, Japan and the other new economic powers emerging in Asia and elsewhere'. This is the Government's view of a Europe 'open for enterprise'. However, not all sectors of industry share this view. DRI Europe, an international forecasting group, claimed in a report issued in July 1988 that the advent of the single market would not bring benefits on the scale envisaged by the Commission, least of all in sectors struggling for survival, such as the car industry. Harmonization of technical standards for and taxes on cars would be slow and incomplete, the report said. The 1992 programme did not envisage a policy for dealing with import threats from outside the Community. There would be cross-border trade distortions if VAT rates on cars were not brought into line, and companies such as Fiat and Renault could suffer sales losses so heavy that the French and Italian governments might try to maintain special restrictions on imports to protect them. Some fear that cross-border mergers in fields from banking to manufacturing will create Euro-conglomerates which will overpower small and medium-sized enterprises (SMEs) unable to compete in terms of resources and capital, even though the Single European Act specifically acknowledged the need to help SMEs in 1992.

The loss of national sovereignty

Even if such gloom is exaggerated, the 1992 process has aroused a widespread feeling (often nurtured by the tabloid press in Britain but also expressed by politicians and commentators) that power is ineluctably slipping out of the hands of national authorities and into those of faceless Eurocrats in Brussels. Pro-European Conservatives like Sir Geoffrey Howe argue that sovereignty is a 'flexible, adaptable organic notion which evolves and adjusts with circumstances'. When Mrs Thatcher resigned, the *Sunday Times*, in an editorial headed 'A Reluctant Goodbye', declared that her determination to defend the British pound and parliament rested on 'misplaced chauvinism', adding: 'It lacks vision or encouragement for our entrepreneurs, who have to trade with Europe, or for the brightest and best of our young, whose careers will increasingly depend on Europe'.

However, some Tories still resent what they see as a transfer of power to Brussels symbolized by plan for a single currency. Sir Keith Joseph wrote in *The Times* on 26 September 1991 that the notion of 'one market, one currency . . . suggests what is false—that a single market can come only with a single currency—and suppresses what seems to be true—that one currency means one government'. In other words, a Europe with a single currency controlled by a European Bank would lead to a European supranational government. Mrs Thatcher continued to speak out in similar terms after her resignation, observing on a tour of the United States in August 1991 that 'Our parliament is 700 years old, and, if its powers are curtailed, then that means curtailing the powers of the British people'.

The Times noted in a leader in June 1991 that, in practice, national sovereignty was eroded by 'every treaty, every negotiation, every military alliance'. But, it added, there are

> thresholds of sovereignty, points at which national electorates lose control over certain economic and political activities . . . Modern nations are not archaic embarrassments to some new international consciousness. They are real expressions of democratic feeling; if suppressed or neglected they will fight back, as they are doing to the East.

Roger Scruton, defining Englishness for the BBC2 series *Think of England* maintained that the English people, 'the most eccentric of peoples', had

> cast away its quirky weights and measures, standardized its goods, forsworn its right to control its frontiers or determine who should dwell within them, subjected its historic common law to the half-baked reasoning of foreign judges, conferred on foreign bureaucrats unlimited right to trample on its national customs, deprived its sovereign of the power to govern and cancelled the centuries-old right of its Parliament to advise, correct and control her.

The case was perhaps best put by Brian Walden, the columnist, in the *Sunday Times* in July 1988, under the headline 'The line must be drawn at rule by Brussels'. After establishing his European credentials ('I admire Dutch tolerance, German cleanliness and efficiency, Italian family life and love of children, French worldliness and realism') Walden continued:

> But a nation is not a mere social arrangement that can be submerged into something better at the whim of planners and bureaucrats. The UK has not managed to solve its own nationality problems . . . Creating a single government for Western Europe is an infinitely more difficult operation than holding the UK together.

Comment of this kind has been encouraged by Delors' observation in June 1988 that an 'embryo' European government would emerge in the 1990s, and that 80% of economic and social legislation would be decided at the European level within ten years. The 1992 programme itself envisages no such development, since it is confined to the creation of the internal market. However, the critics have noticed that the process will not necessarily stop there. As Walden remarked:

> There is no point in subjecting Delors to an abusive tirade, because much of what he says is true. The creation of a single market is bound to mean that many decisions affecting our economic and social life will be taken in Brussels and Strasbourg. British politicians have been very slow to visualize what the new Europe will mean for national parliaments and national sovereignty . . . But I draw the line at a single European government.

The British people, Walden said, had not agreed to such a move when they voted in the 1975 EC referendum:

> and were specifically assured by several pro-Europeans, including me, that no such political arrangement was intended. We must

dig in our heels, before the EC is ruined by the haste and intemperance of political dreamers.

On a different level, the popular press has presented a picture of Britain surrendering sovereignty to Brussels. In August 1988 the *Star* newspaper carried a front-page headline reading '1992 Euro shocker', listing three points: 'Dearer clothes, food and power; our athletes to join Euro-team; Our troops to take orders in German'. 'Mrs Thatcher does not run Britain any more,' the report began:

Nor does the Government. The Civil Service is powerless, and the highest courts in the land can be overruled. This is not the nightmare scenario of George Orwell's *1984*, it is the amazing reality of what life will be like in 1992. For that is the year when Britain will virtually disappear into a United States of Europe.

The *Today* newspaper brought this up to date in June 1991 with what it called 'Delors' Charter':

Finger on our nuclear button in Belgium; taxes and VAT paid straight to Brussels; beer served in litres, yards become metres; British police become part of FBI-style force; our soldiers serve in European Army; compulsory Saturday schooling in German.

A favourite tabloid tactic is to add to such predictions some of the more eccentric proposals advanced by fringe elements in the EC, such as a small group of Euro MPs (who have little real power) obliging British motorists to drive on the right or to cut their lawns between midday and 2 pm on Sundays.

While such reporting has little serious aim (apart from the arousal of indignation) there is genuine political concern among some commentators that by signing the Single European Act EC leaders have gone too far, and have created a monster which may get out of control. The tone was set by the debates in the Commons and Lords in 1986 as the Single European Act passed through both Houses of Parliament. Writing in *The Times* in May 1986, Sir Edward du Cann, MP for Taunton and president of the Conservative European Reform Group, summed up the Act as follows:

The directive powers of the Commission are to be massively enhanced, the national veto is to be reduced in scope, progress toward European political union is to be accelerated. Thus, whether British people approve or disapprove, the establishment of a European super-state is under way.

Sir Edward added: 'Almost overnight and largely unnoticed by our fellow citizens, Britain's right to decide many practical matters, even her own destiny, is being surrendered to the majority vote and the interests of other nations not all of whom share our parliamentary traditions'.

The House of Lords Select Committee appointed to scrutinize the Act concluded that 'in the long term the position of the UK Parliament will become weaker'. Two eminent QCs, Peter Horsfield and Leolin Price, in *The Times* the same month said that the Act involved profound constitutional changes and was a step towards European political union. In the House of Commons this view was most forcefully expressed by Teddy Taylor, Conservative MP for Southend, and a noted anti-Common Market campaigner. 'It would surely be in our national interests if the EC were to resolve its existing problems and implement its existing agreements before seeking further powers,' Taylor wrote to *The Times*:

> Is it wise to give even more power to the EC, which has so abysmally failed to resolve the crisis in its agricultural policy . . . ? More majority voting will simply mean more Euro laws being applied to the UK, which could well be wholly against our wishes or our interests. If this is not a major step towards federation, I wonder what is.

Paul Johnson, the columnist and historian, complained in *The Times* of public apathy as 'fundamental and irreversible changes' were pushed through, partly because of 'the sheer soporific effect of the leaden jargon with which the EC conceals its doings'. The Act was:

> a completely new treaty, which ought properly to have been placed on a level of significance equivalent to that of the original Treaty of Rome . . . When Britain joined the EC we had to accept that membership would involve some limitations to our national sovereignty. But the understanding was that these limitations were finite . . . and that any further limitations would be carefully negotiated by us from a position of strength within the EC.

As the Act passed over the final hurdle at Westminster, approval by the Lords, Lord Denning, former Master of the Rolls, warned that the aim of the Act was 'to transform Europe into a single nation with its own Parliament and its own legislation'. Westminster would become a 'subordinate body'.

For many, the EC is a 'fact of life', but one reluctantly accepted. British assertions of national sovereignty are greeted hypocritically on the Continent, right-wing critics say, since the French and other Europeans are adept at advancing their own national interests while claiming to be *communautaire*. According to Oliver Letwin, formerly a member of the Prime Minister's Policy Unit, fair competition and free movement of capital and labour within the EC under the 1992 programme are welcome, but have to be balanced against the fact that—as Enoch Powell once warned—Britain is losing its national autonomy:

> The idea that a majority group of French, West German, Italian, Belgian, Spanish, Portuguese and Irish ministers sitting behind closed doors in Brussels could pass what is effectively binding legislation on Britain, with our own parliament powerless to intervene, would have struck anyone as a crazy proposition until recently. But this crazy proposition is now a fact.

In September 1988, *The Spectator* declared, after the row over the sacking of Lord Cockfield, that 'there is nothing to be gained from isolation from the Continent, and much to be said for institutionalized co-operation between powers which are geographically and politically close and on the whole friendly'. But it added that it was lukewarm about the European idea:

> Will people really accept that their lives can be ordered by Brussels? Will they only be prepared to accept this if Brussels is controlled by a powerful European Parliament? If so, what will be left of our own Parliament?

The *Sunday Telegraph* editor, Peregrine Worsthorne, argued that much right-wing opinion on the Continent is all too ready to accept 'collectivist' views of 1992, because:

> Quite simply they are not conservative in the way Mrs Thatcher is conservative. They are for the most part Christian Democrat, with deep roots in Catholic social and economic doctrine, which is light years away from Mrs Thatcher's brand of free enterprise economic and social doctrine.

Strong centralizing traditions are common to Left and Right on the Continent, 'making Leon Blum, the great French socialist, at one with Bismarck, the great German reactionary'.

Professor Elie Kedourie of London University, a noted authority on nationalism, agreed that the problem goes wider than arguments over harmonization. Writing in *The Times* in September 1988, he made the point that:

> Whether through good luck or the wisdom of its political leaders, Britain has enjoyed for generations now a stable, constitutional mode of government in which the citizen has not had to fear for his freedom and where legality is the accepted norm and test for all

official action. This is far from having been the case on the
Continent where, since the French Revolution, a disagreeable,
visionary and destructive style of politics has been in the habit of
now and again erupting,

Spain, Greece, Italy and Germany all offer examples of instability and
extremism. 'What is to hold such a disparate union together?' Kedourie
asked. Writing in *The Independent*, Sir William Rees-Mogg, a former editor
of *The Times*, suggested that Delors was trying to impose a socialist view
of 1992, yet 'the European Commission has no remit to re-impose by
subterfuge what Britain has thrown off after disastrous experience'.
Anti-Brussels feeling emerged during the European election in 1989,
following the Government's warning to Brussels not to 'interfere' beyond
its powers. *The Economist* commented that Mrs Thatcher's 'blind spot'
about Europe was lethal, and she was 'ignoring the fact that much of
what is happening in Western Europe is excellently Thatcherite and will
continue to be if only she has the sense to embrace it with a bit of
Continental warmth instead of treating it to unending English *froideur*'.
James Elles MEP wrote in *The Times* on 26 June 1989 that 'The objective
of the EC is not just simply to create an internal market. It is a means by
which its member states can move, step by step, towards closer European
integration, without actually specifying the destination'. But precisely
because of this, thirteen academics, led by Lord Harris of Highcross,
chairman of the Institute of Economic Affairs, in 1989 formed 'The Bruges
Group'—more properly, The Campaign for a Europe of Sovereign States
—to oppose European union in the spirit of Mrs Thatcher's Bruges
speech. (The group had been initiated earlier by an Oxford under-
graduate.) Edward Heath declared that 'any intelligent Conservative'
could support a sharing of sovereignty, adding: 'Of course, if you go to
a member of the British public and say, do you want your British pound
and British pint of beer taken away by a lot of nasty foreign Marxists he
will indignantly reply that no, he does not. But I believe the British
public reject such false popularism, such distortions of the truth for the
patronizing, self-serving hypocrisy that they are'. Jonathan Aitken MP
replied that Britain was in danger of surrendering its sovereignty 'almost
through sleepwalking'. Aitken said he was 'madly in favour of Europe',
with a European wife, children born in Europe and 'lots of European
friends'. But 'I am amazed at the willingness of some politicians to apparently throw out 900 years of constitutional history, headed by a sovereign
parliament, in favour of what is still a European Blancmange . . . The
Single European Act has been used by Delors and many others as a new
Meccano set for constitutional, financial and legal experiments, a good
many of which will turn out to be very damaging to this country' (*London
International*, Summer 1989).

Democratic accountability

Criticisms of this kind carry a great deal of force and express widespread concern about integration. On the other hand, the Act was extensively discussed in Britain and other EC countries (as the comments themselves show) and it was ratified democratically. There was no secret about what it contained. According to an opinion poll published in *The Mail on Sunday* in September 1988, after Mrs Thatcher's speech in Bruges, many Britons now accept a degree of integration with Europe and an erosion of sovereignty. The key question is how the resulting European institutions can be subjected to popular control. The Single European Act does provide for qualified majority voting in the Council of Ministers, and to this extent involves a loss of national sovereignty. On the other hand, joining the EC in the first place entailed some loss of sovereignty, and most supporters of European integration argue that by pooling sovereignty the EC becomes stronger and so more able to promote the interests of all its members. National governments, moreover, retain the right of veto in many vital areas, since the majority voting system applies to internal market matters only. However, there is a widespread perception that EC institutions must be more tightly controlled as European influence in our lives and work increases.

Some anti-EC feeling and comment reflects an unexpressed regret that Britain took the decision to join the Community in 1973. Others accept that EC accession was the right step, but regret that Mrs Thatcher subsequently put her name to the Single European Act, thus allowing the EC to take the process of integration a stage further. However, while such regrets are perfectly legitimate they can have no practical impact, since both the Accession Treaty and the Single European Act are accomplished facts, legally drawn up and ratified after long debate and negotiation. Britain, in the words of one senior EC diplomat, has 'passed the point of no return'.

The answer to fears of loss of control over our daily lives must therefore lie in increasing democratic control over the institutions of the EC, to ensure that EC developments meet British interests and concerns. This is the solution proposed, among others, by Bill Newton Dunn, Conservative MEP for Lincolnshire. The major omission in the 1992 programme, in Newton Dunn's view (which is widely shared by all parties in the European Parliament) is the lack of any provision for ensuring that, as integration proceeds, so democratic control over EC decision making is increased. Proposals are scrutinized at every stage as they pass through the decision-making procedures, particularly when they are approved by European Parliament committees. Nonetheless, in the final analysis decisions are made and proposals passed into law during deliberations of the Council of Ministers, which are confidential.

The argument for retaining confidentiality is that the Council of Ministers is not only a legislature but also a negotiating body, in which minis-ters win and concede points in a way likely to be impaired if the proceedings were made public. British Cabinet proceedings are not open to the press, the argument runs, so neither should those of the EC Coun-cil of Ministers be exposed to the public gaze. In any case, EC ministers all come from national parliaments and are therefore democratically accountable in their own countries.

However, the development of the 1992 process seems bound to lead to further demands for 'accountability', with at least partial media accession to Council meetings, instead of the present system under which Brussels-based correspondents are briefed by national spokesmen and have to find the whole picture (in so far as it can be found) by cultivating official contacts.

On 25 July 1989, as the newly elected European Parliament assembled for the session leading up to 1992, *The Times* noted that Conservative Euro MPs had for the first time been invited to hear the Prime Minister report to the 1922 Committee to increase MEP–MP liaison, but added:

> In practice, Westminster's machinery has been overwhelmed by the quantity and detail of European regulation. The European Parliament has remained weak. In the gap between lies the 'democratic deficit' . . . The approach to monitoring EC regulations taken so far by most Westminster MPs must rapidly change. The work of the select committee on European legislation and debates in the House are adequate only for considering general principles. EC matters need to cease being an alien subject and to be dispersed where they belong—an integral part of almost every aspect of national life considered by the House of Commons.

Attitudes on the Left

The demand for democratic accountability has also been taken up by the political left, and above all by the Labour Party, which, after a long period of hostility towards the EC, has given its support to the 1992 programme while at the same time seeking to ensure that the internal market not only benefits big business but also protects the rights of employees. Most of the Labour Party Group in the European Parliament, paradoxically, remains virulently anti-EC, but national Labour policy has altered.

The key event in the emergence of Labour's new policy was the decision at the beginning of 1988 by Neil Kinnock, the Party leader, to abandon Labour's previous commitment to withdrawing Britain from the EC if it won power. The intellectual ground for the change was prepared in a Fabian pamphlet written by David Martin, MEP, then leader of the Labour Group at Strasbourg, and published in February 1988, which argued that Labour should work with other socialist parties in Europe to 'bring common sense to the Common Market'. The aim, the pamphlet said, should be to increase social spending, redistribute resources as 1992 brought greater prosperity and protect the EC environment. In a preface Kinnock wrote: 'It is surely realistic to acknowledge that Britain's integration with the other European economies by 1990 will have proceeded so far that talk of economic withdrawal is both politically romantic and economically self-defeating'. The aim of socialism, Kinnock declared, was to 'prevent the hardship, exploitation and waste which can result from the operation of unregulated markets'. Labour's view of 1992, in other words, is diametrically opposed to that of the Right, which—in Kinnock's eyes—'puts profit before people'. He concluded that if the Left did not take part in 1992 there would be

> unimpeded movement to the complete economic and political domination of Western Europe by market power, with all of the effects on civil rights, environmental conditions, individual opportunities and collective provision which that implies.
> Leaving the European field to that is no more acceptable than leaving Britain to permanent Thatcherism.

On a visit to Brussels in February 1988 Kinnock followed this up by declaring flatly: 'The prospects for withdrawal in my view are nil'. In September 1988, in a speech to Labour Euro MPs in Glasgow, Kinnock urged all socialists to take part in 1992, remarking: 'If the single market was to mean nothing other than a big finance free-for-all, it would be a social, industrial and environmental catastrophe'. At the Labour Party Conference in Blackpool in October 1988 Kinnock took much the same line, accusing the Government of 'pathetically inadequate' preparations for 1992, and declaring that social justice had to be a central component of the single market if it was not to benefit rich regions and become 'expensive, ugly, a constant source of waste, and a constant source of tension between peoples'.

This appears to be accepted by a broad spectrum of left-wing opinion. In an article in the July–September 1988 issue of *The Political Quarterly* entitled 'Beyond One Nation Socialism: An Agenda for the European Left' Frances Morrell, former leader of the ILEA and a noted left-winger, argued that it was a mistake to examine the reasons for Labour's electoral decline, such as the loss of traditional working class support, in national rather than European terms:

> The shaping of Europe should not be abandoned to the Right. Labour, and indeed all Social Democratic Parties out of office, have a duty to oppose and to lead.

In July 1989 Glyn Ford, new leader of the Labour MEPs at Strasbourg, moved still further from Labour's anti-EC line, saying the Conservatives were 'hardly European' whereas 'we represent the party that is determined to work within the EC'. Kinnock supported this when visiting Strasbourg the same month, but, like Thatcher, was cautious on the pace of economic and monetary union.

In the run-up to the 1992 general election, Kinnock and the Labour Party faced a dilemma in opposing Major and the Conservatives. Though seeking to capitalize on the Tories' difficulties over Europe at the same time they could not afford to be seen as any more 'integrationist' than the government. Kinnock observed of schemes for federalism that 'any attempt to superimpose political union from the top is bound to end in tears'. Equally, monetary union could impose 'tortuous pressures on the British economy'. Kinnock endorsed the concept of a European Bank, but said that exchange rate interventions would have to be supervised by EC finance ministers. George Robertson, Labour spokesman on European affairs, warned that the market could not be left to tackle problems of education, environment or transport: 'At a European level, if you are going to have a single market, then you have to have control'. At the Labour Party conference in October 1991 Kinnock declared that a Labour government would put Britain in the 'first division' of Europe, remarking:

> People look at our society, and they look at our neighbours in the rest of the Community. They see the high standards of training, the quality of child care, the investment in public transport, and they ask: 'Why not here?'

The social dimension: a 1992 Workers' Charter?

Kinnock's lead has been followed by the trades union movement, whose espousal of 1992 was given great encouragement in September 1988, when Delors travelled to Bournemouth to appeal to the TUC to back the internal market. In doing so Delors—a French socialist—indirectly criticized the interpretation of 1992 advanced by Mrs Thatcher, and lent support to the Left's campaign for a 'social dimension'. 'It is impossible to build Europe only on deregulation,' he declared, to an ovation from the trades union delegates:

> 1992 is much more than the creation of an internal market abolishing barriers to the free movement of goods, services and investment. The internal market should be designed to benefit each and every citizen of the Community. It is therefore necessary to improve workers' living and working conditions, and to provide better protection for their health and safety at work.

He assured the TUC that he believed in 'social dialogue and collective bargaining' as pillars of a democratic society. These assertions won Delors

TUC backing and the affectionate sobriquet 'Frère Jacques' (Brother Jacques). He had ceased to be, in the eyes of the Left, a soulless and overpaid international bureaucrat and had become the champion of the workers as the single market approached.

The significance of the change of heart in the Labour Party and the TUC lies partly in its impact on British politics. However, given the Conservative Party's current dominance of British politics, in the long run the most important impact of left-wing thinking on 1992 will be in the European context, where socialist parties are stronger and where some are in power. At the TUC in September 1988, Ron Todd, of the Transport and General Workers Union, speaking for the TUC General Council, called on British trades unionists to link up with their European counterparts to ensure that 1992 was moulded in the right direction. Todd admitted that the TUC had once been 'sceptical about there being any benefits in the European dimension'. But he added:

> The only card game in town at the moment is in a town called Brussels, and it's the game of poker . . . We've got to learn the rules, and pretty fast.

The TUC agreed to set up links with Continental unions to explore the possibilities of Europe-wide collective bargaining with employers, and called on the European Commission to produce a 'European Workers' Charter' to protect employees in cross-border mergers and takeovers.

Such a charter has been considered by the European Commission, and is favoured, in one form or another, by several of the EC countries which at present have socialist administrations. As it happens, three of them—Greece, Spain and France—hold the presidency of the EC Council of Ministers consecutively. Felipe Gonzalez, the Spanish Prime Minister, who held the Presidency in the first half of 1989, is an enthusiastic proponent of the 'social dimension'. When Mrs Thatcher visited Madrid in September 1988 she expressed her opposition to new Europe-wide regulations on company law and worker participation in industry, remarking that the EC term 'social space' was imprecise:

> It is a new piece of jargon. I am never quite sure what it is. But if it means having a regulation on Community company law, then I would oppose that particular thing. I am a democrat and I am a meritocrat and I believe you get on by merit, not by giving particular privileges to one particular group.

Gonzalez, however, insisted that a social dimension to 1992 was indispensable, with employees' rights protected and with help for the socially and economically disadvantaged.

The social dimension figured prominently in the European election campaign, when Michael Meacher, the then Labour employment spokesman, leaked details of a report by a group of EC lawyers showing that Britain lagged behind other EC countries in rights of workers to annual leave, minimum wages and working hours. Norman Fowler, then the Secretary of State for Employment, retorted that economic growth and job creation had brought down unemployment in Britain without the need for regulation or charters. At a meeting in Luxembourg of EC Labour and Employment Ministers in June 1989 he opposed the social charter, which, however, was backed by ten other states (Denmark abstained, saying it had to consult employers and trades unions at home). 'We are being asked to sign a blank cheque before anyone has defined what these rights would be and how much they would cost' Fowler declared. Britain also opposed the related proposal for a European Company Statute (see Chapter 9).

Proposals for a charter tabled in September 1988 by Manuel Marin of Spain, then Commissioner for Social Policy, were restricted to voluntary common measures for training schemes, common standards for social security benefits and common health and safety provisions, to which Britain has no objection. However, France and Germany have since appealed to Mrs Vasso Papandreou of Greece, the present Commissioner, to follow the proposed charter—adopted at the Strasbourg summit at the end of 1989—with binding legislation on social issues and workers' rights by the mid-1990s. Mrs Papandreou issued a revised version of the charter in September 1989. In a letter to *The Times* on 29 June 1989 Norman Willis, then the TUC General Secretary, said the social charter 'would not seek to impose one particular model of worker participation on all member states'. But Mrs Thatcher dismissed the charter as 'backdoor socialism'. Michel Rocard, the then French Prime Minister, memorably mixing his metaphors, accused her of having a view of Europe as 'a jungle, a house with its windows wide open to the winds, a plane without a pilot'. At the Madrid summit in June 1989 the issue was avoided but resurfaced under the French EC presidency in the second half of 1989, when Mitterrand and Rocard actively pursued it in the run-up to the Strasbourg summit in December 1989.

In the course of 1990–91 other EC countries such as Germany and Ireland sided with Britain on the social dimension, arguing that some issues—such as working hours, minimum wages, the rights of part-time workers or pregnant women at the workplace—could not be decided by majority vote, as Mrs Papandreou wanted. On the other hand, Germany, with a strong Christian Democrat lobby against Sunday trading, pressed for a ban on Sunday working as an alleged 'health and safety' measure, a move denounced by Delors as nonsensical. Further workplace legislation, however, was passed by EC employment ministers on the eve of the Maastricht summit in December 1991, in the face of British objections.

The politicization of 1992

These developments show that the single market programme, initially seen as a technical one for harmonization and freer trade across frontiers, has rapidly acquired a party-political dimension as the reality of 1992 approaches. Anxieties on the Right about 'corporate socialism' and inter-ference from Brussels at the expense of British cultural traditions and national sovereignty are matched by concern on the Left that the 1992 agenda has been set by conservative parties in power in Britain and Europe and by big business, which is able to influence both national governments and the European Commission.

The outcome of this debate is not clear, nor can we see how far the debate will shape 1992 and how much it will merely be a domestic political football to be kicked around for domestic political reasons. Speaking to German trades unionists and business executives in Cologne in Sep-tember 1988, Delors responded to criticisms from the Right by attacking the 'verbal excesses of the advocates of deregulation', and called for a 'new Keynes or Beveridge' to lay down a comprehensive EC social and employment programme for 1992, together with a plan for the redistri-bution of wealth. 'We thought we had this debate behind us,' Delors said, 'There can be no Europe without a social dimension . . . Europe must never become an instrument to weaken the trades unions.' The debate is far from over, however, and seems likely to intensify as 1992 approaches.

An indication of how strong the 1992 backlash might become was given in a speech by Sir John Hoskyns, the outgoing Director-General of the Institute of Directors, to an audience of 3,000 business executives in February 1989. Describing the internal market programme as a 'complete fiasco', Sir John attacked the Community and its institutions for 'shifting objectives, bad organization, wrong people, poor motivation, inadequate methods, weak management, personal politics and pilfering on a heroic scale'.

In addition to alleging that 'there are signs that the Brussels machine is becoming corrupted both intellectually and financially', Sir John aston-ished his audience by calling on the Community to scrap its 1992 achieve-ments and start all over again! No less striking was the co-ordinated and instantaneous government assault on Sir John's provocative views.

Sir Geoffrey Howe, the then Foreign Secretary, later told a Birming-ham press conference that: 'It is, quite frankly, perverse and faint-hearted to claim that the single market has been blown off course, or risks being submerged in collectivism or bureaucracy.' These sentiments were also echoed by Lord Young, who accused Sir John of ignoring 'many of the facts', and expressed fears that 'Sir John has been reading too many scare stories in the press and not attending closely enough to what was really happening'.

12 ABOLISHING FISCAL FRONTIERS

The value added tax dispute

Although the European Commission's plans for harmonizing indirect taxation have been seen as a further example of unwarranted attempts by Brussels to extend its authority into areas traditionally regarded as the preserve of sovereign governments, the overhaul of the Community's indirect taxation regime is a logical and inevitable consequence of the agreement by member states to abolish their internal frontiers, as enshrined in the Single European Act. Apart from the objective of reducing the costs imposed on business and commerce of having to pass through border posts, which has been estimated at 1.5% of the value of intra-Community trade, the different rates of indirect taxation among member states and the need to ensure that value added tax (Vat) is remitted on exports and charged on imports is one of the main reasons frontier controls remain in existence. If frontier controls are to be abolished, then rates of indirect taxation must converge, and new mechanisms must be found for preventing fraud and ensuring that national governments are able to levy Vat on consumption.

Rejecting allegations that the harmonization of indirect taxation was little more than an attempt to augment its powers, the Commission insisted that:

> The prime objective is to abolish tax frontiers, in other words, to eliminate the need for checks at internal borders. The Commission's proposals are not therefore designed to achieve tax harmonization for the sake of harmonization . . . The aim is more modest. It is limited strictly to what is needed to remove tax frontiers.

The harmonization of indirect taxation, or more accurately, the approximation of Vat and the harmonization of excise duties is therefore regarded by the Commission as central to the 1992 process.

Nonetheless, for two reasons the tax-harmonization proposals have aroused fundamental passions and fierce opposition, particularly in Britain. Traditionally, taxation has been seen as the preserve of national governments, and therefore free from supranational control or interference. Moreover, the Commission's plans for the approximation of Vat, at least as originally tabled, would mean the end of Britain's cherished zero rating of basic goods such as food, fuel and childrens' clothing—a development any government would regard as politically sensitive, if not potentially explosive. In addition, the harmonization of excise duties, the specific indirect taxes levied on the consumption of certain products such as tobacco and alcohol, will have the effect of bringing down the costs to the consumer of cigarettes, beer and spirits. This has given rise to the charge that 'Brussels' is planning as part of 1992 to increase the prices of food and children's shoes (socially useful products) while reducing those of tobacco and alcohol (socially harmful ones).

Because indirect taxation is one area where the right of national veto has been retained, the proposals put forward by the Commission have to be approved by the Council of Ministers before passing into national law. After a seemingly endless series of negotiations between EC economic and finance ministers, the broad outlines of the new Community indirect taxation regime had emerged by December 1990. New proposals advanced in May 1989 by Mme Christiane Scrivener, the Commissioner for Fiscal Affairs, had already made significant concessions, allowing Britain to keep Vat zero rating on food, children's clothes and other basic items, and by the end of the year a consensus on how the new system of indirect taxation was to be implemented and operated had begun to take shape.

Confusion between new proposals and court rulings

The debate over Vat and 1992 in Britain has been marked by the confusion of two separate points: the 1985 White Paper's plans for the removal of fiscal barriers; and rulings by the European Court on exemptions granted to Britain in 1977, when the Sixth Vat Directive was passed. The first refers to future proposals arising from the Single European Act; the second to a directive which is already in existence. Both tend to be regarded as interference by Brussels in British tax affairs, although this overlooks the fact that Britain has already agreed to the principle of Vat harmonization by putting its name to the 1977 directive (during the last Labour Government).

The 1977 concession does not mean that Britain or any other state is obliged to comply with the White Paper's vision of the removal of all fiscal barriers. Indeed, the Commission's proposals have already undergone a process of modification to meet the objections not only of Britain but also of other countries where Vat rates are either higher or lower than the proposed Vat bands contained in the draft 1992 directive. The Commission can (and does) argue that Vat approximation has long been on the agenda in one form or another. On the other hand, its approach to the problem illustrates the delicacy of the issue, especially the approach adopted in the 1992 White Paper itself.

The White Paper section on fiscal barriers (Section Three) was one of the most controversial aspects of the original 1992 programme. The Commission was well aware of this, as the careful if sometimes argumentative language of the White Paper shows. Section Three was the only one to depart from the overall principle of 1992—that member states should accept common goals and work their way towards them through mutual recognition, with adjustments made afterwards as the realities of the single market developed. Instead, the White Paper made a direct attempt to force EC governments to approximate their indirect tax rates.

It begins by noting that the removal of frontier controls 'is bound to have inescapable implications for the member states as far as indirect taxes are concerned'. In 1968, at the time of the customs union, it was already apparent that 'the mere removal of tariffs' would not create a true common market, and that differences in turnover taxes 'were the source of serious distortion'. The Treaty of Rome itself, the White Paper said, had provided for Commission proposals on the approximation of indirect taxation 'when this was needed for the completion of the internal market' (Articles 99 and 100). This remains the basis of the Commission's drive for Vat approximation: that Vat differentials distort trade in a frontier-free Europe; and that harmonization—or approximation—is necessary for the completion of the single market. Both are distrusted by anti-Marketeers and by a number of EC governments.

Vat has always appealed to EC policymakers as an instrument of fiscal policy because of its relative simplicity—as a principle, that is, not in terms of its complex paperwork for both business executives and Vat inspectors. Now used in all twelve EC states, with Portugal the last to come into line in 1989, Vat is a tax levied at each stage of the process of production and marketing but collected by the government of the country at the point of sale. In practice, however, Vat rates vary considerably from one country to another. A system of limited allowances has been developed for the carrying of tax-free goods across EC borders, but this causes problems for countries like Denmark and Ireland, which have tried (illegally, according to the Commission, which is threatening to take them to the European Court) to restrict such allowances to *bona fide* travellers by imposing arbitrary definitions of what constitutes a traveller.

Steps towards harmonization of indirect taxes

The first major step towards harmonization came in 1967, at the time of the Six, when turnover taxes were replaced by Vat levied on a common basis through a series of Vat directives (the First Vat Directive, the Second Vat Directive, and so on). Three years later, in 1970, came the decision to give the EC its 'own resources'—a common EC fund as opposed to national budgets—by raising revenues based partly on farm levies but mainly on a proportion (up to 1%) of national Vat contributions. This system eventually proved inadequate, and under the Delors reforms of February 1988 has given way to a revised own resources system based partly on Vat and partly on a tax derived from a calculation of gross national product. This more fairly reflects each country's ability to contribute to the EC and, incidentally, creates difficulties for Italy because of the extent of the black economy, making the true Italian GNP almost unknowable. But even under the Delors package, Vat contributions remain a central part of the revenue system.

In 1977 the Sixth Vat Directive laid down the outlines of a common Vat base, yet so sensitive was the issue, and so great the resistance of national governments, that the directive contained a number of loopholes and exemptions, known in EC jargon as 'derogations'. On the other hand, the directive made it clear that such exemptions were only temporary, hence the subsequent cases in the European Court over whether exemptions granted to Britain on medical and social grounds were justified. At the same time, the EC decided to harmonize excise duties, beginning with cigarettes and tobacco, alcohol and hydrocarbon oils. By 1985 the White Paper was able to declare that 'the harmonization of indirect taxation has always been regarded as an essential and integral part of achieving a true common market'. Momentum had been lost between 1977 and 1985, it admitted, but this was due to 'the impact of recession on the economic policies of member states, and preoccupation with other problems'. Progress was now being resumed, 'and we must proceed vigorously if we are to achieve the target date of 1992'.

What are the technical arguments for Vat approximation? EC officials argue that if frontier controls are to be abolished so that people, goods and services can move about within the EC as if it were one country, this clearly affects those controls 'primarily designed to ensure that each member state can collect revenue in the form of indirect taxation'. Whether in the form of Vat or of excise duties, indirect taxes become part of the final price to the consumer. According to the White Paper:

> Different levels of taxation are reflected in different price levels. If the differences in level are substantial, the differences in final prices will also be substantial . . . We need to consider whether or not it would be practically possible, in the absence of frontier controls, for member states to charge significantly different levels of indirect taxation.

The Commission's own answer, unsurprisingly, is no, it would not. Under the Commission's draft Fourteenth Vat Directive—tabled in 1982 and eventually withdrawn in 1987, after much heated debate—EC states would all have had to shift to a system of 'postponed accounting' used in the Benelux states. Under this system, Vat accounting is done at inland tax offices rather than at frontiers. The Commission sought to meet member states' concerns by agreeing that 'some documentation' would still be needed at the border and governments would still have the right to check the movement of goods to prevent fraud. However, the Commission's basic principle remained that Vat incurred by a consumer should be deductible 'irrespective of the member state on which it has been charged'. Under a parallel proposal there would be a computerized central clearing house to ensure that Vat collected in the exporting state but deducted in the importing one was reimbursed to the importing state and not the exporting one. In the end, the Council of Ministers judged that the proposed clearing-house system was too unwieldy and too open to abuse. The Commission's position is that fraud and evasion could best be avoided if the current system of divergent Vat rates was replaced by a common one of approximated rates.

Similar arguments apply to the question of cross-border shopping. Because of the differences in Vat, and hence in prices, people in high-tax countries naturally cross where possible into neighbouring low-tax ones to reap the benefits. Cross-border shopping is particularly intense in Benelux, France and Germany; on the Danish–German border; and between Northern Ireland and the Irish Republic. It applies less to Britain, because of the natural obstacle of the Channel. But arguably, Continental housewives would find it worth making the crossing if British Vat zero rates for 'basic products' were retained after 1992 in an otherwise harmonized EC, and mail order businesses would also benefit. Mothercare—to take one example—would be able to compete with an unfair (and highly lucrative) advantage over Continental mail order firms with a similar speciality in children's clothing and supplies.

Modification of the Vat proposals

In practice, as the fate of the Fourteenth Vat Directive shows, the Commission has found its arguments for harmonization fiercely opposed, and has moved to a policy of 'approximation' instead. This is a concession, but its outlines were already visible in the 1985 White Paper. This conceded that while excise duties could and should be harmonized—which is still the Commission's policy—Vat approximation need only be 'sufficiently close that the operation of the common market is not affected through distortions of trade, diversion of trade or effects on competition'. Opponents of Vat harmonization often point to the example of the United States, where variations exist between the federal states without any noticeable effect on what might be called the single American market. The Commission took this argument and used it for its own purposes, holding up the American system as a model for an integrated Europe—adding, however, that cross-border tax variations must still be limited, with a proposed permitted divergence from the EC norm of plus or minus 2½%. Brussels also now acknowledges that Vat is only one element in the make-up of consumer prices, and that price is only one factor in consumer choice along with service, brand image and convenience: 'Retail markets are often tolerant of quite significant differences in prices'. A further problem admitted by EC officials is that Denmark and Ireland derive a larger proportion of their revenue from indirect taxation than most other EC states (16% to 17%, compared to around 10% in Britain Germany), so that major adjustments for approximation would give Copenhagen and Dublin budgetary problems.

Nonetheless, the Commission has remained determined to bring EC Vat rates broadly into line, whether under the banner of 'approximation' or 'harmonization'. It noted in the White Paper that Vat rates at present vary from zero (in Britain and Ireland) to a high point of 38% in Italy, with Denmark applying a standard rate of 22%.

In July 1987, after much internal discussion at the Berlaymont, Lord Cockfield, the Internal Market Commissioner, announced the Commission's 'approximation' proposals. Vat rates would be grouped into two broad bands: a standard rate of between 14% and 20% and a reduced one of between 4% and 9% on 'items of basic necessity'. The Commission, Lord Cockfield said, was ready to meet the 'particular difficulties' of Britain and Ireland over zero rating by considering temporary exemptions 'where these can be justified, for states for which the proposals could pose political, social or budgetary problems'.

The resulting reaction was, if anything, fiercer than that which greeted the Commission's earlier plans, largely because of the impact on zero rating. Not only would the abolition of zero rating affect lower income groups, the argument ran, it would also affect the economy as a whole, since nearly 30% of all consumer spending in Britain is accounted for by zero-rated goods—i.e. food, energy, children's clothes, water, newspapers, books and drugs. The then Paymaster General, Peter Brooke, declared: 'There is no question of our accepting anything that conflicts with the pledges the Prime Minister has given on our zero rates,' a reference to undertakings given during the 1987 election campaign. Shortly afterwards, Mrs Thatcher confirmed in the Commons that Britain would veto the Vat changes if they were put to the Council of Ministers. Nigel Lawson, the Chancellor of the Exchequer, repeatedly told fellow EC Finance Ministers that the Vat proposal was unnecessary and unacceptable. Lord Young of Graffham restated the British view in *The Times* in July 1988. The Government's rejection of the Vat proposal was 'absolutely final', he said, adding: 'We are not going to harmonize'. Differing Vat rates did not affect competition, he argued—and if distortions did arise, they would, in any case, be corrected after 1992 by market forces. The new Scrivener proposals are the result of the Commission's efforts to meet such objections. Although the issue of Vat rates remained unresolved, ministers had agreed on the means of collection, by maintaining the existing system of leaving Vat on goods and services in the country of consumption, despite Commission objections that this would entail retention of elaborate border controls.

The search for a compromise

The EC's influential Economic and Monetary Committee, composed of senior finance officials from the twelve governments, issued an interim report in April 1988. This sought to balance the opposing views on Vat, arguing that approximation along the lines advanced by Lord Cockfield can be combined with the 'market forces' line of reasoning. On the other hand, the Government's view has received support from leading experts, notably the Institute of Fiscal Studies, which in a report issued in February 1988 agreed that completion of the internal market did not require substantial changes to national Vat systems. The Institute suggested that instead of two broad Vat bands the EC should have common minimum Vat rates, or floors, allowing member states to set higher rates if they wished. It also took issue with the Commission's attempt to legislate for the good of the Community, declaring that if states with high tax rates suffered because of cross-border shopping they had only themselves to blame: 'It is not the business of the Commission to protect member states from the consequences of their own high indirect taxation policies'. It went on to argue that, as an island, Britain was less likely to be affected by cross-border shopping problems—an argument which may lose its force as cross-Channel traffic increases with the building of the Channel Tunnel.

A further compromise suggestion has come from the European Parliament. In July 1988 Alman Metten, a Dutch socialist MEP, proposed two broad Vat bands to replace those of the Commission, one ranging from zero to 6% or 9% and a higher rate of between 16% and 22%—in effect, taking account of the British–Irish zero rating problem and of Denmark's high standard rate of 22%. In October 1988 the European Parliament's committee on fiscal approximation approved this as an amendment to the Cockfield proposals. Ben Patterson, MEP for Kent West (who has himself proposed the retention of zero rating in a pamphlet entitled *Vat: The Zero Rate Issue*), welcomed the idea that zero rating should be a permanent part of the EC Vat system. On the other hand, critics of these compromise proposals argue that a system which tolerates variations of between zero and 22% can scarcely be called 'approximation' any more, let alone 'harmonization'.

The political and business climate in Britain remains suspicious of Vat harmonization, as is shown most vividly by reactions to the European Court's series of rulings on British exemptions under the 1977 directive. As noted earlier, the question of 1977 exemptions is, strictly speaking, separate from that of 1992 harmonization. Yet the two issues are, in a sense, linked aspects of the same basic drive towards harmonization—or approximation. In discussing the 1977 exemptions the White Paper made clear that they were (1) provisional only and (2) part of the wider process leading ultimately to harmonization: '. . .These derogations and social arrangements should ultimately be brought to an end . . . so that a common market permitting fair competition and resembling a real internal market may ultimately be achieved'. The 1977 directive itself stated that exemptions could be maintained until a date 'not later than that on which the charging of tax on imports and the remission of tax on exports in trade between the member states are abolished'. The date is not defined, but EC officials argue that it refers to the completion of the internal market—that is, 1992.

Rulings on the Sixth Vat Directive against Britain

The rulings arrived at by the European Court following cases brought against Britain by the Commission have certainly caused widespread concern in Britain. The rulings have come some ten years after the directive, but the wheels of EC justice grind slowly. In February 1988 the Court ruled that the Vat exemption granted in 1977 for the dispensing of spectacles and contact lenses could not be justified. Backbench Conservative MPs complained that an outside body was dictating to Parliament what taxes it could levy for the first time since the seventeenth-century ship tax. In June the Court caused another political row by ruling that the practice of either zero rating or exempting new commercial construction and certain services to industry (electricity, gas, protective clothing, sewerage, plus news services) was a further unjustified exemption (although it upheld the exemption for private domestic housing as well as for animal feedstuffs and livestock), leading to confusion in the media over whether Britain had 'won' or 'lost'. In the oral hearing in September 1987 the lawyer acting for Britain had argued that not all Vat exemptions in Britain were due to 'a funny Anglo-Saxon habit'.

Following the ruling on new construction, the standard British 15% Vat rate (increased to 17.5% in March 1991) applies to non-domestic construction, and the sale of land for commercial property development, from April 1989. The Court allowed the continued zero rating of private housing, as opposed to commercial building, because Britain was entitled to pursue—on social grounds—'a policy of home ownership for the whole population'. The Government softened the blow to commercial building and services by refunding or partially refunding the extra cost for health authorities and charities, but private schools, hospitals and charities still expressed dismay. (To qualify for a refund the institution in question must be registered for Vat purposes.) Teddy Taylor, MP, giving voice to backbench feelings, recalled in a letter to *The Times* in June 1988 that when the Commons debated the Sixth Vat Directive in November 1976, before its final adoption, the government of the day had repeatedly declared that the British right to retain zero rating was assured. The Court's ruling, Taylor said, was 'one more example of the wishes of the Euro-institutions to extend their powers and control at the expense of sovereign governments'. Responding to this and other charges that the Government had conceded sovereignty over taxation to the EC, Peter Lilley, then Economic Secretary to the Treasury, pointed out that the ruling arose from the 1977 directive, in which the exemptions were not time limited, and that Britain had no alternative but to comply. The European Court is the Court of last resort.

The Cockfield legacy: the logic of approximation

There is, in other words, a clear link—although one not stressed officially—between the various Vat directives which have so far introduced partial steps toward Vat harmonization and the full Cockfield vision, which is seen by the Commission as the logical consequence and fulfilment of earlier directives. The departure of Lord Cockfield and the advent of a new Commissioner for the period 1989–92 signals a change of tone, with Vat harmonization pursued in a less adversarial style. However, the basis of the policy remains the same. If Britain agreed to partial harmonization in 1977, the argument runs, why should it not agree to the end result?

To some extent, the Commission has the new EC law on its side. The Single European Act specifically provided for Vat harmonization as part of 1992. The full passage of Article 99 reads:

> The Council of Ministers shall, acting unanimously on a proposal from the Commission and after consulting the European Parliament, adopt provisions for the harmonization of legislation concerning turnover taxes, excise duties and other forms of indirect taxation to the extent that such harmonization is necessary to ensure the establishment and the functioning of the internal market within the time limit laid down.

The time limit referred to is 1992: the argument therefore revolves around the phrase 'to the extent that such harmonization is necessary to ensure the functioning of the internal market'. Senior British officials continue to argue that it is not necessary: senior Commission officials in Brussels maintain that it is. Britain is not alone in taking its stand. France has also expressed strong reservations about Vat harmonization, largely because the broad bands proposed by the Commission are too broad, and would leave French businesses vulnerable to lower Vat rates levied in neighbouring Germany. Both France and Germany fear that Vat harmonization will force national governments to reshape their fiscal policies because of single market considerations rather than because of priorities set by governments themselves. Martin Bangemann, the German Commissioner and former Economics Minister, is on record as stating that full fiscal harmonization can only come about after 1992, rather than before, since only after 1992 will the full effects of free competition in a frontier-free market become apparent.

Unravelling the deadlock on Vat

Meeting under the Greek presidency on the island of Crete in September 1988, Nigel Lawson, the then Chancellor of the Exchequer, announced a British plan under which there would be a gradual elimination of restrictions on cross-border shopping, a retention of differing rates of excise duty on alcohol and tobacco and a postponed accounting system for Vat to reduce frontier controls. Market forces, Lawson argued, would bring Vat rates into line after 1992. The proposal was given a cool reception, largely because it failed to make provision for the anxieties of other member states over increases in cross-border shopping. Consequently, most economic and finance ministers tended to prefer the Commission's proposals, while insisting that they be made more flexible.

Responding to the evident deadlock, Mme Scrivener did precisely that. In place of Cockfield's two-band Vat principle, at an EC finance ministers' meeting in May 1989, at S'Agaro in Spain, she presented a proposal to introduce a minimum standard Vat rate of 15%, a lower rate or rates for socially sensitive items, and the retention (at least for a transitional phase) of zero rating. In some respects, the proposal was a concession to Britain, although only a partial one, as the list of items to be granted zero-rated status was very limited indeed. The proposal included a gradual elimination of the restrictions on cross-border shopping and a case-by-case negotiation on the harmonization of excise duties. Madame Scrivener said that she had taken the 'market forces' argument into account, prompting Lawson to remark that a British dogmatist (Cockfield) had been replaced by a French pragmatist.

Although far from resolving the issue, the initiative nonetheless contributed to a more concilliatory atmosphere in the negotiations. During further talks in November and December the Commission's broad approach was endorsed by a majority of member states, and at the European Council in Strasbourg in December it was instructed to draw up proposals for the transition. The Commission's blueprint was announced in May 1990, and called for the abolition of all customs procedures governing the movement of goods between member states from January 1993. In effect, the notion of imports and exports within the Community was to become redundant, and the crossing of an internal frontier would no longer attract a tax obligation. Henceforth, people would be free to buy goods in any member state for consumption in any other. In an effort to prevent distortions arising out of different levels of indirect taxation, Vat on certain items (such as cars and mail-order goods) would be applied at the rate appropriate in the country of consumption.

Such transitional arrangements, however, would expire by December 1996. Excise duties were to be harmonized and co-operation between member states' tax administrations to prevent fraud (including exchanges of officials) would be increased. Finally, all frontier documents would be abolished, relieving traders of the legal obligation to complete and submit an estimated 60 million forms a year. The transitionary arrangements were welcomed by Europe's customs officials, and HM Customs and Excise announced that it was preparing to tighten controls on Vat fraudsters, hoping to exploit the internal market by moving 1,500 of their force of 7,000 officers into inland checkpoints in anticipation of a frontier-free Europe.

With the arrangements for implementing the new regime all but complete, attention then focused on the vexed question of Vat rates. Despite the substantial concessions granted to Britain, Norman Lamont, the new Chancellor, continued to insist that market forces must be allowed to determine Vat rates, implying that Britain would veto any attempt by the Commission to legislate on the issue. Britain's position was, however, unacceptable to France, Spain and the Netherlands, all of whom remained anxious about the prospect of an exodus of cross-border shoppers causing havoc to their revenues from Vat and adamant about the need for legislation to prevent member states from manipulating Vat rates.

Six years after the launch of the internal market White Paper, and 18 months before the 1992 deadline expired, final agreement was in sight. After three meetings of economic and finance ministers, held under the Luxembourg presidency in June 1991, the Twelve entered into a political agreement to charge a minimum standard rate of Vat of not less than 15% from January 1993 and binding rates of excise duty on mineral oils, tobacco and alcohol. The agreement requires Germany to increase its Vat rate from 14%, and Spain and Luxembourg to increase their rates from 12%. Member states would be able to choose between two lower rates of around 5% and 6%, while zero rating would be retained on a variety of products for a transitional period, subject to bi-annual reviews. All that remained was to overcome Britain's reluctance to have the entire package codified in law.

Although the original Cockfield twin-band proposals had been modified by the negotiations, the Commission's May 1990 blueprint had emerged from the process virtually intact. However, the Commission's attempt to end zero rating for exports and to charge Vat in the country of origin rather than in the country of destination proved too radical for the member states. Taxation in country of destination will, therefore, continue in the transitionary period from January 1993 to December 1996, although taxation in the country of origin remains the Commission's long-term goal.

Moreover, following the Council's decision in March 1991 to eliminate progressively the financial and quantity allowances for duty-free goods, there can be little doubt that the cherished perk of international travel is nearing the end of its days, even if the practice will not disappear as quickly as the Commission would like. According to Leon Gordon, an advisor to the Commission on indirect taxation: 'In an internal market, where the concept of export–import transactions within it has been made completely redundant, such sales will have no *raison-d'être*'. The point was reinforced by Brian Unwin, the chairman of HM Customs, who observed: 'In pure single-market logic, there can be no justification for continuing to grant tax allowances for crossing fiscal frontiers that no longer exist'. Nonetheless, in October 1991, Britain, Ireland, Greece, Spain and Portugal secured agreement that duty-free shopping must remain for a transitional period after 1993, was subsequently set to last until 1999.

At the back of Treasury minds, however, is the fear that the Commission will not stop at the harmonization of indirect taxes, and that Brussels will revive a forgotten 1975 proposal for co-ordinating direct taxes as well. The 1975 plan envisaged an EC-wide direct taxation band of between 45% and 55%, the logic being that if European economies are to be integrated the taxation of both companies and individuals becomes a Community concern. Before leaving office, Lord Cockfield said that plans for corporate taxes, including a common rate for company profits and dividends, were 'still in the formative stages'.

In addition, Mme Scrivener, complaining of the tendency for inter-company links to develop 'more between the US and Europe than between European countries', revived long-neglected EC proposals for avoiding double taxation of dividends paid by a subsidiary in one state to its parent company in another; deferring tax on company assets in cross-frontier mergers; giving Brussels the power to arbitrate between national tax authorities in disputes over transfer pricing practices involving multinationals; and fiscal consolidation of multinationals' profits and losses. The Commission finally abandoned its attempt to set a single rate of corporation tax in April 1990, although three directives removing the anomalies faced by companies operating in more than one country, as described above, were approved. Commission officials are still tempted by the introduction of a European-wide income tax. Though dismissed by Norman Lamont in June 1991 as 'eccentric', the idea seems destined to resurface in the years ahead.

Checklist of changes

- All member states have agreed to a minimum standard rate of Vat at 15% effective from January 1993.
- Mandatory rates of excise duties for mineral oils, alcohol and tobacco have been agreed, also effective from January 1993.
- Systematic checks at frontiers will be abolished as of January 1993, and all Vat fraud and other monitoring procedures will be conducted inland.
- Cross-border duty-free shopping will survive the abolition of internal frontiers in 1993, but only for a transitional (if protracted) period.
- New initiatives designed to harmonize direct taxation are also likely in the longer term.

13 A TRANSPORT POLICY FOR EUROPE

Trains, boats and planes in the single market

Charles de Gaulle's once-famous image of a *Europe des patries*—a continent riven by territorial boundaries, ideological tensions and a formidable array of water, mountain and land barriers—is slowly giving way to the vision of a Europe *sans frontières*. The cumulative effects of the internal market programme, the determination of the six members of the European Free Trade Association to participate in the process of integration it offers and the collapse of the East European and Soviet dictatorships is giving substance to the once-unimaginable idea of an economically, politically and geographically integrated Europe from the Atlantic to the Urals. But while the dramatic events which have unfolded in Eastern Europe and the Soviet Union have been dominating newspaper headlines, comparatively little attention has been paid to the more prosaic developments which are progressively eliminating the so-called 'missing links' in Europe's transport infrastructure.

Nonetheless, the historic natural barriers which have inhibited Europe's political and economic integration for decades, from the English Channel to the mountain ranges of the Alps and the Pyrenees, and the water masses of the Baltic Straits to the physical isolation of Greece (in the sense that it has no common border with any other EC country), are being overcome one by one. Viewed in isolation, each of these great physical barriers would appear to have little more than regional consequences, impairing the movement of goods and people between one neighbouring country and another. Taken collectively, however, they have acted as fetters on trade and commerce across the continent, while at the same time condemning the outer regions to bear the economic costs of geographical marginalization, known in Eurospeak as 'peripherality'.

The Channel Tunnel is perhaps the most well known of these great civil engineering projects. In an influential report published in 1990 by the Royal Institution of Chartered Surveyors (*Transport in the Nineties: The Shaping of Europe*) transport analyst Terence Bendixson described the Channel Tunnel as the single most expensive addition to Europe's transport infrastructure, and 'the first great infrastructure project to come out of the new Europe'. While the description may be tinged with hyperbole, the consequences are not. Completion of the Channel Tunnel will reinforce the historically dominant trading relationships within the so-called London–Frankfurt–Milan golden triangle at the very moment when northern Europe's economic pre-eminence is being challenged by the emergence of a European high-tech Sun Belt running along the Mediterranean from Barcelona to Trieste and by the lure of new economic opportunities in the east.

Attention is now being focused on the second of Europe's great physical barriers—the Alps. Because of the lack of additional capacity on the three main Alpine passes, the Simplon, the Gothard and the Brenner, which serve the flow of people and goods between Germany, Italy and Austria, ambitious proposals are being examined to excavate three new tunnels. Similarly, since the accession of Spain and Portugal, work has begun on taming the Pyrenees. Plans have already been developed for new and expanded road and rail tunnels, aimed at integrating the Iberian peninsula with the road and rail networks of the rest of continental Europe. Farther north, work has begun on the Scanlink project, a composite programme of road and rail bridges across the Baltic designed to link the Scandinavia peninsula with Denmark and mainland Europe. Funds from the European Investment Bank are also being used to upgrade the Autoput, Yugoslavia's equivalent of the M1, and the only road link between Greece and its European partners. Finally, Karel van Miert, the new Transport Commissioner, has drawn up ambitious plans for improving road and rail links between the EC and its eastern neighbours.

With the exception of the Channel Tunnel, however, most of these schemes are in their formative stages and face formidable financial and technical difficulties. With scant financial resources of its own to spend on transport infrastructure projects, the Commission's role in such schemes is, at best, marginal and, at worst, non-existent. There is little doubt that Brussels is eager to make a contribution towards the elimination of Europe's missing links, but the overriding priority remains the completion of the internal market in air, rail, road and sea transport before the 1992 deadline expires.

Honouring the Treaty of Rome

Before publication of the Internal Market White Paper the prospects for any significant progress towards the liberalization of the Community's heavily regulated air transport, road haulage, shipping and rail network systems—not to mention the creation of a genuine common transport policy—seemed negligible. Transport policy (or, more precisely, the lack of it) had become the single greatest failure of the EC. The architects of the European Community attached so much importance to transport as a means of promoting European economic integration that it was given its own chapter in the Treaty of Rome. Yet 30 years after the creation of the EC the highly prized goal of a coherent Community-wide transport policy still remained confined to the ever-receding horizon, with member states pursuing independent (and often conflicting) transport policies, united solely by their scant regard for the interests of the Community as a whole.

The failure of member states to deal effectively with the difficult issues involved in laying the foundations for a more efficient Community transport system has exacted a heavy toll. Community governments, businesses, employees and consumers have all had to bear the costs of fragmented, inefficient, poorly planned, unnecessarily expensive and environmentally insensitive transportation systems, while frequently being unaware or indifferent to the consequences of their actions. On the rare occasions that the *status quo* has been challenged, governments have all too often responded with the indignant defence that 'the traffic does flow'. So it may, at least most of the time, and especially if one is not trying to leave Heathrow in July or August, driving to work in the morning rush hour or bringing an articulated lorry through Italian frontier controls. However, as the Commission has been arguing for decades:

> If one takes a closer look it becomes apparent just how inefficient the conditions are. They make transport more expensive and in many cases slow down the integration of the Community.

Writing in *European Affairs* in autumn 1988 Stanley Clinton Davis, the then European Commissioner for Transport Policy, asked whether one could envisage a common policy for the free movement of products, services and citizens without a corresponding policy for the transport systems which carried them. Yet paradoxically:

> Road transport continued to be controlled by a complex system of licences effectively isolating each national market from its neighbours; civil aviation policy operated on a purely national basis designed to protect the national flag carrier against allcomers— sometimes offering better terms to American or Singaporean carriers than fellow Europeans—with a whole web of agreements between governments and airlines. Each member state had its own maritime policy, and the railway systems maintained the pattern of arm's length co-operation which had reached its peak in the nineteenth century.

Even before the internal market programme made a fresh attempt to create a common transport policy, a series of developments had emphasized to member states the growing urgency of abandoning shortsighted national protectionist policies and embarking on concerted action to solve the Community's increasingly acute transport problems. Following the example of deregulation of the US air transport industry (which resulted in considerable increases in efficiency, substantial decreases in air fares and a significant expansion of the number of passengers), its European counterpart began to face growing criticism—principally from consumer lobbies—demanding an end to the air transport cartel which had kept air travel prices at extortionate levels for the few who could afford to pay and far out of reach for most European citizens.

Almost simultaneously, the absurdity of member state road transport policies, which effectively cut the Community's road network into twelve incompatible segments, was highlighted by a series of expensive and time-consuming blockages at frontier crossings during the early part of the decade and discredited by the flourishing black market in cross-frontier permits needed to transport goods into other member states. Likewise, following the contraction of the European steel industry, the decline in consumption of coal and iron ore left Europe's merchant marine fleets in a state of chronic overcapacity. This problem was further exacerbated by the growing tendency of the centrally planned and developing countries to exclude Community fleets from their domestic trade. Member states were thus presented with little option other than to look to the European Commission to protect the interests of their shipping fleets in trade negotiations with the Community's trading partners around the world.

In 1984 the European Parliament initiated legal proceedings against the Council of Ministers in the European Court of Justice for its failure to carry out the provisions in the Treaty of Rome calling for the creation of a common transport policy. To the embarrassment of the governments of the member states, the Court found that the Council had been negligent in its duties, and ruled that its defence—namely, that it had proved too difficult to agree on a common policy—was completely unacceptable. The Council was now under a legal obligation to overcome such obstacles, a task greatly facilitated by the ratification of the Single European Act and the introduction of qualified majority voting.

In addition to symbolizing the end of Britain's physical isolation from Continental Europe, the decision to build the Channel Tunnel opens up the possibility of bringing new life to Europe's ailing rail networks. The construction of high-speed rail systems between Europe's capital cities would at last enable these networks to compete effectively with air travel in speed, cost and comfort, thereby offering a commercial opportunity for Europe's historically indebted rail transport systems and helping to relieve some of the pressures faced by the air transport sector in the process.

Finally, the growth of tourism in Europe over the past 20 years (particularly in Britain, where the advent of the package holiday has had a profound effect on popular attitudes to Continental Europe) has helped to break down many of the traditional prejudices held by the peoples of Europe against each other. In 1985 140 million Europeans took at least one holiday, and over 20% of this total went to another member state. Three out of every four Britons have now visited at least one Community country, suggesting that the old Victorian adage—'fog in the Channel, Continent cut off'—has long been obsolete. Furthermore, Europe's cultural diversity, natural wealth and rich historical heritage are likely to prove a powerful magnet for the continued expansion of tourism in the decades ahead.

These developments have helped to focus attention on the urgent reforms needed to develop the Community's transport system, which, after all, makes a greater contribution to Community GDP than agriculture and which provides employment for millions of workers either directly or through other key sectors heavily dependent on it, such as the car, aviation, shipbuilding, construction and steel industries. Consequently, although only half-way through the internal market programme, and with much remaining to be done, the Commission had already made a number of impressive breakthroughs which had eluded Community politicians for decades.

Railways and the Channel Tunnel

The subterranean rendezvous in December 1990 between Graham Fagg and Phillipe Cozette, the two construction workers chosen to chip away the last few feet of chalk separating the British and French tunnelling teams working under the English Channel, heralded the end of Britain's 8,000 years of physical isolation from Continental Europe. After successive financial crises and widespread scepticism over the project's viability, the two construction workers earned a place as a footnote in history by making the first dry-land crossing between the British Isles and the European mainland since the end of the Ice Age. The Channel Tunnel, which had been made possible by the 1987 agreement between Mrs Thatcher and President Mitterrand to grant approval for the construction of a privately financed fixed link under the Channel, had become a fact, and Britain was henceforth inextricably linked to Europe.

When Eurotunnel's new shuttle trains begin operations in June 1993 motorists and hauliers will be able to make fast, reliable and competitively priced journeys between the two Channel Tunnel terminals at Folkestone and Calais, both of which will be served by new and upgraded motorways linking them into the British and French national road systems. In addition, the Channel Tunnel will provide the railways with an unprecedented opportunity to challenge the dominance of air transport by offering international passenger services between London, Paris and Brussels. Plans to build a new network of high-speed railway lines linking the three cities are already well advanced, with the French link expected to be completed in 1993 and the Belgian one by 1996.

Britain's high-speed link between London and Folkestone is unlikely to be completed before 2005, following the government's decision to adopt an easterly rather than a southerly approach. British Rail is, however, spending £1.5 billion upgrading existing lines so that international services can begin as soon as the Channel Tunnel opens. When all the new high-speed lines are in operation, rail passengers will be able to travel between London and Paris in 2 hours 45 minutes, and between London and Brussels in 2 hours 15 minutes. Plans for through-services on the existing east- and west-coast main lines, linking Scotland and the regions with a variety of Continental destinations, have also been proposed.

British Rail's £1.5 billion package for the first phase of international services includes a new £120-million station at Waterloo, about £15 million of which will be spent on a new station frontier-control facility. Although much of the argument over whether Britain is entitled to retain frontier controls after 1992 appears to have dissipated following the government's assertion that nothing in the Single European Act prevents it from carrying out spot checks, it would seem that Community nationals disembarking at Waterloo will be required to pass through traditional frontier posts. Home Office officials maintain, however, that any immigration or security checks that are carried out will be kept to a minimum, and will possibly be 'even faster then those conducted at airports'.

The new London–Paris–Brussels service could be merely a sample of what is to come. In January 1989 the Community of European Railways, an organization of the twelve EC national rail companies, along with those of Austria and Switzerland, announced plans for a transcontinental high-speed rail network linking Europe's main urban areas by 2025. The proposals envisaged the construction or upgrading of some 20,000 miles of track, which would be capable of providing passengers with 190 mph rail services, thereby reducing many existing journey times by half. Rail planners presented the proposals as a means of reversing the ailing fortunes of Europe's railways by enabling them to compete with air transport, and predicted that the new high-speed system would act as a powerful catalyst for economic and regional integration in the twenty-first century, in much the same way as the construction of national rail networks had promoted an economic boom in the nineteenth.

The proposed high-speed rail network would help to relieve increasing air and road congestion which has been estimated to cost 3.1% of EC gross national product a year in wasted time and energy, and, at the same time, bring about substantial environmental benefits in the form of reduced pollution and damage to the countryside. However, the entire network is expected to cost somewhere in the region of £100 billion, and apart from the embryonic high-speed service between London, Paris and Brussels, there has been little indication that Europe's national rail networks are prepared to co-operate, much less to generate the resources to make the vision of Europe's transcontinental rail network a reality. Hitherto, the national rail organizations have been little more than state-controlled bureaucracies, burdened with decades of accumulated debt, with little or no incentive to operate on a commercial basis or to market their products through mergers or joint ventures across frontiers.

Although a number of national rail organizations have crossed the threshold into the age of high-speed trains, following the precedent set by Japan with the Shinkansen 'bullet train' between Tokyo and Osaka in 1964, such endeavours have not extended beyond state borders. For example, the French Train à Grande Vitesse network, launched in 1981 with a new service between Paris and Lyons, and the German InterCity Express, launched in 1991 between Hamburg and Munich, are incompatible. The new French trains cannot run on the German high-speed network because the power supply is different, while the new German trains cannot run on the French network because they are too heavy. In addition, while the track guages in most member states are the same, their loading gauges, which determine the height and width of locomotives and rolling stock that can be taken through tunnels, along platforms and past other lineside structures, vary considerably. Consequently, unless the existing infrastructure is demolished and rebuilt to common European standards, the national rail organizations face the prospect of remaining prisoners of their nineteenth-century origins.

The cost of such an undertaking would, however, be prohibitive. As a result, the only way out of the impasse is to ensure that any new lines are built with the European dimension in mind. The proposed high-speed service between London, Paris and Brussels, for example, is a case in point. The new fleet of Transmanche Supertrains which are being built for the international service will be designed to run three different power systems. Plans to build a new high-speed line between Madrid and Seville are being developed in the context of linking the new to the French high-speed network. In addition, it would not be impossible to design a new fleet of trains capable of running on both the French and the German high-speed networks, assuming that French and German pride towards preserving the integrity of their own national achievements can be overcome.

In January 1989 the European Commission produced a draft directive on railways designed to foster such cross-border co-operation. The proposal called for the abolition of existing state rail monopolies by separating ownership of railway infrastructure from the provision of services. It envisaged the creation of track authorities responsible for maintaining network infrastructure, thereby enabling state and private companies to compete with each other to provide services. Accumulated debts were to be progressively written off, and subsidies for loss-making but socially necessary services were to be strictly regulated. Admittedly, the proposal had shortcomings, not least in establishing an equitable way of deciding how to integrate the competing services offered by rival companies into a coherent timetable. For most member states, however, the idea of challenging established national rail monopolies was anathema.

Although by 1991 the Commission had made some progress towards the objectives of the Internal Market White Paper, the goal of creating a single market for transport remained distant. During a meeting of transport ministers in Luxembourg in June 1991, Malcolm Rifkind, Britain's new Transport Secretary, gave vent to his frustrations. 'I find it astonishing,' he said, 'that countries prepared to discuss a single currency and political union are incapable of implementing their commitment to the internal market by the end of next year.' He added: 'It is not enough simply to express aspirations, we have an obligation to create a single market by the end of next year.' Rifkind's outburst was in part prompted by the British government's evident frustration and embarrassment at having to deal with what it saw as a Community mesmerized by the high ground of political and economic union, while, at the same time, content to ignore the nuts and bolts of creating the single market.

Nonetheless, the following day, EC transport ministers took their first step towards creating a single market for railways by abolishing the monopoly of member states to provide rail services on their national networks, in the process laying the foundations of a trans-continental high-speed railway. Under the agreement, national rail monopolies are henceforth required to account separately for their infrastructure and operating costs, thus making it possible for new operators to be charged fairly for providing new services. In addition, joint ventures between companies of more than one member state have the right of access to the rail networks in other member states. As a result, for example, from January 1993 British Rail and Deutsche Bundesbahn will now be able to form a joint company to provide international passenger services between Britain and Germany, with an automatic right of transit through France.

Furthermore, plans to stimulate modern techniques of freight distribution have also been agreed. Commission proposals to create a network of 30 international freight routes, designed to promote the growth of combined transport—a technique for shifting freight from road to rail by enabling the bulk of the journey to be carried out by rail and final leg of the journey to be carried out by road—have been accepted by member states as a means of reducing traffic congestion on national motorway networks. From January 1993 any company providing combined transport services will have the automatic right of access to the rail network of other member states. Finally, transport ministers agreed to begin work on harmonizing standards for new rolling stock and lineside structures.

The air transport sector

Because governments exercise sovereignty over their own airspace in a way similar to that enjoyed over their physical territory, entry into a national airspace has to be authorized by its respective government. Few governments, however, are equipped to carry out this function, and so they allocate the task to their national carriers (most of which are state-owned), who are empowered to negotiate terms governing capacity, fares, landing and take-off rights with other national carriers—subject to approval of member state governments. Out of a desire for a comfortable life, and in an effort to guarantee themselves a stable income, national carriers have traditionally granted landing rights to one foreign carrier in return for reciprocal landing rights in its country of origin. The two airlines have then entered into negotiations about flight prices and schedules and confirmed the deal by dividing the income generated between them on a 50–50 basis.

This formula was duplicated with the national carriers of every other country, thereby creating a powerful cartel throughout the international air transport industry which ensured the least possible competition between national airlines. Air fares were thus determined by cosy mutual agreements which deprived any new airline wanting to compete on somebody else's route the right to gain access to the market. The result, especially after deregulation of the US air transport sector, was that a passenger seeking the cheapest flight from, for example, London to Madrid would have to go via New York. Just as the railway networks were the pride of states in the nineteenth century, so the national air carriers became the symbol of state virility in the twentieth, and governments were reluctant to sanction any liberalization that might jeopardize the viability of their own airlines.

Admittedly, charter airlines are now firmly established, but they have done little to promote price competition between scheduled airlines, who still cater almost exclusively for the business traveller. Confident that their position was unassailable, the Community's national carriers had little incentive to introduce any change. In 1974, however, the first breach in the air transport sector's protected market was made following a ruling by the European Court of Justice that civil aviation was not exempt from the competition provisions of the Treaty of Rome. This ruling was given added force in 1986 in a case brought by the French travel agency Nouvelles Frontières, in which the Court confirmed that the Community's competition rules applied to the skies.

A bilateral agreement between Britain and the Netherlands in 1984, which opened up the market for new carriers, resulted in the introduction of cheaper fares between London and Amsterdam, and a 10% increase in passengers almost overnight. Flag carriers were soon forced to follow suit, but the arrival of discount fares was invariably surrounded by innumerable restrictions in an attempt to limit their effect on flag carriers' standard prices. Discount fares were merely a small hole in the cartel's dyke, but they were, nonetheless, the first significant erosion of the industry's power to set prices independently of market forces.

The combination of the Court's rulings, the determination of the Commission to create an internal market for transport in the air as well as on the ground, the emergence of small independent carriers challenging the dominance of the established airlines and the relentless assault on the air transport cartel by European consumer groups had finally put the Community's air transport industry on the defensive. In an attempt to drive home its advantage, the Commission made a two-pronged assault on the air transport sector by trying to agree an air transport liberalization package in the Council of Ministers while simultaneously threatening legal action against the Community's national carriers under Article 85 of the Treaty, should the negotiations fail. Once the national carriers had backed down and had recognized the authority of the Commission to enforce the competition rules, attention turned to the discussions between member states over price fixing, capacity and revenue sharing, in anticipation of the long-awaited arrival of the age of cheap air fares for millions of European travellers.

However, despite the furore raised by the airline companies, the changes demanded by the Commission could hardly be described as revolutionary. The main elements of the package provided for the abolition of the clauses in their bilateral agreements which formed the cornerstone of the air transport cartel (the so-called 50–50 deals), guaranteeing flag carriers only 45% of capacity for a two-year period, falling to 40% in the third year. It also sought to establish freedom of entry for new carriers on major routes, and to open up services between major hub and regional airports, and the introduction of discounts of up to 45% on normal economy class fares subject to certain restrictions. The proposals were very different from the creation of a European air space and the dismantling of the principle of bilateralism upon which the air transport cartel rested.

Consumer organizations, sceptical that acceptance of the package would lead to any significant reform of the structure of the European air transport industry, warned of a possible sell-out, and demanded that the Commission avail itself of the power conferred on it by the Community's competition rules. The Brussels-based consumer organization, BEUC, a consortium of consumer groups drawn from all over the Community, warned that: 'Whilst the gradual spread of lower fares continues, the resistance to any real change by the majority of scheduled airlines has now become so apparent that a satisfactory outcome in the Transport Council, without Commission and Court action, is impossible'. BEUC insisted that only the unimpeded freedom of new airlines to compete with established operators would open up the air transport sector to the rigours of competition, and demanded the full application of the Treaty's competition rules in place of the proposed 'watered-down agreement' being tabled by the Commission.

As member states gathered in Luxembourg in June 1987 for a crucial transport ministers' meeting the Commission was confident that the air transport liberalization package would finally get their approval. It acknowledged that its proposals were modest, and that the airlines would need time to adjust to a new competitive environment, but maintained that acceptance of the package would be a major first step along the road to more substantive reform.

However, just as the member states were about to put their signatures to the historic agreement an unexpected diplomatic row between Britain and Spain over whether Gibraltar Airport should be included in the package delayed the deal for months. Because the majority voting provisions of the Single European Act did not come into effect until 1 July, Spain was able to exercise a veto over the package. Señor Jesus Ezquerra, the Spanish minister responsible for conducting the negotiations with Britain over the status of Gibraltar, maintained that the land on which Gibraltar Airport was built was not ceded to Britain under the 1713 Treaty of Utrecht.

Portraying Britain as a neocolonialist power refusing to give up the ill-gotten gains of centuries past, Ezquerra insisted that Madrid could not sign an agreement covering Gibraltar without enshrining its present status in Community law, and demanded that Gibraltar be excluded from the deal. British ministers, infuriated at Ezquerra's decision to introduce a long-running bilateral dispute into a Community context, emphasized that Madrid had already accepted Gibraltar's status when it ratified Spain's accession agreement, and, for good measure, discreetly drew attention to Spain's Moroccan enclaves, Ceuta and Melilla, to demonstrate that one former colonial power was at least as bad as the next. However, Ezquerra could not be appeased, the deadline expired and the Commission was forced to redraft its proposals and present them to the European Parliament and the Council of Ministers, as required under the new procedures of the Single European Act. Only the consumers' organizations, which regarded the package as a betrayal of consumer interests in any case, had a kind word for Ezquerra.

When the package came up again for approval in December 1987 Ezquerra failed to put in an appearance, and the deal finally went through. Its provisions were more or less identical to those on the table in June, covering air fares, capacity sharing and market access, and the application of the competition rules to the air transport sector. Only services between member states were subject to the deal, while the application of the competition rules was limited to scheduled airlines alone. The package was the first effective inroad into the power of member states to control their scheduled airlines and introduced competition into what Commissioner Sutherland had once described as 'the most uniquely anti-competitive cartel in Europe'.

As of 1 January 1988, a common bilateral procedure for the approval of discount and deep discount fares became effective throughout the Community and a timetable established for the phasing out of capacity-sharing arrangements between the major airlines. Under that timetable national carriers are entitled to only 40% of route capacity, and the Commission hopes that even this protection will be abolished by the 1992 deadline. Routes between most major hub and regional airports have been opened up, and procedures for applying Articles 85 and 86 to the air transport sector have also been established.

However, it is clear that the major airlines still regard the prospect of across-the-board lower fares as anathema. Despite the adverse effect of the lower fares charged by some of the smaller airlines on flag carrier profits, few have been forced to fundamentally overhaul their price structures. Indeed, most have done their utmost to resist reducing prices by trying to attract customers, especially business executives, with greater comfort and style. As Sir Colin Marshall, the chief executive of British Airways, said in an interview with *The Times* in October 1988: 'We are in business to make money. Low fares are available—at the back of the aircraft'. But greater competition in the post-1992 era could force many companies to trim their generous travel budgets, adding considerably to the downward pressure on prices.

As an indication of the Commission's determination to introduce greater competition in the air transport sector, the Belgian national carrier, Sabena, was fined £65,000 in November 1988 for refusing to give the Irish-owned air liner, Ryanair, access to its computer reservation system because the Dublin-based company was offering cut-price flights. The Commission's action followed a dawn raid on Sabena's headquarters the previous year, and was the first occasion on which the Community had exercised its new powers against an airline involved in anti-competitive behaviour.

As Community citizens were anxiously awaiting the arrival of the age of cheap air travel the Association of European Airlines (AEA), which represents 21 airlines responsible for approximately 90% of Europe's air traffic, began to issue a series of warnings about the shortcomings of the internal market programme. At its annual conference in Paris in April 1988 Karl-Heinz Neumeister, the Secretary General of the AEA, warned that the Commission's fiscal harmonization proposals would be a step backwards for the air transport industry. Once the internal market programme is completed, all intra-Community flights will be classified as domestic and therefore subject to Vat. However, Neumeister pointed out that the possibility of different rates within the lower 4% to 9% Vat band between member states would actually be a step away from a perfectly harmonized market, currently at 0%. Consequently, there was a need to maintain the zero rate or at least introduce a single rate throughout the Community.

Furthermore, Neumeister predicted that the abolition of internal frontier controls would require the expansion of the domestic sections of airports, while the introduction of new routes and more flights was likely to lead to a considerable expansion in demand, and yet few governments were planning to increase existing airport and runway handling capacity. Perhaps most important of all, the Secretary General drew attention to a major anomaly in the internal market programme which allowed member states to continue exercising sovereignty over their own air space (effectively fragmenting Europe's air space into twelve segments), a situation which was widely regarded as the major cause of the delays experienced by air travellers in the summer of 1988. In 1987 air traffic movements were already at levels forecast for 1991, and Neumeister predicted that the situation would only get worse until the member states overcame their traditional reluctance to relax control over their own air space:

> We would like to see an integrated European air traffic control system with co-ordinated plans, and at least working with the same standards. Perhaps we should give Eurocontrol the task it was originally designed to have: to co-ordinate and control the air traffic flows in Europe. Are we going to have the single market on the ground and still divide the skies?

In July 1988 the European Parliament accepted Neumeister's challenge by calling for the merging of Europe's air traffic control systems into a single Community network, under the authority of the Netherlands-based organization, Eurocontrol, which is already responsible for monitoring and predicting daily air traffic flows. Unfortunately, there was little to suggest that member states are prepared to accept the one remedy for freeing the Community's congested skies. Then in September, Paul Channon, then Secretary of State for Transport, gave the first indication that Britain was seriously considering the creation of a central unit responsible for flight planning in Europe. The issue was discussed by EC transport ministers meeting in Frankfurt in November, when the Commission formally proposed to member states that they create a single European air traffic control system based on Eurocontrol. By July the following year, when tens of thousands of tourists again faced lengthy delays at British airports, Community transport ministers agreed to a £40 million scheme setting up a centralized airflow management system based at Eurocontrol. However, while the new system will undoubtedly help to reduce departure delays, it is unlikely to be fully operational before 1992.

Meanwhile, the European Court of Justice had ruled the previous April that virtually all air fare price-fixing arrangements could be in violation of Community competition rules. Encouraged by a ruling which indicated that price-fixing arrangements on routes within member states (as well as those to non-Community destinations) were possibly illegal, the Commission announced three months later its intention to press ahead with phase two of the air-transport liberalization programme. In January 1990 Karel van Miert, the Transport Commissioner, proposed that member states should cede their right to negotiate air routes with the rest of the world to the Commission. If accepted, the proposal would give Commission officials the power to bargain with the government's of the world's carriers, such as those in America and Asia, granting routes and landing rights in the Community in exchange for reciprocal rights outside the Twelve.

Moreover, the Commission would also be able to exploit its collective negotiating position to open up competition inside the Community by using the attractive incentive of access to third-country airports to open the domestic markets of individual member states. The Commission is particularly keen on extending what are known as 'fifth freedom rights' —the right of an airline in one member state to pick up passengers in a second member state and deposit them in a third. As van Miert pointed out, the United States has 18 such routes in the Community, granting it fifth freedom rights, while Community carriers have no such privileges in the United States (not counting fifth freedom rights between the continental United States and Puerto Rico).

By the summer of 1990, however, most observers were becoming more sceptical of the Commission's ability to increase competition in air transport, and thus pave the way for the seemingly elusive era of cheap air fares. Indeed, the trend towards concentration, such as Air France's plans to take over its domestic rival UTA and Inter Air, and the proposed joint venture between BA, KLM and Sabena, were seen by many critics as a rearguard action by national governments to strengthen their national carriers by reducing competition.

Such enthusiasm for the liberalization of air transport was not shared by the industry, whose operators were becoming increasingly anxious about the potential growth of a Community bureaucracy governing the sector. These fears materialized in October 1990, when the Commission announced its proposals for rationing landing rights in Europe's congested airports. The objective was to ensure that smaller carriers were given fair access to the limited number of take-off and landing slots needed to run services, an objective described by one airline as like telling department stores that they had to hand over large areas of their floor space to smaller High Street rivals in the interests of fair competition. Nevertheless, in December 1990, the proposals were adopted. Under the new rules, surplus take-off and landing rights are to be put in a pool for distribution among carriers, half of which must go to new entrants, while proposals for cheaper fares can only be blocked by the so-called 'double disapproval' principle, which requires national governments at either end of the route to withhold their authorization.

Iraq's invasion of Kuwait in August 1990 and the subsequent Gulf War, increasing oil prices and collapse in demand for air travel were to cast an ominous shadow over the Commission's attempt to open up air transport. The crisis confronted airlines across the world with sudden and potentially huge losses, and many were to go out of business. In an effort to help European airlines to overcome the crisis, the Commission proposed a series of measures, including the temporary suspension of the competition laws to enable airlines to create joint ventures on loss-making routes, which were generally greeted with scorn by the industry. When British Airways announced its decision in the summer of 1991 to withdraw from air routes to the Republic of Ireland, a route which had been opened to competition from allcomers in 1985, many observers feared that the Commission's air-liberalization initiative was going to prove as disruptive to European air transport as the US government's earlier air-liberalization programme had been in North America. By May 1991 van Miert was openly saying that the third and final air-liberalization or 'open-skies' package was in trouble.

However, such pessimism turned out to be premature. In July 1991 van Miert tabled the Commission's final air-liberalization package, calling for the establishment of common criteria for licensing Community air carriers, open access to routes for all new carriers, recognition of the principle of double disapproval on fares and the introduction of cabotage —the right to pick up passengers and freight in a second member state destined for a third. Surprisingly, the AEA gave the open-skies proposal a cautious welcome, although the organization continued to have reservations about forcing existing carriers to cede their rights to surplus landing and take-off slots. The package would, in effect, give airlines the freedom to set fares themselves, subject to regulation by market forces, although approval from member states is unlikely to be forthcoming until well into 1992.

Road transport and coastal trade

One of the most pervasive barriers to free trade in the Community is the technically illegal system of bilateral licences governing the European road haulage industry. Road haulage companies obtain the right of access to the roads of other member states on the basis of a licence obtained from its national department of transport. These, in turn, are arranged through a series of annual bilateral negotiations between member states, which determine the number of licences that are to be made available. In 1986, for example, Germany granted 91,000 licences to Italian road haulage companies, while Italy granted 145,000 licences to German ones. But the system has long been denounced, principally by Britain, as iniquitous, inefficient and one which protects the interests of the larger member states at the expense of their smaller neighbours.

Road haulage, which accounts for about £322 billion of intra-Community trade, is by far the most important artery along which trade between member states flows, and it is long overdue for reform. However, the Commission's proposals to create an internal market for road haulage were regarded by Germany as a serious threat to its own heavily protected industry. The politically powerful German road haulage lobby, fearful that much of its road haulage trade would slip away to its more efficient Dutch and Belgian competitors, adamantly opposed any liberalization before progress had been made on harmonizing the industry's operating conditions, notably lorry and fuel taxes and drivers' terms of employment.

Under pressure of legal action from the Commission, and a persistent refusal by Britain to accept anything less than the complete implementation of the Commission's liberalization proposals, the Germans finally conceded at the Transport Council in Luxembourg in June 1988. The deal, which was widely seen as a major breakthrough for the internal market programme, committed member states to the complete abolition of quotas to Community and non-Community destinations by 1 January 1993, and required the Commission to specify the harmonization measures needed to ensure fair competition among road haulage companies by June 1991.

By the time the quota system is abolished, Community road haulage companies will be able to avail themselves of the freedom to make as many journeys as they like, anywhere in the Community. Far from increasing the number of articulated lorries on Europe's roads, the internal market in road haulage will automatically lead to a reduction of the number of empty lorries (estimated by the Commission to be around one in three), due to existing restrictions on trade conducted in other member states. In 1990, member states agreed to the progressive introduction of cabotage, which will enable, for example, a British road haulage company delivering a freight consignment from Manchester to Munich to be able to compete with local German firms for business between, say, Frankfurt and Hamburg. Despite attempts by British road hauliers to obtain government approval for an end to the derogation which imposes a 38-tonne limit on lorries on British roads by 1992 (thus bringing them into line with the 40-tonne ceiling enforced in other member states), Paul Channon managed to retain the derogation until 31 December 1998, on the grounds that the government's bridge-strengthening programme would not be completed until that date. Proposals to liberalize bus and coach transport have, however, been less successful. Attempts by one member state to introduce scheduled bus and coach services in other member states are still subject to prior government approval, which can often be refused if the proposed service competes with existing services.

Similarly, Britain has been less successful in convincing its partners of the need to abolish restrictions on Community ships trading along each other's coastlines. Britain, Ireland, Belgium and the Netherlands are the only countries that grant foreign vessels the unrestricted right to pick up and deliver loads between ports on their coastlines, known as coastal cabotage. Most of the Southern European states, fearful of increased competition, continue to reserve coastal trade for domestic shipping. If progress is not forthcoming Britain is likely to implement those provisions of the 1988 Merchant Shipping Act which grant it the power to demand reciprocal treatment. However, proposals to remove overcapacity in the inland waterways industry, caused largely by the decline of heavy industry, were adopted in 1990, enabling member states to scrap an estimated 1,600 surplus vessels—most of which were antiquated river barges—and thereby help the inland waterways to adjust to changing market circumstances. Similarly, following earlier attempts to halt the decline in Europe's merchant fleet, the Commission is now also seeking approval for a new Community shipping register and Community flag.

Finally, in 1989 van Miert was able to secure approval from member states to establish a new Community infrastructure fund. Although the sums involved are relatively small compared to other Community funding schemes, this is at least a beginning, and will no doubt expand as increasing demands are placed on it. The fund's first three-year action programme, which covers the period from 1990 to 1992, is designed to provide capital for high speed rail link projects, new Alpine and Pyrenean road and rail passes, the upgrading of the North Wales coastal road linking Ireland with the rest of the Community and improved road and rail links between the two formerly estranged halves of Europe.

Travel and tourism

Tourism now accounts for almost 5% of the Community's gross domestic product, is responsible for some 5.5 million jobs and is expanding constantly. An estimated 75% of Britons have visited at least one Community country, while the average Briton has visited 3.5 member states. The Community has spent millions of pounds developing a tourist infrastructure (holiday villages, pleasure harbours, ski-lifts and hotels) through the regional development funds and the European Investment Bank in an attempt to provide new employment opportunities and relieve some of the congestion in the more popular and overdeveloped resorts.

The Commission has also attempted to make life easier for tourists by introducing the Community passport, and producing brochures giving detailed information on existing border-crossing formalities, duty-free allowances and the availability of health care. Further publications listing places of interest such as museums and art galleries are in preparation, as are plans to produce a standardized classification of Community hotels (priced in ECUs) and a directive regulating the package holiday industry.

By 1992 millions of travellers and holidaymakers will be deprived of their duty-free allowances (now regarded as the legitimate booty of foreign travel) if the Commission's proposals on fiscal approximation are implemented. Yet the abolition of duty-frees is unlikely to be the unmitigated disaster predicted by the pro-duty-free lobby. Admittedly, Community-wide duty-free sales are estimated to be worth about £2 billion a year, and their demise, only as far as intra-Community travel is concerned, will have a significant impact on the revenues of short-haul ferries, charter airlines and regional airports.

However, everyone involved in the duty-free industry accepts that abolition is merely a question of time, and are already planning ways of compensating themselves for lost revenues. British ferry companies are planning to introduce a new generation of floating department stores for cross-Channel shoppers. Built from modified roll-on–roll-off ferries, the offshore superstores are likely to make extensive use of franchises, similar to those already in operation at most Community airports, to sell a wide selection of discount consumer products.

James Hannah, Sealink British Ferries' corporate communications director, is convinced that there are great opportunities for skilful marketing to a captive audience. Pointing to the success of franchising operations at airports, Hannah said that:

> Dublin Airport, for example, is now selling more black silk lingerie than many major High Street stores. It's quite a phenomenon. I suspect it's the only chance businessmen get to buy their wives a gift.

These sentiments are also shared by Graeme Dunlop, managing director of P&O European Ferries, who told *The Times* in an interview in June 1988:

> We are making our plans now on the assumption that the European internal market will be a reality in 1992. If we are going to survive, it's the only prudent course to take.

Indeed, in the face of the threat posed by the Channel Tunnel, the cross-Channel ferry companies have had to transform the way they do business. In 1988, James Elles, the Conservative MEP for Oxford and Buckinghamshire, was, with some justification, able to describe passing through the port of Dover as similar to going through an 'East European' border post. Elles demanded to know why the British ports were unable to introduce simplified frontier procedures, similar to the red and green channels used at major airports. By 1991, however, the ferry companies had been able to bring about significant reductions in the formalities and time taken to pass through Dover's port facilities.

Despite the generally optimistic prospects for the European tourist industry, greater mobility throughout the Community has brought with it the serious and growing problems of hooliganism and drunken rowdiness. These are by no means confined to British tourists, although the reputation is. During her visit to Spain in September 1988 Mrs Thatcher felt compelled to apologize to Felipe Gonzalez, the Spanish Prime Minister, for the behaviour of the small minority of British holidaymakers who have been responsible for disfiguring many Spanish resorts in recent years. Mrs Thatcher made it clear, however, that the Spanish authorities had her personal support in taking severe action against the trouble-makers. It may eventually be necessary to consider a Community initiative designed to temporarily deprive those Community nationals unable to behave responsibly in other member states of the right to travel in the internal market, perhaps through the issue of EC identity cards, withdrawable in the event of damage or nuisance to property or persons.

Checklist of changes

- The European Commission's determination to create an internal market for air transport will further erode the restrictive practices of the European air transport industry.
- There will be increased freedom of entry for independent air carriers on major European air routes.
- Services between major and regional airports will be progressively increased.
- National carriers seeking to restrict competition from the new independent carriers will find themselves subject to substantial fines imposed by the Commission for violating the Community's competition rules.
- The availability of discount fares can be expected to multiply as a result of increased competition from the new independent carriers.
- In an effort to ease the congestion in Europe's crowded skies, pressure for a single integrated European air traffic control system will result in the creation of a central unit responsible for flight planning in Europe.
- There will be an internal market for road haulage following the abolition of the system of national quotas for the road haulage industry.
- European road haulage companies will have complete freedom of destination within the Community.
- Coastal trade will also be opened up to free competition.
- Duty-free allowances for travellers will come to an end following the harmonization of member states' varying rates of indirect taxation.

14 SATELLITE BROADCASTING

Television technology in the 1990s

Towards the end of the 1980s Europe's audiovisual sector had clearly arrived at a cultural, technological and economic crossroads. The national film and television industries, which had flourished since the Second World War—largely, though by no means exclusively, within the confines of national boundaries—were suddenly confronted with the imminent arrival of a European-wide market for films and television and the broadcasting and reception equipment needed to transmit and receive them. As in so many areas of human endeavour, the rapid pace of technological development had, seemingly overnight, led to the internationalization of the entire audiovisual industry. By contrast, the legal and regulatory framework which governed the way in which the audiovisual sector operated in the individual member states continued to function along national lines. Unless the essentially national character of regulation was brought into line with the new international character of broadcasting, the long-term prospects of the Community's audiovisual sector were in danger.

The need for a new framework

Of all the internal market directives contained in the White Paper programme, few aroused as much passion as the European Commission's efforts to create a single market for satellite broadcasting without frontiers. Supporters of the Commission's unprecedented entry into the television broadcasting sector characterized the initiative (in imagery similar to that used in Hollywood's portrayal of the last days of General Custer) as Europe's heroic last stand against the twin assault of American cultural imperialism and Japanese technological dominance, and the only real hope of saving Europe's ailing cinema film and electronics industries from extinction.

This vision of the Community's predicament was not shared by everyone. Some member states, principally Britain, Denmark and Germany insisted that there was no compelling case for Community legislation in the field of satellite broadcasting and challenged the competence of the Commission to legislate on cultural matters. Many of the new English-language satellite companies endorsed the Commission's broad objectives, but were deeply opposed to the way in which it has set about putting them into practice. Finally, over the past few years there have been many prophets of doom, predicting that the age of satellite broadcasting will destroy civilization as we know it by submerging national values and culture in a tidal wave of smut, pornography, gratuitous violence, low-budget soap operas and game shows, manipulative advertising and, to cap it all, US-style television evangelists.

Passion aside, the Community was confronted by a series of wide-ranging changes in the audiovisual sector which it could do nothing to prevent. The rapid pace of technological change in the field of telecommunications had already conferred on satellite broadcasters the ability to ignore national boundaries and reach audiences of continental proportions. The so-called 'footprint' of satellite transmissions cannot be held up at national border controls for inspection by customs officers before being granted or refused permission to enter.

However, because of the great variation in national regulations governing television broadcasts, particularly on advertising, programming and public morality, the technical ability of the new satellite companies to reach large numbers of people was constrained by their legal obligation to respect the differing regulations of the various member states. Unless satellite broadcasters comply with national regulations, the cable companies who relay the satellite transmissions into our homes can be effectively prohibited from doing so. Even in the case of direct broadcasting by satellite (where viewers can pick up transmissions themselves after installing the necessary receiving equipment) the member states are capable of preventing transmissions which violate national law through the Community's legal system and, theoretically, by the use of sophisticated jamming techniques.

If the extraterrestrial technological advances were not to be stillborn as a result of divergent terrestrial regulations, twelve national systems had to be replaced by one set of common rules governing satellite broadcasting. Addressing the Independent Broadcasting Authority on the sensitive question of advertising regulations in April 1985, Dr Ivo Schwartz, the Commission official responsible for overseeing the Community's satellite broadcasting initiative, said:

> Given the reality of communication satellites and continental wide cable television, as well as the imminence of direct broadcasting by satellite, the Commission believes that it is essential to institute as quickly as possible a minimum of rules for European advertising within which the providers of commercially supported programmes may freely operate. Such limited approximation will make it possible that from then on, only the rules of the country of transmission shall apply to cross-border advertisements.

The same principle would also be applied to the European content of programming schedules, public morality and the protection of minors.

However, the Commission maintained that the audiovisual challenge faced by the Community goes far beyond the mere legal mechanics of creating a single unified market for satellite broadcasting. Europe is also confronted by a series of cultural, scientific, technical, industrial and commercial challenges, in which the United States and Japan clearly have the advantage. The Commission has forecast that somewhere in the region of 200 new satellite channels could be available by the 1990s. The very rapid growth in the number of broadcasting hours available is already beginning to generate an almost insatiable demand for new programming material, which European countries are unable to satisfy at competitive prices. Similarly, the expansion of satellite broadcasting has already begun to create new markets for transmission equipment and mass markets for receiving equipment. These new markets could provide a great stimulus to Europe's electronics industry, creating thousands of new jobs in the process. However, many EC and national officials feared that, unless the Community is able to respond to these challenges, the benefits of a single market for satellite broadcasting will be enjoyed only by film studios in Hollywood and consumer electronics companies in Tokyo.

Television without frontiers

The challenge to the Community's competence to legislate in the field of satellite broadcasting was effectively undermined following the adoption by all member states of the Internal Market White Paper, which made explicit reference to the need to create an internal market for cross-frontier television broadcasting. Furthermore, the Commission was able to point to its obligation under Article 3 of the Treaty of Rome, requiring it to approximate national laws 'to the extent required for the proper functioning of the common market', and Articles 59–62, which prohibit member states from exercising their supervisory powers to restrict trade in goods and services on a discriminatory basis. As 'services' include television broadcasting, these articles collectively confer on the Commission the authority to propose legislation regulating satellite broadcasting between member states.

They also provide the legal basis on which the satellite broadcasters themselves, even in defiance of the wishes of national governments, can demand access to audiences throughout the Community. However, member states retain the legal right to impose non-discriminatory restrictions on foreign and domestic broadcasters in the interests of public policy, security and health, or because of the need to protect copyright, until such times as the various national laws had been harmonized. As a result, by the time the satellite broadcasters had acquired the technical ability to reach European-wide audiences it was not only incumbent on the Commission to provide the necessary regulatory framework for them to do so but had also become a race against time to put this framework in place before or shortly after the satellite stations were operational.

The urgency of this task was emphasized by the collapse of Europa-TV in November 1986. A group of networks from five member states had combined in an attempt to launch the first public broadcasting service as an alternative to the growing number of private, commercial stations. Using the latest technology for dubbing and subtitling, Europa-TV transmitted multilingual broadcasts to some 5 million homes in the Community. But after running up debts in excess of £25 million, the Netherlands pulled out, and the initiative came to a halt. According to the testimony given by a Commission official to the House of Lords Select Committee on the European Communities in 1987:

> Europa-TV faced formidable difficulties obtaining access to existing cable networks because of conflicting advertising regulations in West Germany, Belgium, Ireland, Denmark and even in its host country the Netherlands. It failed because it could not generate sufficient advertising revenues.

Following publication of the Commission's 1984 Green Paper on television without frontiers and extensive consultations with member states (including the various professions involved in the television industry), the Commission tabled a draft directive on satellite broadcasting in June 1986, later revised in March 1988. Behind the proposed legislation lay the conviction that the Community was more than merely an organization of states; it was also a union of peoples. The emergence of cross-frontier television broadcasting would reinforce the creation of the internal market by providing companies with access to a single market of 320 million consumers through satellite advertising. However, it also contained the rather visionary notion that new communications satellites would also provide the means by which the peoples of Europe would become more familiar with each other as a result of exposure to their different television cultures, thereby reinforcing (or, perhaps more realistically, at least making people aware in the first place) that they shared a common economic and cultural identity.

The directive is designed to enable satellite broadcasters to transmit programmes anywhere in the Community without restriction or interference from other member states provided that they meet certain minimum requirements governing the European content of programming, the organization of advertising breaks, copyright protection, public morality and the protection of minors. The directive also applied to ground-based broadcasters if their transmissions can be received in neighbouring member states. Lord Cockfield attached particular importance to the directive, regarding it as the 'flagship' of the entire internal market programme, and called for prompt action by the member states to implement the proposal which was already a year behind schedule. However, the draft legislation met with bitter opposition when ministers first discussed it in March 1988. From the outset, Britain had objected vigorously to any attempt to introduce programme quotas. Ministers made no secret of their conviction that the proposal was one of the most élitist and paternalistic documents ever produced by the Commission. It was denounced as an example of 'European cultural imperialism', and Britain felt that it had no alternative but to put all its hopes for a more liberal satellite broadcasting system on the rival convention being drawn up by the 21-member Council of Europe in Strasbourg.

Quotas, advertisements and copyright

Within three years of the March proposal being adopted, all satellite broadcasters would have been required to reserve at least 60% of their air time for feature films made in the Community or in association with members of EFTA and the Council of Europe. The proposal had nothing to do with abolishing barriers to the free movement of television across frontiers. In fact, it purposely sets out to achieve the exact opposite. Its overriding objective was to stimulate the European film industry by protecting it from foreign competition and providing it with a guaranteed part of the European market. The Commission maintained that such action is necessary because:

> Frequent warnings are heard about the dangers of the cultural
> domination of one country by another in motion pictures, although
> this is not a problem between member states. As for the production
> of television programmes within the Community, no individual
> member states are predominant. Statistics on the films broadcast
> on television in member states show that the proportion of films
> from other member states is regrettably small. However, most of
> the films shown come from a single non-member country, the
> US.

The main source of such warnings are the French and Italian film industries, who were already facing difficult times and feared that they would have to close if they were forced to compete with their American counterparts. Writing in the spring 1988 edition of *European Affairs*, Jack Lang, the National Secretary for Culture and Youth in the French Socialist Party, while paying tribute to the achievements of the American film industry attacked the view expressed by Britain that the new satellite broadcasting companies should be allowed to decide for themselves what proportion of their broadcast material came from within or outside the Community. Lang insisted that:

> At a time when Europe, the cradle of Western civilization, loses
> control over one of the main areas in which contemporary

culture is being made, the audiovisual, one can no longer react aesthetically to such liberal or ultra-liberal ideologies. Reality demands that concrete steps be taken as quickly as possible.

By which he meant quotas.

In defence of the proposal, Lord Cockfield maintained that the quota plan was not so much anti-American as pro-European. Commission officials, however, acknowledged that the 60% quota would present severe difficulties for specialized film channels, and indicated that a limited number of derogations or exemptions could be incorporated into the directive. However, such concessions did little to allay the anxieties of satellite and ground-based broadcasters, who feared that the Commission was asking them to drink a cup of hemlock in the name of the defence of European culture.

In 1987, for example, the BBC screened 709 feature films, of which 409 were made in the United States. Both Sky Channel, owned by Rupert Murdoch, and SuperChannel, owned by Richard Branson in association with an Italian company, are also heavily dependent on US feature films. The same applies to every other English-language satellite station planning to launch new stations, even the non-English-language ones showing dubbed or subtitled US films. Whatever the critics of the US film industry may say, American feature films are extremely popular all over Europe, and the attempt to restrict them to 40% of the European market would have deprived the new satellite stations of the large-scale audiences and advertising revenues needed to make them economically viable. After all, what one cannot see on television one can usually pick up in a High Street video shop.

The Commission argued that Britain's opposition to the quota plan was dogmatic, and points out that the Independent Broadcasting Authority (IBA) already accepts the principle of quotas by requiring 86% of all programmes on ITV and Channel 4 to come from Community sources. However, Britain insists that this is a regulation enforced by the IBA, and apart from specifying that a 'proper proportion' of all broadcast material should be Community sourced, broadcasters should be free from government or Commission interference to decide what that level should be. The problem faced by the Commission, however, is that it is not self-evident what a proper proportion means. Twelve member states would produce twelve different definitions, effectively creating a new barrier to satellite broadcasting across frontiers. At the same time, no amount of compulsory screening will make European-made films any more popular.

The Commission's proposed regulations on satellite advertising received a considerably less hostile reception from most member states. The directive established a maximum threshold of 15% a day or 18% an hour of total programming time which can be allocated to broadcast advertising. Any station transmitting above these thresholds can be prohibited by the member states. Governments retain the right to impose more stringent conditions on domestic broadcasters serving national audiences if they so wish. The directive no longer required broadcasters to group advertisements at the end of programmes, as specified in the 1986 version. Under the terms of the revised directive they were granted the option of broadcasting commercial breaks in concentrated blocks or periodic slots, provided that the 'integrity' of programmes was maintained and as long as programmes were not interrupted excessively. Advertisements must not fall below prevailing standards of decency or exploit the immaturity of minors.

Britain seemed to be quite content with the directive's provisions on broadcast advertising, in contrast to those incorporated into the Council of Europe's convention on satellite broadcasting. The government had originally agreed with the convention, primarily because of its opposition to the Community's proposed quotas and in the hope that it would prove to be a more liberal regulatory system. However, to the consternation of Downing Street, the Germans, urged on by domestic press barons who did not want to see their advertising revenues jeopardized by competition from the new satellite television stations, were able to insert into the draft convention a provision requiring satellite broadcasters to bunch commercial breaks in a 'block' at the end of programmes. Consternation turned to exasperation in the summer of 1988, when the Germans, without success, tried to have the same restrictions that were incorporated into the draft convention also applied to the draft directive.

Britain, as well as the other member states opposing this provision, was not obliged to sign or ratify the Council's convention. Yet too many refusals to sign would have undermined the entire purpose of the agreement, as individual member states would be forced to embark on bilateral negotiations with their European neighbours. Long before the convention was due to be ratified in November 1988 it was clear that the proposal was deadlocked.

Although ministers were unable to reach a consensus on the convention during their subsequent meeting in Stockholm, there was a considerable convergence of views between Britain and Germany on advertising breaks. Britain appeared ready to accept that 'serious' programmes should not be interrupted more than once every 45 minutes, while Germany seemed content with allowing more frequent advertising breaks for less serious programmes. Nevertheless, France still expressed grave reservations about allowing too much imported US broadcast material into the Community, and seemed to be determined to hold out for a quota of at least 50% of all programmes broadcast to be of Community origin. With agreement still out of reach, ratification was postponed until June 1989. The Commission, however, saw the impasse over the convention as an opportunity to rewrite their own draft directive and regain the initiative in the rivalry between the two organizations to create Europe's satellite broadcasting system for the twenty-first century.

In the summer of 1988 Commission officials let it be known that a plan to split the draft directive in two was being given serious consideration. The scheme would enable the Commission to deal separately with the issues of programme quotas and advertising regulations. If accepted, it would mean that the Commission could press ahead with issuing a directive on satellite broadcast advertising for an industry whose development was outstripping the ability of Community and national legislators to regulate it, while allowing the vexed issue of programme quotas to be given a reduced priority for EC cultural affairs ministers to sort out at their leisure. However, officials realized that the major obstacle in the way of the proposal would be the objections of France and Italy, who appeared to remain adamant over their demand for Community quotas.

Gradually, however, it began to occur to the French authorities that quotas and advertising restrictions could mean the end of the new satellite companies. If broadcasters could not transmit the kind of material likely to attract mass audiences, and if restrictive advertising regulations forced the advertisers to seek other outlets, then there would be no new satellite stations, and certainly no new money with which to stimulate the output of the ailing European film and audiovisual industry. In February 1989, EC trade ministers (taking their cue from the Rhodes summit meeting) managed to agree on a compromise on the controversial issue of quotas, allowing satellite broadcasters to transmit a 'majority' of European-made programmes 'where practical', thereby eliminating Britain's objection to the imposition of legally enforceable quotas. Unfortunately, the compromise began to unravel in June, due to last-minute reservations by Paris. The issue fell to France to resolve during its Presidency of the Council of Ministers.

In October, during a ministerial meeting in Luxembourg, the seemingly interminable wrangle of cross-frontier broadcasting regulations was finally laid to rest. On a majority vote, the ministers agreed to the 50% European programming restriction, and at the same time accepted that legal imposition of the quota was a 'political' measure, and thus legally unenforceable. Welcoming the agreement, Richard Dunn, chairman of the ITV Association said: 'ITV does not believe the directive will have a detrimental effect on our current practices in terms of advertising, programme content, and origin. We can certainly live with it'. The US, however, immediately expressed its hostility to the measure, and announced its intention to bring the issue before the disputes panel of the General Agreement on Tariffs and Trade.

The Commission believes that the existing system of copyright protection is also a potential barrier to the free movement of programmes across frontiers, and wants to replace it with one that allows satellite and cable companies to broadcast or retransmit any programme after two years, while ensuring adequate remuneration for copyright holders. The Commission argues that once a programme has been placed in the public domain in one member state, copyright regulations should not be used as a method of preventing it from circulating around the other member states. According to one Commission official: 'Once you have taken the fundamental decision to market your service, you cannot rely on national frontiers—in this case through intellectual property rights—to divide the market'.

The system would operate on the basis of voluntary contractual agreements between the copyright owners and broadcasters, sponsored by the individual member states. Broadcasters would have an automatic right to a licence on the copyright if terms could not be agreed within the two-year period. However, anyone broadcasting a programme before the two-year period had expired, or with the intention of depriving the copyright holders of their legitimate remuneration, would be liable to court action in the appropriate member state. The Commission acknowledges that without a system for providing authors, performers and copyright holders with equitable remuneration there would be a detrimental effect on the very industry responsible for generating the programmes needed to fill the new programme schedules. Consequently, copyright must be adapted to reflect the needs of the modern audiovisual age. Britain, however, has opposed the initiative on the grounds that copyright cannot be considered a barrier to trade.

As soon as the dust from the argument over quotas had begun to settle, a new dispute emerged over the Commission's attempts to regulate advertising. In August 1990 it was discovered that Brussels was drafting legislation restricting or prohibiting the advertising of alcohol, tobacco, certain foods, pharmaceuticals and children's toys throughout the Community. Britain's Advertising Association, the industry's trade body, warned that, if implemented in its draft form, the directive would cost the industry hundreds of millions of pounds a year in lost revenues. The plans also aroused great anxiety throughout the Community's television, press and magazine industries, all of whom would be faced by declining income from advertising if the Commission's plans were approved.

The row provoked a bitter debate on the role and influence of advertising, which is still generating more heat than light. On the one hand, it is evident that manufacturers of tobacco products, as with any other product, wish to be able to advertise across frontiers because they believe that such techniques will help to generate sales. This does not, of course, apply to the state-owned tobacco companies in France, Italy, Spain and Portugal, who support stringent restrictions on cross-frontier tobacco advertising because they do not want to see their protected market shares eroded by increased foreign competition. On the other hand, it is difficult to explain consumer choices by reference to advertising alone, as many other factors are involved. Until recently, for example, there were no cigarette advertisements in the Soviet Union or Eastern Europe, but sales have been increasing steadily for decades. Commission officials, along with members of the European Parliament, are still wrestling with the task of reconciling changing social attitudes towards tobacco and alcohol with the revenue-generating needs of the advertising industry. As yet, there is little indication that a compromise is at hand, although new restrictions on cross-border advertising seem inevitable.

Quantity versus quality

If the Commission's estimates are realized and there are some 200 new television stations by the 1990s what will they be broadcasting into our homes? Not enough new material is being produced to fill the existing satellite stations' schedules with new programmes, and many critics fear that an excessive proportion of what we get when the new stations are operational we will probably have seen already, and much of the remainder will be cheap imported soap operas, game shows and serials from the United States, which we will not want to watch in any case. Many fear that the age of satellite telecommunications will represent a giant step forwards for technology, matched only by a giant step backwards for culture.

Fearing the worst, the critics have predicted the end of the expensive quality programmes and the various wildlife documentaries, and because of the competition for advertising revenue, broadcasters will be compelled to fill their air time with popular and inexpensive off-the-shelf reruns. In short, satellite broadcasting will become little more than 'chewing gum for the eyes', and will probably turn us all into vegetables.

It is precisely this anxiety that has prompted the Commission to advocate the introduction of quotas in an effort to stimulate the European film and audiovisual products industry. Having created a single audiovisual market, the Commission wants to have sufficient European products to fill it with, and 'ensure that the new televisual media continue to reflect the Community's cultural diversity and richness, and that the large market does not simply operate to encourage a search for the audiovisual lowest common denominator'. However, there is no guarantee that the Commission's attempts to provide a stimulus for Europe's film and programme makers will prove successful. The French have never shown much of a liking for German serials, Holland is only going to have a a very limited interest in Portugal's news and Britain is unlikely to get too enthusiastic about Greek game shows. Even if some magic formula was found that overcame such national dispositions, it would be many years before there was sufficient material to satisfy the needs of the proliferating satellite television stations.

However, the experience of satellite broadcasting to date, while hardly a triumph, is far from being the unmitigated disaster the pessimists had predicted. Admittedly, the launch of SuperChannel was greeted with almost universally poor reviews, and the lack of late-night advertising forced it to reduce its transmissions from 24 to 20 hours a day. During the summer of 1988 most of its programme schedules were made up of old ITV–BBC reruns like *Some Mothers Do 'ave 'em*, *The Professionals* and *Spitting Image*. However, it has also shown some of the classics of television from the 1950s like *The Twilight Zone*, while its nightly 30-minute European news broadcast (since sadly abandoned) was thoroughly professional, with a breadth of outlook often lacking in British television news programmes.

Similarly, Sky offers a mixture of the high and lowbrow. In the summer of 1988, before it became generally available in Britain, Sky's schedules were filled with many childhood favourites like *Dr Who*, *Lost in Space* and *Fantasy Island*. It has bought in a number of old US programmes like *Hawk*, *Wanted Dead or Alive* and *Hogan's Heroes*, which put many of America's more recent offerings to shame. Sky has also broken new ground with its *Earth Watch* environmental programme and its current affairs programme *Roving Report*. Since linking up with the Arts Channel, viewers have also been able to see a broad selection of classical music, opera and jazz—albeit after midnight. Many adults have objected to what they regard as excessive amounts of music broadcast by satellite channels —a criticism not shared by the Community's teenagers.

The calibre of advertising, by any standard, is atrocious, and is in desperate need of improvement. Nothing much could be done for washing-powder advertisements, which seem unable to break out of the traditional formula in which a housewife compares a new version of the old brand-name to an unnamed rival and decides to go for the newly packaged old washing powder which, as a result of successive unexplained biological breakthroughs, is now washing clothes nuclear-white. Such advertisements are undoubtedly destined to remain appalling, no matter what language they are in. However, for Britain's advertising companies, who, in the words of one observer, have already managed to send the nation to work on an egg and succeeded in getting a respectable proportion of British holidaymakers onto the beach before the Germans, the European advertising market could provide new, interesting and potentially rewarding challenges.

Amid great publicity, Rupert Murdoch's satellite television service was formally launched in Britain in February 1989, with four new channels providing general entertainment, sport, films and a 24-hour news service. The joint venture between Murdoch (who owns *The Times*) and Alan Sugar, the chairman of the Amstrad consumer electronics company, had produced the satellite dishes viewers needed to receive the new channels for around £250, and Britain's satellite television revolution began in earnest. Sky's programmes included newly imported American serials such as the comedy *Wings*, the law drama *Equal Justice*, the mini-series *Lonesome Dove*, many of Hollywood's latest releases and a few British offerings such as *Sale of the Century*. Many critics attacked the new service for targeting the lower end of the market and for failing to produce any new programme ideas. Meanwhile, sales of satellite dishes continued to mount.

The launch of British Satellite Broadcasting (BSB) in April 1990, which provided five new channels of films, sport, light entertainment and current affairs, inaugurated a fierce commercial battle between the two rival satellite companies. BSB, which was owned by a consortium of media groups, including Pearson (owners of the *Financial Times*), Reed International, Granada and Chargeurs, attempted to pitch its product towards the upper end of the market. With both companies confronted by huge start-up costs, mounting operating losses and breakeven dates that were years away, they rapidly became bitter opponents in the struggle for control of the British satellite market. Along with multi-million pound promotion schemes, the two companies traded personal abuse and libel writs, leaving the existing terrestrial channels unscathed.

While observers were debating whether there was room for two satellite stations in Britain, the multi-billion-pound satellite war was brought to an abrupt end with the merger of the two companies in November 1990. Three weeks of secret negotiations led to the creation of a new company, British Sky Broadcasting (BSkyB), in which Sky and BSB shareholders each hold 50% of the combined assets and obligations. But while the merger eased the financial crisis facing the two fledgling satellite companies, it also created many political and legal difficulties.

Roy Hattersley, the shadow Home Secretary, condemned the merger, and threatened to break up large-scale media empires if Labour came to power by seeking an enquiry by the Monopolies and Mergers Commission into 'overlapping' television and newspaper ownership, 'with the intention of breaking up unacceptable concentrations of power'. Critics of the deal demanded to know how it was possible to allow Murdoch, who owns one-third of Britain's national newspaper market, to have a satellite monopoly as well. What was not widely appreciated, however, was that what was seen as a monopoly in Britain amounted to a miniscule share of the satellite television market in Europe, where the competition was widespread—and growing. Separately, the two companies would probably have bled each other to death. Together, they provide Britain with a presence in the new European satellite television industry, and have a prospect of mounting an effective challenge against the existing BBC–ITV duopoly. The European Commission could find no grounds to vet the merger. In a separate action in February 1991, however, Eurosport, the joint venture between Sky, the BBC and the European Broadcasting Union, was prohibited on the grounds that it was likely to 'restrict and distort competition within the Community'.

However, there were more substantive criticisms of the merger. Lord Thompson of Monifieth, a former chairman of the IBA (now the Independent Television Commission) and the Liberal Democrat spokesman on broadcasting, said that the Sky–BSB merger would be 'a setback for prospects of wide screen, high-definition television of the future, in which Britain is a leader'. Before the merger, BSB broadcasts (via the Marco Polo satellite) had been using a new set of technical standards, known as D-Mac, which provides a 35 mm picture quality and stereo sound (although few viewers were equipped with television sets able to receive it). By contrast, Sky broadcasts, via the Astra satellite, use the conventional transmission standards, known as Pal. But the merger required BSB to switch over to Astra, raising fears in some quarters that the new high-definition television technology would fail to receive the boost it needed to become commercially viable.

Under an agreement with the Independent Television Commission, BSkyB will continue to broadcast the merged programme output on the Marco Polo satellite until the end of 1992. The new company also undertook to supply owners of BSB 'squarials' with the Sky satellite dishes needed to receive the Astra signal. Immediately after the merger, Comet, the High Street electrical retail chain owned by Kingfisher, obtained a High Court writ against BSkyB for £6 million in damages for a breach of contract which left it holding obsolete stocks of BSB satellite dishes, although an out-of-court settlement was finally reached in October. In addition, Philips, the Dutch electronics multinational, issued a £100-million law suit because of the losses it expected to incur as one of the manufacturers of D-Mac technology.

However, as BSkyB began to deal with the political and legal implications of the merger the government was faced with a new problem presented by the emerging satellite broadcasting industry—pornography. The issue came to a head in June 1991, when David Henry, a Scottish businessman, announced plans for a new channel called 'After Twelve', which would provide viewers with 'the sort of material they might find in *Playboy* magazine'. The tabloids seized on the announcement, calling Henry: 'TV's Mr Porn—the man who is going to bring bonking onto British TV sets'. In fact, similar material has been available on a number of channels using the Astra satellite for some time. An article in the *Sunday Telegraph* pointed out that British viewers had long been able to watch 'adult movies' on Filmnet, a Belgian company broadcasting to Scandinavia, and *Tutti-Frutti*, an adult game show from Germany. Pointing out that 'The BBC shows "art films"—it does not show contestants whipping off their blouses on game shows', the article described such programmes as 'the first wave in the tide of pornography that many claimed would engulf British living rooms once satellite TV arrived'.

Harmless fun or degrading dirt? The 1989 broadcasting directive prohibits the transmission of pornographic programmes unless they have been approved by one member state. Clearly, however, definitions of pornography vary. What might be acceptable in one country could easily be seen as offensive in another. In fact, British viewers are not supposed to be able to receive Filmnet at all, but word of its availability created a flourishing black market in the pirate decoders needed to receive it. Kenneth Baker, the Home Secretary, and Jacques Delors, the President of the European Commission, promptly received strongly worded letters from Mary Whitehouse, the President of the National Listeners and Viewers' Association. But many critics of the directive characterized the government's response as similar to 'bolting the gates after the stable was empty'. Others pointed out that no-one was being compelled to watch such programmes, and insisted that what people do in their own home is their own affair.

The availability of pornography was not the only issue that generated public debate about the arrival of satellite broadcasting. Some observers suggested that the anticipated widespread appeal of satellite television was wholly misconceived. It was pointed out, for example, that viewers in the Netherlands had no less than 21 channels to choose from, yet the two main channels accounted for almost 90% of television audiences. In addition, the situation was similar in the United States, where cable stations had been in operation for many years. There was also a body of evidence that suggested that family television viewing times had been declining in the face of competition from videos, and that the new satellite stations were likely to find it extremely difficult to win these audiences back.

Writing in *The Independent* in July 1991, Steven Barnett, the Director of the Henley Centre's media group, argued that the predicted arrival of the age of satellite broadcasting in Britain was 'pie in the sky'. He dismissed the idea that Britain was on the threshold of a multi-channel television revolution, described the sale of satellite receiving equipment as proceeding at 'a crawl' and ridiculed forecasts that there would be 8 million satellite dishes on British homes by the mid-1990s as 'fallacious'. Responding to Barnett's article, John Clemens, the Chairman of Continental Research and a Fellow of the Institute of Practitioners in Advertising, accused the Henley Centre of misrepresenting the statistics. Clemens pointed out that satellite dish sales had grown from 63,000 to 1.5 million in two years. By contrast, video recorders (launched in 1977) took five years to reach 1.5 million sales, while colour televisions (begun in 1967) took four years to reach 1 million sales. By August, when the *Financial Times* published its monthly satellite sales monitor, 1.7 million homes had access to satellite television, while installations of satellite receiving equipment had increased by a staggering 80% in 12 months. At the time the monitor was published, one in every ten Britons lived in a home with multi-channel television. The age of satellite television, for better or worse, had already arrived in Britain.

High-definition television

Long before the arguments over programme quotas, advertising regulations and declining moral standards in broadcasting, the European Commission had embarked upon an initiative to avert what was described at the time as a potentially devastating technological challenge from Japan. In the face of increased competition from some of the newly industrialized countries in the Far East, a number of Japanese electronics companies took a decision in the early 1970s to abandon the market for traditional television sets to their more cost-efficient neighbours and to concentrate on developing a new generation of high-definition television (HDTV) sets that would offer the viewer 35-mm picture quality and stereo sound. In 1985 Japan submitted its own technical standard for HDTV (known as Muse) to the International Radio Consultative Committee (CCIR), the world broadcasting organization, as the first step towards making the Japanese standard the world standard.

For Europe's struggling electronics companies the implications of Japan's attempted demarche were profoundly disturbing. The proposed HDTV standard would significantly increase the number of lines that go to make up a television picture, and would establish the technical parameters for television sets in the same way that the VHS standard has set the technical parameters for video recorders. If Japan succeeded in getting its standard adopted, Japanese electronics companies would have pulled off one of the biggest commercial coups in the history of consumer electronics, forcing other electronics companies to produce their equipment to Japanese standards, thereby enabling Japanese companies to dominate the industry well into the next century. In addition, Europe's 140 million television sets would have been made obsolete overnight, as they would not be able to receive the new HDTV broadcasts.

At the CCIR's annual assembly in Dubrovnik in May 1986 the European electronics companies argued against Japan's all-or-nothing approach, and put forward the case for a more evolutionary approach that would be compatible with existing television receiver sets. Europe's leading consumer electronics equipment manufacturers joined forces under the Community's Eureka telecommunications research and development programme in a bid to perfect the new HDTV technology before the Japanese. In the same year, Council adopted a directive on common technical standards for direct broadcasting by satellite (known as the Mac-packet family of standards), requiring all new satellite broadcasting companies to use the D-Mac technology. The D-Mac standard was not a fully fledged HDTV standard but it is superior to the existing conventional Pal standard, and was widely regarded as a stepping-stone towards the ultimate goal of HDTV.

The 1986 directive, however, contained a fundamental flaw. It did not apply to Astra, which is classified as a telecommunications, not a broadcasting satellite, and is thus exempt from the directive's provisions. With the 1986 directive due to expire at the end of 1991, the Commission was presented with a second opportunity to help provide a boost to the new European technology, an initiative vigorously supported by Philips, the Dutch electronics firm, and Thompson, its counterpart in France, both of whom had invested heavily in HDTV. But Société Européene des Satellites, which owns the Astra satellite, to which there were some two million subscribers at the beginning of 1991, feared that the Commission was trying to phase out Pal in favour of the new transitionary standard. Moreover, after the debacle of BSB, one of the first satellite companies to use the new transitionary standard, some critics accused the Commission of promoting a 1960s-style industrial policy which would increase the cost of receiving equipment and depress growth in the new satellite market.

Under the draft directive tabled in June 1991 by Filippo Maria Pandolfi, the Commissioner for Research and Development and Telecommunications, all new satellite broadcasting companies are required to use the new D-Mac standards from January 1993, while manufacturers must incorporate D-Mac decoders in new television sets wider than 22 inches from the same date. In addition, the Commission offered some £350-million worth of incentives for research into equipment that would allow satellite companies to broadcast in both standards simultaneously, and gave assurances that companies broadcasting in Pal would not be forced to switch over to D-Mac.

However, the compromise satisfied no-one. John Redwood, Britain's Trade and Industry minister, accused the Commission of trying to compel broadcasters and consumers into accepting the new standards. French and Dutch ministers demanded assurances about when and how Pal was to be phased out, while the satellite companies, many of whom were prepared to broadcast in both standards, remained anxious that the Commission would try to force the new standards upon them. Moreover, a report published in August by the independent consultants, Coopers & Lybrand, suggested that the Commission's HDTV strategy would cost European taxpayers, broadcasters and consumers up to £15 billion over a ten-year period in upgraded equipment. In the absence of a workable agreement between manufacturers, satellite operators and broadcasters, the Commission appeared reluctant to press ahead with its proposals, raising the prospect of the 1986 directive lapsing without anything to replace it.

By December, however, agreement was in sight following Pandolphi's decision to relax the provisions of the proposed HDTV directive. Under the revised formula, all new satellite services are required to broadcast in D-Mac, as the transitionary stage to full HDTV technology, But existing broadcasters will be allowed to transmit in Pal indefinitely, with no obligation to broadcast simultaneously in both standards. Admittedly,

Pandolphi's concession falls short of the industrial strategy advocated by France, and the broadcasters and satellite companies have still to put their signature to a legally binding memorandum. But the prospects of their doing so have never looked more optimistic.

Checklist of changes

- There will be considerable expansion in the number of satellite television channels available to viewers.
- Satellite broadcasters will have the right to transmit television programmes anywhere in the Community, provided that they meet certain minimum requirements.
- Broadcasters will be obliged to reserve a specified quota of their air time for feature films made in the Community.
- Television advertisers will have the option of grouping commercials into blocks or slots, and will be required to abide by prevailing standards of decency.
- Satellite and cable companies are expected to have an automatic right to broadcast or retransmit any programme within two years of original transmission, as long as adequate remuneration for the programme copyright holder is provided.
- New regulations are expected on cross-frontier advertisements for alcohol, tobacco, certain foods, pharmaceuticals and children's toys.
- Viewers could benefit from a considerable improvement in television picture and sound quality if the implementation of high-definition technology is commercially successful.

15 REGIONAL DEVELOPMENT

Economic cohesion and the North—South divide

Complementing the European Commission's attempt to increase the competitiveness of European industry through the 1992 programme is a parallel effort to reduce the economic disparities that exist both between and within the Community's rich and poor regions. The objective, in brief, is to ensure that the integrated market develops cohesively. Hence the jargon words 'cohesion' or 'convergence' for the 1992 policy of avoiding a North—South divide or 'two-speed Europe' in which the Northern states (Britain, France, Germany, Denmark and the Benelux countries) enjoy most of the economic benefits of the single market while the Southern states (Greece, Spain, Portugal, parts of Italy and the Irish Republic) lag behind. The Commission provides economic assistance to the regions by means of grants from three distinct but related funds—the European Regional Development Fund (ERDF), the European Social Fund (ESF) and the guidance section of the European Agricultural Guidance and Guarantee Fund (EAGGF), which are collectively referred to as the structural funds.

Preventing the emergence of a North—South economic divide is, however, only one of the overall objectives of the structural funds. Partly on British insistence, the definition of economic cohesion has been broadened to include the redevelopment of declining or depressed rural and urban areas in Northern countries, such as parts of Scotland and the run-down industrial towns and derelict urban areas of Britain. To equip the Commission for the task of ensuring that the Community developed cohesively, the Council of Ministers, after much resistance from some of the Northern member states, agreed to double the money made available to the structural funds to some £9 billion by 1992. In addition, the administration of the funds has been overhauled to ensure a more co-ordinated and coherent approach to regional development by focusing on a programme rather than a project-based approach to aid distribution.

Applications for economic assistance from the structural funds, which must normally be made by government departments, local authorities and other publicly funded organizations, are required to satisfy at least one of five objectives or categories, defined by the Commission as:

Category **One**: To assist those regions whose development is lagging behind.

Category **Two**: To revitalize regions affected by serious industrial decline.

Category **Three**: To combat long-term unemployment.

Category **Four**: To integrate young people into the job market.

Category **Five**: To adjust agricultural structures and develop rural areas.

Generally, although there are exceptions, each of the three funds is restricted to certain areas. The ERDF covers Categories One and Two, the ESF Categories Three and Four and the EAGGF covers Category Five. Consequently, while all the UK qualifies for assistance under Categories Three and Four and parts of it qualify for support under Categories Three and Five, only Northern Ireland qualifies for help under Category One.

During a lunch for British Brussels' correspondents shortly after taking up his new post as the Commissioner for Regional Development, Bruce Millan, Labour's former Scottish Secretary, expressed surprise at the media attention given to Leon Brittan, the UK's senior commissioner. 'He may have got the top job but I've got all the money,' Millan said wryly. The Commissioner's sense of humour was to be sorely tested, however, in a long-running dispute with Whitehall over how money from the structural funds was to be used. From the outset, Brussels has insisted that support from the structural funds, unless otherwise agreed, must be provisional on co-financing from member states. According to the Commission's guidelines on EC loans and grants:

> It is an important principle of Community aid that it supplements rather than replaces resources allocated at national level. In almost all cases Community aid must be additional to and matched by at least an equivalent amount of money from national resources.

British Treasury officials, however, disagree—and therein lies the origins of a dispute over what has come to be known in Eurospeak as 'additionality'.

Cohesion: reducing regional disparities

The aim of 1992 is to bring all areas of the EC up to a high standard of living and economic growth, largely by raising extra revenue and distributing it around the Community on the basis of priorities decided by successive EC summits and implemented in detail by the European Commission. Whether throwing money at the problem in this way will prove effective is a moot point: as with any aid programme, there is ample scope for abuse or misuse. Widespread fraud in the southern countries—especially Italy and Spain—where agricultural funds are concerned does not offer an encouraging example, and the Commission lacks the resources or the powers to carry out adequate inspections to ensure that funds are properly used. On the other hand, the regional and social funds already have a record of achievement, and British citizens are often unaware that motorway schemes, youth training programmes or urban regeneration projects have been funded wholly or partly by the EC.

The commitment to 'cohesion' pre-dates the 1992 programme but has been given added impetus by the single market. In its current form it stems not only from the original Cockfield 1992 programme but also from the Single European Act. The Commission has always been conscious of the North–South problem, and Delors has made 'cohesion' something of a personal crusade. The 1985 White Paper referred to the issue in its introduction in the following terms:

> The Commission is firmly convinced that the completion of the internal market will provide an indispensable base for increasing the prosperity of the Community as a whole. The Commission is, however, conscious that there may be risks that by increasing the possibilities for human, material and financial services to move without obstacle to the areas of greatest economic advantage, existing discrepancies between regions could be exacerbated and therefore the object of convergence jeopardized. This means full and imaginative use will need to be made of the resources available through the structural funds. The importance of the funds will therefore be enhanced.

Shorn of Eurospeak, this conveys the Commission's fundamental worry that money and resources will move towards the more prosperous north in the EC after 1992, with the southern states—and backward regions—unable to stand up to cross-border competition. This anxiety has also been strongly expressed by the southern countries themselves, not least by Greece—which held the presidency of the Council of Ministers in the second half of 1988—and Spain, which had the presidency in the second half of 1989. As a consequence, many 1992 directives (for example, the directive on the liberalization of financial services by July 1990) contain exemptions for the southern states, to allow them a 'breathing space'. Other exemptions originate from the accession terms negotiated by the southern countries. On the other hand, all these exemptions are provisional, and it is assumed that in due course (in the later 1990s, perhaps) the southern economies will be strong enough to co-exist with other European economies in a frontier-free commercial environment.

Increasing the structural funds

To achieve this, the EC 'structural' funds are being increased, so that the southern states and backward regions can benefit from greater investment and—with the aid of the regional and social funds—stage an economic recovery. The White Paper referred, rather coyly, to the importance of 'enhancing' the funds. What the Commission really wanted, however (and achieved at the important Brussels summit of February 1988), was to increase the funds substantially, and even to double them—a proposal resisted at first by Britain and other states but eventually agreed as part of the Delors reform package which followed the Single European Act and 'cleared the way' for 1992 legislation.

Even the Act avoids direct reference to a 'doubling' of the structural funds. The relevant section (Title Five) notes that

> In order to promote its overall harmonious development, the Community shall develop and pursue its actions leading to the strengthening of its economic and social cohesion . . . In particular, the Community shall aim at reducing disparities between the various regions and the backwardness of the least-favoured regions.

To achieve this, the EC states undertook to co-ordinate their economic policies in such a way as to avoid a North–South split, although it was not altogether clear what this meant in practice. More immediately, the EC was committed under the Act to making better use of the three 'structural funds': the European Agricultural Guidance and Guarantee Fund; the European Social Fund; and the European Regional Development Fund, as well as loans from the European Investment Bank. Article 130c outlined the purpose of the regional fund in particular: 'The European Regional Development Fund is intended to help redress the principal regional imbalances in the Community through participating in the development and structural adjustment of regions whose development is lagging behind, and in the conversion of declining industrial regions'.

So far so good: but the Act went on to authorize the Commission to submit 'a comprehensive proposal to the Council, the purpose of which will be to make such amendments to the structure and operational rules of the existing structural funds as are necessary to clarify and rationalize their tasks in order to contribute to the achievement of the objectives . . . and to increase their efficiency'. In practice, Delors and the Commission wanted nothing less than to double the funds so that 1992 could go ahead without major disruption and the further creation of regional imbalances.

The European Regional Development Fund

The structural funds had been operating for ten years before the 1992 process began. Yet oddly enough, the need to redress regional imbalances to prevent one part of the EC developing faster than another (or rather, to bring more backward regions up to the higher levels of development) was not foreseen in the Treaty of Rome, which has no separate clause on regional problems. The preamble refers to the need for the EC to 'ensure harmonious development by reducing the differences existing between the various regions', and in the 1960s there were plenty of examples of backwardness—in the low-subsistence agriculture of the Italian south, in depressed coalmining regions in Belgium and the Ruhr, and in central France. Some funds were channelled through the European Investment Bank (EIB).

However, the ERDF was only created in the mid-1970s, after the Six had grown to Nine with the addition of Britain, Ireland and Denmark in 1973. Britain, although not one of the underdeveloped regions on a par with the Southern states, did (and still does) have important areas of both rural and, above all, industrial decline, including Northern Ireland —which is still singled out as a high-priority area for regional aid under the 1992 programme, partly with the political aim of promoting harmony between the conflicting Ulster communities. Denmark had a poor region in Greenland—it subsequently left the EC after a local referendum; and the Republic of Ireland, for its part, had a low per capita income and added to the weight of what was to become the 'southern bloc' with the entry of Greece in 1981 and Spain and Portugal in 1986.

What had started as mainly a 'rich man's club' in 1957 had become a much more diversified Community by the 1970s and 1980s. It quickly became apparent after 1973 that the 'less favoured' EC regions were either backward rural areas with high unemployment levels and poor communications and transport, largely in the south, or—no less important to Britain, Germany, France and Belgium—regions which were formerly thriving centres of traditional industries, such as iron and steel, but which had increasingly fallen on hard times because of changes in global trading patterns and competition from outside Europe, with a consequent cost to Europe in unemployment, economic decline and social malaise.

However, the allocations made to member states under the regional fund, set up in 1975, were not universally regarded as fair or just. The practice was that member states propose projects—a new motorway, inner-city developments, irrigation schemes—and the Commission decides which projects are worthy of the most support. Both public authority and commercial projects can qualify. However, in the early days the Commission took the view that each country should have a part of the regional aid funds, even if Country A's depressed regions were far better off than those of Country B. In practice, it is true, most of the aid between 1975 and 1985 (one eighth of the EC budget) ended up in the regions which arguably needed it most: the Italian Mezzogiorno; Greece; Ireland; Britain (including Northern Ireland); and the French overseas departments, which also count as EC territories.

The allocations, however, needed adjustment, and at the time of the 1992 White Paper in 1985 the rules were changed to give each country a maximum percentage of the regional fund budget rather than a fixed annual quota. The maximum percentage of the ERDF budget allocated to Britain was 19.31% and the minimum guaranteed 14.48%. This compares favourably with the 9.96% upper limit allocated to France, the 3.40% given to Germany and even with the 10.64% allocated to Greece or the 14.20% for Portugal. Only Spain and Italy had higher allocations than Britain, with upper limits of 23.93% and 28.79%, respectively. Following the Brussels agreement of February 1988 the Commission proposed a new system under which it would reserve to itself 15% of the structural funds to ensure a fair redistribution of wealth, while issuing 'indicative allocations' for the remaining 75%. In practice, 'indicative allocations' have been equivalent to the old quotas, which remain informally in force.

The southern states also benefit from a separate fund known as the Integrated Mediterranean Programmes (rather amusingly abbreviated to IMP), which derive from the accession terms negotiated by Greece, Spain and Portugal and which benefit selected Mediterranean regions through a system of grants and loans (the French Mediterranean regions also receive IMP funds).

In addition, the European Social Fund—which, unlike the regional fund, was included in the terms of the Treaty of Rome—has the principal aim of encouraging job creation in areas of high unemployment, partly through retraining schemes. The Fund's importance has grown together with unemployment, so that it now accounts for almost the same proportion of the EC budget as the regional fund. The Government's Youth Training Scheme, for example, was established with help from the EC Social Fund—although again, not many people are aware of this. The Fund also helps to retrain employees unfamiliar with new technologies, migrant workers and women whose families have grown up and who return to full- or part-time employment only to find that techniques and work patterns have changed.

The February 1988 Brussels Agreement

The key question as 1992 approaches is whether the Commission and Council will succeed in further developing these funds to prevent a North–South division, or whether the less-advantaged regions will fall further behind as free competition benefits those economic sectors most prepared for it. The decision to double the structural funds by 1992 has certainly improved the chances of avoiding a 'two-speed' Europe. Taken in February 1988, it appears to have surprised even those—like Delors —who had sponsored the proposal. On the other hand, the increase in regional and social spending is directly related to the Delors package's overhaul of EC finances. Europe can only spend more on its regions because it is increasing the revenues coming into central EC funds while at the same time cutting back on farm spending under the Common Agricultural Policy, despite protests from EC farmers and farm ministers.

The decision, in other words, only came after the Northern countries, with Britain heading the campaign, had insisted that extra regional spending was a luxury the EC could only afford once other expenditure (above all, farm support) had been brought under control. The Commission, for its part, recognized that budgetary reform was needed if the 1992 programme—regional aid included—was to be based on a 'sound economic footing'.

The process of bringing EC spending under control to allow for greater regional aid, and the framework programme for technological research, dominated the last four years of the 1980s, just as the preceding four had been overshadowed by the question of the British budget rebate. The crisis really came in June 1987, at the Brussels summit marking the end of Belgium's EC presidency, when Mrs Thatcher demanded 'good house-keeping' in the EC before budgetary increases for 1992 could be contemplated. Chancellor Kohl of Germany declared Bonn's willingness to increase the regional and social funds by up to 50%, but Mrs Thatcher declared that the CAP had to be curbed first, and there was, in any case, room for improvement in the way the existing structural funds were administered. 'The EC is not a mechanism for redistributing wealth, it is a common enterprise for producing it' was her spokesman's terse comment.

The result was a 'Maggie versus the Rest' summit, in which Mrs Thatcher held out against a compromise package because it lacked budgetary rigour, arguing—correctly—that she was 'doing the Community a service'. At Brussels, Mrs Thatcher was mocked by Jacques Chirac, the former French Prime Minister, for taking a 'housewifely' view of the budget. A senior British diplomat at the EC subsequently compared Mrs Thatcher—rather more admiringly—to a nanny: 'She says to the others, if you don't eat your porridge up now you'll have to eat it cold tomorrow'. The alternative, Britain insisted, was EC bankruptcy as expenditure continued to exceed revenue.

On the eve of the next summit, in Copenhagen in December 1987, France and Germany suggested a compromise, allowing states to escape farm spending cuts 'in exceptional circumstances'. Sir Geoffrey Howe, the then Foreign Secretary, replied on Britain's behalf that there was no point in filling the proposed spending deal with loopholes 'like a motheaten sock'. The British solution lay in strict ceilings on farm output, known as 'stabilizers', coupled with a German-backed scheme for taking land out of production (set aside, and an altered revenue system, as devised by the Commission, to include a GNP tax), provided that there was no consequent alteration for the worse in the British budget rebate agreed in 1984. In the end, Copenhagen failed, but the debate was better tempered, and the leaders moved closer to agreement, with the summit vowing to take action when it reconvened in special session in Brussels in February 1988, under German chairmanship.

The extraordinary Brussels summit, when it met, was on the verge of breaking up several times, with French leaders taking a hard line against farm cuts because of the impending French presidential election and Mrs Thatcher still insisting that the regional funds could not be increased by more than 50% to 60%. Chancellor Kohl, after allowing the summit to drift, held separate talks with his fellow leaders—'confessionals' in EC jargon—to break the deadlock. In the final negotiation Chirac went one better (or worse) than his earlier 'housewife' epithet when, late at night on the second day, he shouted a crude French word (*couilles*) across the table at Mrs Thatcher after she had accused him of holding up the deal by going on interminably about non-arable products.

In the end, the February 1988 summit reached an historic deal. With last-minute concessions on all sides—not least from Mrs Thatcher—it finally reformed EC finances along the lines of the original Delors plan, thus not only allowing for a doubling of the structural funds by 1992 but also 'clearing the way for 1992' as a whole, in the Prime Minister's own words. The Brussels agreement included:

1 An overall increase in the EC budget from £31 billion in 1988, to £37 billion in 1992, with revenues based not only on Vat but also the GNP tax (the resulting mix producing revenue equivalent to 1.9% Vat);
2 Preservation of the British rebate, which Mrs Thatcher said had saved British taxpayers £3 billion over three years;
3 Legally binding limits on cereals and other crops, with the proportion of farm spending in the budget to decline from two thirds to 56% by 1992; and, above all,
4 A rise in the structural funds to £9.5 billion a year by 1992, or over a quarter of the budget, with most of the new aid going to Portugal, Ireland, Spain and Greece.

Britain and the structural funds

Since the Delors reforms, the argument has mainly been over the official definition of a 'less-developed region' and of a 'depressed industrial area', defined in the summit conclusions as an area with unemployment higher than the Community average. There is concern over the Commission's interpretation of this to mean that the very poorest EC regions should be developed first to help them to cope with 1992. The Commission proposed giving most of the new money to 'Category One' regions, in which per capita income must be below 75% of EC average (with only Northern Ireland among the British regions therefore qualifying for high-priority Category One). The Government objected in the Council that other British regions deserved special treatment—rural Wales, the Highlands and Islands of Scotland (which officials had hinted would be Category One), parts of Devon and Cornwall, and inner-city 'black spots' in London, Liverpool, Manchester and elsewhere.

In late 1988 a further difficulty arose over British objections to public spending being taken into account in the allocation of structural funds. The Commission, for its part, does not want to see member states using regional funds as an excuse to cut public spending.

British special pleading—accompanied by special pleading from other countries—has had some effect, partly because the logic of earlier regional grant awards supports the British case. The Highlands alone received £100 million over the first ten years of the ERDF, with EC cash supporting projects like the new Perth-to-Inverness trunk road. Neither Scotland nor Whitehall was keen to lose this support. The government aim was (and is) to maintain a situation in which Britain was a major recipient of structural funds, and especially ERDF cash. According to figures published by the Commission, in the first ten years of the ERDF Britain was near the top of the league of aid recipients, with over £3 billion in aid. The initial Commission list of regional aid recipients in March 1988 gave the whole of Greece, Ireland and Portugal as 'Category One' regions, together with regions of Spain and Italy, Corsica, the French overseas departments and Northern Ireland. However, Britain has since been given assurances that other of its regions—including both rural areas and those of industrial decline—will benefit substantially from the new funds, up to Britain's allotted ceiling, even if they are in Category Two rather than Category One. Under the new criteria, Category Two covers areas of industrial decline, defined as areas where there has been higher than average unemployment for more than three years, or where there has been an 'observable fall' in industrial employment.

In the spirit of 1992 Kent County Council has joined forces with the regional Council of the Pas de Calais (Nord) to apply to Brussels for £1 billion worth of aid over a ten-year period to help develop the infrastructure on both sides of the Channel for the Channel Tunnel. On the other hand, under the new criteria neither Kent nor the Pas de Calais qualifies as a high-priority depressed region in terms of regional aid—although both qualify for Social Fund cash.

In other words, the new approach to the expanded structural funds —concentrating resources on the most backward areas—still gives rise to concern in Britain. The government has put forward plans for including areas of 'high deprivation' such as Merseyside and Strathclyde in future EC aid allocations to Britain. Some areas (Cornwall is one example) have even launched their own campaigns to ensure they do not lose out in 1992. Cornwall received £125 million worth of aid from the ERDF between 1975 and 1985, but the decline of tin mining and other local industries has brought continuing high unemployment.

The government's anxieties about losing out because of the overhaul in the way the structural funds are managed was, however, overshadowed by a more pressing argument over the way the funds were used. In July 1990 Millan announced that Scotland and Yorkshire were to receive an additional £44.3 million in regional aid for a variety of job creation, economic regeneration and transport improvement programmes. The announcement followed an unseemly row between Brussels and Whitehall over the vexed question of additionality, one that was to resurface the following year. By the summer of 1991, newspapers were reporting that Britain's depressed regions were being prevented from claiming hundreds of millions of pounds in structural fund aid because of the government's tight control of public spending. Although the Commission had agreed a total budget of £850 million in ERDF aid for Britain in the three years leading up to 1993, only £350 million had actually been handed over. As local councils were forced to stay within the spending ceilings imposed under the new Community Charge, or poll tax, many councils found themselves unable to raise the co-financing they needed to release Community funds. Consequently, some £500 million was held up in administrative limbo, jeopardizing numerous projects in the Black Country, Merseyside and West Cumbria.

Similarly, in July, Millan announced a total of ECU 1.87 billion in aid for other member states, while refusing to release £100 million designated for depressed coal-mining regions in Britain under Category Two because he was not convinced that the government would use the money in addition to—rather than as a substitute for—national funds. Disputes between Brussels and London over the principle of additionality also extended to the ESF, which is designed to provide assistance for the long-term unemployed and youth unemployment, with particular attention to women, migrant workers and the disabled. In September, *The Times* reported that a confidential study prepared on behalf of the Commission by Coopers & Lybrand, the firm of management consultants, had concluded that some £200 million in social fund grants should be paid direct to training and employment councils, local authorities and voluntary organizations because the government had taken the social fund money and used it to replace part of its own training budget which would have been paid for by the Treasury.

Britain does not benefit from the guidance section of EAGGF aid as much as it does from ERDF and ESF assistance. About 7.5% of the fund's guidance section—by far the smallest part of EAGGF—will go to Britain, mostly to rural areas in Scotland, Wales, Devon and Cornwall. The bulk of EAGGF is used (squandered some would say), on intervention and export subsidies to help stabilize the market. Guidance section cash is designed to help rural communities to diversify away from traditional forms of production to new ones of agricultural activity such as forestry, while, at the same time, preserving the fabric of rural society. However, this can be expected to change significantly under new proposals designed to bring about a radical overhaul of the CAP.

All previous attempts to reform the CAP (notably in 1973, 1978, 1986 and, most recently, in 1988) have met with little success. In January 1991

Ray MacSharry, the Agricultural Commissioner, forecast that the CAP would cost the EC £5.6 billion, thereby breaching the ceiling imposed on agricultural spending at the EC summit in February 1988. By the summer, both the Commission and the member states had begun to accept that the CAP's central problem of overproduction had to be tackled, although some member states, notably Britain, were opposed to the Commission's proposed remedy. Nonetheless, in addition to external pressures for reform, internal reform pressures were also mounting—not least because the policy of spending 80% of EAGGF cash on subsidizing the richest 20% of farmers (most of whom are located in the northern states) made a mockery of the goal of fostering economic cohesion and avoiding a North–South divide. The MacSharry reforms, which include penalties in place of incentives on overproduction, are likely to cost more in the short term. But once spending on agricultural production declines, substantial sums of money should be released for the three structural funds.

Helping the North to help the South

On balance, the doubling of structural funds by 1992 will benefit Britain as well as the southern countries. Whether it will succeed in achieving Delors' aim of averting a North–South split in the integrated European market remains to be seen. One often-overlooked aspect of the increase in structural funds is that British and other northern companies can benefit from aid granted to the southern countries by entering into joint ventures which have the approval of Brussels and which draw on regional fund allocations. This is a particularly attractive proposition to companies which specialize in development aid projects in underdeveloped economies but which have been adversely affected by problems in the Third World, such as indebtedness or the decline in oil revenues. EC officials argue that many southern countries in the EC will have to turn to northern companies for help in development, since the funds they are likely to receive under the social and regional fund reforms will exceed the capacity of local industry and commerce to meet the challenge (for example, in construction). It is already becoming clear, however, that to benefit from 1992 joint ventures in the south, British companies would do well to have close arrangements with local firms in Spain, Greece, Portugal or Southern Italy, and will probably gain the most benefit if they have a local subsidiary.

The DTI—which has a projects and export policy division dealing with 1992 joint ventures—has warned that other north European countries such as Germany or the Netherlands will not be slow to seize this 1992 opportunity. Will the tables eventually be turned, with southern EC companies which benefit from increased EC aid becoming strong enough to challenge northern European firms on their home ground under the rules of the single market? In the short run it is unlikely, but if the integrated market develops after 1992 to the benefit of the south, the north may find its present superiority under challenge, not least from countries like Spain, which have a policy of economic dynamism backed by a great desire to prove to the rest of the EC—and the world at large —that they are part of a modern European economy and culture. If skills, labour and plant—including high-tech industries—move south in the integrated market, Spain and Portugal, and perhaps southern Italy, could become the European equivalent of the American Sun Belt.

Not all scenarios are so optimistic. At Madrid in June 1989, Bruce Millan, the Commissioner for regional development, said structural funds reform was 'off to a good start' and 'going pretty well to schedule'. He outlined a possible stark alternative to southern enrichment, however, saying the Commission had serious doubts about 'further concentration of resources in major central conurbations' in rich northern areas because of pollution, traffic congestion and poor housing. The Commission, Millan said, wanted 'a more centrifugal view of Europe' in the 1990s because of the danger of a cycle of decline in less-developed and depressed industrial regions if economic expectations were not met and then fell. The rich areas, from southern England to northern Italy, would be unable to sustain the pressures of migration from a declining south, and the 'rich centre' would then itself fall into a cycle of overcrowding and decay. To avoid this, the regional funds needed yet more cash, and new technology and market economics must be exploited to show that peripheral regions could be just as competitive as central regions.

During a visit to London in June 1991, Millan was asked whether the Commission was mapping out policies for the structural funds in the period after 1993. Responding with some caution, the Commissioner said:

> I have always taken the view that we cannot talk about a real
> Community if you have the disparities that we have at the present
> time. Therefore, if we are moving towards closer political
> integration, as well as closer economic and monetary integration,
> that has to be accompanied by continued efforts to remove the
> disparities between member states.

Spain, Portugal, Greece and Ireland were insisting that additional help would be needed if they were to avoid being caught in the second tier of a two-speed Europe, the Commissioner added. Spain has even gone so far as to suggest the creation of a new 'cohesion fund' to act as a sort of wealth-redistribution mechanism. Indeed, the Spanish government has indicated that its support for closer economic and political union will depend to a considerable degree on even larger transfers of wealth from more developed northern countries to their less-developed southern neighbours. Partly in response to such anxieties, the Commission asked national governments in May 1991 to submit medium-term economic strategy or convergence plans to Brussels by the end of 1991, as a prerequisite to moving on to stage two of EMU.

Satisfying the economic aspirations of the Community's poorer regions will, however, be but one of the tasks facing the Commission in the years after 1992. Closer economic ties with the six members of the European Free Trade Organization (EFTA), together with the impending association agreements with Eastern European countries such as Poland, Czechoslovakia and Hungary, will undoubtedly entail new economic development responsibilities and even greater calls on the resources of the structural funds, which will have to be borne by the more prosperous members of the EC.

Checklist of changes

- The Community's structural funds have been doubled to £9 billion in an effort to ensure that the poorer regions also benefit from the single market programme's aim of increasing economic growth.
- The structural funds will be targeted towards assisting those regions whose economic development has lagged behind, revitalizing the regions experiencing industrial decline, reducing unemployment and developing rural areas.
- Most of the new funds will go to Category One regions, for which only Northern Ireland qualifies in the UK. The UK will, however, benefit considerably from assistance to declining industrial areas, anti-unemployment programmes and rural development schemes.
- Companies in the more developed countries will be able to benefit from the funds allocated to poorer ones by participating in urban and rural development projects.
- Financial resources allocated to the structural funds are likely to be increased again after 1992, in an effort to meet the demands for additional assistance to the Community's poorer regions and to help East European countries to make the adjustment to free market economies.

16 PROTECTIONISM AND TARIFFS

The risks of Fortress Europe

Efforts to regenerate the EC's original vision of creating a common market entailed a wide range of implications for the world beyond Europe's borders, although little attention was paid to this so-called external dimension when the Internal Market White Paper was published in 1985. But while the European Commission would undoubtedly have preferred to focus its limited negotiating resources on the internal aspects of the single market, a succession of events in the outside world was to deny it any such luxury. In addition to fending off allegations from around the world that the new drive for European integration was inherently protectionist, the Commission found itself on a collision course with the United States in the closing stages of the Uruguay Round of international trade talks over the EC's reluctance to undertake a wholesale reform of the Common Agricultural Policy. In December 1990 the Uruguay Round, which promised to do for the world what the single market promised for Europe, was on the verge of collapse and Europe was being singled out as the guilty party.

Moreover, the Commission's attempts to redefine the nature of the Community's relationship with the neighbouring European Free Trade Association (EFTA) was suddenly overtaken by the eagerness of some EFTA states to abandon their allies unilaterally and opt for full membership of the EC. Although the Community appeared initially to favour the deepening of existing institutional and economic bonds between member states over the creation of new ties with non-member status, the collapse of the East European dictatorships, followed by the end of Communism in the Soviet Union, confronted EC decision-makers with a radically different Europe to that with which they were familiar when the old Cold War certainties were still in place. Consequently, as well as facing the prospect of a wave of accession applications from EFTA, Commission officials suddenly realized that they could be facing a similar onslaught from the East. Finally, while Brussels was struggling to find ways of bringing the fledgling East European democracies into the Community's orbit, Third World countries began to express fears that their meagre amounts of aid and assistance would dry up as financial resources were increasingly diverted to provide support for Eastern Europe and the Soviet Union.

A Fortress Europe

Complete and effective implementation of the internal market pro-gramme will have a number of profound implications for the global econ-omy and for the Community's world-wide trading partners. The gradual removal of Europe's internal barriers to trade will create the single largest advanced industrial market in the world. An integrated European econo-my could act as a major stimulus to world trade or it could become a major obstacle in the path of such expansion. Decisions about who has access to this market, and on what terms, will affect millions of people, from the humble banana producers of the Caribbean to the giant trading houses of the Far East, all of whom depend on a healthy and expanding trading relationship with the European Community for their livelihoods.

The ink on the Internal Market White Paper was barely dry before some observers had begun to complain. The European Commission found itself accused of turning its back on the world by planning to increase trade between the member states at the expense of business with their traditional trading partners, and of scheming to restrict access to the internal market to only those countries that granted the Community reciprocal access to their own domestic markets in return.

From Australia to Latin America and Japan to the United States, many were alarmed at the prospect that, as Europe's internal barriers began to crumble, they would be replaced by a unified external one designed to limit the benefits of the internal market to a new 'Fortress Europe'. Busi-ness executives began to express anxieties that, once the external barrier was in place, the Community would have the power to dictate who should be let in and who should be kept out.

These fears were increased by a series of articles in some of the world's leading business publications predicting the worst. In May 1988 the influential Hong Kong-based *Far Eastern Economic Review* ran as its cover story an eight-page account of how Europe was preparing to steal the initiative from the dynamic, newly industrialized countries of the Pacific Rim, and bring the centre of gravity of international trade back to the Old World. Warnings that 'the Fortress Europe of such simple protection-ism as national quotas could give way to a complex citadel of Europrotec-tionism, enshrined in Community-wide quotas, a generally stiffer trade policy, and less liberal policies towards outside investment' almost seemed calculated to confirm the international business community's worst fears.

At the same time, the European edition of the *Wall Street Journal*—published just as the controversial trade bill with protectionist clauses was passing through the US Congress—predicted that the next frontier of protectionism would be found emerging from the borders of Europe. It insisted that the combination of the EC's historical record, especially the Common Agricultural Policy, which it called 'a black hole of protectionism', and the growing pressure from European car manufacturers, financial institutions and other industrial sectors for Community help in the face of external competition would turn the internal market programme into one of the most restrictive initiatives ever implemented by a regional trading group, precipitating a new and vicious round of trans-Atlantic trade wars.

Much influential US opinion concedes that the European Commission, along with the General Agreement on Tariffs and Trade (GATT), is one of the leading advocates of free trade in the international community yet remains convinced that, without any legislative power of its own, the Commission would soon fall victim of the protectionist instincts of member states. However, US attitudes to 1992 are by no means uniform. For the giant corporations like IBM and Caterpillar, who have regular access to the Commission, the internal market programme is seen as a great opportunity. For the small and medium-sized exporting companies, whose access to information about the Commission's activities is considerably more limited, the fear of being excluded from the internal market is very real. Such anxieties have undoubtedly been increased by political rhetoric and alarmist newspaper reports, such as that in the *Wall Street Journal*, which reminded its readers that 'Protectionism is as much a part of the European business climate as the three-hour lunch'.

A new strategy for external trade

Much of the blame for such visions can be attributed to the Commission. The Internal Market White Paper failed to address itself adequately to the vital issue of the external implications of the 1992 programme. The whole question was neatly averted with a passing reference to the necessity of replacing the separate national import policies with unspecified 'temporary measures'.

Under Article 115 of the Treaty of Rome, member states are granted the right to impose quantitative restrictions against each other on imports from third countries. They are also empowered to inspect intra-Community trade in order to establish the origin of a given import, and thereby prevent what is known as trade deflection, the ability of external exporters to gain access to the protected market of one member state via the unprotected market of another.

However, a central part of the internal market programme is the abolition of frontier controls, and as Article 115 relies on these to monitor intra-Community trade from third countries, it will have to be gradually phased out. The White Paper, however, gave no indication of how the Commission intended to deal with the problem posed by the different policies member states have adopted towards third-country imports. Will the restrictions on, for example, imports of cars adopted by one member state (whether through quotas, tariffs or voluntary export restraints) have to be adopted by every other member state? Will the member state in question have to abolish its national restriction and bring it into line with everybody else? Or will there be some sort of compromise between the two extremes? If so, what will be the level and nature of Community protectionism on 1 January 1993?

These were the kinds of questions being asked by the international business community when the Commission began to give the first indications of the strategy on external trade that it was in the process of evolving. In his various addresses, Willy de Clercq, then Commissioner for External Relations, began to make much use of the word 'reciprocity', indicating that external trade relations were to be based on the principle 'You scratch my back and I'll scratch yours'. On one occasion de Clercq said bluntly, 'If our partners want to take advantage of our integration, and profit from the dynamism it will create, they will have to co-operate with this effort and be determined to open up their markets on equivalent terms', effectively confirming the worst suspicions of business executives around the world. In a keynote speech in London in July 1988 de Clercq attempted to dispel some of the fears prompted by his earlier comments.

> The Community is already the world's largest trading partner. Our exports of manufactured goods represent 26% of those of the OECD countries, compared with 14% for the United States, and 17% for Japan. Our share of world exports of services is even greater. As a result, we have a vital interest in the maintenance of a worldwide liberal trading system.

Having reaffirmed the Community's commitment to an open trading system, de Clercq then went on to outline three principles that would guide the Commission's external trade policy in the run-up to 1992 in practice. In the first place, he acknowledged that the internal market programme would automatically lead to the reinforcement of the external identity of the EC as a result of the phasing out of Article 115. However, he insisted that the Community would adhere to its commitments under the current round of trade-liberalization talks being held in Geneva under the auspices of the GATT not to introduce any new protectionist barriers.

He also made it clear that as the GATT does not yet cover trade in services, the Community saw no reason why the benefits of internal liberalization 'should be extended unilaterally to third countries'. Asked what this meant in concrete terms, the Commissioner illustrated the point by saying that any American or Japanese bank already resident in one member state would not be allowed to expand into other member states, unless Community banks were granted the same privileges in return. Britain was especially unhappy about the use of reciprocity as a means of securing access to foreign markets, as this was likely to invite retaliation which could harm British interests, particularly in the financial services sector. In August 1988 Sir Nicholas Goodison, the former chairman of the London Stock Exchange, expressed Britain's fears by warning the Commission that any attempt to put a 'ring fence' around European financial markets would 'lull Europeans into a false sense of security'.

Finally, de Clercq confirmed that the wide divergence between the import arrangements of the 12 member states would have to be eliminated. In most cases, import restrictions could be abolished without difficulty. However, he insisted there were a number of 'hard-core cases' where abolition would cause considerable hardship in some member states, and that national protective measures would have to be replaced by 'appropriate measures at Community level' for a transitionary period.

Shortly thereafter, the Commission gave the first indication of its plans for one of these so-called hard-core cases. These call for the complete abolition of all the fiscal and technical regulations fragmenting the European car industry and a severe restriction on state subsidies. The Commission also proposed to replace the quantitative restraints imposed on Japanese car exports by Britain, France, Italy, Spain and Portugal by a Community-wide ceiling of one million units per annum until 1992, in order to give European manufacturers time to adjust to the new climate of international competition. The Commission maintained that this is the only way that member states could be cured of their addiction to quantitative restrictions in the car sector.

The proposal represented a compromise between the two extremes of outright abolition and permanent Community quotas outlined above, and was even seen by some as the model solution for all other divergent national import arrangements. But the question of what level of access to grant Japanese car exporters proved to be so politically sensitive between those favouring a high degree of protection and those in support of a more liberal import system that the Commission was forced to postpone repeatedly the publication of the Community's strategy towards Japanese car imports.

In December 1989, and in the face of repeated demands from European car producers, the Commission finally agreed that a transitionary period would be needed to protect EC car manufacturers after 1992, and that this should take the form of a voluntary export restraint (VER). The following February, Japan let it be known that it would accept VERs, much to the Commission's relief. Japan's Ministry of International Trade and Industry (MITI) urged Japanese car manufacturers not to increase sales to the Community, though made clear that such arrangements would no longer be acceptable at the turn of the century. When the details of the deal were published in August, Japanese officials were clearly unhappy about the length of the transitionary period, although relieved that Japanese car production in Britain and Spain (known as transplants) could circulate freely around the Community. France and

Italy, however, continued to insist that the Commission had given too much away.

In many respects, the conflict over Japanese car exports, and the level of protection demanded by some European producers after 1992, highlighted one of the central dilemmas faced by the internal market programme. While the Commission was eager to reduce the level of protection in order to increase the Community's long-term competitiveness, countries like France and Italy were deeply alarmed at the industrial restructuring and large-scale job losses that such a policy entailed. In July 1991 Raymond Levy, the chairman of Renault, warned that the European car industry would have to shed 'several hundred-thousand' jobs in order to fend off the competition from Japan, and few politicians could ignore the electoral consequences of job losses on such a scale. But the alternative to industrial restructuring was to maintain obsolete high-cost plants with large public subsidies. Hitherto, protectionism has rarely encouraged manufacturers to become more competitive, and considerable sums have been squandered in the process.

Despite his protestations to the contrary, in the eyes of many critics de Clercq's three principles collectively constitute a violation of the spirit of the GATT. That system, which has been struggling to overcome the increase in protectionism throughout the world, is based on the principles of non-discrimination and multilateralism. By contrast, the de Clercq system of international trade asserts its commitment to multilateralism where possible, but makes no attempt to hide its readiness to revert to discrimination and bilateralism where necessary. Admittedly, the GATT does not yet cover trade in services, but the willingness of the world's largest trading bloc to show its strength in a pursuit of its own self-interest does not bode well for the future of an international trading system, already under severe strain from the increasing temptation of nation states to resort to bilateral solutions to trade difficulties.

The main reason the Internal Market White Paper had not dealt effectively with the problems posed by the strengthening of the Community's external identity was that it was an entirely new area of Community competence, in which definitive policies are still in the process of being formulated. In September 1988, however, EC external relations policy underwent a major transformation following a ruling by the European Court of Justice, which conferred on the European Commission the right to take legal action and impose fines on non-Community companies that violated EC competition laws.

The decision was the first to grant the Community powers in the highly sensitive area of extra-territorial jurisdiction, and was seen by legal experts as one of the most important rulings by the Luxembourg-based court—effectively granting the Community global jurisdiction. The ruling followed an appeal by a group of wood-pulp producers from the United

States, Canada and Finland against punitive price-fixing fines levied on their exports to Community manufacturers in 1984.

The producers (most of whom are based outside the EC) initiated legal proceedings against the Commission on the grounds that it had no authority to interfere in the activities of companies operating outside the EC. In a preliminary ruling earlier in the year, the court said that the Commission did have the power to take action against non-EC companies engaged in price-fixing or market-sharing conspiracies if it believed that 'free competition within the Community would be affected'. The ruling was based on the highly controversial US 'effects doctrine', granting American authorities the power to regulate foreign companies whose activities outside the United States have a damaging impact on domestic ones.

However, in what legal experts interpreted as an attempt to avoid the potentially divisive issue of infringing the sovereignty of other nation states the final judgment made no reference to the so-called effects doctrine. Instead, the court based its decision on the consequences of external activities inside the Community, arguing that 'the decisive factor is the place where the agreement is implemented'. The court found that 'where wood pulp producers sell directly to the Community and engage in price competition in order to win orders from those customers, that constitutes competition within the common market'.

At the time, observers acknowledged that the distinction between price-fixing agreements and their place of implementation was little more than a legal fiction, but it did enable the court to avoid dealing with the effects doctrine. Morever, the implications of the decision were far-reaching, as the Commission can now exercise jurisdiction over the supply of all raw materials to the EC.

Europe and the Uruguay Round

When the eighth round of international trade-liberalization talks were inaugurated in Punta del Este, Uruguay, in 1986, few observers expected them to be completed by the time the four-year negotiating timetable expired. Indeed, given the nature, complexity and range of conflicts involved in global trade, most analysts were astonished that they had begun at all. Under the auspices of the GATT the so-called Uruguay Round was initiated by President Ronald Reagan in an effort to inhibit growing protectionist pressures in Congress, to extend the global trade rules to new areas such as services and to reverse what has become known as the 'new protectionism', the increasing tendency of countries to take refuge from foreign competition in an elaborate series of semi-permanent non-tariff barriers such as voluntary export restraints—a technique often referred to as 'managed trade'.

The GATT (a specialized agency of the UN, based in Geneva) had come into being in 1948 in an effort to prevent a repetition of the growth of protectionism in the 1920s and 1930s that had contributed to the Great Depression and to build up an international momentum in support of the principles of free trade. The GATT, the nearest the world has to a legal framework for international trade, is based on the two core principles of reciprocity and non-discrimination. In essence, the trade rules require that what you do for one country you must do for all others at the same time. Consequently, if country X decides to reduce its tariff barriers for a specific product for country Y, then that bilateral agreement must also be applied to every other country in the international trading system, a practice known as the most favoured nation (MFN) principle or multilateralism.

During the 1950s and 1960s much of the GATT's efforts were spent on eliminating export quotas. The so-called Kennedy Round of GATT negotiations launched in 1962, for example, was designed to prevent the introduction of the EC's new external tariff from provoking a global increase in protectionism. However, in the face of falling rates of economic growth, rising unemployment and intense domestic pressures to protect indigenous industries from foreign competition, the 1970s and 1980s witnessed an alarming increase in the growth of non-tariff barriers and a tendency to abandon the MFN principle in favour of bilateral trade accords. In addition to arresting these tendencies, the Uruguay Round also set itself the ambitious task of extending the GATT rules to trade in agriculture, textiles, services and intellectual property rights—all hitherto beyond the reach of the multilateral trading system. But if the developing economies were to make concessions granting the developed economies access to their potentially multi-billion pound markets in, for example, financial services, the developed economies would also have to make concessions—particularly in the field of agriculture, where the cost of global protection in the form of production and export subsidies was running in excess of £100 billion a year. It was evident from the outset, therefore, that powerful vested interests were at stake, and that the negotiations were going to be difficult at best and acrimonious at worst.

For most of the Uruguay Round's four-year negotiating period little was heard of the talks. But in October 1990 an apparently intractable conflict within the EC over agricultural reform propelled the issue into the headlines and cast a shadow over the prospects for the Uruguay talks and the future of the global multilateral trading regime itself. In the face of demands from the United States and the Cairns Group (an organization made up of 14 leading agricultural exporters, including Australia, New Zealand, Canada, Argentina, Brazil, Chile and Indonesia) for a 75% cut in domestic production subsidies and a 90% cut in export subsidies, the Community was torn between the advocates and the opponents of reform. Ray MacSharry, the new Commissioner for agriculture, had proposed a 30% cut in production subsidies, which was instantly rejected by Germany, France and Ireland. Moreover, the United States and the

Cairns Group refused to entertain MacSharry's 30% offer as a serious proposition and denounced the failure to address the question of export subsidies, leaving the Commission to face mounting domestic and international criticism.

By November, Arthur Dunkel, the chain-smoking multi-lingual director of the GATT, had alarmed everyone by alleging that the EC's intransigence was threatening the future of the world trading system. The EC finally overcame its internal deadlock in the same month, after no less than seven meetings between agricultural ministers, in which Germany, France and Ireland accepted the Commission's 30% cuts package. But the agreement did little to appease the Community's foreign critics. During a tour of EC capitals, Clayton Yeutter, the US agriculture secretary, warned of the 'high political price to be paid by the Community' if the talks failed. 'If the reform that is achievable is the amount encompassed in the EC proposal, then it simply isn't worth it. I'd rather simply forget the whole thing and go about protecting our interests in our own way,' he said defiantly.

As more than 100 GATT delegations arrived in Brussels for the Uruguay Round's 'final' set of talks in December, an estimated 30,000 farmers from all over the world demonstrated their opposition to the proposed subsidy reductions on the streets of Brussels. Police fired tear gas and used water cannon to disperse protesters who had burnt tyres and ripped up traffic lights. From their perspective at least, the outcome of the Brussels talks was a victory, albeit a hollow one. Because EC governments refused to sacrifice the interests of its 10 million farmers, the Uruguay Round, the largest and most ambitious negotiation ever undertaken by a group of sovereign states, was postponed indefinitely. The United States promptly announced its intention to impose 200% punitive levies on a range of EC agricultural exports. The Commission, deeply embarrassed at being held responsible for the collapse of the talks, tried to talk up its free trade credentials by emphasizing its support for liberalizing services, which the United States had originally opposed. Meanwhile, trade experts warned of the potentially catastrophic consequences if the multilateral trading system was replaced by a series of semi-autarkic trading blocs, and Arthur Dunkel was left to find a way of salvaging something from the wreckage.

While the EC continued to insist that 90% cuts in export subsidies and 75% cuts in production subsidies were unrealistic, the US administration's fast-track authority (the procedure by which Congress waived its right to amend the GATT treaty when it was finally ready to be submitted for approval) was due to expire in March 1991. Without this authority, Congress would tear the trade treaty to shreds, thereby undermining the prospects for ratification in other countries. But there was little point in obtaining an extension of the fast-track procedure if the trade talks remained deadlocked over agricultural reform. That impasse was overcome in February 1991, when Dunkel managed to talk the Community into accepting 'binding commitments' to reduce production and export subsidies and improve market access, which enabled President Bush to secure a two-year extension of his negotiating authority.

Nonetheless, transatlantic relations continued to deteriorate over the agriculture issue, with US and EC trade negotiators frequently unable to bring themselves to speak to each other. In a fit of exasperation in May, Dunkel hit out at both sides, saying that US–EC relations were 'bedevilled by accusations, self-righteousness, mutual misunderstanding and an inability to distinguish between special-interest pleading and the public good'. It is a sterile procedure, he insisted, 'for the main trading nations to throw figures backwards and forwards, as if merely winning the numbers argument somehow supplies an answer to the real challenges of the Uruguay Round'. Addressing his criticisms directly to Washington and Brussels, Dunkel added: 'Let us be in no doubt, the days of passing the buck all around the globe as a means of avoiding the crucial political challenges in trade policies are long gone'.

Despite pleas from the OECD in June and the leaders of the Group of Seven industrial nations in July to put completion of the GATT talks at the top of the international diplomatic agenda, farm subsidies remained the make-or-break issue. MacSharry's 30% cuts were adopted by the Commission in July. The scheme called for the deepest price cuts in agricultural support ever contemplated by the Commission, coupled with full compensation for small farmers, and scaled compensation for larger farmers taking land out of production. Although designed to end the 20% over-production of agricultural produce in the EC and abolish export subsidies, Britain, which had long campaigned against the more blatant absurdities of the CAP, found itself in the awkward position of opposing the reforms because they would cost more to implement and would discriminate against the larger, more efficient farms. Responding to the Commission's proposals, John Gummer, Britain's Agriculture Minister, said: 'We oppose them, we hate them, and we consider them dead'. In short, Britain feared that the reforms would 'maintain in perpetuity a peasant society'.

By November, the GATT talks passed another deadline, and still no resolution of the conflict between Washington and Brussels was in sight. Even more alarming was the growing feeling in the US that perhaps it was time to abandon the multilateral trading system and concentrate on building the North American Free Trade Agreement between the US, Canada and Mexico. A new deadline was set for December, and trade negotiators betrayed a rare hint of optimism after the US moderated its demands for cuts in agricultural subsidies and Germany showed the first signs of abandoning France in its opposition to reform. Dunkel drew up another compromise document, known as the 'final act', calling on both the US and the EC to make further concessions. But December passed without agreement, and with it, commentators feared, the last chance of a rapid breakthrough, especially as President Bush's fast-track mandate would run out in the spring. As 1992 progressed, America would become increasingly preoccupied with the US presidential election, while the EC concentrated on completing the internal market and choosing a new Commission. Few 'wanted the trade talks to collapse or to be postponed, but with Washington and Brussels increasingly focusing on internal matters, the omens were not good. A breakthrough was likely, however, only if the draft compromise was improved, thereby giving the US and Europe some face saving concessions.

The European Free Trade Association

Few countries outside the European Community have been forced to think harder about the external implications of the internal market programme than the six-member EFTA. Formed in 1960, following ratification of the Stockholm Convention the previous year, EFTA was basically a reaction to the creation of the EC three years before. The EC and EFTA reflected the two conflicting visions of Europe's future which were fighting for ideological ascendancy in the immediate post-war period. The first saw Europe moving in the direction of economic and political union, with supranational institutions in a federation of states, while the second had the more modest ambition of creating a loose commercial association, thereby enabling its members to preserve their traditional economic relations with other parts of the world.

Despite initial rivalry and suspicion, each survived to become the other's most important trading partner. Following the implementation of the 1972–3 free trade agreements between the two trading blocs, the volume of two-way trade flourished. In 1986, 25% of EC exports went to EFTA countries (more than the Community's exports to the United States or Japan) while 50% of EFTA exports went to the EC. Overall trade was valued at £120 billion. All seemed rosy—until the Commission published the internal market White Paper. Now, the Community's drive for economic integration by 1992 could mean the end of EFTA.

Composed of six small but highly industrialized countries—Austria, Finland, Iceland, Norway, Sweden and Switzerland—EFTA has been struggling to define its identity in relation to its larger and more powerful regional neighbour before the 1992 deadline expires. Will EFTA be allowed to preserve intact its privileged access to the Community's internal market? If so, will the member states be prepared to enact the same legislative programme of physical, technical and fiscal harmonization measures being implemented by the EC in order to be able to avail themselves of the Community's largesse? If not, will the organization break up as some or all of its members join in the headlong 'rush for Brussels'?

Prior to the publication of the White Paper, the two halves of Western

Europe had already been moving in the direction of increased economic co-operation. At the first ministerial meeting between the two groups in Luxembourg in April 1984 they announced their intention to create by the 1990s a 'European Economic Space', made up of all 18 nations. The most tangible expression of this rather vague rhetoric to date was the inclusion of EFTA in the Community's Single Administrative Document arrangement for simplifying the amount of documentation required for the cross-frontier transportation of goods, due to be phased out at the beginning of 1993.

At the first ministerial meeting between the two organizations since the announcement of the White Paper programme, held in Brussels in February 1988, the two groups reaffirmed their commitment towards the creation of a common economic space, later renamed the European Economic Area (EEA) so as not to imply a *'vacuum'*, and identified a number of areas for further co-operation, including common rules for technical standards, rules of origin and greater openness in the field of public procurement and state aids. However, by the time de Clercq met EFTA ministers in Tampere in June it was already clear that the Community was determined to impose strict limits on the extent to which EFTA could benefit from the creation of the internal market.

De Clercq, with a remarkable tendency for formulating principles in batches of three, enunciated another set of guidelines around which the Community's relations with EFTA would be organized:

1 Priority to internal market considerations over EFTA at all times;
2 The preservation of EC sovereignty to make decisions regardless of the extent of co-operation with EFTA; and
3 The maintenance of a balance of advantages and obligations between the two groups in any agreements made between them.

In addition, de Clercq told the EFTA nations that they must recognize 'that there is a difference between the European Economic Area [EEA] and the internal market, and only member states can expect to participate fully in the internal market'.

De Clercq's three principles may well have come as a shock to EFTA members, but the indications had been obvious for some time. Like most organizations, the Community's resources of time and manpower are limited, and any endeavour to incorporate EFTA into the internal market programme would divide the Community's attention from the primary task in hand. Equally, EFTA was free to mirror Community harmonization legislation if it so wished, but having done so it could not then expect to veto or influence any subsequent decision by the Community to alter or amend any part of the programme in any way it saw fit.

Finally, the Community insisted that it was entitled to benefit as much as EFTA from any closer association between the two trading blocs. This particular issue had already become the source of considerable friction within the Community. A number of the southern member states, anxious that they would not be able to compete with the more advanced economies of EFTA, had complained bitterly about the Commission's granting favours to rich non-member states instead of doing more to help the poorer member states. Spain, particularly, accused EFTA of seeking a free ride on the EC by wanting preferential access to the benefits of the internal market while remaining free of the financial burdens imposed on member states, such as the cost of the CAP. Indeed, this feeling is so strong that British Conservative MEPs openly refer to EFTA as EFRA— the European Free Ride Association.

Consideration has been given to the possibility of EFTA making financial contributions to regional development in the Community's poorer regions by way of compensation for the privileges of access to the internal market. Much of the controversy has since been taken out of this issue following the decision by the Council of Ministers during the February summit meeting in Brussels to double the structural funds to some £9 billion by 1993, most of which will go to the poorer member states.

The idea of paying a premium to the Community in exchange for certain privileges neatly encapsulates many of the dilemmas faced by EFTA nations in the run-up to 1992. Because of its determination to preserve its sovereignty over decision making the Community could not permit EFTA to say how the money was spent. However, ceding the power of decision making to Brussels represents a fundamental loss of sovereignty, far more serious than anything sustained by members of the Community—who at least play a part in the decision-making process. Such problems have already caused a debate in many EFTA member states (particularly Austria, which formally applied for membership in July 1989, and Norway, which is expected to follow suit in the near future) about the possibility of accession to the EC. However, while the Community could not possibly embark on yet another round of accession negotiations prior to 1992, it has accepted EFTA's initiative, announced after its summit meeting at Oslo in March 1989, to improve economic and institutional ties between the two blocs.

In November, Frans Andriessen, the new External Relations Commissioner, announced plans for a new round of EC–EFTA talks, designed to create a "common economic space" between all 18 countries, thereby extending the benefits of the single market to the Six without undermining the autonomy of existing EC institutions. The talks, which were initially expected to last for a year, began when foreign ministers from all 18 countries met to discuss the creation of new institutional relationships between the two organizations. The aim was to establish rules for allowing goods, capital, services and labour (collectively known as the four freedoms) to circulate freely around the combined market of some

380 million people without compromising the sovereignty of either organization.

Because the Community's negotiating mandate prohibited the Commission from diluting the EC's decision-making autonomy, Brussels came up with the novel idea of creating special consultation bodies which would allow EFTA to 'shape but not make' Community decisions. But by the summer of 1990, serious disagreements had broken out between the two bodies, principally because of EFTA's desire to acquire some form of joint decision-making and its reluctance to be subjected to EC competition policy. The impasse raised the spectre of a collapse in the talks and a spate of unwanted accession applications. At the same time, a report published in August by the House of Commons Trade and Industry Committee called on the government to support the eventual entry of all EFTA countries into the Community, and dismissed the EEA negotiations as an 'unsatisfactory alternative'.

Although by May 1991 Commission officials had given a pledge to allow EFTA to follow its own trade policies towards the outside world after 1992, there was a widespread feeling that the EC–EFTA negotiations were about to collapse as EFTA members began to reconsider their earlier opposition to full EC membership. The EEA talks had been designed to forestall EFTA accession applications while the Community concentrated on completing the internal market. Now the EEA was being increasingly seen as a step towards full membership, and an unsatisfactory one at that. The EEA would not create a full customs union between the EC and EFTA, while EFTA states would only be allowed a say and not a vote in EC decisions. Understandably, Austria, Sweden, Switzerland and Norway, had begun to ask themselves what was the point—why not wait until the internal market was completed and apply for full membership?

Nonetheless, the EEA talks proved to be a constructive forum in the attempt to clarify a trio of issues which continued to cause friction between the two trading blocks, known as the 'cash, cod and trucks' disputes, which, in any case, would have to be settled before full EC membership could be agreed. Spain and Portugal were still arguing for additional economic assistance from EFTA in the form of soft loans and grants in exchange for access to the internal market, the Community wanted access to Nordic fishing grounds and Brussels was eager to negotiate transit rights for EC trucks traversing Austria and Switzerland. Although progress on these issues was slow, it no longer seemed beyond reach. Moreover, the vexed question of how to give EFTA a say in EC affairs without compromising the Community's decision-making authority was resolved in May, when the two agreed to create a new EEA panel, made up of five EC and two EFTA judges, who would be responsible for passing judgments on breaches of EEA rules. By now, however, the Commission's original goal of forestalling a wave of EFTA accessions seemed less important than laying the groundwork for further enlargement.

The final breakthrough came in October, after a marathon 16-hour negotiating session in Luxembourg, when foreign ministers from the two trading blocs signed the agreement creating the 18- (19, including Lichtenstein) nation European Economic Area, the largest internal market in the world, stretching from the Arctic to the Mediterranean. When the new agreement comes into effect in January 1993 it will bring into being an internal market of 380 million people, accounting for 40% of world trade. The breakthrough was reached after EFTA states made a series of key concessions. All EFTA members accepted demands from the EC's southern states for substantial economic assistance in the form of soft loans and grants; Switzerland and Austria conceded an increase in the number and weight of EC lorries crossing their frontiers; Norway granted increased access to its fishing grounds for British fishermen. In return for a commitment to adopt all EC single market legislation, EFTA countries were given unimpeded access to all aspects of the internal market. The agreement is expected to lead to a substantial increase in trade between the two organizations. Further, Britain's banks and insurance companies are expected to benefit substantially from the EEA, as they will now be granted access to EFTA's lucrative financial services sector. EFTA will not be able to participate in the EC's decision-making process until after accession (expected some time in the 1990s). Nonetheless, as far as trade in goods, services, capital and labour are concerned, 'they are in' as Frans Andreissen, the External Relations Commissioner, said.

The United States and the EC

Most American business executives, accustomed to thinking about the EC in terms of Eurosclerosis (a wasting disease attributable to endemic labour rigidities, rampant protectionism, an elemental fear of competition and, of course, the proverbial three-hour lunch) have been caught off-guard by the Community's version of *perestroika*. The initial reaction to the internal market programme was one of profound scepticism, but that has since given way to the conviction that the EC is in the process of erecting a giant industrial version of the CAP.

It took the US Administration over three years to make its first official response to the Community's internal market programme. That reaction finally came in August 1988, in an address given by Peter McPherson, a deputy secretary of the US Treasury Department, to the Institute of International Economics in Washington, DC. McPherson's speech betrayed a deep ambivalence towards the goals of the 1992 programme. On the one hand, he welcomed the Community's new initiative to the extent that it would help to promote economic growth in the EC, increase the demand for US exports and thereby help to reduce the US trade deficit, which had reached a staggering $170 billion in 1987. However, he gave a clear warning that the process of internal liberalization must not succumb to the temptation for greater external protection. If in abolishing the divergent import arrangements of individual member states the Commission opted for a common commercial policy that reflected the demands of its more protectionist members, McPherson left the Community in no doubt that the United States 'would respond'. Turning to the vexed issue of reciprocity, he insisted that any attempt to implement such a policy would provoke a serious deterioration in transatlantic trade relations.

The problem to be resolved lay in the conflicting approaches taken by each trading bloc to external trade. The Community's insistence on reciprocity appeared, on the surface, innocuous—if you grant us access to your market we will grant you access to ours. What could be more equitable? However, it failed to acknowledge that in countries like the United States there are stringent regulations governing interstate trade and commerce. US banks, for example, are not free to operate in any state they choose. The Community's demand for reciprocal treatment would mean revising federal and state banking laws to allow European banks greater privileges than those enjoyed by US ones. Hence the US Administration's insistence on the principle of national treatment, whereby foreign companies are governed by the same rules as domestic companies.

However, while warning the Community that 'the creation of a single market that reserves Europe for the Europeans would be bad for Europe, bad for the United States and bad for the multilateral economic system' McPherson had little to say on the Omnibus Trade Act, just then approved by the US Congress. This grants the President powers to employ sanctions against countries running chronic and persistent trade surpluses with the United States. The EC, for example, had a large $21 billion surplus with the US in 1987, and would seem to be a prime target for US retaliation.

The Trade Act is a clear indication that the United States has decided to take a more aggressive approach to reduce its trade deficits with its major trading partners. However, predictions that the move is the first step in a transatlantic trade war, possibly leading to the dissolution of the Atlantic Alliance, seem to be little more than an exercise in hyperbole. As one senior US official said:

> The US trade bill is nowhere near as onerous as it once was. Similarly, 1992 is not going to turn out to be Armageddon. Trade negotiators are sensible people who are not going to go around slashing each other's wrists. The international trading system is simply too important to sabotage.

Indeed, many Europeans have expressed fears that the large US and

Japanese companies will be the primary beneficiaries of the completion of the internal market. Many US corporations have been operating in Europe for decades (a few for considerably longer), and most are often more at home with the European way of doing things than companies from individual member states. De Clercq, however, has dismissed these fears as groundless, and insisted that:

> There is no *a priori* reason to suppose that the subsidiaries of American or Japanese companies operating in the Community will do better or worse than European-owned companies. Europe will be neither a fortress nor a sieve.

Europeans have yet to be convinced.

Nevertheless, the protectionist debate has continued unabated. By the summer of 1989, mutual recrimination between Washington and Brussels over the issue reached the level of a transatlantic propaganda war. Publication of the US National Trade Estimates Report in May, which singled out the Community for a host of restrictive practices, was matched two days later by the publication of a 41-page report by the Commission accusing the United States of more or less the same thing. However, as Commission officials were quick to point out, while the EC report merely described US protectionist practices, the US report triggered those provisions in the 1988 Trade Act which set in motion potential retaliatory action. But despite continued attempts by the Commission to convince foreign trading partners that the Community will not retreat behind a protectionist wall, many, particularly the United States and Japan, remain profoundly suspicious of Brussels' intentions.

An analysis of EC trade policy, published by the GATT in April 1991, threw light on how it was possible for the Community to be described as a supporter of free trade and protectionism at the same time. The report dismissed the Fortress Europe allegation, and pointed out that there had been no increase in the overall level of EC protection. Nevertheless, the GATT accused Brussels of targeting protection towards certain areas of industrial activity, notably car production, consumer electronics, and agriculture, in which the Community faced strong external competition. Highlighting the contrast between the EC's internal and external trade policies, the report said that Brussels had erected a 'complex hierarchy' of preferential trading agreements which had introduced a 'strong element of discrimination' into the multilateral trading system. The GATT was particularly critical of VERs (on the grounds that they could become permanent) and the extensive use of anti-dumping procedures, and called on the EC to match its internal integration with 'a parallel lifting of its external barriers, and closer adherence to the fundamental principles underlying the multilateral trading system'.

The Commission reacted strongly to the GATT report, and criticized it for being 'unbalanced'. Brussels insisted that temporary bilateral export restraints were permissible under GATT rules, pointed out that it was the largest importer of world food products (50% of which entered the EC duty free) and highlighted its record on imported textiles, which had increased 300% since 1976. The report did little to strengthen the EC's case in its periodic trade skirmishes with Washington. But while US anxieties over the potential threat of EC protectionism remained, the earlier paranoia had all but disappeared. The same could not, however, be said of Tokyo.

Japan and the EC

The US approval of the internal market programme (albeit with reservations) has been echoed by the Community's other major trading partner, Japan. During a major speech at the Mansion House in London in May 1988 Noboru Takeshita, the former Japanese Prime Minister, issued an unprecedented call for the strengthening of relations between Japan and the Community in an effort to remedy what he described as the 'weak link' in the US/EC/Japanese economic triangle. Displaying some of the growing concern in Tokyo over the protectionist tendencies inherent in the internal market programme, Takeshita also said that the Community had a responsibility to maintain an open stance towards the global economy as 1992 approaches.

Takeshita's concerns were more than academic. The EC has registered a series of bilateral trade deficits with Japan in recent years (which exceeded £14 billion in 1987), and the Commission has reacted by persuading the Japanese government to accelerate the opening up of its domestic market to Community imports and by inaugurating a severe restriction on imported components destined for Japanese manufacturing facilities located inside the Community.

Since the integration of the internal market programme the Commission has imposed a series of large anti-dumping duties on Japanese goods, including dot matrix printers, electronic typewriters, photocopiers and electric scales, produced by so-called 'screwdriver plants'. The Commission argues that its action is justified, because Japanese companies are trying to evade the Community's anti-dumping duties on imported finished products by building manufacturing facilities inside the EC and then supplying them with Japanese-made components at low prices.

The GATT rules allow countries to impose anti-dumping duties on products sold at below the cost of production where such action is causing hardship for domestic manufacturers, but the Japanese insist that the Commission has taken no account of the difficulties they face locating reliable Community component suppliers in the period immediately after a new manufacturing facility has been established in a member state. Moreover, the Japanese emphatically deny that they have been importing components at prices below those being charged in the Japanese market in an effort to secure an unfair advantage over Community producers, and appealed to GATT's anti-dumping panel to pass judgment on the legitimacy of the Community's action.

In March 1990, when the GATT finally delivered its judgment, the Commission was thrown into a state of confusion. The GATT disputes panel said that the so-called anti-circumvention duties were inconsistent with international trade, as the levies were not customs duties imposed at border posts but internal taxes, and therefore discriminatory. The decision effectively destroyed the EC's defences against what it regards as unfair competition from Japanese and Asian manufacturers. Brussels insisted that the GATT's anti-dumping procedures were ineffective without anti-circumvention levies, and accused the GATT of failing to address itself to the real problem posed by 'screwdriver plants'.

The issue is likely to remain highly sensitive and politically charged. A number of member states are making great endeavours to obtain Japanese investment to help reduce their levels of unemployment. Britain, particularly, has been competing with some of its Community partners to become Japan's gateway to Europe, and is distinctly unhappy about the way the Commission's anti-dumping policy has developed. Alternatively, many industrialists insist that Japanese 'screwdriver plants' are undermining the foundations of local industry, and are a major contributory factor to the very unemployment problem they purport to resolve.

In October 1988, for example, the French government made public its determination to impose restrictions on exports of the British-made Nissan Bluebird car in order to protect French car makers from Japanese competition. Initially (and unofficially) the Commission indicated that such action would be illegal under the free circulation of goods provisions of Article 30. Although, as a result of intense diplomatic pressure from France, the Commission was forced to 'rephrase' its assessment of the French plan, there seemed little doubt that once France appeared before the European Court of Justice it would be forced to back down. The row was, however, illustrative of the deep reluctance on the part of member states to subject their national industries to increased competition.

Yet if the logic of the internal market programme is to be applied systematically, European industrialists have little option but to adjust to the effects of competition from Japanese companies, or indeed any other foreign competitor. Assuming that Japanese companies are not increasing their penetration of European markets by unfair means, European producers must become equally competitive or accept that they lack any comparative advantage in particular manufacturing sectors, and divert their resources to those areas where they can compete more effectively. In the words of one leading economist, where the Community lacks comparative advantage, protection is costly.

At the end of the European Council meeting in Rhodes in December 1988 the EC issued a communiqué on 'Fortress Europe', in an effort to convince the United States and Japan that they would not be discriminated against as a result of the abolition of internal barriers to trade. The communiqué asserted that: 'The internal market will not close in on itself . . . 1992 Europe will be a partner not a Fortress Europe'. Mrs Thatcher had argued for a reference to the internal market programme serving as a model for the rest of the world in the interests of free trade, thereby thwarting attempts by Mitterrand and Gonzalez to give greater prominence to the concept of reciprocity. However, there could be little doubt that the communiqué was as much a reminder to EC member states of the Community's commitment to free trade as an attempt to appease Europe's major trading partners.

Tensions between the free trade and protectionist wings of the Community, particularly over Japanese imports, continue to sour relations between Brussels and Tokyo. In May 1991, Edith Cresson, the French Prime Minister, made matters worse by launching a new tirade against the Japanese, describing them as 'ants'. The outburst followed Cresson's earlier calls for the EC to rally to the defence of Europe's car and electronics industries by providing itself with a new industrial policy. But her attempts to bully the Commission into adopting a more protectionist disposition towards Japan were to no avail, while her choice of words did little to improve the tenor of EC–Japanese relations or contribute towards a resolution of the complex trade tensions between them.

The Soviet Union, Eastern Europe and the EC

The Community's drive for economic integration, allied to EFTA's determination to ensure that it was not excluded from the benefits integration would bring, have been complemented by the opening up of a new chapter in relations between Brussels, Eastern Europe and the Soviet Union. The process began in a modest way at a ceremony in Luxembourg in June 1988, when the EC and the Soviet-led trading bloc, Comecon, signed a declaration of 'mutual recognition', thus ending almost 30 years of unremitting enmity between the two. Although described by Lord Plumb, the former President of the European Parliament, as 'destined to change the map of Europe', it was soon overshadowed by a series of developments in Eastern Europe and the Soviet Union that really were to open up the prospect of a Europe from the Atlantic to the Urals.

President Gorbachov's ascent to power in 1985 is widely acknowledged as the catalyst which liberated Eastern Europe from four decades of Communist rule, thus paving the way for increased co-operation between the two formerly estranged halves of Europe. But how this process was to be managed presented decision-makers in Brussels with a host of new challenges. The rapid pace of the democratization process in Eastern Europe (particularly the tearing down of the Berlin Wall in November 1989) provoked an anguished debate over whether it was possible to reconcile the Community's attempts to 'deepen' the relationships between existing member states with the growing desire to 'broaden' its relationship with the new East European democracies.

At the beginning of 1990, while Comecon members were negotiating the demise of the state trading organizations, the EC started to focus its attention on the so-called second generation of trade agreements with Eastern European countries, designed to introduce real pricing, currency convertibility and recognition of private ownership, and to prevent a wave of premature accession applications. Discussions also began on how to provide the Soviet Union with the short- and long-term economic assistance needed to accelerate economic and political reforms. Both sets of negotiations were conducted against a background of sporadic demonstrations over price rises, which highlighted the vulnerability of former command economies and their fledgling democratic governments attempting to make the transition to a free-market system.

The creation of the European Bank for Reconstruction and Development, based in London, and an increase in funds for the European Investment Bank, based in Luxembourg, were a first step towards providing the urgent funds to finance long-term investment needs and short-term consumption aspirations. However, the funds available were a drop in the ocean compared to what many economists predicted would be needed to help the economies of Eastern Europe and the Soviet Union during the difficult transition from command to market economies. In addition, there was a clear reluctance on the part of some advanced economies to become involved with large-scale macro-economic adjustment programmes in the Soviet Union, which the United States and Britain in particular felt would be better left to the IMF and the World Bank (WB), after there had been more progress with economic reform.

Washington and London's opposition to Moscow's application for full membership of the IMF and WB in July 1991 was motivated not out of any residue of hostility towards the Soviet Union, as some critics maintained, but because of a fear that scarce financial resources would be squandered in supporting an obsolete economic system. Besides, full membership requires the disclosure of gold and foreign currency reserves and a wealth of statistical information about economic performance which, because of the breakdown of the old centrally planned economy, the Soviet Union was hardly in a position to provide. Nevertheless, after the abortive hard-line Communist coup in August 1991 there was a widespread feeling that something more should be done. Western businesses were clearly elated by the collapse of the coup but few felt secure enough to rush in with proposals for new joint ventures. Business conditions had deteriorated alarmingly before the coup, and many expected that it would be many years before any recovery would be in sight. Although East–West joint ventures had increased from 23 in 1987 to 3,000 by 1991, they still accounted for a miniscule portion of Soviet economic activity.

The attempted coup certainly provoked the European Commission into urging EC governments to embrace a more flexible attitude towards the new association agreements with Eastern European countries. Talks on the second-generation association agreements with Hungary, Poland and Czechoslovakia had become embroiled in a series of narrow disputes over accepting their coal, steel, textile and agricultural exports. In September, the Commission proposed an extension of the Community's relationship with the Eastern European democracies, including trade concessions to conclude the association talks with Hungary, Poland and Czechoslovakia, the extension of associate status to Romania and Bulgaria, and the opening of trade talks with Albania and the newly independent Baltic states. After much wrangling, the new association agreements with Czechoslovakia, Hungary and Poland were signed in December. But the difficulty in arriving at an agreement caused considerable resentment in Prague, Budapest and Warsaw over the apparent contradiction between the EC's enthusiastic support for political and economic reforms and its reluctance to back them up with increased access to its markets.

In addition, Frans Andreissen forecast that the wave of accession applications anticipated from EFTA and Eastern Europe would force the Community to convene yet another intergovernmental conference, probably some time in the mid-1990s, in order to overhaul the institutional structure of the EC before enlargement could take place. Otherwise, the Community would face the impossible task of trying to make decisions with up to 24 member states, 30 Commissioners and 1,200 MEPs. 'It is quite clear that the present institutional structure is not conceived for a Community of 24 members or more,' he said. Revolution in Eastern Europe had, therefore, brought the Community to the crossroads between deepening and widening, making it difficult to proceed with the former without at least taking into consideration the consequences of the latter. Meanwhile, John Major urged his Community partners to agree to full EC membership for the Eastern European countries and the Baltic Republics 'as soon as they are ready, politically and economically'. Admittedly, that might not be for many years, but the recommendation held out the prospect of slowing the more federalist impulses of some of the other EC member states.

The decision in October to grant the Soviet Union associate membership of the IMF may have fallen far short of Gorbachov's original request. But it did give the Soviet Union access to some of the world's top advisors on how free-market systems function, and opened the way for the transfer of thousands of Western technical advisors specializing in everything from banking systems to infrastructure projects. Gorbachov's pleas for large-scale direct aid (such as his request for £12 billion in economic assistance made at the end of the G7 summit meeting in London in July) met with less success—despite protests from Germany, France and Italy. The G7 countries were, however, forced to make some provision for helping the Soviet Union to overcome its shortage of foreign currency, which it needed to service its £34 billion external debt. Nevertheless, James Baker, the US Secretary of State, remained determined to adhere to the terms outlined in the G7 meeting, warning that:

> You're not going to see the Soviet Union succeed economically through the mechanism of free cheque writing on the part of others. There have to be fundamental free market reforms.

Money mountains were ruled out, but substantial amounts of short-term emergency aid had been pledged by the United States, Europe and Japan.

An increasing number of critics, however, were beginning to express fears that the approach of the Western industrial democracies was dangerously over cautious. In November, the UN Economic Commission warned that Eastern Europe, and the disintegrating Soviet Union, were spiralling downwards towards a 1930s-type economic depression. Unless far greater levels of economic assistance were forthcoming—at the least along the lines of the Marshall Plan after the Second World War—the East European and Soviet economies would continue to contract, popular support for economic and political reforms would evaporate and the new democratic impulses would be extinguished by a return to authoritarian government. Western attempts to respond effectively to this challenge are likely to become the dominant theme in international relations during the 1990s, the outcome of which will affect relations between east and west into the 21st century.

The Third World and the EC

Under the arrangement known as the Generalized System of Preferences, most developing countries are permitted to export specified amounts of their manufactured products to the EC with a partial or total reduction of customs duties. But the 69 members of the African, Caribbean and Pacific group of nations (or ACP states) are granted quantity-free access for their exports to the Community under the provisions of successive five-year trade accords known as the Lomé Conventions. In contrast to normal trade agreements between developed nations, the Lomé Conventions are not based on the principle of reciprocity, and are therefore regarded by the European Commission as one of the EC's most important mechanisms for promoting economic developments in the Third World.

The origins of the Lomé Conventions stem from an obligation felt by the former colonial powers who now make up the EC to assist their former dependencies. The Fourth Lomé Convention came into being in 1990, and, in contrast to its predecessors each of which ran for a period of five years, the current convention will last until the year 2000. The Lomé Conventions have been the focus of increasing criticism, not least from the recipient countries themselves, who have long regarded the conventions as a modest attempt to provide the ACP countries a guaranteed market for their exports, and so enable them to earn the hard currency needed to reduce the burdens imposed by heavy external debt (estimated to be in excess of $150 billion at the end of 1991). More recently, the conventions have come under heavy criticism from a variety of Western aid groups for failing in their primary objective of promoting economic development.

However, because of the internal market programme, and the necessity of creating a common commercial policy towards third country imports, the negotiations for the Fourth Lomé Convention created great anxiety among the ACP states. Many of these countries have benefited from preferential access to particular EC markets. The Windward Islands, Jamaica and Belize, for example, have been able to export bananas to Britain for decades under extremely favourable terms. Under the new harmonized external trade arrangements, preferential treatment on a national basis will be eliminated. But although the new convention stipulates that 'no ACP state shall be placed . . . in a less favourable position than in the past or present', Britain's Overseas Development Institute (ODI) forecasts a re-direction of trade away from traditional suppliers towards intra-EC trade. In a report published in October 1991 the ODI predicted that the most far-reaching effect on developing countries will be the progressive dismantling of traditional bilateral ties, in which exporters of certain products (notably bananas and fish) are likely to suffer. At the same time, however, exporters of coffee, tea and cocoa are likely to benefit because the harmonization of excise duties will lead to reductions in taxation levels.

The negotiations preceding the signing of Lomé Four (which provides some 12 billion ECUs in aid over the ten-year period) were accompanied by some awkward questions from non-governmental organizations specializing in aid and development. In addition to pointing out that the conventions have failed to improve per capita food production, aid agencies accused the Lomé treaties of confining ACP states to the export of a handful of primary commodities that have kept exports of finished products to the Community at roughly 3% to 4%. Moreover, while the ACP states have failed to diversify their production, nominal increases in aid have been eroded by inflation and population growth. In addition, although the general principles behind the aid programmes are 'progressive', they have been criticized for concentrating on prestige projects (such as building hydroelectric dams) at the expense of providing low-technology solutions which are more likely to improve the quality of life.

Most criticism is, however, reserved for EC food aid programmes, and their relationship with the CAP. Food aid accounts for roughly 33% of all EC development aid, which is spent on wheat, dairy products, rice, sugar and vegetable oil. While few would question the efficacy of emergency or disaster relief, aid agencies argue that the disposal of EC agricultural surpluses simply depresses domestic food prices, and takes away the incentives local farmers need for self-sufficiency. Moreover, the dominance of dairy products in EC food aid shipments (which are high in price but low in volume) have been singled out for reflecting the EC's need to dispose of its surpluses rather than meeting the requirements of food-deficit countries. Without a fundamental reform of the CAP, a re-evaluation of the objectives of EC development aid and a wholesale increase in the number of officials implementing Community aid programmes, aid agencies remain doubtful of the Community's ability to promote genuine development in the Third World.

Checklist of changes

- The abolition of internal barriers to trade will be accompanied by a strengthening of the Community's external identity.
- National import quotas (such as those which currently exist for cars) will be phased out gradually and replaced with EC-wide quotas for a transitionary period.
- There will be increased economic co-operation between the EC and EFTA under the EEA arrangements, although many EFTA countries are likely to submit accession applications after 1993.
- There is likely to be an increase in the number of US and Japanese companies locating themselves in Europe in an attempt to capitalize on the benefits of European economic integration.
- The wave of accession applications from EFTA countries is likely to be followed by a second one of accession applications from East European states, principally from Hungary, Czechoslovakia and Poland.

17 COMMON FOREIGN AND DEFENCE POLICY

Towards a European army?

The question of a common European defence—largely theoretical until a few years ago—has been given added impetus by upheavals both inside and outside Europe requiring a cohesive European response. The Gulf War against Iraq in early 1991 brought British and French forces into a major Middle Eastern conflict alongside the United States, but, at the same time highlighted the fact that a common European approach to defence was still in the early stages. For Euro-sceptics (Mrs Thatcher among them) the Gulf conflict proved that a common European defence was a chimera. Others argued the reverse: that the Gulf War demonstrated how far moves towards a common defence policy needed to be speeded up. The Franco-German proposal for a joint army corps as the nucleus of a future European armed force put common European defence at the top of the agenda at the NATO summit in Rome in November 1991, with Britain criticizing the Franco-German move and arguing that nothing should be done to undermine the existing Atlantic Alliance.

Within Europe, the disintegration of Yugoslavia and its descent into civil war in the course of 1991 also underlined emphatically the urgent need for a common EC foreign and defence policy. Under the Dutch presidency in the second half of 1991, the EC intervened directly in Yugoslavia through diplomatic mediation, while also giving serious consideration for the first time to the formation of an EC peace-keeping (or even peace-making) force. The chosen instrument was the Western European Union (WEU), to which nine of the twelve EC nations belong, and which had, in any case, been gradually emerging as the EC's defence arm after years on the sidelines. In the event, given the reservations of Britain and others, the WEU confined itself to the sending of ceasefire monitors. But on several occasions in the summer and autumn of 1991 EC foreign and defence ministers (meeting as the WEU) drew up plans for a force of armed bodyguards to protect the 200 white-clad monitors, with further contingency plans for developing the bodyguards into a peace-keeping operation.

This is a striking development for the EC. Noel Malcolm, in *The Spectator*, saw such moves as the precursor of a European army, 'with jeeps and armoured cars decked out with little dark-blue and gold-star flags'. Hans Dietrich Genscher, the German Foreign Minister, spoke of a European Security Council, with a force of EC 'green berets' to match the 'blue berets' of UN peace-keeping operations.

A European army in fact remains a long way off. Nonetheless, even though three EC countries—Ireland, Denmark and Greece—are not part of the WEU, the WEU has, in effect, become the accepted defence forum of the Community. In the aftermath of the Gulf War and the beginning of conflict in Yugoslavia, in October 1991 Britain and Italy presented a joint paper to EC foreign ministers, accepting that closer political union embraces 'a stronger European defence identity'. Britain proposed a WEU 'European reaction force' for use anywhere in the world where 'the interests of WEU members or peace-keeping operations are threatened'.

Roots of a common European defence

As with other aspects of European unity, the trend towards a common defence can be traced to the Single European Act. This provided the germ for a common security policy. 'Security' is a wider and more political term than the purely military concerns of 'defence'—but the two concepts overlap, and, under pressure of events, the distinction has become blurred. At Maastricht, it was agreed that EC foreign and security policy would be dealt with though 'systematic co-operation' between states, rather than through EC institutional mechanisms. On the other hand, the Council of Ministers can agree—by unanimous vote—on the principles of joint action in foreign policy, with the actual implementation of that policy requiring only a majority vote. Some see this as the thin end of a wedge leading to a more integrated foreign and defence policy. Maastricht also agreed that the Western European Union would be 'developed as the defence component of the European Union', although the WEU is also to serve as the means of strengthening the European pillar of the Atlantic alliance, and WEU decisions 'shall not affect the obligations of certain member states to NATO'. The treaty foresees 'the eventual framing of a common defence policy, which might in time lead to common defence'. In January 1992 Delors noted that when that day came, the French nuclear deterrent (he did not mention the British) should be put at the disposal of the EC as a whole. This is unlikely, given national feeling in Britain and France over nuclear deterrence, and the complexities of joint control. A joint nuclear policy would follow anyway from common defence, with shared aims and military strategies. So far the EC seems to share common conventional defence aims, but has a varied approach to conflicts such as the Yugoslav civil war.

A European defence union was attempted (unsuccessfully) in the 1950s, foundering both because of the lack of political union to underpin it and of the complexities involved in combining the differing defence interests and technologies of the European states. There was also the difficulty of reconciling European defence with the functions of NATO. This problem remains, especially as France continues to press for a European defence distinct from NATO and the United States. But it is perhaps becoming less intractable as NATO redefines its role as the Western defence alliance in the wake of the collapse of Communism in Eastern Europe and the dissolution of the Warsaw Pact.

As defence priorities are re-examined, the prospect of sharing military costs through European co-operation in armaments design and manufacture has clear attractions. Even before the crises in Yugoslavia and the Gulf, this trend gained impetus when the Europeans found themselves not consulted by the United States at the time of the 1986 Reykjavik Reagan–Gorbachov summit. Europeans were shocked into taking the question of European defence interests more seriously, despite strong Danish and Irish reservations (because of their traditional neutrality) and a traditional EC reluctance to become involved in defence issues.

The process began as early as October 1987. When EC foreign ministers met for their semi-annual informal get together at the seaside resort of Nyborg in Denmark, one of the top items on the agenda was Gorbachov's speech at Murmansk, offering the West a pact on the partial demilitarization of seas in the Nordic area. The offer was considered and rejected, on the grounds that it merely reiterated a long-standing Soviet proposal, and would not materially add to Western security. What was worth noting, however, was that the EC was discussing an East–West defence and security issue. Between 1987 and the treaty-revising Maastricht summit on economic and political union in December 1991, arguments for a common defence gathered force. But it is still unclear whether the focus should be the EC Council of Ministers; the WEU; bilateral defence co-operation (with the Franco–German Defence Council as a model); or the 'European pillar' of NATO, with the Euro-Group of European defence ministers and officials acquiring an expanded role.

The Anglo–Italian EC paper on defence of October 1991 (disliked by France) suggested a combintion of the WEU and the 'European pillar', to bridge the EC–NATO gap. France, Germany and Spain issued a statement of their own in Paris the same month which made no mention of NATO;

> To come closer to European union, with a federal vocation, we
> recall that the implementation of a foreign and security policy is a
> necessary component of political union. Such a policy must include
> all questions relating to security and defence, with the aim in future
> of a common defence.

Of the Twelve, Ireland is neutral and a non-NATO member; Greece, although in NATO, has taken a maverick line more favourable to both the Soviet Union and the radical Arab states than that of other Western nations; while Denmark—also a NATO member—leans towards neutralism, and has a sizeable minority opposed to Denmark's membership of both the EC and NATO.

Common foreign policy

The question of formulating a defence or security policy is directly related to—indeed, grows out of—the EC's history of gradual, often crab-like moves towards a joint foreign policy, culminating in the growing importance of the EC foreign policy structure known as 'European political co-operation' (EPC, or somewhat inelegantly, POCO). Political co-operation meetings are usually held at foreign minister level, with the assistance of foreign ministry political directors responsible for POCO co-ordination. Discussion of security issues in this context is justified by the reference in the Single European Act to the need for 'closer co-operation on questions of European security' within the political co-operation framework.

The record of EC co-operation in foreign policy has been mixed. EC states remain divided over how they should proceed towards 'closer co-operation' in security, as well as over the difference between what is meant by 'security' and what is meant by 'defence'. The concept of a defence union to accompany economic and political union arouses fundamental issues of national sovereignty, since defence and foreign policy —like taxation—are normally considered the prerogative of national governments and therefore 'no-go' areas for the EC.

'Political co-operation' is a relatively recent invention, with its origins in the Davignon Report of 1970 rather than in the Treaty of Rome. Viscount Davignon of Belgium (later an EC Commissioner) was asked by The Hague EC summit of 1969 to put together a team of senior foreign ministry officials (he was himself in the Belgian foreign ministry at the time) to report on ways of increasing EC co-ordination in foreign policy. Despite objections on grounds of national sovereignty, the Davignon Report recommended the 'harmonization' of foreign policy views and— where possible—joint decisions on matters affecting the foreign policy interests of Europe as a whole. A number of countries (led by France) opposed the idea on the grounds that, whereas individual states had foreign policy interests, Europe as a whole did not. Nonetheless, the proposal was adopted, with provision for twice-yearly meetings of EC foreign ministers to discuss 'political co-operation' questions.

Subsequent events provide an object lesson in the way in which harmonization proposals tend to be agreed by the EC, with member states entering reservations which eventually become eroded or appear irrelevant. Initially, France made sure that a rigid distinction was drawn between 'political co-operation' meetings—held in the member state holding the Council of Ministers presidency—and normal EC Councils. At first, the distinction was strictly enforced: long-serving EC officials recall that foreign ministers used to hold their regular sessions in Brussels or Luxembourg and then depart, with their staffs, for the country holding the presidency in order to put their 'political co-operation' hats on. Eventually, however, this practice came to be regarded as wearisome and unnecessary, and the situation became blurred, making such elaborate arrangements seem quaint or redundant. French opposition declined after the death of de Gaulle, and it became common for foreign ministers to mix normal EC business with foreign policy (most often, by discussing foreign policy matters over lunch). More recently, East–West issues and matters related in one way or another to defence, security or the common fight against terrorism have come onto the agenda, thus completing the original Davignon vision. 'It is simply not realistic to expect EC foreign ministers, who may have just come from a United Nations meeting in New York, a Western economic summit or a NATO Council to confine themselves to the EC budget' one senior diplomat in Brussels argues, 'They are bound to carry on discussing issues of vital concern to the West and to Europe in particular—and increasingly that means defence issues.'

Under the Single European Act, a political co-operation secretariat was set up in Brussels to help the foreign ministry of the presidency country to co-ordinate foreign policy. The foreign minister of the presidency country speaks for the EC as a whole in the United Nations. In theory, at least, the Twelve work out a joint approach to international issues at the UN and vote together in the UN General Assembly; similarly the EC takes a common line on human rights and related issues at the Vienna European Security (CSCE) Conference. EC summits and foreign councils make declarations on global issues, from Afghanistan to the Middle East, and EC foreign ministers hold regular meetings with their counterparts from regional groupings (the Gulf, Central America, ASEAN, etc.). These declarations have sometimes been influential: the 1980 Venice summit declaration on the Middle East still reverberates in the region because of its implicit suggestion that the Palestine Liberation Organization (PLO) should take part in the peace process, provided it recognized the right of all states in the region (Israel included) to live within secure borders.

The EC has also taken limited sanctions against various states in an attempt to use its political and economic power for agreed European aims: for example against Libya and Syria over terrorism; against Iraq after its invasion of Kuwait in August 1990; and against South Africa over apartheid. Such sanctions have had mixed results (EC sanctions against Argentina in support of Britain during the 1982 Falklands War fell apart altogether).

Foreign policy, for the most part, still rests on perceived national interests. Splits in Europe over how to deal with Iran and the hostage crisis in Lebanon provided a case in point, with nations disagreeing on whether and how to deal with hostage-takers. Britain and France still have world roles and links which echo past glories and responsibilities;

Germany looks to the east; Spain, Italy and Greece all have special links with the Arab world and the Mediterranean; Denmark feels the attraction of the Nordic states and, more recently, the newly independent Baltic states, too. Danish ties with Scandinavia are formally acknowledged by the EC (for example, in allowing Denmark to maintain special trading and border arrangements with its Nordic neighbours).

NATO and the American presence in Europe

A common European defence, by contrast, was in the spotlight even before the end of the Cold War, because of a growing movement in the United States—not least in Congress—to oblige 'the Europeans' to shoulder more of the Western defence burden, 'roles, risks and responsibilities' in NATO jargon. In fact, the European members of NATO already contribute 90% of NATO's manpower in Europe and almost the same percentage of the Alliance's tanks, artillery and combat aircraft. Nonetheless, American demands for a larger European defence effort reflect a general rethinking in the Western Alliance, encapsulated by the Rome NATO summit of November 1991 and President Bush's offer the previous month of substantial unilateral cuts in the US nuclear arsenal, forcing the post-coup leadership in Moscow to match and even to exceed the proposals. The new East–West climate and the restructuring of NATO has led to the reorganization of NATO forces, with the emphasis on a British-led rapid reaction force able to intervene flexibly in conflicts. The decisive move away from Soviet Communism which followed the failed Moscow hardline coup of August 1991 confirms that the West need no longer assume a Soviet threat to Western Europe of the kind which has hitherto dominated NATO thinking.

On the other hand, Western strategic planners remain wary of instability in the former Soviet Union, and continue to regard a powerful independent Russian republic under Boris Yeltsin as a potential threat, especially since Yeltsin's Russia deliberately draws on the glories of the imperial Russian past for inspiration. There is thus no question of a total US withdrawal from Europe. But troop levels are being reduced under the Conventional Forces in Europe (CFE) agreement signed in September 1990, with the United States and the Soviet Union reducing forces in Central Europe to a ceiling of 195,000 each. As the US Presidential campaigns in 1988 and 1992 both show, it has become common in the United States to argue that, although the depth of American involvement in European defences was justified after the Second World War, the world has moved on in the past four decades. In 1988, the North Atlantic Assembly declared in its report *NATO in the 1990s* that a 'new transatlantic bargain' had to be struck. The European response has been to look for ways of meeting the American demand for fairer 'burden sharing' within NATO while, at the same time, exploring avenues towards a joint European defence—sometimes, paradoxically, to the alarm of the United

States, which wants Europe to pay more for its own defence but does not relish the thought of a European defence body emerging as a counter-weight or alternative to NATO itself.

Senior NATO and, indeed, EC officials (although this is less true of the French) remain anxious to preserve the transatlantic aspect of defence. Manfred Worner, the NATO Secretary General, noted in September 1990 —during the Gulf crisis—that while the EC must clearly 'take over greater responsibility for its defence', this did not mean 'decoupling' Europe from the United States. Similarly, Tom King, the Defence Secretary, observed when presenting the UK Defence White Paper in July 1991 on the 'peace dividend' resulting from the end of the Cold War:

> Building totally distinct West European entities, involving the eventual absorption of the WEU by the Twelve, would be disruptive of NATO. It would result in at least two classes of NATO European states and would erode the principle of equal security for all.

However, General John Galvin, the NATO Supreme Commander in Europe, upset the EC by suggesting in the *Washington Post* in October 1991 that US troops might have to stay in Europe, because 'the Euro-peans' had a long history of fighting each other that was not necessarily at an end.

The Western European Union

Efforts to develop an EC defence dimension have tended to focus on the Western European Union, which groups together Britain, France, Germany, Italy, the Benelux countries, Spain and Portugal, a total of nine out of the twelve EC states. The WEU was founded by the Treaty of Brussels in 1948 (the founding members were Britain, France, Belgium, the Netherlands and Luxembourg), and first expanded in 1954, when West Germany and Italy joined. The 1950s were not, however, a pro-pitious time for European defence efforts, as is shown by the fate of the proposed European Defence Community (EDC), which was set up in 1952 by France, West Germany, Italy and the Benelux states but which collapsed when the French National Assembly voted against ratification of the EDC Treaty two years later (West Germany joined the other Western nations in NATO shortly afterwards).

Unlike the abortive EDC, the WEU survived, with offices in both Paris and London, albeit in somewhat dormant form until it was revived in 1984 at foreign minister level. It has since been further strengthened under a triple impulse: the need to forge a closer European defence identity at a time when the superpowers are concluding far-reaching disarmament agreements directly affecting European interests: common European interests in areas outside Europe, notably the Gulf, with its vital oil supplies to Western Europe (less vital to the United States): and the fact that two European powers, Britain and France, have independent nuclear deterrents which could be used for European as well as national defence but are not yet included in the terms of reference of any wider international arms control process.

A key move in the development of the WEU came in March 1987, when Sir Geoffrey Howe, the then Foreign Secretary, in a speech to the Institute of International Relations in Brussels called for a European defence strategy, with the WEU headquarters moved from Paris and London to Brussels. This proposal, much resisted by the French, would bring the WEU institutions closer to NATO—and to the EC. In October 1987 at The Hague the WEU launched a 'Platform on European Security Interests', which recalled 'our commitment to build a European Union in accordance with the Single European Act, adding that the construction of an integrated Europe 'will remain incomplete as long as it does not include security and defence'. While partnership with the United States remained vital, 'we intend to develop a more cohesive European defence identity'. This declaration did much to revitalize the WEU. But it was the Gulf conflict of 1990–91 and the EC's efforts to resolve the Yugoslavian crisis in 1991 which brought the WEU out of the shadows and into the headlines.

The Gulf War and the EC

Iraq's invasion of Kuwait in August 1990 was the first major test of Europe's new cohesion in defence. During the crisis Mrs Thatcher, the then British Prime Minister, was scathing about EC disunity, as indeed she was later, observing in March 1991 in a speech in the United States that, once again, only America had proved capable of defending world freedom. 'Perhaps the most extraordinary suggestion yet to come out of Brussels,' she said, 'is that the disunity and half-heartedness of most European nations during the Gulf crisis demonstrates the need for a united European foreign and defence policy.' John Major, her successor, agreed. In January 1991, with the war at its height, he told the Commons there was 'a considerable disparity in the extent to which individual European countries have committed themselves . . . political union and a common foreign and security policy in Europe will have to go beyond statements and extend to action'. Only Britain and France, of the EC nations, sent troops on any scale, although Germany—after much debate —sent warplanes to Turkey and contributed financially to the war effort. There was particular anger in Britain over Belgium's reluctance to supply the UK with much-needed ammunition. France, too, was initially reluctant to become involved, and—without telling its EC partners—sought to avert war at the last moment with behind-the-scenes approaches to Baghdad through third parties at the UN.

The EC's initial emphasis was on economic sanctions rather than military action, with foreign ministers meeting in August 1990 to embargo purchases of Iraqi and Kuwaiti oil (the latter then under Iraqi control), freeze Iraqi assets in Europe, ban (rather belatedly) European arms sales to Iraq and suspend all trade with Baghdad. At the International Institute for Strategic Studies (IISS) in London in March 1991, after Iraq's surrender, Delors observed that the conflict had been a reminder of the need for a common European defence, not least because European interests— no longer directly threatened by Communism—were clearly at risk from other quarters such as the Middle East. The decision by Britain and France to send troops to guard Kurdish 'safe havens' in northern Iraq after the war was taken at an EC summit in Luxembourg in April 1991, at which John Major proposed the havens as a way of protecting Kurdish refugees fleeing persecution by Saddam Husain.

The Yugoslav civil war

The EC also faced a test of resolve in the subsequent crisis in Yugoslavia. The Gulf War involved a threat to European interests, not least because of European dependence on Middle Eastern oil supplies. But the Yugoslav civil war, caused by declarations of independence by Slovenia and Croatia, was the first serious shedding of blood on the European continent itself since the end of the Second World War. 'This is the hour of Europe, not the hour of the Americans,' Jacques Poos, the Luxembourg Foreign Minister, declared as the Yugoslav crisis began in the first half of 1991, during Luxembourg's EC presidency. Many doubted the wisdom of venturing into the morass of South Slav nationalisms dating back to the bitterness of the Serbian–Croatian conflicts of the Second World War and, even earlier, to the ethnic rivalries of the Austro–Hungarian Empire. But pressure grew for 'Europe' to solve a European conflict which threatened to spill across borders—to Italy or Hungary, for example. The EC withheld aid and low-rate credits to Belgrade (the capital of both Serbia and the Yugoslav federation) perceiving Greater Serbian nationalism to be one of the causes of the tragedy.

However, most EC states balked at German proposals for outright recognition of Croatia and Slovenia. France and the UK judged it wiser to preserve some form of Yugoslav federalism in the interests of future stability, while Spain feared that recognizing new states would encourage Spanish separatists such as the Basques. Instead, the EC established a Yugoslav peace conference in The Hague, chaired by Lord Carrington, sent several peace missions to Belgrade headed by Hans van den Broek, the Dutch Foreign Minister, negotiated a series of ceasefires, and sent monitors to supervise the fragile truces which followed.

The Dutch EC presidency in the second half of 1991 proposed an EC peacekeeping force of 25,000, but the WEU, at the end of September 1991, described this as 'long-term planning' for a 'worst-case scenario', and opted instead for a strengthened monitoring force. In October 1991 Lord Carrington and van den Broek persuaded Slobodan Milosevic, the

Serbian leader, to abandon his aim of a 'Greater Serbia' and acknowledge that internal borders could not be changed by force (a cardinal EC and CSCE principle), the eventual aim being 'self-determination' for Yugoslav republics, perhaps within a much looser form of federation. Douglas Hurd, the Foreign Secretary, declared that Yugoslavia could not be held together by force and 'those republics which decide for independence will get it'—eventually.

What is striking is that the Yugoslav crisis set a precedent for EC intervention in European disputes, even where they arise outside the EC itself. In Yugoslavia the EC, acting as the regional supra-national body, assumed a mediation role hitherto confined to the United Nations. But it was, in the end, the UN rather than the EC which arranged with both Serbs and Croats for a peacekeeping operation. Yugoslavia, moreover, threatened the very principle of common EC foreign policymaking just at the moment when it had been formulated at the Maastricht summit in December 1991. Chancellor Kohl pledged German recognition of Croatia and Slovenia 'by Christmas,' a move described by *The Times* as 'Germany's Balkan folly'. Lord Carrington warned it would prolong the war, and could encourage demands for recognition from other republics. Nonetheless EC foreign ministers, taking Bonn's lead, agreed to recognise the breakaway republics by 15 January 1992, provided they met agreed EC criteria for independence, including democratic rule, respect for human rights and the safety of ethnic minorities. A Yugoslav federal air force rocket attack on an EC helicopter on 7 January, in which four Italians and a Frenchman were killed, underlined the risks taken by EC monitors—including, for the first time, the risk of death and injury in a European rather than national cause. In early 1992 Cyrus Vance negotiated a ceasefire on behalf of the UN, and all parties—except hardline leaders of Serbian enclaves in Croatia—agreed to the deployment of a UN peacekeeping force of 10–15,000 men. The EC duly recognised Croatia and Slovenia as independent states, but Greece blocked proposals for recognising Macedonia.

Bilateral defence co-operation

NATO foreign ministers meeting in Copenhagen in June 1991 (and the Rome NATO summit of November in the same year) duly recognized the progress of the EC toward a common foreign and security policy, declaring that this would be reflected in the strengthening of the European pillar of NATO. At the same time, in addition to joint defence efforts, European defence policy is based on national conventional forces, plus the deterrent provided by the British and French nuclear forces (at present under national control, and, in the British case, assigned to NATO). Thinking of this kind has been encouraged by the development of limited forms of cross-border defence co-operation, notably Anglo-French and Franco-German. In his Brussels speech in 1987, Sir Geoffrey

Howe noted that France was moving tentatively away from the notion of a 'national sanctuary', protected by the *force de frappe*, towards the concept of a nuclear force for the protection of both Germany and France, and possibly of Western Europe as a whole.

Other bilateral moves include exploratory Anglo-French talks on nuclear co-operation—for example, joint targeting of the sovereign nuclear deterrents—and the formation of a joint Franco–German army corps at Strasbourg. This follows the creation of a Franco–German brigade—part of the 1988 Treaty renewing the 1963 Elysée Treaty—based at Boblingen, near Stuttgart, with 4,000 men plus light tanks and artillery. French and German forces have also held large-scale manoeuvres in Bavaria. The Atlantic Assembly's report *NATO in the 1990s* went further, and suggested building on the Franco–German example to form a European brigade drawn from the national armed forces of Europe. Such moves are clearly designed in part to coax France back into the orbit of Western defence structures, if not into the integrated military structure of NATO, which the French left in 1966. There are also moves towards Anglo–German bilateral co-operation within NATO, although such co-operation falls short of the Franco–German link and no Anglo–German brigade is envisaged at present.

Nation states remain reluctant to pool national resources in so sensitive an area as defence. There can be few more potent symbols of nationhood than a country's armed forces. The formation of a European brigade, let alone a European army, is as fraught with difficulty as the formation of a European police force to combat crime and terrorism in a border-free Europe. Defence expenditures vary widely from country to country, with the military budget amounting to 4.7% of GDP in Britain, 4.0% in France, 3.0% in Germany, 2.2% in Italy and 2.1% in Denmark. Britain, for its part, continues to place high value on its military co-operation with the United States. Anglo-French talks on British use of a French air-launched 'stand-off' nuclear missile to replace ageing British free-fall nuclear bombs have run into difficulties because the French ASMP rocket, used on Mirage fighters, has a range of 150 miles rather than the 300 miles Britain wants, and does not have radar-foiling 'Stealth' technology of the kind developed in America.

The impetus towards common defence

For all these difficulties, the impetus towards a common European defence is strong. David Greenwood, Director of Defence Studies at Aberdeen University, argued as long ago as 1988 that the transatlantic partnership was 'unhealthily unequal'. That American power and technology dominates NATO, for example, breeds 'European resentment', while the fact that the United States has what it sees as a disproportionate share of the burden of defending the West fosters 'American disenchantment'. Western Europe, Greenwood suggests, must develop not only a more assertive personality but more durable defence structures. He proposes three purposes for this: co-ordination of policy; co-operation in arms procurement; and collaboration in defence industry production.

The case for intra-European co-operation in arms procurement is particularly compelling, since 'no country in Western Europe can afford the price of self-sufficiency in weapons research, development and production'. NATO has a procurement agency in the form of the Independent European Programme Group (IEPG), and projects such as the Euro-Fighter testify to the growing importance of collaborative projects. But NATO officials want far more in the way of weapons harmonization, with a common defence research programme and a central register of defence requirements to match defence industry production and development.

François Heisbourg, director of the IISS also believes that constructing an effective 'European pillar' of NATO would be 'a logical corollary to ventures leading to the creation of a single unified European market after 1992', despite the differing national defence goals of Britain, France and Germany. The impetus towards European defence need not weaken the transatlantic alliance, which has so far survived tensions not only in defence matters but also in trade and finance, with US–European strains arising over protectionism and the dollar, and over regional conflicts.

The main problem lies within Europe, which is having to face up to the consequences of the collapse of Communism in the east, extensive nuclear and conventional disarmament, and the need to extend security structures to former Communist countries in Eastern Europe. Despite upheavals in Russia and Eastern Europe there is still insufficient common ground on defence between France and Britain, and between the two European nuclear powers and a reunified Germany.

A convincing collective European defence policy, like an effective joint European foreign policy, can only come about when Europe is fully integrated politically and economically, in accordance with the vision outlined at Maastricht. A European Defence Union, in other words, will be possible when the 1992 process is completed: it is very unlikely to precede it.

This need not, however, prevent the European nations from making preparatory moves now towards greater co-operation in arms procurement and other defence fields, thus laying the foundations for some form of closer defence integration to accompany other aspects of the 1992 phenomenon. In the end, in defence as in the political, economic and technological fields, Europe will progress as far and as fast towards union as its peoples and its politicians want. An integrated Europe of 320 million people not only has the potential to challenge the US and Asia in trading terms, it also contains within it the seeds of a powerful and technologically advanced defence bloc. As with a European Bank and single currency, whether the EC should have a European army will, in the end, be a political decision, and will partly depend on whether the EC widens its membership to the point where a joint defence force becomes too unwieldy to contemplate.

Checklist of changes

- Foreign policy co-operation to be increased.
- Defence and security policy to be co-ordinated more closely.
- Moves toward European defence to be based on Western European Union (WEU) within overall NATO framework.
- NATO to bring Eastern Europe closer to Western alliance through new East–West Co-operation Council.

18 TOWARDS A COMMUNITY OF THIRTY

The problem of EC enlargement

The 1992 programme, as originally conceived, did not anticipate the changes which were to take place in Eastern Europe in 1989, in Germany in 1990, and in the Soviet Union in 1991. Nor did it anticipate the list of applications for EC membership from countries as far apart as Malta and Sweden, and the creation of a European Economic Area through the October 1991 deal with EFTA, giving the seven EFTA nations and their 60 million people 'unimpeded access' to the single market and bringing them closer to EC membership. The EC has had to adjust its plans in the light of this redefinition of what is meant by a European 'community'. The paradox is that even a Community of Twelve is finding integration a complex and arduous task—yet the closer that integration looms, the more attractive it appears to those outside the 'magic circle', not least in Eastern Europe and EFTA, and even in the former Soviet Union.

In Western Europe, 1992 promises to make already successful economies even more prosperous. In Eastern Europe, by contrast, statues of Lenin have been toppled and symbols of the hammer and sickle thrown on the scrap-heap. In a manner and speed which would astonish the EC's founders, what began as an enterprise of Six, then Nine and now Twelve may come to embrace all or most of the Continent. In October 1991 Delors called on the EC to prepare for a Community of 24 or even 30 members, noting in the Paris-based magazine *Belvedere* that a 'new political and institutional programme' would be needed for this after Maastricht.

Delors's answer to the collapse of Eastern Europe and the growing demand from EFTA countries such as Sweden and Austria for EC membership has been to devise a system of 'concentric circles' with the Twelve at its core, EFTA countries in the second ring, and Eastern Europe in the outer ring. This presumes, however, that both the EFTA nations and the East Europeans will be satisfied with various forms of association with the EC. Already, with Soviet troops due to leave Poland altogether at the end of 1992 and Germany by 1994, the East Europeans are looking to the EC and NATO for some form of security umbrella to fill the vacuum left by the disintegration of the once-familiar post-war system of military blocs. The East European ethnic conflicts since the fall of Communism, especially in Yugoslavia, have reinforced this trend, with Jozsef Antall, the democratic Prime Minister of Hungary, calling for the nations of East and Central Europe to be in both the EC and NATO.

The future of Europe is 'a question now posed in the broadest terms since the end of the Second World War' *The Times* said in an editorial entitled 'Germany and Europe' in November 1989 as the Berlin Wall started to crumble. Since 1989 the 'other Europeans' have risen with remarkable speed and determination to throw off the Communist system imposed on them after the Second World War. Even in the Soviet Union —or the 'ex-Soviet Union'—Communism collapsed following the abortive and counter-productive coup of August 1991, when hardliners —including the then heads of the armed forces and the KGB—miscalculated disastrously in trying to overthrow President Gorbachov, introducing instead a new era of freedom built on the defiance of the coup by Boris Yeltsin and the Democrats who control the Russian Federation. The failed coup also gave the final push to persistent efforts by the Baltic Republic—often in the face of bloody suppression by Moscow—to regain their independence. Other republics, too, from the Ukraine to central Asia, have proclaimed independence, leaving Gorbachov with the task of trying to bring about some new form of political federation and economic union.

This has re-opened the question of what is meant by 'Europe', and of what is to be the link between the EC and its East European neighbours. The seismic shifts in European political geology have exposed differing attitudes on the part of key EC states. Britain, for example, urges a cautious approach to economic and monetary union within the EC as it tries to evaluate the new situation. France, by contrast, wants faster integration to ensure that Germany, united since October 1990, remains firmly anchored in the Community and is not tempted by virtue of its historical links with Eastern Europe to contemplate if its future, too, might not lie more in Eastern Europe.

After the thaw

Formally speaking, the end of the Cold War dates from the Malta summit between Bush and Gorbachov in December 1989, when Bush gave approval for German reunification provided Germany remained within NATO and the EC. Gorbachov at first resisted this, but in July 1990 agreed with Kohl that a united Germany could stay in NATO, provided that the combined German army was reduced from 600,000 to 370,000 and that no NATO troops were moved into former East Germany. Gorbachov agreed in turn to withdraw Soviet troops from East Germany over a period of three to four years. The end of the Cold War, and the collapse of both Comecon and the Warsaw Pact, were codefied in a new 'Charter for Europe' signed by leaders from East and West (and the neutral countries of Europe) at the Paris Conference on Security and Co-operation in Europe in November 1990.

The rush to German reunification became inevitable as thousands of young East Germans began to flee through the crumbling borders in the autumn of 1989, some pouring through the newly opened Hungarian border with Austria, others leaving by special train after taking refuge in West German embassies in Warsaw and Prague. Street protests against the East German regime took place in East Berlin and Leipzig, leading to the fall of Erich Honecker, the Communist leader who had once vowed that the Berlin Wall (the so-called 'Anti-Fascist Protection Barrier') would last 100 years. Overwhelming popular demand for change also engulfed detested Communist regimes across Eastern Europe, with the first non-Communist government in Eastern Europe since the Second World War taking office in Poland in August 1989. The term 'People's Republic' became redundant, and Communist parties reconstituted themselves as socialist parties, either suffering ignominious defeat in elections or forced into coalitions with parties of the centre and right. In the words of Gennady Gerasimov, then the Kremlin spokesman (and subsequently Soviet ambassador to Portugal), the 'Brezhnev doctrine' used to justify the 1968 invasion of Czechoslovakia to 'preserve socialism' had been supplanted by the 'Sinatra doctrine'—letting East Europeans 'do it their way'.

The EC Dublin summit of April 1990 welcomed the advent of democracy in Eastern Europe and the prospect of German reunification. Western fears of German resurgence surfaced in Britain in July 1990, however, when Nicholas Ridley, a government minister, told *The Spectator* that the European Monetary System was a 'German racket' designed to take over the whole of Europe. He also referred explicitly to Hitler and concentration camps, suggesting—in an apparent reflection of Mrs Thatcher's own thinking—that some aspects of 'the German character' might not have changed for the better. His resignation followed promptly.

However, in August 1990 the EC's conditions for German unity were worked out: special tariffs between the Soviet Union and former East Germany would continue for two years, and, because of the immense problems of absorbing antiquated East German industries and sub-standard goods, Germany would be given temporary exemptions from some EC directives. On pollution, factories in the eastern half of Germany have three years beyond the 1993 deadline to comply with EC directives limiting sulphur dioxide emissions. As part of his bid to reunify Germany despite the economic and fiscal costs involved, Kohl insisted that the almost valueless Ostmark should be exchanged one for one with the powerful deutschmark when German currency union was declared in the summer of 1990 (at a stroke delivering a death blow to what remained of eastern Germany's ramshackle economy). Political unification followed in October 1990, with elections throughout Germany in December, Kohl and the Christian Democratic Union (CDU) winning in both West and East.

In the year that followed, economic strains became evident as Treuhand, the government agency for privatizing and funding eastern German companies, struggled to unite a dynamic western economy and a moribund eastern one. At least for a time, Kohl, once feted in Leipzig and Dresden, became the target of abuse. Economic difficulties also gave rise to social pressures, including violence against foreign immigrants in eastern German states such as Saxony. In the Soviet Union, Gorbachov was criticized by hardliners for 'losing Germany' to the West—indeed, such charges became part of the move to oust him in August 1991. But when accused of 'losing' Eastern Europe, Gorbachov retorted:

When you say this is a collapse of socialism, I counter—what kind of socialism? A variety of the Stalinist authoritarian and bureaucratic system which we ourselves have abandoned.

At his historic encounter with Pope John Paul II in the Vatican on the eve of the 1989 Malta summit Gorbachov spoke of the need to find 'solutions to common European problems' based on 'respect for peoples' national, state, spiritual and cultural identity'.

Nonetheless, the euphoria which greeted the exhilarating sight of young Germans from east and west sitting atop the once-feared Berlin Wall on 10 November 1989 and hacking away whole chunks of it has given way to more considered rethinking on Europe. Both the special EC summit in Paris eight days after the Berlin Wall was breached and the Strasbourg summit of December 1989 were dominated by the need to react to change in Eastern Europe, and by the desire to ensure that a united Germany did not either return to the militarism of the German past or—as a new German economic giant of 80 million people—upset the European economic and political balance, traditionally based on the Anglo–French–German triangle. The Strasbourg summit endorsed German reunification, provided it was 'peaceful, democratic and honoured existing treaties', and at the same time sought to bind Germany further into the EC by setting a date for the intergovernmental conference to discuss treaty revision and economic and monetary union: the Rome summit of December 1990. The summit also approved the creation of a new European Bank for Reconstruction and Development (EBRD) to assist East European economic recovery. This was founded amid much ceremony in London in April 1991. It is headed by Jacques Attali of France.

In 1992 the new democracies of Eastern Europe are still struggling to establish both mature political systems and stable banking and industrial systems. Poland, Hungary and Czechoslovakia have successfully conducted elections and begun to privatize industries and encourage Western investment. But other East European nations such as Romania are still undergoing periodic upheavals, and have less securely founded pluralism. Indeed, the tradition of authoritarian rule, which pre-dates the Communist era, remains strong in Eastern Europe, especially in the Balkans. The descent of Yugoslavia into civil war has been of particular concern to the EC, leading to direct EC involvement (see Chapter 17). Forty per cent of Yugoslavia's exports go to the EC, which, apart from the disintegration of the federation, is worried by Yugoslavia's hyper-inflation and $17 billion foreign debt.

An obvious way for the EC to reinforce East European democracy lies in economic and financial investment. The EBRD draws capital of £7 billion from 41 countries, and numbers EC institutions among its shareholders. It offers a combination of investment in new infrastructure and private investment in East European economies. British companies have been in the forefront of investment in Eastern Europe, although Germany dominates the East European market, from banking and insurance to cars and supermarkets. Douglas Hurd told the Institute of Directors in February 1990 that investment in Eastern Europe was a question of 'getting in on the ground floor, at the start of something which is going to lead to an immense expansion of markets for goods and services'. On the other hand, much of the infrastructure, manufacturing and distribution systems in Eastern Europe remains backward, and it will be some time before work practices, professional attitudes and consumer expectations match those of the West. Foreign investors remain wary because of bureaucratic and time-consuming ways of doing business: direct investment in Eastern Europe only amounted to $1 billion in 1991, with lending from state and private banks amounting to $13 billion—a lower figure than expected. General Electric, which bought Tungsram, the Hungarian light-bulb manufacturer in 1989, has had to prune both management and workforce to streamline the company. Like many East European firms, Tungsram operated as a subsidized social complex, with schools, sports facilities, kindergartens and holiday homes connected to the enterprise (*Economist Survey of Business in Eastern Europe*, September 1991).

The demand of East European countries such as Poland for access to West European markets, meanwhile, has exposed protectionist tendencies among the Twelve and has led to the charge that the EC, while wishing to encourage democracy in the East, is less willing to pay the economic price involved. This debate came to a head in September 1991, when the Commission proposed a reduction in import levies on agricultural products from Hungary, Poland and Czechoslovakia of 60% over three years. Coal quotas would be phased out over three years and textile quotas over five—proposals which aroused fears that Western Europe would be flooded with cheap East European fuel and clothing, in the process undermining Portuguese textile workers, French farmers, German miners and British fruit growers.

At a meeting in Paris in September 1991 John Major sought to per-suade a reluctant President Mitterrand that Poland should be allowed to sell its beef within the EC. 'There is no point in giving countries aid and then denying them trade access,' Major said. East and West should be brought together in a common home numbering 400 million citizens: 'We must be prepared to widen our horizons and widen our membership'. France eventually agreed to Polish beef imports, provided French farmers were compensated. But the Polish beef argument was symptomatic of the gap between the ECs 'wideners' such as Major, who want to see the EC include Eastern Europe in some way, and the 'deepeners' such as Mitterrand, who believe that the EC in its present form must achieve full integration before expansion can be considered. As *The Times* observed in September 1991, while the EC had multiplied its moral, financial and political commitments to Eastern Europe, 'from the Baltics to Albania', after the abortive Moscow coup, and had provided substantial aid to help Eastern Europe make the difficult transition to the free market, at the same time it was maintaining protectionist barriers against East European exports. 'Europeans should remember their history . . . In the 1930s pro-tectionism deepened the economic depression, which fed nationalist extremism and plunged the world into war.'

Towards a 'greater Europe'?

The EC dilemma over 'widening' and 'deepening' in relation to Eastern Europe also affects the aspirations of the many other European nations now lining up to submit membership applications. Sweden, which in 1990 was still declaring its neutrality to be incompatible with EC inte-gration, a year later asked for membership, with pressure from Swedish industry sweeping most other considerations aside. Stockholm's pro-EC tilt was further confirmed when the Social Democrats lost to the Centre-Right in the September 1991 elections. The Commission gives its opinion on the Swedish application in the spring of 1992, and on Malta and Cyprus in the winter of the same year. (Turkey has already been told that its application is, for the time being, inappropriate.)

The Commission's view, however, remains that no applications can be seriously entertained until the current process of treaty revision and political and monetary integration is completed—the mid-1990s at the earliest. In July 1991 the Commission's opinion on Austria's application was that, although Austrian entry would involve few economic problems, Austrian neutrality remained an obstacle (in view of plans for a common defence policy) and that Austria could not be allowed in until the treaty revisions begun at Rome in December 1990 and continued at Maastricht in December 1991 had come to fruition.

With the EC thus still an exclusive club, some of the countries outside the magic circle (and some within) have begun to form regional associ-ations. The Alpen–Adria association groups together with Croatia,

Slovenia, five of the Austrian Lander (states), three of Hungary's western regions, four of Italy's northern regions, and one German Land (Bavaria), with common problems relating to tourism, the environment, sport and energy on the agenda. The Pentagonale group brings together Italy, Austria, Czechoslovakia, Hungary and Yugoslavia, with Poland making the group a Hexagonale. A Black Sea Economic Co-operation agreement, still under discussion, would group Turkey, Bulgaria, Romania and the Soviet Union. Austria has also proposed a Danube association from Bavaria to Moldavia to promote trade and tourism along the Danube River.

The fear, however, is that without the powerful influence of the EC, with its democratic procedures and economic stability, East and Central Europe could fragment, with ethnic rivalries and feuds resurfacing after years of Communism, during which they were suppressed. Indeed, to some extent, this is already happening. There is also the danger that the darker side of nationalism will rear its head. On a visit to Poland at the time of the breaching of the Berlin Wall in 1989 Chancellor Kohl declared that the Germany of today was not the old one of dark excesses, but a Germany of democratic and Christian values, of which the EC integration process was a guarantee. 'We want European union, the United States of Europe,' Kohl declared firmly, 'The EC was, is, and will stay open for other democratic countries in Europe—Warsaw, Moscow, Prague, Budapest and Vienna are as much part of Europe as Brussels, London, Paris, Rome and, of course, Berlin.' The EC must 'approach with imagination and flexibility those Central and East European states which are embarking on deep reforms of their politics, economy and society'.

Yet Kohl's reference to 'dark excesses' strikes a chord, even causes a shiver in those parts of Europe whose present borders are the result of cruel and barbaric rule by Nazi and Stalinist totalitarianism. The democratization of Eastern Europe has raised not only the question of borders but also the even deeper question of whether the process of integration in Western Europe, founded on common democratic values, can be extended to the rest of Europe, perhaps even to Moscow, where such values have often had only shallow roots.

As Donald Cameron Watt, Professor of International History at the LSE, put it, freer travel across East–West borders opens up a vision of Europe as 'a total free-trade area', with 'its peoples living together in comparative amity, free from fear of war or violence, its security forces reduced to the minimum to combat civil war and international crime, the frontiers open, and the public, not excluding salesmen and investors, travelling freely'. Yet Europe was still obsessed with memories of '1870, 1914 and 1939'. As the Soviet empire crumbled, old national frictions were emerging: the Hungarian minority in Romania, the German minority in Silesia, the Albanians in Yugoslavia. Transnational management and planning were needed to tackle the legacy of Stalinist governments which had polluted and impoverished everything they touched. As Watt says:

Within French and Polish hearts, at levels much deeper than
reason, talk of German reunification stirs images of the Gestapo . . .
of the midnight knock on the door and the sealed train to the death
camp. Pessimism sees ahead of us a Central Europe no longer
dominated by the long shadows of 45,000 Soviet tanks or 1,400
Lance missiles, but still divided, disappointed and embittered
with ancestral memories and hatreds.

Lord Callaghan, the former Labour Prime Minister, sounded a similar
warning in the House of Lords: the Cold War, and Moscow's iron grip
on Eastern Europe, had 'kept many of Europe's ancient antagonisms and
feuds in the deep freeze'. The loosening of that grip could mean 'the
Balkanization of Eastern Europe, for some of those countries do not have
long experience of the conventions and constraints that a democratic
system imposes'.

Behind the challenge for the EC in rethinking the single market, in
other words, is the question of whether the process of integration started
by Monnet and Schuman, and taken up by Delors, will prove equal to
the weight of European history, a history in which rivalry and bloodshed
have figured more often than co-operation, with a consequent cost in
human pain and division.

If a 'greater Europe' is achieved, on the other hand, it would have a
total GDP twice that of the United States by the early part of the next
century, according to some forecasts. Delors told the German magazine
Der Spiegel in October 1991 that economic and monetary union should
lay the foundations of a European superpower of the future. Douglas
Hurd, in June 1991, observed that the EC was trying to manage the
'enormous and welcome changes' which had broken the old mould
before the new mould had had time to set. But he added: 'I do not see
that the Europe of Twelve can shut the door of membership for any
length of time against fully qualified European democracies which are
anxious to join, whether they are in EFTA or in Central Europe'.

The key difference between the East European frictions of today and
those of the past is that the EC now offers a model of prosperity and
democracy at a time when the climate of world opinion is forcing authoritarian systems to give way to those based on human rights and the
rule of law. The vision beckons of a Greater Europe embracing Poland,
Hungary, Czechoslovakia, the Baltic states, and perhaps other parts of
the former Soviet Union. As *The Independent* noted in June 1991, 'One of
the paradoxes of today's turbulent new Europe is that the various small
entities and nationalities struggling out from under the embrace of centralized power would like nothing better than to join the EC'. This, the
paper said, suggested that people who had actually lived under centralized power, and hated it, did not share the Thatcherite view of the
EC as a centralized superstate. On the other hand, they will have to wait

outside the 'inner circle' of the EC until the 1992 process, and plans for economic and monetary union associated with it, have made clear what kind of European federation is likely to emerge for them to join in the 1990s.

EC—EFTA: the wider single market

In October 1991 the seven EFTA nations—Austria, Finland, Iceland, Liechtenstein, Norway, Sweden and Switzerland—finally agreed the terms of a pact with the 12 EC members, giving the EFTA countries access to the single market and creating the world's richest free-trade zone, a 'European Economic Area' (EEA) from the Arctic to the Aegean, to take effect at the same time as the EC single market on 31 December 1992. The EC and EFTA between them account for nearly 45% of world trade. Delors observed that the pact would provide a 'trial run' for EFTA countries such as Austria and Sweden which wanted full EC membership. Frans Andriessen, the Commissioner for External Affairs, also noted that the former communist countries of Eastern Europe might use the new trade zone as a stepping stone to EC membership.

Under the EEA accord, EFTA countries are obliged to incorporate EC single market legislation into their national statutes, including company law, consumer protection, social policy and environmental protection measures, to ensure harmonization. The complex documents laying down conditions for the EEA amount to 40 protocols and 20 annexes. The final obstacle to the pact was removed when Austria agreed that Greece could have an extra 2,000 permits for lorries crossing the Alps, provided it also agreed to transport more of its goods by rail rather than road, so as not to clog up the trans-Alpine routes. The EC countries have guaranteed access to Nordic fishing grounds, while EFTA will provide £1.7-billion worth of soft loans and grants to the poorer southern EC countries such as Portugal.

There are limits to the EEA. For example, only goods produced within the EEA can circulate freely, not goods imported from outside. Equally, common EC policies such as the CAP will not apply to the EFTA countries. However, the EFTA countries, including not only Austria and Sweden but Finland and Norway as well, have made it clear they will not in the long run be content with membership of a 'halfway house' to EC membership but would like to enjoy the benefits of full membership. The implications of such ambitions for future common policies in sensitive areas like defence and foreign policy are profound. Shortly after the EEA deal was announced Britain and Germany revealed they were planning joint diplomatic missions to independent Soviet republics as a first step toward pooling their foreign services in some parts of the world. Such initiatives in common foreign policy would become far more complex in an EC of 24 or more. As for Eastern Europe, EC officials want to see far greater evidence of moves toward economic and political stability before membership is countenanced, and NATO (at the Rome summit of November 1991) similarly offered 'consultative' or 'liaison' status to the East Europeans through a new 'Co-operation Council'. The likely end result, some years in the future, is an enlarged European structure, from economics to defence, in which an inner core of nations—the Twelve—continue to control the key decision-making institutions.

Checklist of changes

- New co-operation agreements with Central European countries to allow Poland, Hungary and Czechoslovakia greater access to EC markets.
- Formation of European Economic Area (EEA) by EC and EFTA creates world's largest single market.

CONCLUSION
Britain and the Reshaping of Europe

The Europe of today is the result of three years of political upheaval which amount to the biggest change in the region since the Second World War and the division of Europe that followed it. The changed Europe of 1992–93 has new underpinnings: a united Germany, achieved despite doubts not only in the former Soviet Union but also in France and Britain; the emergence of East European democracies from the ashes of Communism and the break-up of the Soviet Union; closer ties between EFTA and the EC; and—altered by these cataclysms, but not knocked off course by them—the development of a single market in Europe, giving rise to ambitious plans for economic, monetary and political union.

This Europe is the backdrop for a tug of war between the federalist view of EC integration as originally conceived for an EC of Twelve, and the desire of nation states to retain their individuality and traditions while pooling resources economically to gain the benefits of a single market. In the end, the tensions this engenders seem likely to lead to compromise: an enlarged Community in which the vision of a centralized European superstate—never seriously advanced in any case except by a few Euro-fanatics—fades into the background, while at the same time harmonization and the creation of cross-border political and monetary institutions make the wider Europe far more than a mere free-trade zone. Common policies on matters from defence to immigration and working practices to transport will be limited by practicalities and national differences. But they will exist, and with them the concept of a United States of Europe.

The post-Maastricht debate on Europe can be presented too much in terms of Britain versus the Rest. Germany has its doubts about the pace and nature of economic and monetary union, and the link between EMU and political union. France, for its part, is beginning to realize the implications of federalism, implications to which Britain has been alert for some time. After years in which France presented itself as more 'pro-European' than any other EC nation, the French woke up in the course of 1991 to the fact that they, too, had objections to 'interference from Brussels'. It took the decision by a British Commissioner—Sir Leon Brittan—to veto the purchase by Aerospatiale of the Canadian firm de Havilland on monopoly grounds to bring French concerns into focus. Angry French farmers' demonstrations against attempts to reform the CAP (and the import of British lamb) had a similar effect. As John Laughland pointed out in *The Spectator* (19 October 1991), there has never been a detailed debate on 1992 in France on the scale of the British debate.

British federalists who warn us that we might miss the [1992] train say that if France can accept federalism, so can we: but the truth is that the French media, parliament and public opinion have hardly given the matter a thought.

All EC nations have their views on the single market, all have hopes and fears. France, Spain and other countries are as concerned as Britain about the need to control drugs, terrorism and crime after 1992—and whether such controls should be for the EC or co-operation between governments. Germany is worried about the impact on previously highly protected sectors such as transport and insurance, and is keener than France on enlarging the Community to incorporate Eastern European countries. Most EC countries, moreover, have a far worse record than Britain when it comes to observance of EC law and the Treaty of Rome.

Even the stereotype of the insular Briton unable to speak European languages and secretly wanting to draw up the Channel drawbridge has its Continental counterpart. Anyone who has observed German tourists in Spain or Italy will note that the German capacity for speaking foreign languages is not much greater than our own. On many Continental trains, passport and customs checks are minimal already. Yet anyone taking a train from France to Italy, or from Italy to France, along the Riviera Coast, having to change at the border and pass through customs only to find that trains on either side of the border do not connect, will reflect that the French and Italians also have a long way to go before they regard one another as part of the same internal market. There is the danger that, contrary to the idealism of its founders, the EC will degenerate into xenophobia as nationalist feelings come to the fore in a belated backlash against 1992. Attacks on immigrants in France and Germany have been directed not only against Arabs and North Africans but also, in some cases, against southern Europeans. Anti-Semitism and xenophobia have resurfaced in France, Poland and Austria.

Nationalism and European identity
Nonetheless it is in Britain that awareness of the broader implications of the single market have been most acutely felt. When in October 1991 Carlo Ripa di Meana, the Italian EC environment commissioner, asked Britain in a personal letter to Major, to halt important road and rail projects so that the environmental effects could be studied, the reaction in Britain was vociferous. 'Fury over the Euro-Meddlers' ran the headline in *The Evening Standard*, reporting that backbench MPs thought Brussels had gone 'power mad' and should be 'curbed'. John Major described the Commissioner's action as 'astonishing', adding 'this is absolutely how the European Commission ought not to behave, and I have told them so'. Senior lawyers however, including Sir Gordon Slynn, the British judge at the European Court of Justice, pointed out that Ripa di Meana

was fully within his rights in asking for the environmental impact to be assessed. 'It is as plain as a pikestaff', Sir Gordon told the Law Society annual conference in Brussels. 'You cannot say, "No surrender of sovereignty". It has gone, in a limited way. Pooling of sovereignty is a better expression'.

In her speech on Europe at Bruges, Mrs Thatcher poured scorn on the idea of an 'identikit European personality . . . To try to suppress nationhood would be highly damaging . . . Europe will be stronger precisely because it has France as France, Spain as Spain, Britain as Britain, each with its own customs, traditions and identity'. Yet Jacques Delors, at the opposite end of the Euro-spectrum, also acknowledges that national traditions will persist long after 1992. Perhaps as a Frenchman, he could hardly do otherwise: 'Naturally there is the question of national identity,' he told *Le Monde*. 'But in my concept of Europe the French will remain French, France will still be France. Quite simply, the French will also belong to a second country called Europe.

This is in line with Lord Cockfield's theory that the creation of a United Europe is analogous to the creation of the United Kingdom. Scots, Welsh and English owe fundamental loyalty to the United Kingdom, pay taxes to its government and are ready, if necessary, to don military uniform to defend it. Yet they do not cease at the same time to owe often intense regional loyalty to Scotland, Wales or England. There is no reason, in this view, why they should not in future owe a triple loyalty: to region, country and Europe as a whole. The trend in Eastern Europe and the ex-Soviet Union is towards local nationalism; equally, the Scottish National party advocates an independent Scotland within a barrier-free EC. The desire for national independence often goes hand in hand with a desire for membership of the wider Europe. The two are not necessarily incompatible.

It is in any case questionable to what extent the British are 'anti European'. Opinion polls conducted by Euro-Barometer, the EC's own polling organization, consistently show a majority of British respondents in favour of some form of European unification. A MORI poll published in *The Mail on Sunday* shortly after the Bruges speech produced similar results, with a majority of those questioned favouring unity up to and including a single currency, a result which suggests that anti-EC rhetoric is not necessarily a vote winner. As Christopher Huhne observes in his monograph on *The Forces Shaping British Attitudes Towards the EC* (Centre for European Policy Studies, Brussels, CEPS Paper No. 23, 1985), Britain is an island,

but an island with a long tradition of trade and exchange with the continental mainland . . . the degree of foreign travel, the increasing willingness to learn other European languages and the opinion poll evidence all suggest that the British people's attitudes would be unfairly characterized as isolationist.

Opinion polls in the run-up to Maastricht tended to reinforce this. For that matter, Mrs Thatcher as Prime Minister was not an isolationist. At Bruges she said:

> We British are as much heirs to the legacy of European culture as any other nation. Our links to the rest of Europe, the continent of Europe, have been the dominant factor in our history . . . And let me be quite clear: Britain does not dream of some cosy, isolated existence on the fringes of Europe. Our destiny is in Europe, as part of the Community.

Britain is inextricably enmeshed in the economic and political machinery of the EC, and plays a major role in it.

The appalling behaviour of British football hooligans on the Continent, and the drunken rampages of young British 'holidaymakers' in Spain, reflect a contemptuous and ignorant attitude towards fellow Europeans as well as personal inadequacy and social malaise at home. On the other hand, the modern generation of professional Britons is far less influenced by stereotypes of 'Continentals' than previous generations, and more likely to view Europe in terms of business and money-market opportunities. It's an approach that is relatively hard headed and unsentimental, and unimpressed by narrowly 'nationalist' values. To a degree, Mrs Thatcher's rhetoric masked the fact that she took a full and exhaustive part in EC decision making, often improving the end result by leavening wilder EC proposals with common sense and experience. John Major and Douglas Hurd played a similar role over Maastricht. As Hurd put it in a speech to the Atlantic Commission in The Hague, just before Maastricht, 'thoroughness and thoughtfulness should not be mistaken for reluctance and rejection'. Just as the internal market programme and the Single European Act both bear British hallmarks, not least in the emphasis they place on de-regulation, so, too, the treaties on monetary and political union are shaped by the British debate. This is hardly surprising. As Tom Hutchinson, a director of ICI and chairman of the CBE Europe Committee, points out, over 50% of British trade is with fellow Community states.

Britain, the EC and national sovereignty

Nonetheless, Britain is widely perceived as the country most resistant to European integration. The history of Britain's relationship with the EC —late application, rejection, accession, re-negotiation, budget rebate squabbles, objections to the single currency and to extra powers for the European Parliament—has produced a Europhobia in which Britain's natural reaction to EC proposals tends to be 'no' rather than 'yes but'. It's a position that derives from a number of geographical and political facts: that as an island race, the British do not feel culturally European; that by virtue of empire and historic links Britain has looked in the past as much, if not indeed more, to the US and to the Commonwealth as to its immediate European neighbours; that its role as the dominant world power of the nineteenth century has led Britain even today to play a global rather than purely European role in matters of defence; similarly, that sterling is a world currency as well as a European currency. In short, that in significant ways, Britain is *in* Europe but not *of* it.

There is, in consequence, a trend in British opinion which fears that, instead of 'willing and active co-operation between independent sovereign states', something more like a 'European super-state' will emerge. After resigning as Prime Minister Mrs Thatcher continued to warn against a federal superstate which would undermine NATO, exclude Eastern Europe and jeopardize the GATT negotiations. 'It is time to recognize even in Brussels that the age of empire is past', Mrs Thatcher declared in Chicago in June 1991. During the run-up to Maastricht Douglas Hurd used similar language, objecting to the use of the phrase 'a union with a federal goal' in the draft treaty. 'We do not intend to be committed to the implications which the phrase "federal goal" carries in the English language,' Hurd said. 'Federal has come to mean something tight and integrated in English.'

Though the Commission promotes symbols of European nationhood —the EC flag, the European anthem (Beethoven's 'Ode to Joy')—in reality the process of forming a European identity has barely begun. To suggest, as the Commission did in newspaper advertisements, that all Europeans should share in the glory of medals won by the Twelve at Olympic games, is counterproductive, since for many national feeling is expressed above all through sport—and will continue to be long after 1992.

Yet the single market and the Channel Tunnel will between them bring immense psychological changes in their wake, as the British adjust to having an umbilical cord tying them to the Continent. There is already a breed of businessmen who commute across the Channel, and British property developers—and house buyers—are moving into the Pas de Calais and the Boulogne area. This kind of cross-Channel fertilization will be commonplace.

Does this make inevitable something approaching a United States of Europe? Mrs Thatcher as Prime Minister thought not, and many still share her views. Others, by contrast, believe union of some kind is both inevitable and desirable. The case has been most forcefully put by Germany's Chancellor Kohl, who, as a Christian Democrat, is ideologi-aligned with the Conservative Party but nonetheless reflects German enthusiasm for European integration. In a speech in Brussels in October

1988, Kohl spelled it out graphically. Kohl said fiscal harmonization was indispensable in 1992. As for the fight against crime and terrorism, he called for a European police force along US lines, adding, 'I know this idea has far-reaching consequences, but the nature and size of the challenge we face leaves us no choice'. On defence, Kohl suggested the eventual creation of a European Army. Finally, the loss of sovereignty involved in 1992 was counter-balanced by a gain in pooled sovereignty. When President Mitterrand was presented, with Kohl, with the Charlemagne Prize at Aachen in November 1988, he defined the EC goal as 'one currency, one culture, one social area, one environment'.

'Socialist central control' and the European super-state

The process outlined by Kohl and Mitterrand and taken further in the inter-governmental conferences on monetary and political union in 1991 – 92 does not quite add up to a United States of Europe—but it is a step along the road. Part of the problem is that neither the phrase 'an ever-closer union' laid down in the Treaty of Rome preamble nor the goal of 'European Union' enshrined in the Stuttgart summit declaration of 1983 have ever been properly defined. This gives room for conflicting interpretations, including the Thatcherite 'nightmare' of a 'socialist' and 'collectivist' European superstate run from Brussels. At the Conservative Party Conference in Brighton in October 1988 the Prime Minister gave the formula a new twist: 'We haven't worked all these years to free Britain from the paralysis of socialism only to see it creep in through the back-door of central control and bureaucracy from Brussels'.

The choice, Thatcher said, was between two Europes: 'One based on the widest-possible freedom for enterprise, and one governed by socialist methods of centralized control and regulation'. The choice is not a real one, however. The 'social dimension' involves EC law in employer–employee relations, but few Continental leaders, whether of the left or right, would regard this as 'collectivist'. Most Continental systems rest on a political culture of consensus. For example, Kohl presides over a Centre–Right coalition which accepts worker participation in industry—Mitbestimmung—as much as the opposition Social Democrats do. The effect of the single market, German industrialists believe, will be to reduce over-protection of employees rather than the reverse. All EC leaders are committed to free enterprise capitalism, as is Delors, even though he is a French socialist by origin. Few EC countries have reacted with the same horror as Britain to EC social policies such as the maximum working week or the increase in maternity benefits for pregnant working women agreed in November 1991. Speakers at the CBI annual conference in November 1991 welcomed the single market but expressed concern about the additional business costs of the social charter, for example in overtime payments.

To some extent, generalized attacks on 'rule from Brussels' articulate a British aversion to the involvement of 'foreigners' in domestic British affairs. But to call European federalism 'socialist' is to confuse the issue. What such attacks really express perhaps is disagreement with the kind of federalism espoused by Christian Democrats such as Kohl and Wilfried Martens, the Belgian Prime Minister. Shortly after Bruges, Martens said elimination of trade barriers would make closer political unity inevitable, leading to 'some form of loosely constructed federal European government' responsible for economic affairs as well as for defence and foreign relations. Martens agreed with 'apprehension about an unbridled European bureaucracy' and 'centrally imposed over-regulation', but came to the opposite conclusion to that drawn by the Euro-sceptics. The answer lay in an all-European executive body 'answerable to a genuinely European and sovereign legislature'. National states would retain some powers to control crime and immigration, and, 'given Europe's history, steeped in diversity, a highly decentralized form of government is undoubtedly preferable'. But European government there would be.

The Commission, stung by the charge that the EC is controlled by 'appointed bureaucrats', has also joined the debate. To focus on the Commission, officials point out, is to ignore the Council of Ministers and the Parliament, which take decisions for the Twelve as a whole. The Commission's real aim is to enhance competition and enterprise, limit central regulation 'to the minimum level required for coherence', and give the regions a greater say in their own economic development. But many believe the Commission is too powerful, 'inserting itself into the nooks and crannies of everyday life' as Douglas Hurd put it during a clash with Delors at a pre-Maastricht meeting of EC foreign ministers.

Federalism: the end of the nation state?

Writing in *The Times* in October 1988, Peter Sutherland, the former Commissioner for Competition, called for 'a reasoned debate, avoiding emotional polemics' on how Europeans could deal with the loss of sovereignty flowing from 'our common commitment to the 1992 programme'. He continued,

> It is important to remember that with the ratification of the European treaties, concessions of sovereignty to autonomous European institutions have already occurred. An embryonic federal structure is in place, even if its powers are confined to certain areas . . . There is no vast bureaucracy in Brussels which seeks to impose itself on member states. It is inconsistent to criticize the institutions of the Community for being appointed rather than elected democratically and at the same time to ignore the claims of the European Parliament for powers which alone can develop control on a common European basis.

It's a view shared by Delors. Speaking to the Belgian newspaper *Le Soir*, he said, 'It is the Council and not the Commission which takes the real decisions. It is regrettable that attacks on the Brussels bureaucrats have become a scapegoat and a way of avoiding having to give concrete answers to what should be done to implement the Single European Act'.

But the problem of the 'democratic deficit' is not so easily solved. If transfer of sovereignty is inevitable, is the right answer to devolve further powers from Westminster, the Bundestag and the Assemblée Nationale, for example, to the European Parliament? The same Britons who supported European unification in the MORI post-Bruges opinion poll obviously thought not. 67% opposed giving greater power to Strasbourg, with only 25% in favour. Sheer volume of work, and the integration process, are pushing the European Parliament towards more frequent sessions—perhaps two weeks a month instead of one—and will almost certainly push it towards meeting in Brussels rather than Strasbourg. This is not the same, however, as the evolution of a European Government.

The idea of a European government in any case arouses horror in some quarters. In an article in *The Times* in response to Commissioner Sutherland, William Cash, Conservative MP for Stafford and a member of the Commons Select Committee on European Legislation, claimed European federalism was being introduced by stealth:

> The EC in principle has just about the right framework now. It will develop and must be reformed. The advantages it offers will help us to compete successfully with other continental giants. But political union on the same scale is unnecessary, and could provoke unwelcome hostility.

In November 1991 Nigel Lawson, who as Chancellor of the Exchequer had fought for British entry into the ERM, said in *The Evening Standard* that to go on from ERM membership to a single currency would risk breaching the principle that a government should be democratically elected and able to carry out the wishes of its people. If nations were denied their identity, the 'ugliest manifestations of nationalism' would come to the fore. 'Nothing could be better calculated to encourage the growth of M. Le Pen's Front National in France and its unpleasant counterparts elsewhere in the Community than the creation of full monetary and political union,' Mr Lawson wrote. Douglas Hurd also noted that to attempt common EC control of immigration was to try mistakenly to 'harmonize history' when asylum policy ought to be based on national backgrounds and conditions.

Yet according to Sir Leon Brittan, Britain's senior EC Commissioner:

> We have long since abandoned the idea that our sovereignty is absolute, neither to be shared nor diluted by one jot or tittle. We

joined the Community precisely because we decided we would be stronger as a country if some decisions were taken on a European basis . . . We would not now be contemplating the privatizing of a profitable British Steel Corporation if there had not been a powerful European steel regime able to bring about the necessary and painful changes required in the steel industry throughout Europe.

Some who are unhappy about the transfer of sovereignty fall back on a cautious 'step-by-step' approach. On the other hand, as Sir Nicholas Henderson, former British Ambassador in Bonn, Paris and Washington, and chairman of the Channel Tunnel Group, points out, 'a step-by-step approach is very reasonable, but it is also reasonable to believe that the steps must be leading somewhere'. He adds 'For many of the peoples of Europe the nation state has proved in this century to be not only inadequate to their needs, but disastrous. Without wishing to sacrifice national tradition or nationhood, they aspire to a new and wider identity'.

What is needed, in other words—especially in an era when there is likely to be further pooling of security and defence interests—is a redefinition of the nation state itself. In their study of *Options for British Foreign Policy in the 1990s* (Royal Institute for International Affairs) Christopher Tugendhat and William Wallace confront this head on:

There is now a structural contradiction not only between the logic of international industrial and economic integration and the national framework of popular loyalty, but also between the increasing integration of defence and security policies and the underlying rationale of the nation state. The force of this contradiction has not yet filtered through to the British electorate.

Defining Europe: the global context

One side-effect of Mrs Thatcher's approach was that it helped to bring home to British voters that the underpinning of the nation state—popular loyalty to the state within defined borders, management of common economic resources within the same borders, taxation to raise revenues, the maintenance of nationally defined police and armed forces—needs re-examining as some of these functions begin to take on a pan-European character. Traditionally, a nation defines itself by what its citizens have in common, or—though this is not quite the same thing—by the ways in which it differs from other nations. Ultimately, nation states are given internal coherence by their response to perceived external threats. In the past, such threats, whether commercial or military, have come to Britain from across the Channel, in centuries of commercial and military rivalries with France, Germany and other Continental countries.

To some extent, both the EC and NATO draw their *raison d'etre* from the need to ensure that the countries of Europe remain locked into intimate alliances which make cross-border European conflicts less likely, perhaps impossible. In the absence of an old-style Soviet threat, but with control of nuclear weapons causing new anxiety as the Soviet empire breaks up, the EC and NATO are still needed to provide internal security: hence the establishment at the Rome NATO summit of November 1991 of a 'North Atlantic Co-operation Council' to embrace East and Central Europe, the Soviet Union and the independent Baltic states as well as Western Europe and the US. Conversely, the perceived commercial threat—again to Europe as a whole—comes from the United States and Japan. Europe itself, meanwhile, grows more compact: the Channel Tunnel will reduce train journey time between London and Paris from 5½ hours to 3, between London and Brussels from 5 hours to 2½, and between London and Amsterdam from 10 hours to 5. Planned east–west motorways should also make trade and other contacts more coherent.

Certainly, the rest of the world has come more and more to look on Europe as a unit, and deals with it as such. The United States, Japan, and EFTA have been increasingly alarmed at the prospect of being shut out of 'Fortress Europe', with the EC building up barriers against the outside world while demolishing frontiers inside the Community. World competitors fear that in sectors such as cars and textiles EC quotas, replacing national ones, will be geared to the most protectionist EC states; that non-EC companies with subsidiaries in Europe will have to prove that their products have a 'minimum local content' and therefore count as European; and that the single market integration programme in services such as banking and insurance is premature when the GATT is still discussing an international liberalisation regime.

Yet increasingly, the Commission uses the term 'foreign' in official documents to mean 'non-EC'. The reaction of EFTA countries, many of which border directly on the EC, was first to draw closer to the EC and then, in a headlong rush, to apply for full membership. It remains to be seen how far the creation of a European Economic Area bringing EFTA into the single market will satisfy countries like Austria, Sweden and Norway. Non-EFTA countries know they will have to wait much longer: Turkey's application for membership, made in April 1987, has been put on ice by the EC until the mid-1990s at the earliest. On the other hand the EC made considerable efforts to bring Greece, Spain and Portugal— all of which had recent undemocratic records—into the Community, and it is increasingly difficult to argue that, say, the Scandinavian countries do not qualify. Denmark is already in the club; Sweden, though not a member, is unquestionably a powerful commercial force within the EC. As for Norway, it was only in 1988 that Mrs Gro Harlem Brundtland, the Norwegian Prime Minister, made it clear that Oslo had no desire to re-open the wounds of the 1972 referendum campaign, when Norway narrowly turned down membership. She even rebuked 'impatient voices in EFTA countries calling for a direct, bilateral approach to the issue of membership'. Now Oslo is as eager as Stockholm to join.

The United States remains suspicious that the single market spells protectionism, and views EC enlargement with mixed feelings. On the one hand any reinforcement of European democratic values in the aftermath of the collapse of Communism is welcomed; on the other, the Bush administration does not want to compete with a European leviathan. It already regards 'the Europeans' as more difficult to negotiate with in the GATT talks than the Japanese. As for defence, as Bush put it at Rome in November 1991, 'If you don't need us any longer, say so'. Every European leader including Chancellor Kohl, replied that while a united Europe was impossible without a united European defence, it was also impossible without an American presence.

Maastricht

Making industry and commerce more competitive on a European rather than national basis will also have painful consequences as well as benefits within Europe itself. This—together with belated resentment over the partial loss of political sovereignty—could lead to a popular backlash against integration. According to Sir John Harvey-Jones, former chairman of ICI, 'We are looking at a degree of attrition that we have not experienced at any time. In my judgment, at least half the European companies will disappear'. The EC has twelve major boiler-making companies, the United States only six: the EC has ten competing turbine manufacturers, the US only two. Something will have to give, and the consequences could be traumatic. Hence the Commission's concern over a 'social dimension' to soften the blow. Hence also the argument that the single market inevitably entails monetary union, which, in turn implies close co-ordination of economic and social policy, if not a supranational body to supervise such co-operation.

As Roy Denman, the former EC Director General for External Affairs, observes, it is ironic that as one kind of union is falling apart—the Soviet empire—another is taking shape in Western Europe. But the British horror of federation, Denman suggests, produces amusement across the Channel, 'Switzerland is a federation—but the citizens of Geneva and Unterwalden do not go to bed at night gibbering with terror at the prospect of a superstate in Berne'. Since the 1950 Coal and Steel Community, a European federation has been the long-term aim, in one form or another. As Denman observes,

> When businessmen can trade as easily between Hamburg and
> Lyons as they can between the states of the American union,
> they will not long put up with the expense and inconvenience of
> separate currencies. But a single currency means a single

economic policy, and that cannot be controlled by non-elected bureaucrats in Brussels. This means the start of a federal union, which means a common defence and foreign policy, which will probably happen in the next five to six years . . . Unfortunately the British attitude to the unification of Europe has been that of the Victorian mother who summons her nanny and instructs her to find out what the children are doing and tell them to stop it.

Conversely Sir Alan Walters, writing in *The Times* in October 1991, admitted he had been wrong to maintain that monetary union would prove a virtual impossibility 'because it would inevitably imply a centralization of power in Brussels which would be quite unthinkable to the peoples of Europe and particularly to the British'. The idea of a single currency had won far more support among businessmen and voters than he would have believed possible. He continued to insist, however, that, 'the economic union of Europe does not require a monetary union, and certainly not a single currency'. Furthermore, as economic union would be accompanied by political union, he repeated his warning that, 'the inevitable tensions and frictions between nations and groups in any conglomerate can be contained only if the central authorities practise light government . . . From the best intentions, I fear, a European leviathan will emerge to plague us all'.

Clearly the debate over Britain's role in a unified Europe is far from over. Indeed, as Maastricht showed, it has in some senses only just begun.

From Maastricht to Lisbon and Edinburgh

The Maastricht agreement, John Major said as the summit ended in December 1991 and Portugal prepared to take over the EC Presidency, was 'a good agreement for Europe and for the United Kingdom', one which 'safeguards and advances our national interests'. It was 'game, set and match for Britain'.

Was it? Major's skill in negotiation, and his non-strident tone, allowed an unusual deal to be struck in the early hours of the third and final day of the summit, with Britain opting out not only of plans for a single currency—which had been expected—but also out of the social chapter giving the EC competence in labour-management relations and working conditions. Major's style won him applause in his own party, and quelled the threat of a rebellion by arch-Conservative anti-federalist campaigners such as Norman Tebbit when the Commons voted on Maastricht shortly afterwards. On the other hand, the Maastricht treaties undoubtedly moved the EC as a whole—Britain included—farther down the road to a European Union. Similarly, while attention was focused on the social charter and the single currency, Britain gave significant ground in other areas such as common defence and the powers of the European Parliament. Maastricht also signalled a future European citizenship, and marked a shift toward a role for the EC in education and health.

Major's tennis metaphor, Ian Davidson wrote in *The Financial Times*, suggested he,

> did not seem to understand the difference between winning and losing . . . The Maastricht agreement must be considered, by any rational measure, one of the most important events in post-war European history. This is a treaty which will lead to a single currency in Europe in just over seven years, as well as to the gradual development of a common foreign and defence policy. If this programme is adhered to, the European Community will be well on the way to becoming a sort of federation.

What Maastricht highlighted, as Piet Dankert, a Dutch minister, pointed out, was the 'cultural difference' between Britain and most of its EC partners, above all Germany, for whom extension of EC powers is an article of faith. In the end it was the alliance built between Major and Kohl which made compromise possible. Yet as Germany increasingly dominates European policy, from Yugoslavia to interest rates, Britain seems likely to be pulled along in its wake, perhaps coming to accept a degree of European Union even in areas where Major stood his ground in December 1991.

The Maastricht deal on social policy, with the eleven forming their own 'European Social Community' to legislate on the labour market, was forged by Chancellor Kohl and Ruud Lubbers, the Dutch Prime Minister and summit host, who between them persuaded President Mitterrand that the best course was to let Britain opt out altogether. The CBI and leading British employers expressed relief. Michael Howard, the Employment Secretary, pointed out that foreign investors would regard Britain with favour because of lower labour costs and less rigid workplace rules. On the other hand, if the eleven go ahead with plans for works councils or harmonized legislation on part-time workers, trades union pressure on employers in the UK to match such measures will increase. British employers with Continental subsidiaries will in any case have to observe the new rules. Labour condemned the government for 'consigning Britain to the slow lane of a two-speed Europe', and vowed to impose tough social legislation on coming to power. Portugal continued to press during 1992 for EC legislation on maximum working hours, using majority voting rules under health and safety provisions, with Britain countering that such matters properly required a unanimous vote. The Maastricht compromise looks set to become a legal battleground, with critics arguing that Britain is infringing single market competition rules by maintaining labour laws which give it an unfair advantage over the other eleven.

On the single currency, too, the pressure will be on Britain to fall into line. It remains unclear how or indeed whether most EC states will meet the criteria laid down for economic convergence. Equally unclear at present is how the European Monetary Institute (EMI), the precursor of the European Bank, is to manage member states' foreign exchange reserves. But at Maastricht France and Italy between them secured German consent to an 'irreversible' move toward a European Bank and single currency, spelling the end of the all powerful Deutschmark, despite constant German worries—based on the relationship in German history between currency weakness and political instability—about currency stability. 'The end of the D-Mark' was the banner headline in the German mass circulation daily *Bild*.

It is true that Kohl failed to ensure the kind of political union treaty he had wanted as a *quid pro quo* for concessions on monetary union. But he won greater powers for the European Parliament, through the 'Negative Assent Procedure' giving Strasbourg the right to negotiate directly with the Council of Ministers the changes it wants to see made in EC laws—and the right to veto bills which fail to make such changes. Because of British sensitivities over the concession of sovereignty involved, this power is referred to in the treaty merely as 'the procedure laid down in article 189b'. But in plain terms it amounts to co-decision making for Strasbourg in key areas: the internal market, consumer protection, the free movement of labour, company establishment, treatment of foreigners, vocational training, public health, infrastructure projects, structural funds, international agreements, the rights of European citizens, and the harmonization of electoral systems for European elections (which could mean the introduction of PR into the UK).

On defence, too, Britain gave ground. The role of NATO is maintained, but the EC's common foreign and security policy is to 'include all questions related to the security of the European Union, including the eventual framing of a common defence policy, which might in time lead to common defence'. Tentative as the wording is, it is not altogether what Britain wanted. Nor did Britain particularly want the treaty to define the Western European Union as 'an integral part of the development of the European Union', which can request the WEU 'to elaborate and implement decisions and actions of the Union which have defence implications'. The foreign policy procedure requires unanimity on matters of principle, with majority voting only on the technicalities of implementing policy. Yet with the ink on the Maastricht treaties barely dry, at the end of December 1991, Germany succeeded in steamrolling the EC into recognition of Croatia and Slovenia by the middle of January 1992, this very much against the better judgement of Douglas Hurd, who observed wearily: 'It was a compromise, it always is.'

As the 'European Union' was being outlined at Maastricht, three of the former Soviet republics, led by Boris Yeltsin's Russia, were forming the new Commonwealth of Independent States at Minsk. By the end of

December, the Commonwealth had taken shape with the signing of a new treaty at Alma Ata and the resignation of Gorbachov and the formal dissolution of the Soviet Union. A new form of federation is being created in the East; but it looks for inspiration to the West. Poland, Hungary and Czechoslovakia all want EC membership following their new association agreements, signed just after Maastricht. While at the new NATO Co-operation Council at the end of 1991, Yeltsin astonished NATO officials by formally applying for Russian membership of the western alliance. History has been stood on its head.

As the European Union sketched at Maastricht and developed at Lisbon under Portugal's presidency in June 1992 takes shape, can Britain —itself chairing the EC in the second half of 1992—stand aside? Nicholas Ridley, writing disapprovingly of Maastricht in *The Times* (12 December 1991), described the thrust of EC policy as federal: 'The Community will enter upon stages two and three of the Delors plan for an economic and monetary union with a single currency and an independent central bank. This, inevitably, means the transfer of control of economic policies to the centre, and the end of the sovereignty of national parliaments over interest rates, exchange rates and budget deficits. It reduces them to the status of rate-capped county councils'. Ridley's fear is of a 'corporatist, regulated EC' whose protectionism makes a mockery of GATT, as opposed to 'a Europe open to all European states to join, with a free and open market both internally and externally, voluntarily co-operating on a range of subjects from immigration to foreign policy'. There is also an overriding fear—shared by many in the US—of Germany as the new European superpower.

Such views are rejected by Labour, the party which once wanted Britain out of the EC altogether. Rebutting Ridley's arguments, Gerald Kaufman, the shadow foreign secretary, declared in *The Times* (13 December 1991) that a Labour government would want to join the other eleven in common social policies, because

> in a single market with a single currency, working people in every kind of occupation require protection from the unbridled activities of commerce and industry . . . Community best practices will apply for all workers in countries which subscribe to the social charter, which simply provides an updated and Europe-wide extension of the kind of enlightened social protection pioneered by the Tory party's revered icon, Disraeli.

As for the ECU, Kaufman wrote, even investors wishing to profit from low labour costs would 'think twice before investing in a country outside the single currency area'.

Maastricht undoubtedly moved the agenda forward. Not so long ago the debate was over whether the pound should join the ERM; now, although arguments continue over interest rates and devaluation, the debate is over whether the pound should give way to a single European currency by 1999 at the latest. As *The Times* observed in an editorial after Maastricht, 'Where Britain's interests will lie by then it is impossible to say, which was precisely Mr Major's point.' Maastricht had been a 'job well done', but there were collective challenges beyond Maastricht such as the completion of the single market, the Uruguay round of GATT, and the problem of Eastern Europe. It was 'time for Europe to get down to real business'. Or, as *The Wall Street Journal Europe* put it, Maastricht did not create a United States of Europe, but it did amount to 'an economic and political transformation which will make it possible for the EC to embrace new members without crippling its decision-making structures . . . Maastricht has given the EC a road map for the next decade'.

The Portuguese Presidency in the first half of 1992 had budgetary reform and justice for the southern countries as well as the momentum of the single market at the top of its agenda. It falls to Britain, at the Edinburgh EC summit in December 1992, actually to usher in the single market. Germany and France have no monopoly on European credentials: it was Germany which broke ranks over Yugoslavia, and which used new ecological packaging laws to turn back goods, while France, as *The Times* observed at the beginning of 1992 'has given short shrift to the principle of collective industrial policy in its creation of a new nationalised electronics cartel'. To succeed, the single market needs the full co-operation of all Twelve—with Britain playing the role of 'good but sceptical European'.

Appendix 1   EUROPE'S TOP 20 COMPANIES

Company	Country	Turnover (£ million)	Profits (£ million)
Royal Dutch/Shell Group of Companies	UK/Netherlands	59,416	8,566
British Petroleum	UK	41,711	3,439
Daimler Benz	Germany	29,593	1,675
IRI	Italy	28,343	539
Fiat	Italy	25,489	2,607
Volkswagen	Germany	23,557	1,327
Unilever	UK	22,258	2,255
Siemens	Germany	21,535	1,470
Veba	Germany	18,895	1,046
Nestlé	Switzerland	18,773	1,974
Renault	France	18,696	1,042
ENI	Italy	18,211	2,390
Philips	Netherlands	17,107	555
Peugeot	France	16,391	1,782
BASF	Germany	16,137	1,141
Elf Aquitaine	France	16,053	1,080
Electricité de France	France	15,766	2,329
Hoechst	Germany	15,527	1,377
RWE	Germany	15,220	843
B.A.T. Industries	UK	15,027	1,347

Source: *The Times 1000*.

Appendix 2   EUROPE'S TOP 20 BANKS

Bank	Country	Assets (£ billion)
Crédit Agricole	France	150.5
Banque Nationale de Paris	France	143.6
Deutsche Bank	Germany	138.5
Barclays	UK	134.9
Crédit Lyonnais	France	130.7
National Westminster Bank	UK	121.1
ABN Amro Holding	Netherlands	120.6
Société Générale	France	109.0
Dresdner Bank	Germany	98.0
Union Bank of Switzerland	Switzerland	94.7
Paribas (Cie Financière de)	France	86.0
Swiss Bank Corporation	Switzerland	78.1
Suez (Cie de)	France	77.6
Commerzbank	Germany	74.7
Bayerische Vereinsbank	Germany	71.2
Istituto Bancario San Paulo di Torino	Italy	66.9
Midland Bank	UK	66.2
Rabobank	Netherlands	62.0
Crédit Suisse	Switzerland	60.9
Bayerische Hypotheken und Wechselbank	Germany	60.4

Source: *The Times 1000*.

Appendix 3　VAT RATES IN THE EC

Country	Lower	Standard	Higher	VAT as percentage of GDP
Belgium	1–6	19	25	7.67
Denmark	None	22	None	9.84
France	2.1–13	18.6	25	9.19
Germany	7	14	None	6.34
Greece	3–6	16	36	
Ireland	0–10	23	None	8.22
Italy	4–9	19	38	5.48
Luxembourg	3–6	12	None	6.04
Netherlands	6	18.5	None	6.83
Portugal	8	17	30	—
Spain	6	12	33	—
UK	0	17.5	None	5.22

Source: *Taxation in the Single Market*.

Appendix 4　EUROPEAN COMMISSION DIRECTORATES GENERAL

DG I	External Relations
DG II	Economic and Financial Affairs
DG III	Internal Market and Industry
DG IV	Competition
DG V	Employment, Social Affairs, Education
DG VI	Agriculture
DG VII	Transport
DG VIII	Development
DG IX	Personnel and Administration
DG X	Information and Culture
DG XI	Environment, Consumer Protection, Nuclear Safety
DG XII	Science and Research
DG XIII	Telecommunications, Information Industries, Innovation
DG XIV	Fisheries
DG XV	Financial Institutions and Company Law
DG XVI	Regional policy
DG XVII	Energy
DG XVIII	Credits and Investments
DG XIX	Budgets
DG XX	Financial Control
DG XXI	Customs Union and Indirect Taxation
DG XXII	Co-ordination of Structural Instruments
DG XXIII	Small and Medium Enterprises (SMEs)

Secretariat General
Spokesman's Service
Interpreting and Conference Service

Statistical Office
Official Publications
Source: European Commission.

Appendix 5 USEFUL 1992 CONTACTS AND ADDRESSES

Commission of the European Communities:
rue de la Loi 200
1049 Brussels
Belgium
Tel: 010 322 235 1111

EC UK Information Offices:
8 Storey's Gate
London SW1P 3AT
Tel: 071-222 8122

4 Cathedral Road
Cardiff CH1 9SG
Tel: 0222 371631

7 Alva Street
Edinburgh EH2 4PH
Tel: 031 225 2058

Windsor House
9–15 Bedford Street
Belfast
Tel: 0232 40708

European Business Information Centres:
Scottish Development
   Agency
Rosebery House
Haymarket Terrace
Edinburgh EH12 5EZ
Tel: 031 337 9595

Birmingham Chamber of
   Industry and Commerce
PO Box Harborne Road
Birmingham B15 3DH
Tel: 021 454 6171

Northern Development
   Company
Bank House
Carilo Square
Newcastle-upon-Tyne
Tel: 091 261 0026

Department of Employment
Small Firms and Tourism
   Division Limited
Ebury Bridge House
Ebury Bridge Road
London SW1W 8QD
Tel: 071-730 5874

European Documentation Centres in the UK:
The Library
University of Aberdeen
Meston Walk
Aberdeen AB9 2UB
Tel: 0224 4021

Library
Wye College
Wye
Ashford
Kent TN25 5AH
Tel: 0233 812401 × 242

University Library
University of Bath
Claverton Down
Bath BA2 7AY
Tel: 0225 826826 × 559

The Library
Government Publications
   Dept
Queens University
Belfast BT7 1LS
Tel: 0232 245133

William Kendrick Library
Birmingham Polytechnic
Birmingham B42 2SU
Tel: 021 356 6911

Main Library
University of Birmingham
PO Box 363
Birmingham B15 2TT
Tel: 021 414 3344 × 58

J B Priestley Library
University of Bradford
Richmond Road
Bradford BD7 1DP
Tel: 0274 733466

The Library
University of Sussex
Brighton BN1 9QL
Tel: 0273 678159

Law Library
University of Bristol
Queens Road
Bristol BS8 1RJ
Tel: 0272 24161

The Library
University of Cambridge
West Road
Cambridge CB3 9DR
Tel: 0223 61441

Arts and Social Studies
   Library
University College
PO Box 430
Cardiff CF1 3XT
Tel: 0222 874262

The Library
University of Essex
PO Box 24
Colchester CO4 3UA
Tel: 0206 862286

The Library
New University of Ulster
Coleraine BT52 1SA
Tel: 0265 4141

Lanchester Polytechnic
Priory Street
Coventry CV1 5FB
Tel: 0203 24166

University of Dundee
Perth Road
Dundee DD1 4HN
Tel: 0382 23181 × 4101

Official Publications Section
University Library
Stockton Road
Durham DH1 3LY
Tel: 091 374 3041

Centre of European Studies
University of Edinburgh
Old College
South Bridge
Edinburgh EH8 9LY
Tel: 031 667 1011

Centre for European Legal
   Studies
Exeter University
Law Faculty
Rennes Drive
Exeter EX4 4RJ
Tel: 0392 77911

The University Library
University of Glasgow
Hillhead Street
Glasgow G12 8QE
Tel: 041 339 8855 × 67

George Edwards Library
University of Surrey
Guilford GU2 5XH
Tel: 0483 571281

Brynmor Jones Library
University of Hull
Cottingham Road
Hull HU6 7RX
Tel: 0482 46311

The Library
University of Keele
Staffs
Tel: 0782 621111 × 300

Library Building
University of Kent
Canterbury
Kent CT2 7NU
Tel: 0227 66822

University of Lancaster
Library
Lancaster LA1 4YX
Tel: 0254 62501

The Library
Leeds Polytechnic
Calverly Street
Leeds LS1 3HE
Tel: 0532 462925

University of Leeds
20 Lyddon Terrace
Leeds LS7 9JT
Tel: 0532 31751

University Library
University of Leicester
University Road
Leicester LE1 7RH
Tel: 0533 522044

Liverpool and District
Science
and Industry Research
Council
Central Libraries
William Brown Street
Liverpool L3 8EW
Tel: 051 207 2147

EC Unit Room 61
Polytechnic of Central
London
309 Regent Street
London W1R 8AL
Tel: 071-580 2020

The Library
Queen Mary College
Mile End Road
London E1 4NS
Tel: 081-980 4811

The Library
Polytechnic of North London
Prince of Wales Road
London NW5
Tel: 071-359 0941

Reference Division
Department of Printed Books
Overseas Section
British Library
Great Russell Street
London WC1B 3DB
Tel: 071-323 7602

The Library
RIIA
10 St James Square
London SW1Y 4LE
Tel: 071-930 2233

European Depository Library
Central Reference Library
City of Westminster Library
St Martin's Street
London WC2 7HP
Tel: 071-798 2084

British Library of Political
and Economic Science
The Library
10 Portugal Street
London WC2A 2HD
Tel: 071-405 7686

The Library
Loughborough University
of Technology
Loughborough LE11 3TU
Tel: 0509 222344

John Rylands Library
University of Manchester
Oxford Road
Manchester M13 9PP
Tel: 061 273 3333

The Library
Newcastle Polytechnic
Ellison Place
Newcastle-upon-Tyne
NE1 8ST
Tel: 091 232 6002 × 4136

The Library
University of East Anglia
University Plain
Norwich NR4 7TJ
Tel: 0603 56161 × 2412

The Library
University of Nottingham
Nottingham NG7 2RD
Tel: 0602 506101 × 374

Bodelian Library
University of Oxford
Oxford OX1 3BG
Tel: 0865 277201

Frewen Library
Portsmouth Polytechnic
Cambridge Road
Portsmouth PO1 2ST
Tel: 0705 827681 × 401

The Library
University of Reading
Whiteknights
PO Box 223
Reading RG6 2AH
Tel: 0734 874331 × 131

The Library
University of Salford
Salford
Lancs
Tel: 061 736 5843

The Library
Sheffield City Polytechnic
Pond Street
Sheffield S1 1WB
Tel: 0742 20911 × 2494

Faculty of Law
University of Southampton
Southampton SO9 5NH
Tel: 0703 559122

The Library
University of Warwick
Coventry CV4 7A

British Library
Document Supply Centre
Boston Spa
Wetherby
LS23 7BQ
Tel: 0937 546045

Robert Scott Library
Polytechnic of
Wolverhampton
St Peters Square
Wolverhampton WV1 1RH

Source: European
Commission

**Private EC Consultancies
and Advisers:**
Allott & Lomax
Fairbairn House
Ashton Lane, Sale
Manchester M33 1WP
Tel: 061 962 1214

Advocacy Partnership
Limited
16 Regency Street
London SW1P 4DB
Tel: 071-630 1235

Ceres
Station House
Station Road, Wylam
Northumberland NE41 8HR
Tel: 0661 853982

CSM European Consultants
Limited
Eagle House
109 Jermyn Street
London SW1Y 6HB
Tel: 071-839 4544

CTA Economic Export
Analysts Limited
96 London Road
Reading RG1 5AU
Tel: 0734 66 8381

David Perchard Associates
23 Kingsbury Avenue
St Albans AL3 4TA
Tel: 0727 43227

European Strategy Council
18 Bolton Street
London W1Y 7PA
Tel: 071-493 0049

GJW Government Relations
64 Clapham Road
London SW9 0JJ
Tel: 071-582 3119

Galactic Trading Company
Limited
European Trade Index (1992)
38–40 Clareville Street
London SW7 5AW
Tel: 071-244 8697

Halcrow Fox & Associates
Vineyard House
44 Brook Green
London W6 7BY
Tel: 071-603 5783

Hambros Bank Limited
41 Bishopsgate
London EC2P 2AA
Tel: 071-588 2851

McAvoy Wreford Bayley
36 Grosvenor Gardens
London SW1W 0ED
Tel: 071-730 4500

Randall's Parliamentary
Service
7 Buckingham Gate
London SW1E 6JY
Tel: 071-828 2277

Sallingbury Casey Limited
25 Victoria Street
London SW1H 0EX
Tel: 071-799 1020

Spicers Centre for Europe
Information Division
4th Floor
Cavendish House
Albion Street
Leeds LS1 6AG
Tel: 0532 442629

SRI International
Menlo Park House
4 Addiscombe Road
Croydon CR0 5TT
Tel: 081-686 5555

Westminster and Whitehall
Consultants Limited
25 Victoria Street
London SW1H 0EX
Tel: 071-222 2025

Appendix 6 THE SECOND DELORS COMMISSION 1989–92

1 **Jacques Delors** (France) President of the European Commission
2 **Christiane Scrivener** (France) Fiscal Affairs and the Customs Union
3 **Martin Bangemann** (Germany) Internal market
4 **Peter Schmidhuber** (Germany) Budget
5 **Leon Brittan** (UK) Competition Policy and Financial Services
6 **Bruce Millan** (UK) Regional Development
7 **Abel Matutes** (Spain) Mediterranean Policy, Relations with Latin America, and North –South issues
8 **Manuel Marin** (Spain) Co-operation and Development (Lomé), and Fish.
9 **Carlo Ripa di Meana** (Italy) Environment, Nuclear Safety, and Civil Protection
10 **Filippo Maria Pandolphi** (Italy) Science, Research and Development, Telecommunications, and Joint Research Centres
11 **Frans Andriessen** (Netherlands) External Relations
12 **Henning Christopherson** (Denmark) Economic and Monetary Affairs, and Co-ordination of the Structural Funds
13 **Raymond MacSharry** (Ireland) Agriculture
14 **Antonio Cardosa** (Portugal) Personnel and Administration, Energy, and Small and Medium Enterprises
15 **Vasso Papandreau** (Greece) Employment, Industrial and Social Affairs, and Education
16 **Karel Van Miert** (Belgium) Transport, Credit and Investment, and Consumer Protection
17 **Jean Dodelinger** (Luxembourg) Audio Visual and Cultural Affairs, Information and Communi-cation, and Citizens' Europe

---

Appendix 7 SELECT BIBLIOGRAPHY

The basic texts for 1992 remain the European Commission's White Paper *Completing the Internal Market*, June 1985; the Commission's Mid-Term Report on the Internal Market, December 1988; and the Treaties establishing the European Communities, incorporating the Single European Act and the Treaty of Rome, all issued by the Office for Official Publications of the European Communities, Luxembourg.

Other useful publications include:

Europe Without Frontiers—Completing the Internal Market, Commission of the European Communities, 1987.

The European Challenge 1992: The Benefits of a Single Market, by Paolo Cecchini and others, Wildwood House, 1988.

Pocket Guide to the European Community, by Dick Leonard, Basil Blackwell and The Economist Publications, 1988.

The EEC: A Guide to the Maze, by Stanley Budd, Melville Crawford Associates, Edinburgh, 1985.

The Economics of the Common Market, by Dennis Swann, Penguin, 1984.

Europe: More than a Continent, by Michael Butler (former UK Ambassador to the EC), Heinemann, 1986.

Making Sense of Europe, by Christopher Tugendhat (former Commissioner), Viking, 1986.

Europe's Domestic Market, by Jacques Pelkmans and Alan Winters, Chatham House Papers No. 43, Royal Institute of International Affairs, 1988.

The European Community. Past, Present and Future, edited by Loukas Tsoukalis, Blackwell, 1983.

The European Community: Progress or Decline? by Karl Kaiser, Royal Institute of International Affairs, 1983.

1992: Implications and Potential, by James Elles, Conservative MEP for Oxford and Buckinghamshire. The Bow Group, 1988.

VAT: The Zero Rate Issue, European Parliament discussion paper, by Ben Patterson, Conservative MEP for Kent West, 1988.

Common Standards for Enterprises: Document, Commission of the European Communities, Florence Nicolas, Office for Official Publications, Luxembourg, 1988.

Vacher's European Companion (quarterly), 29 Tufton Street, London SW1P 3QL.

Eurojargon: A Dictionary of EC Acronyms, Abbreviations and Sobriquets, by Anne Ramsay, Capital Planning Information, The Grey House, Broad Street, Stamford, Lincs PE9 1PR.

Europe 1992 Directory, published by Coventry Polytechnic Commercial Development Unit, Priory Street, Coventry CV1 5FB, in collaboration with the DTI Information Technology Unit.

Finance from Europe: A guide to loans and grants from the European Community, Commission of the European Communities, London.

Appendix 8 HIGHLIGHTS OF THE SINGLE EUROPEAN ACT

Article 8a
The Community shall adopt measures with the aim of progressively establishing the internal market over a period expiring on 31 December 1992, in accordance with the provisions of this Article and of Articles 8D, 8C, 28, 57(2), 59, 70(1), 83, 99, 100a and 100b and without prejudice to other provisions of this Treaty.

The internal market shall comprise an area without internal frontiers in which the free movement of goods, persons, services and capital is ensured in accordance with the provisions of this Treaty.
Article 8b
The Commission shall report to the Council before 31 December 1988 and again before 31 December 1990 on the progress made towards achieving the internal market within the time limit fixed in Article 8a.

The Council, acting by a qualified majority on a proposal from the Commission, shall determine the guidelines and conditions necessary to ensure balanced progress in all the sectors concerned.
Article 8c
When drawing up its proposals with a view to achieving the objectives set out in Article 8a, the Commission shall take into account the extent of the effort that certain economies showing differences in development will have to sustain during the period of establishment of the internal market and it may propose appropriate provisions.

If these provisions take the form of derogations, they must be of a temporary nature and must cause the least possible disturbance to the functioning of the common market.
Article 99
The Council shall, acting unanimously on a proposal from the Commission and after consulting the European Parliament, adopt provisions for the harmonization of legislation concerning turnover taxes, excise duties and other forms of indirect taxation to the extent that such harmonization is

necessary to ensure the establishment and the functioning of the internal market within the time limit laid down in Article 8a.

Article 100a

1 By way of derogation from Article 100 and save where otherwise provided in this Treaty, the following provisions shall apply for the achievement of the objectives set out in Article 8a. The Council shall, acting by a qualified majority on a proposal from the Commission in co-operation with the European Parliament and the Economic and Social Committee, adopt the measures for the approximation of the provisions laid down by law, regulation or administrative action in Member States which have as their object the establishment and functioning of the internal market.

2 Paragraph 1 shall not apply to fiscal provisions, to those relating to the free movement of persons nor to those relating to the rights and interests of employed persons.

3 The Commission, in its proposals laid down in paragraph 1 concerning health, safety, environment protection and consumer protection, will take as a base a high level of protection.

4 If, after the adoption of a harmonization measure by the Council acting by a qualified majority, a Member State deems it necessary to apply national provisions on grounds of major needs referred to in Article 36, or relating to protection of the environment or the working environment, it shall notify the Commission of these provisions.

The Commission shall confirm the provisions involved after having verified that they are not a means of arbitrary discrimination or a disguised reaction on trade between Member States.

By way of derogation from the procedure laid down in Articles 169 and 170, the Commission or any Member State may bring the matter directly before the Court of Justice if it considers that the Member State is making improper use of the powers provided for in this Article.

5 The harmonization measures referred to above shall, in appropriate cases, include a safeguard clause authorizing the Member States to take, for one or more of the non-economic reasons referred to in Article 36, provisional measures subject to a Community control procedure.

Article 100b

1 During 1992, the Commission shall, together with each Member State, draw up an inventory of national laws, regulations and administrative provisions which fall under Article 100a and which have not been harmonized pursuant to that Article.

The Council, acting in accordance with the provisions of Article 100a, may decide that the provisions in force in a Member State must be recognized as being equivalent to those applied by another Member State.

2 The provisions of Article 100a(4) shall apply by analogy.

3 The Commission shall draw up the inventory referred to in the first subparagraph of paragraph 1 and shall submit appropriate proposals in good time to allow the Council to act before the end of 1992.

Article 148

1 Save as otherwise provided in this Treaty, the Council shall act by a qualified majority of its members.

2 Where the Council is required to act by a qualified majority, the votes of its members shall be weighted as follows:

Belgium	5	Ireland	3
Denmark	3	Italy	10
West Germany	10	Luxembourg	2
Greece	5	Netherlands	5
Spain	8	Portugal	5
France	10	United Kingdom	10

For their adoption, acts of Council shall require at least:

—fifty-four votes in favour where this Treaty requires them to be adopted on a proposal from the Commission,

—fifty-four votes in favour, cast by at least eight members, in other cases.

3 Abstentions by members present in person or represented shall not prevent the adoption by the Council of acts which require unanimity.

Declaration on Article 8a of the EEC Treaty

The Conference wishes by means of the provisions in Article 8a to express its firm political will to take before 1 January 1993 the decisions necessary to complete the internal market defined in those provisions, and more particularly the decisions necessary to implement the Commission's programme described in the White Paper on the Internal Market.

Setting the date of 31 December 1992 does not create an automatic legal effect.

Declaration on Articles 13 to 19 of the Single European Act

Nothing in these provisions shall affect the right of Member States to take such measures as they consider necessary for the purpose of controlling immigration from third countries, and to combat terrorism, crime, the traffic in drugs and illicit trading in works of art and antiques.

Appendix 9 GLOSSARY OF EC TERMS

ACP states
The 66 African, Caribbean and Pacific countries party to the Lomé Convention
ACPM
Advisory Committee on Programme Management
Additionality
Using EC funds to augment national funds
Agrimed
Mediterranean Agriculture
Aqua Europa
European Federation for Water Treatment
ASSILEC
Association of Dairy Industries of the EC
BCC
Business Co-operation Centre
BEUC
European Bureau of Consumer Councils
BRITE
Basic Research in Industrial Technologies for Europe
BTR
Basic Technological Research
CAOBISCO
Association of the Sugar Products Industries of the EC
CAP
Common Agricultural Policy
CARICOM
Caribbean Community and the Common Market
CCC
Consumer Consultative Committees
CCT/CET
Common Customs Tariff/ Common External Tariff
CEFIC
European Council of Chemical Industry Federations
CEN
European Committee for Standardization
CENELEC
European Committee for Electrotechnical Standardization
CEOP
European Committee of Workers' Co-operative Production Societies

CERN
European Nuclear Research Centre
CFP
Common Fisheries Policy
CICI
Confederation of Information Communication Industries
CID
Centre for Industrial Development
Cohesion
A term meaning reduction in disparities between regions
Comecon
Council for Mutual Economic Assistance
COMETT
Community in Education and Training for Technology
Comitextil
Co-ordination Committee for the Textile Industries of the EC
COPA
Committee for Agricultural Organizations in the EC
CORDI
Advisory Committee on Industrial Research and Development
COREPER
Committee of Permanent Representatives (i.e. EC ambassadors in Brussels)
Co-responsibility levy
A tax paid by farmers as a contribution towards the cost of storing farm surpluses
COST
Committee on European Co-operation in the field of Scientific and Technical Research
CPC
Community Patent Convention
CRM
Committee for Medical and Public Health Research
Democratic deficit
The need for greater democratic accountability of EC institutions as a result of European integration
DG
Directorate General

EAGF
European Agricultural Guidance and Guarantee Fund
ECB
European Central Bank
ECE
Economic Commission for Europe (UN)
ECSC
European Coal and Steel Community
ECU
European currency unit (mecu = million: becu = billion)
EFTA
European Free Trade Association
EIB
European Investment Bank
EMCF
European Monetary Co-operation Fund
EMI
European Monetary Institute
EMS
European Monetary System
EMU
Economic and Monetary Union
EP
European Parliament
EPC
European Political Co-operation
EPU
European Political Union
ERASMUS
EC programme to promote student mobility
ERDF
European Regional Development Fund
ERM
Exchange Rate Mechanism
ESA
European Space Agency
ESC
Economic and Social Committee
ESCB
European System of Central Banks
ESPRIT
European strategic programme for research and development in information technology

ETSI
European Telecommunications Standards Institute

ETUC
European Trades Union Confederation

EURATOM
European Atomic Energy Community

Eureka
European programme for high-technology research and development

Euro-Coop
European Community of Consumer Co-operatives

Eurofer
European Federation of the Iron and Steel Industry

EUROPMI
European Committee for Small and Medium-sized Industries

EUROSTAT
The Community's statistics office

EVCA
European Venture Capital Association

FAO
Food and Agricultural Organization (UN)

FAST
Forecasting and Assessment in Science and Technology

FIPACE
International Federation of Self-generating Industrial Users of Electricity

FIPMEC
International Federation of Small and Medium-sized Enterprises

GATT
General Agreement on Tariffs and Trade

GSP
General System of Preferences.

IDN
Integrated Digital Network

IEA
International Energy Association (OECD)

IGADD
Intergovernmental Authority on Drought and Development

IGC
Intergovernmental Committee

IMF
International Monetary Fund

IMP
Integrated Mediterranean Programmes

IPM
Integrated Pest Management

ISDN
Integrated Services Digital Network

IT
Information Technologies

ITTTF
Information Technology and Telecommunications Task Force

JET
Joint European Torus

JRC
Joint Research Centre

LDCs
Least Developed Countries

MCA
Monetary Compensation Amount

MFA
Multi-Fibre Arrangement

MFTA
Medium-term Financial Assistance

MGQ
Maximum Guaranteed Quantity

MS
Member States of the EC

NCI
New Community Instruments (EIB)

NGO
Non-governmental Organization

OCTs
Overseas Countries and Territories

OECD
Organization for Economic Co-operation and Development

OJ
Official Journal of the EC

POCO
see **EPC**

QR
Quantitative Restrictions

RACE
Research and development in advanced communications technologies for Europe

SCAR
Standing Committee on Agricultural Research

SEA
Single European Act

Set aside
Taking land out of production

SMEs
Small and medium-sized businesses

STABEX
Stability in Export Revenue (Lomé Convention)

Stabilizer
A mechanism for controlling farm output

STMS
Short-term Monetary Support

Subsidiarity
Taking decisions at the lowest possible level

Sysmin
System for Safeguarding and Developing Mineral Production

Systran
Co-ordination of National Policies Relating to Machine or Machine Assisted Translation

UKREP
United Kingdom Permanent Representation to the EC (i.e. the British Embassy to the EC)

UNICE
Conference of Industries of the European Communities

Vat
Value Added Tax

WEU
Western European Union

Appendix 10 EC SUMMITS 1983–92

Stuttgart, June 1983 (West German presidency): Agreed budget needs reform, especially in view of coming enlargement, and Common Agricultural Policy must be brought into line with market realities.

Athens, December 1983 (Greek presidency): Stuttgart declaration reaffirmed.

Fontainebleau, June 1984 (French presidency): Principles of budgetary discipline agreed; British budget rebate agreed.

Dublin, December 1984 (Irish presidency): Laid down internal market without frontiers and the key to growth and jobs.

Milan, June 1985 (Italian presidency): Disagreement over Single European Act giving European Parliament more power and defining 1992 as date for completion of internal market.

Luxembourg, December 1985 (Luxembourg presidency): Single European Act finally agreed.

The Hague, June 1986 (Dutch presidency): Limited sanctions against South Africa. Budget reform deferred.

London, December 1986 (British presidency): Further progress on internal market and Community co-ordination against threat of terrorism.

Brussels, June 1987 (Belgian presidency): Disagreement (Thatcher veto) over proposed budget reform based on package put forward by Jacques Delors, the president of the European Commission. Britain said farm controls too weak.

Copenhagen, December 1987 (Danish presidency): Further refinement of Delors reforms, but still not enough to satisfy Britain. Agreement to hold extraordinary summit in Brussels in February 1988, to solve the crisis before the Hannover summit of June 1988 and the passing of the presidency to Greece.

Brussels, February 1988 (German presidency): Delors reforms agreed.

Hannover, June 1988 (German presidency): Delors Committee on Economic and Monetary Union set up. 1992 declared 'irreversible'. Delors confirmed as President of the European Commission for a second term.

Rhodes, December 1988 (Greek presidency): Presentation of European Commission's mid-term report on progress towards the completion of the internal market by 1992. 'Slippage' identified as cause of growing concern.

Madrid, June 1989 (Spanish presidency): Delors report on economic and monetary union debated. First stage adopted.

Paris, December 1989: special one-day summit, called after upheavals in Soviet bloc, agreed to link economic aid to Eastern Europe to political reform.

Strasbourg, December 1989 (French presidency): Endorses principle of German reunification, sets date for intergovernmental conference to reform the Treaty of Rome, and approves the creation of a European Development Bank and the European Social Charter.

Dublin, April 1990 (Irish presidency): Welcomes changes in Eastern Europe and impending reunification of Germany. Agrees need for further IGC on political as well as economic union.

Dublin, June 1990 (Irish presidency): Hears first report on treaty revisions. Thatcher raises no objections to report on political union.

Rome, October 1990 (Italian presidency): Called to discuss aid to the Soviet Union but sets timetable for economic and monetary union: European Bank to begin in 1994, single currency in 1997. Angry Thatcher condemns summit for 'putting the cart before the horse'.

Rome, December 1990 (Italian presidency): First appearance by John Major as Prime Minister, seen as more 'flexible' than Thatcher. Summit agrees to establish two IGCs on political and economic union to prepare draft treaty revisions to be put to summit one year later, at Maastricht. Discusses impact of Gulf crisis on Europe.

Luxembourg, April 1991 (Luxembourg presidency): Agrees Major initiative on 'safe havens' for Kurds in northern Iraq and EC aid for Kurdish refugees.

Luxembourg, June 1991 (Luxembourg presidency): Considers Luxembourg presidency texts for draft treaty amendments. Major objects to word 'federalism'. Economic convergence agreed as condition for single currency.

Maastricht, December 1991 (Dutch presidency): Debate on federalism, powers for European Parliament, common foreign and defence policy, co-operation on immigration and crime, timetable for European Bank and single currency comes to a head.

Lisbon, June 1992 (Portuguese presidency): Portugal in EC chair for first time since joining EC in 1986. Deals with consequences of Maastricht before handing over to UK, which is in chair for the run-up to 31 December 1992 and the single market.

Appendix 11 PERCENTAGE OF WORLD TRADE HELD BY PRINCIPAL TRADING NATIONS 1989

Country bloc	Imports	Exports
EC	16.2	15
US	15.6	12
Japan	7	9.1
USSR	3.8	3.6
Canada	3.8	3.8

Source of EC imports

EFTA	22.8
Japan	10.3
Latin America	5.8
ACP	4.4
USSR	3.4

Destination of EC exports

EFTA	25.9
US	18.8
Japan	5
Latin America	3.6
ACP	3.4
USSR	2.9

Source: *Europe—World Partner*, Commission of the European Communities.

Appendix 12 UK REGIONS ELIGIBLE FOR REGIONAL FUNDS

Category 1: Northern Ireland.
Category 2: *England*: Northumberland, Tyne and Wear, Durham, Cleveland, Humberside, South Yorkshire, West Yorkshire, Nottinghamshire, Greater Manchester, Lancashire, Merseyside, West Midlands, North Yorkshire, Lincolnshire, Derbyshire, Cheshire, Shropshire, Staffordshire, Warwickshire, Cumbria and Nottinghamshire. *Scotland*: Fife, Central, Strathclyde, Tayside, Lothian, Dumfries and Galloway. *Wales*: Gwent, Mid-Glamorgan, West Glamorgan and Clwyd.
Category 5: Devon, Cornwall, Plymouth, Bude, Bodmin, Liskeard, Newquay, Redruth, Cambourne, Falmouth, Helston, Penzance, St Ives, Scilly Isles, the Highlands and Islands and rural Wales.

The whole of the UK qualifies for assistance under categories 3 (to combat long-term unemployment) and 4 (to integrate young people into the job market).

Appendix 13 DECLARATION OF THE EUROPEAN COUNCIL ON EUROPE AND THE WORLD (RHODES, DECEMBER 1988)

1 Reaffirming its commitment to achieve concrete progress towards European Unity on the basis of the Single European Act,
—determined to strengthen and expand the role of the European Community and its Member States on the international political and economic stage, in co-operation with all other States and appropriate organizations,
—and aware that the completion of the internal market in 1992, which is already inspiring a new dynamism in the Community's economic life, will equally affect the Community's political and economic role in the world,
—the European Council reaffirms that the Single Market will be of benefit to Community and non-Community countries alike by ensuring continuing economic growth. The internal market will not close in on itself. 1992 Europe will be a partner and not a 'Fortress Europe'. The internal market will be a decisive factor contributing to greater liberalization in international trade on the basis of the GATT principles of reciprocal and mutually advantageous arrangements. The Community will continue to participate actively in the GATT Uruguay Round, committed as it is to strengthen the multilateral trading system. It will also continue to pursue, with the United States, Japan and the other OECD partners, policies designed to promote sustainable non-inflationary growth in the world economy.
2 The Community and its Member States will continue to work closely and co-operatively with the United States to maintain and deepen the solid and comprehensive transatlantic relationship. Closer political and economic relations with Japan and the other industrialized countries will also be developed. In particular, the Community wishes to strengthen and to expand relations with EFTA countries and all other European nations which share the same ideals and objectives. Open and constructive dialogue and co-operation will be actively pursued with other countries or regional groups of the Middle East, and the Mediterranean, Africa, the Caribbean, the Pacific, Asia and Latin America, with special emphasis on interregional co-operation.
3 The European Council emphasizes the need to improve social and economic conditions in less-developed countries and to promote structural adjustment, both through trade and aid. It also recognizes the importance of a continuing policy to tackle the problems of the highly indebted countries on a case-by-case basis. It looks forward to the successful conclusion of the negotiations for the renewal of the Convention between the European Community and its 66 African, Caribbean and Pacific partners during the coming year.
4 The European Community and its member states are determined to play an active role in the preservation of international peace and security and in the solution of regional conflicts, in conformity with the United Nations Charter. Europe cannot but actively demonstrate its solidarity to the great and spreading movement for democracy and full support for the principles of the Universal Declaration on Human Rights. The Twelve will endeavour to strengthen the effectiveness of the United Nations and to actively contribute to its peace-keeping role.
5 Against the background of improved East–West relations, the European Council welcomes the readiness of the European members of the CMEA to develop relations with the European Community and reaffirms its willingness to further economic relations and co-operation with them, taking into account each country's specific situation, in order to use the opportunities available in a mutually beneficial way.
   The European Council reaffirms its determination to act with renewed hope to overcome the division of our continent and to promote the Western values and principles which Member States have in common. To this effect, we will strive to achieve:
—Full respect for the provisions of the Helsinki Final Act and further progress in the CSCE process, including an early and successful conclusion of the Vienna follow-up meeting;
—The establishment of a secure and stable balance of conventional forces in Europe at a lower level, the strengthening of mutual confidence and military transparence and the conclusion of a global and verifiable ban on chemical weapons;
—Promotion of human rights and fundamental freedoms, free circulation of people and ideas and the establishment of more open societies; promotion of human and cultural exchanges between East and West;
—The development of political dialogue with our Eastern neighbours.
6 The European Community and the Twelve are determined to make full use of the provisions of the Single European Act in order to strengthen solidarity among them, co-ordination on the political and economic aspects of security, and consistency between the external policies of the European

Community and the policies agreed in the framework of the European Political Co-operation. They will strive to reach swift adoption of common positions and implementation of joint action.

7 The European Council invites all countries to embark with the European Community as world partner on an historic effort to leave to the next generation a Continent and a world more secure, more just and more free.

Appendix 14   DECLARATION ON ECONOMIC AND MONETARY UNION ADOPTED BY THE EUROPEAN COUNCIL (MADRID, JUNE 1989)

1 The European Council restated its determination to progressively achieve economic and monetary union as provided for in the Single European Act and confirmed at the European Council in Hannover. Economic and monetary union must be seen in the perspective of the completion of the internal market and in the context of economic and social cohesion.

2 The European Council considered that the report by the committee chaired by Jacques Delors, which defines a process designed to lead by stages to economic and monetary union, fulfilled the mandate given to it at Hannover. The European Council felt that its realization would have to take account of the parallelism between economic and monetary aspects and allow for the diversity of specific situations.

3 The European Council decided that the first stage of the realization of economic and monetary union would begin on 1 July 1990.

4 The European Council asked the competent bodies to carry out the preparatory work for the organization of an intergovernmental conference to lay down the subsequent stages: that conference would meet once the first stage had begun and would be preceded by full and adequate preparation.

Appendix 15   DECLARATION ON THE THREE STAGES TO ECONOMIC AND MONETARY UNION ADOPTED BY EUROPEAN COUNCIL WITH BRITAIN DISSENTING (ROME, OCTOBER 1990)

For the final phase of Economic and Monetary Union, 11 member states consider that the work on the amendment of the Treaty will be directed to the following points:

- For economic union, an open-market system that combines price stability with growth, employment and environmental protection and is dedicated to sound and sustainable financial and budgetary conditions and to economic and social cohesion; for monetary union, the creation of a new monetary institution comprising member states' central banks and a central organ exercising full responsibility for monetary policy. The monetary institution's prime task will be to maintain price stability. The institution as such, as well as the members of its council, will be independent of instructions. It will report to the institutions which are politically responsible.

With the achievement of the final phase of economic and monetary union, exchange rates will be irrevocably fixed. The Community will have a single currency—a strong and stable ECU.

The second phase will start on January 1 1994, after:
- The single market programme has been achieved;
- The treaty has been ratified, and, by its provisions;
- A process has been set in train designed to ensure the independence of members of the new monetary institution;
- The monetary financing of budget deficits has been prohibited and any responsibility on the part of the Community or its member states for one member states debt precluded;
- The greatest possible number of member state's have adhered to the ERM.

The European Council recalls that, in order to move on to the second phase, further satisfactory and lasting progress towards real and monetary convergence will have to be achieved, especially as regards price stability and the restoration of sound public finances.

At the start of the second phase, the new Community institution will be established. This will make it possible:
- To strengthen the co-ordination of monetary policies:
- To develop the instruments and procedures needed for single monetary policy;
- To oversee the developments of the ECU.

At the latest within three years of the start of the second phase, the Commission and Council of the monetary institution will report to the EcoFin and the General Affairs councils on the functioning of the second phase and on the progress made in real convergence in order to prepare the decision concerning the passage to the third phase.

The treaty may lay down transitional provisions for the successive stages of Economic and Monetary Union according to the circumstances of the different countries.

The United Kingdom is unable to accept the approach set out above.

But it agrees the overriding objective of monetary policy should be price stability; the Community's development should be based on an open-market system; that excessive budget deficits be avoided; and that there should be no monetary financing of deficits nor the assumption of responsibility on the part of the Community or its members states for one member's debts.

The UK, while ready to move beyond stage one through the creation of a new monetary institution and a common Community currency, believes that decisions on the substance of that move should precede decisions on its timing. But it would be ready to see the approach it advocates come into effect as soon as possible after ratification of the necessary treaty provision.

Appendix 16 SUMMARY OF THE MAASTRICHT SUMMIT

ECONOMIC AND MONETARY UNION

The key changes to the treaty at Maastricht are contained in article 109F, which defines the irreversible switch to a single currency for an as-yet unknown number of EC states. The important addition was the British opt-out protocol.

The second stage of European monetary union will start in 1994, with the creation of the European Monetary Institute (EMI), and all governments 'shall endeavour' to avoid excessive budget deficits. In 1996, the European Commission and the EMI will report on the fitness of each state for inclusion in the ECU zone. Stiff criteria include low inflation and stable exchange rates.

At the beginning of 1992, the criteria were met by only three of the 12 EC economies. In December 1996, an EC summit will see whether that number has reached seven. If it has, a majority vote will decide the start date for the 'third stage', a single currency. Otherwise, the European central bank will start work in the middle of 1998 and 'the third stage will start on January 1 1999'. No minimum number of states will be required.

The British protocol is attached to the treaty, with footnotes on the purchase of second homes in Denmark and the coinage of San Marino. Britain must say before December 1996 if it intends to merge its currency, but is 'under no obligation to do so'.

SOCIAL CHAPTER

The summit reached a solution whereby social policy was removed from the treaty on political union. Eleven of the 12 EC members adopted a special social policy of their own, including majority voting on 'working conditions'. This may raise more legal problems than the political log jam it was designed to break.

Two annexes were attached to the treaty at the last moment, and a six-clause chapter on social policy shrank to one sentence. Five draft pages expanding EC powers over employment and welfare law became: 'Present EC treaty provisions unchanged (c.f. Annex 111).' The annex has a protocol noting that 'eleven member states wish to make policies not applicable to Britain.' The text says: 'The United Kingdom shall not take part in the deliberations on and the adoption of the Commission proposals relating to fields covered by the above-mentioned agreement'.

FOREIGN AFFAIRS

Britain succeeded in limiting majority voting by requiring that a unanimous vote be required to agree the framework of a joint foreign policy. It agreed, however, that the implementation of policy could by majority vote. The article describing the organisation of European defence was also a compromise. Both France and Germany, arguing for the foundations of a European defence run by the EC, and Britain and Italy, countering with demands that anything agreed should be complementary with NATO, gave ground. The wording implies that the EC will absorb the Western European Union, which will acquire greater status. The exact relationship between NATO, the WEU and the EC remains to be established.

EUROPEAN PARLIAMENT

The summit agreed a compromise under which the Council of Ministers will try to agree legislation with the 518-member Strasbourg assembly. If all else fails, for the first time, the parliament will be able to veto a measure in areas that fall under the new scheme, known as 'Article 189B procedure'.

This veto can apply to most new EC powers to be decided by qualified majority vote. These include: measures to complete the single market; consumer protection; free circulation of workers; 'rights of establishment' (of professionals and businesses); treatment of foreign nations, education; vocational training; research and development; programmes for environment policy; trans-European transport; telecommunications; health; and culture.

The parliament has won a veto over research and development, but Britain has retained a national veto on these.

IMMIGRATION

The treaty binds Community members into taking common action on asylum policy, immigration, and the fight against drugs and fraud; and co-operation between customs services, between home affairs and justice ministries in fighting crime, and between police in combating terrorism and international crime.

Britain made significant concessions in giving the Commission a say in this field, and in introducing qualified voting. On a common visa policy, the Commission will propose a list of countries whose citizens need visas to enter the EC, which the Council of Ministers must approve unanimously. But paragraph 2 of Article 100C says: 'In the event of an emergency situation in a third country posing a threat of a sudden inflow of nationals from that country into the Community, the Council may, acting by a qualified majority . . . for a period not exceeding six months, introduce a visa requirement for nationals from the country in question'.

COHESION

The question of 'cohesion'—the demand by poorer, southern countries, led by Spain, for greater transfer of money from the richer north—was removed from the main treaty.

It was included instead as a protocol that promises a 'thorough evaluation' of structural funds in the course of 1992 to see whether they are enough to support EC goals of social and economic cohesion. A general review is scheduled for 1993 under new EC budget procedure.

A new Cohesion Fund will be set up by the end of 1993 to provide money for the environment and trans-European networks (transport, telecommunications and energy). It will go to countries with a per capita GNP of less than 90% of the EC average. The protocol insists that these countries move towards economic convergence as specified in the EMU section of the treaty.

ENLARGEMENT

The summit issued a declaration reaffirming its readiness to open negotiations with any democratic European country applying for membership. The Twelve said talks could begin as soon as the EC terminated negotiations on its own budget and related issues in 1992. This means Sweden and Austria, whose applications are already on the table, may begin talks before 1993.

The final declaration omits reference by name to Sweden and Austria, which has been specifically mentioned in the original draft, so as not to be seen to discriminate against Turkey, Malta and Cyprus, which have also applied to join but whose accession the EC is in no hurry to consider. The declaration noted the consitutional role of the European Parliament in ratifying all accession and association agreements.

INDEX

(Entries in bold type indicate a chapter/section devoted to the subject entry. For names of Europe's top 20 companies and banks, see Appendices 1 and 2.)